CATHONOMICS

CATHONOMICS

HOW CATHOLIC TRADITION CAN CREATE A MORE JUST ECONOMY

ANTHONY M. ANNETT

GEORGETOWN UNIVERSITY PRESS / WASHINGTON, DC

The publisher is not responsible for third-party websites or their content. URL links were active at time of publication.

Library of Congress Cataloging-in-Publication Data

Names: Annett, Anthony, author. | Sachs, Jeffrey, writer of foreword.
Title: Cathonomics : how Catholic social thought can create a moral economy / Anthony M. Annett ; foreword by Jeffrey D. Sachs.
Description: Washington, DC : Georgetown University Press, 2021. | Includes bibliographical references and index.
Identifiers: LCCN 2021000275 | ISBN 9781647121426 (hardcover) | ISBN 9781647121433 (ebook)
Subjects: LCSH: Economics—Religious aspects—Catholic Church. | Neoliberalism—Religious aspects—Catholic Church. | Church and social problems—Catholic Church.
Classification: LCC BX1795.E27 A55 2021 | DDC 261.8/5—dc23
LC record available at https://lccn.loc.gov/2021000275

∞ This paper meets the requirements of ANSI/NISO Z39.48-1992 (Permanence of Paper).

23 22   9 8 7 6 5 4 3 2   First printing

Printed in the United States of America

Cover design by Jeff Miller, Faceout Studio
Interior design by BookComp, Inc.

We must regain the conviction that we need one another, that we have a shared responsibility for others and the world, and that being good and decent are worth it. We have had enough of immorality and the mockery of ethics, goodness, faith and honesty.

—Pope Francis, *Laudato Si'*

CONTENTS

FOREWORD

Readers of all faiths and backgrounds, from professional economists and ethicists to students and concerned citizens in all parts of the world, will benefit enormously from *Cathonomics* and its wonderful introduction to the social teachings of the Catholic Church. The global turmoil of recent years—including COVID-19, wars without end, climate upheavals, and widespread social unrest—are symptoms of a world in ethical crisis. We have the wealth and the know-how to achieve a prosperous and sustainable world for all, yet we lack the consensus on how to address our pressing and growing woes. Even worse, the polarization and ideological battle lines are becoming starker as the global challenges have grown.

The core problems we face are not due to the lack of technical solutions or scarcity of vital resources and finances. Solar and wind energy, for example, can provide environmentally safe power to meet the world's energy needs hundreds or even thousands of times over, if we deploy these energy sources properly, instead of relying on dangerous fossil fuels. Our land, water, and food supplies can meet the food and other needs of all the world's people, indeed with far healthier diets than today, if we use these resources wisely and with less waste and with due regard for nature. And in a world in which a few hundred people have more than $7 trillion of combined wealth (!), we can finance the urgent needs of the world's poorest people.

Our core challenges are ethical and organizational. We human beings, acting together through our families and communities, our governments, and our global organizations, most important the United Nations, must choose to do the right things, both individually in our personal behavior and together as citizens and members of society. These challenges are ethical—to promote the common good—and organizational, to create institutions that turn ethical choices into human well-being.

Cathonomics offers us practical solutions based on the great ethical wisdom of the Church's social teachings. This remarkable body of thought is a great gift to humanity. It draws on the wisdom of the ancient Greeks, the Jewish prophets, the teachings of Jesus and the Gospels, the thoughts of the Church Fathers, and the magnificent synthesis in the philosophy of Saint Thomas Aquinas. Late in the nineteenth century, Pope Leo XIII turned to Aquinas's great teachings to help the Church to address the ethical challenges posed by industrialization. Annett powerfully recounts how a series of great papal encyclicals, starting with Leo XIII's *Rerum Novarum (Of New Things, 1891)* and continuing till today with Pope Francis's remarkable encyclicals *Laudato Si'* and *Fratelli Tutti*, have addressed the ethical challenges raised by the modern world economy and the new geopolitics. The Church's social teachings that have emerged from this remarkable series of reflections over 130 years offer the world a profoundly wise vision of humanity, one that inspires us to overcome self-defeating egoism and narrowmindedness in order to foster a peaceful, inclusive, and sustainable world. Not only that, this great body of thought offers very practical guidance and pastoral wisdom on how these great goals can be achieved.

Cathonomics carries forward the aspirations of Ethics in Action, a program in recent years that brought together scholars, educators, and theologians to help identify and foster a global ethic grounded in the Church's social teachings and the great virtue traditions of other religions and cultures, including of Asia, Africa, and Indigenous nations. In all of these great virtue traditions, human beings are called on to reach fulfillment and happiness through compassion, love for the poor, respect for peoples of other cultures and nations, and responsible stewardship of nature. The remarkable chancellor of the Pontifical Academy of Sciences, Marcelo Sánchez Sorondo, hosted the meetings of Ethics in Action and inspired all of us with the glories and joys of soaring ethical thought and applications in action.

As *Cathonomics* demonstrates, the Church's social teaching has helped both to inspire and to promote the United Nations in its efforts to build a world of universal human dignity and sustainable development, according to the aspirations of the Universal Declaration of Human Rights, the Millennium Development Goals, and the Sustainable Development Goals. Pope Francis's *Laudato Si'* and *Fratelli Tutti*, Annett shows, offers us great guidance in promoting a world of environmental responsibility and universal fraternity across nations and cultures.

Readers of *Cathonomics* will be dazzled and inspired to join a dialogue about the human good that has been underway since Aristotle walked in the Lyceum of Athens and Jesus delivered the Sermon on the Mount. Most important, readers will gain practical insights from the Church's social teachings to help find a way out of our current global cul-de-sac. Pope Francis and the Church's unwavering defense of human dignity inspire us to move beyond our throwaway culture and the globalization of indifference. Annett shows persuasively how this great ethical wisdom can guide practical action to achieve a world economy that is prosperous, inclusive, and sustainable; that is, a world economy that serves the common good.

—Jeffrey D. Sachs

PREFACE

On February 28, 2014, a stooped and aged Pope Benedict XVI walked out of the Vatican and out of his papacy. He stepped down because he felt he no longer possessed the physical or mental strength needed to govern the Church. Yet this humble gesture turned the Church upside down. It was the first voluntary resignation of a sitting pope in almost six hundred years. It was a big deal. It would change the papacy. It would change the Catholic Church. And it would change my life too.

A few weeks later, on March 13, the assembled cardinals elected as pope someone few people had heard of: the archbishop of Buenos Aires, Jorge Mario Bergoglio. Pope Francis. It was immediately obvious that he was a pope of firsts. He was the first Jesuit pope, and the Jesuits were sometimes viewed with suspicion by more conservative corners of the Church for their passionate advocacy of social justice and the rights of the poor. Bergoglio is also the first pope to hail from the new world, from Latin America, a vital center of global Catholicism in the twenty-first century.

Bergoglio also stunned the Catholic world by being the first pope in history to choose the name Francis. He did this to honor the humble saint of Assisi—as he put it, "the man of poverty, the man of peace, the man who loves and protects creation."[1] He later recounted that as his election seemed assured, his friend Cardinal Cláudio Hummes of Brazil urged him not to forget the poor. At that moment, he decided he would be Pope Francis—the pope of the people, the pope of the poor, the pope of the planet.

From his first moment on the balcony after this election, people were enthralled by his humility, his simplicity, his tendency to speak plainly. While Pope Benedict was a learned theologian who seemed most comfortable in a classroom setting or a seminar, Pope Francis delighted in being among ordinary people. He would be a pastoral pope whereby gestures were as important as words, and—as he liked to put it—reality was more important than ideas. He chose to live simply, forsaking the apostolic palace for the spartan accommodation of a Vatican boardinghouse. He called on the ministers of the Church to get outside of their comfort zones and go to the margins of society; shepherds, after all, should "smell of the sheep." He called on cardinals, bishops, and priests to be less worldly, ambitious, and self-referential; to emphasize God's mercy instead of rigidity; and to spread joy rather than acting like "sourpusses."[2]

For Francis, the most important thing was to have a poor Church for the poor. It was important to be with the poor, live with the poor, learn from the poor. As bishop of Buenos Aires, he prioritized ministry to the slums and was rarely seen on the media or among Argentina's chattering classes. As pope, he spoke out for the poor, the marginalized, the indigenous, migrants and refugees. He condemned what he called an economy of exclusion, a globalization of indifference, a throwaway culture, and the denigration of our common home. He called for the poor to become dignified agents of their own development, for a rejection of a technocratic zeal for ceaseless economic growth in pursuit of insatiable appetites, and for global cooperation to solve the socioenvironmental crisis that threatens our collective future.

In some of his most prophetic language, delivered at a speech to the poor of Bolivia in 2015, the pope denounced the current economic model: "The first task is to put the economy at the service of peoples. Human beings and nature must not be at the service of money. Let us say NO to an economy of exclusion and inequality, where money rules, rather than service. That economy kills. That economy excludes. That economy destroys Mother Earth."[3]

Needless to say, such unflinching moral language and such passionate advocacy have earned the pope some powerful enemies, especially among corporate interests, fossil fuel companies, and ideological libertarians. Popes are not supposed to talk like this, they claim: they should be concerned with saving souls.

Yet Pope Francis is proving to be the prophet we need. He is touching into something deep in the zeitgeist—a feeling that our global economy is on the wrong path, driven by the wrong values, headed in the wrong direction. I would argue that we are going through an inflection point right now. For the past four decades, the dominant orthodoxy has come to be known as neoliberalism—the premise that free markets and free flows of goods and capital, unrestrained by government interventions, represent the best route to rising prosperity.

But the results are in, and this narrative has now been largely discredited. As has been well documented, inequality is skyrocketing, and the global elites and large corporations are running away with the lion's share of the gains from prosperity. In a world of vast riches, hundreds of millions of people live in extreme poverty, barely able to survive from day to day, let alone have access to goods like healthcare and education. In wealthier regions, the combination of rapid technological change and financial globalization is hollowing out jobs and whole communities, forcing workers into dead-end service or gig jobs, with low wages and paltry protections. All over the world, the increasing political power of the wealthy is biasing policy away from an expansive notion of the common good toward their own particular financial interests—so much so that some have argued that the superrich are retreating from society to their own enclaves, with little sense of responsibility to their fellow citizens, national or global. And the values of neoliberalism tell them that these outcomes are just, reflecting a meritocracy and the fruits of hard work. At the same time, financialization has led to increasing fragility, as evidenced by the global financial crisis of 2008—again, the fruits of neoliberal values, the notion that the pursuit of short-term self-interest is good for everyone. And looming over all of this is the climate emergency. In a very real sense, our turbocharged global economy since the industrial revolution has been driven by the incredible energy that can be harnessed from burning fossil fuels: coal, oil, and gas. But this is an addiction that is proving almost impossible to kick and is turning out to be a collective act of self-sabotage with the poor on the front lines.

Things are changing. The COVID-19 crisis in particular has shone some powerful high beams on these giant flaws and on how more and more people realize that the current model is untenable. The economic, social, and environmental fractures are too large to ignore any longer.

For decades, economists have played handmaiden to this economy. But there seems to be a new springtime in the air. Even before COVID, there was growing recognition that free market zealotry has failed us, especially through its promotion of exclusion, inequality, financial instability, and environmental devastation. A host of prominent economists called for a new approach to economics, including a new approach to *teaching* economics.

The same seems to be happening on the policy front. On both Left and Right, there is a sense that the market alone cannot bring about true well-being and is responsible for a host of pathologies. While there remain differences in ideology, many are now calling for a return to the kinds of social democratic policies that held sway after the war, for reinvigorated communities fertilized by a robust civil society, and for a more holistic way to measure well-being rather than merely wealth or GDP. All sides can see the writing on the wall.

There is a clear danger here. Times of deep economic anxiety always present an opening for demagogues with simplistic solutions, who seek to build common cause by demonizing the other—whether they be ethnic minorities, immigrants, or rootless global elites. Extremism is rising all across the world—chiefly on the Right, but the Left cannot be too far behind. The lessons of history are not encouraging in this regard.

Here's what I've noticed: The question of values tends to play second fiddle in the reform agenda. It is not entirely missing, but it never treated in a detailed, rigorous, or systematic way. Numerous people have recently called for a better grounding of economics in ethics, most recently Paul Collier, while Nobel Prize–winner Jean Tirole has called for a new economics rooted in the common good.[4] But fully worked-out alternative ethical paradigms are rare.

My contention in this book is that an alternative paradigm is hidden in plain sight, and Pope Francis offers a clue to where it can be found. This is the key point: the pope's denunciations of the moral failures of our global economy do not exist in a vacuum. They are not merely the reflexive judgments of a religious leader. They are instead a reflection of some rather ancient wisdom—the wisdom embodied in a corpus of knowledge that has come to be known as Catholic social teaching. This tradition offers a humane and virtuous approach to economic life based on a set of principles rigorously built up from first principles and laid down in a series of remarkable documents over the past 125 years—from the industrial revolution through to the age of sustainable development.

As I will point out, this approach to economics—what I have impishly dubbed *Cathonomics*—has even older pedigrees: on the one hand, the Hebrew Scriptures, the Christian New Testament, and the writings of the early Church Fathers; and on the other hand, the virtue ethics associated most clearly with the philosopher Aristotle. Indeed, one of the great accomplishments of the towering medieval theologian Thomas Aquinas is that he managed to synthesize these two traditions, and this synthesis continues to inform how Catholics think about economics. The goal of this book is to deploy ancient wisdom in the service of contemporary economic problems.

I want to be clear, however: I am no theologian, and this is not a work of theology. It is meant as an elaboration of a set of moral principles than can help us achieve a safer, healthier, fairer, and more humane global economy. If you are a Catholic, you might find in this book an invitation to explore some of the sadly neglected aspects of your religious tradition. But this book is also written for non-Catholics too, for people of all faiths and none. The principles that I will enunciate, and the application of those principles to the economic problems at hand, can be assessed solely on their own merits and without reference to the confessional claims of the Catholic faith. The only article of faith you need to accept is that economics built on faulty ethics is a recipe for disaster—as indeed we are seeing to our great detriment.

◇

I noted at the outset that the election of Pope Francis also changed my own life. Let me conclude this short preface by introducing myself. I am an economist by training, having grown up in Ireland and moved to the United States in 1993 to pursue a PhD. I hail from a working-class background. Both of my parents left school at age twelve, and I was the first in my family to go to college: Trinity College Dublin. My college years would be familiar to anyone from a similar background—a sense of imposter syndrome combined with a sometimes-comical lack of the social capital needed to navigate this strange new world. But on top of that, the economics I studied left me unfulfilled. I opted for economics—in Ireland, you choose your course of study in first year and stick with it for four— because I was always interested in how to improve the lives of people, including the kinds of people I grew up with. But the neoclassical economics I learned seemed rather impractical and out of touch with the reality experienced by so many.

And yet I stuck with it. More than that, actually; I studied it for four years as an undergraduate and then for a two-year master's degree at Trinity College Dublin. Following that, I did my PhD at Columbia University in the areas of macroeconomics and political economy. Looking back in honesty, I never became more comfortable with neoclassical economics, especially in terms of the trend toward mathematical formality. I stuck with it because I figured I could get a job with it. As a working-class kid, I simply did not see a route to employment with the subjects that really interested me: history, theology, and philosophy.

The job I ended up with was at the International Monetary Fund (IMF). As a twenty-eight-year-old, it was an exciting new world—well paid, with the opportunity to travel around the world and be at the center of economic policymaking. At that time, I had bought into the nostrums of neoliberalism—hey, it was the nineties, after all! Everything changed for me with the global financial crisis, though. What for most of my colleagues was an economic crisis requiring technical policy solutions was for me an ethical crisis requiring the reembedding of economics in a better ethical worldview. Needless to say, most people at the IMF thought I was a little "out there" . . .

When I started looking for alternative paradigms, I was drawn immediately to Catholic social teaching. It had always hovered somewhere in my background, though in my neoliberal days I regarded it as somewhat quaint and unrealistic. But now, as I explored it afresh, I came to the conclusion that it offered a superior ethical basis from which to guide the global economy than neoclassical economics. Little did I know it at the time, but I was on a path that would ultimately take me out of the IMF.

By this stage, my job was speechwriter to the managing director. In this role, I served two different individuals: Dominique Strauss-Kahn and Christine Lagarde. It was a role that suited me well—somebody with a flair for writing, more creative than the average IMF economist, and more rooted in the humanities than the sciences. I remain proud of the work I did during those years. I was instrumental in pushing the institution to pay more attention to such topics as inequality, climate change, and the need for ethics in finance.

As I hinted, though, the election of Pope Francis changed everything. When I watched him come onto the balcony to greet well-wishers for the first time, I felt that my life would change too. But I didn't know how at the time. It would take over a year to figure that out. At the end of 2014, I took a leave of absence from the IMF to work with Jeffrey Sachs, of Columbia University, on the intersection of ethics, religions, economics, and sustainable development, in tandem with a remarkable institution called Religions for Peace. This initiative was centered on Pope Francis's most important document to date, *Laudato Si'*, issued in 2015.

Along with key partners such as Religions of Peace and hosted by bishop Marcelo Sánchez Sorondo, the chancellor of the Pontifical Academies of Sciences and Social Sciences at the Vatican, we formed an initiative called Ethics in Action. The goal was to bring together religious leaders from all of the major traditions—plus leading economists, philosophers, theologians, development experts, educators, business leaders, labor leaders, activists, and Indigenous representatives—to come up with a shared moral framework for sustainable development, especially as encapsulated by the seventeen Sustainable Development Goals approved by the United Nations in September 2015 (at a session in which Pope Francis gave the keynote speech). These goals are predicated on the idea that economic prosperity can never again be divorced from social inclusion and care for the planet. The results of this initiative can be seen in both a free online course and a book. Many of the ideas in this volume arose in the meetings of Ethics in Action, and I thank the participants for excellent discussions and collegiality. I learned so much from them.

There are a few people I need to thank by name, without whom this journey could not be possible. In particular, I thank Jeffrey Sachs for his great wisdom, guidance, and moral compass. Every day he reminds me of the kind of economist I want to be, one who has truly made a difference in the lives of people. I thank Bill Vendley, former secretary-general of Religions for Peace, for many great discussions on what a "virtue-based economics" might look like. I thank Bishop Marcelo Sánchez Sorondo, chancellor of the Pontifical Academy of Sciences and Social Sciences, our gracious host for Ethics in Action and a great moral leader in his own right. I thank Stefano Zamagni, president of the Pontifical Academy of Social Sciences, for providing helpful comments on an earlier draft. I thank the wonderful people at the European Forum Alpbach for inviting me to teach a seminar for two years in a row—out of which grew this book. I thank my friends Aniket Shah, Laura Segafredo, Sharon Paculor, and Gabriella Marino for many fun and fruitful discussions in both New York and Rome. Going back further in time, I thank the late Richard R. Roach SJ for introducing me to Catholic social teaching when I was a PhD student in the nineties. Last but not least, I thank my wife, Tram. For everything.

This brings me to the present juncture. I have now left the IMF to work full time on what I am passionate about: reforming economics to help create, in the words of Pope Francis, "another type of progress, one which is healthier, more human, more social, more integral."[5] This is what this book is all about. I had fun writing it. I hope you can join me for the ride.

Notes

1. Pope Francis. "Audience to Representatives of the Communications Media."
2. For more on Pope Francis the man and the reformer, see Ivereigh, *Great Reformer,* and *Wounded Shepherd,* n.p.
3. Pope Francis, "Participation of the Second World Meeting of Popular Movements."
4. Tirole, *Economics for the Common Good*; Collier, *Future of Capitalism.*
5. *LS,* 112.

1

The Old Stuff

Where It All Comes From

I mentioned in the preface that when Pope Francis talks about the economy, he is not speaking in a vacuum. He is not giving his mere personal opinion. What he says has deep roots in Catholic social teaching. These roots go back thousands of years to the twin sources of Hebrew Scriptures and the thought of Aristotle, continue with Jesus and the New Testament, move into the early Church, and culminate in the high synthesis of Saint Thomas Aquinas. The goal of this chapter is to provide an overview of this deep and broad history.

The Hebrew Scriptures

About a decade ago, the British historian Diarmaid MacCulloch penned an expansive book with a thought-provoking title: *A History of Christianity: The First Three Thousand Years.*[1] MacCulloch chose this title to underline the direct continuity between the tradition of the Hebrew Scriptures and the newly emergent Christianity. Nowhere is this clearer than in the obligation toward our fellow human beings and indeed all of creation.

Judaism was born out of the historical experience of marginalization and vulnerability. No phrase is more recurrent in the Hebrew Scriptures than a reminder that the Jewish people were once slaves in the land of Egypt; this is repeated thirty-six times. This history gives rise to a moral obligation to love the poor and the excluded.[2] In the Jewish tradition, this notion of justice to the poor became paramount, as—over and over again—God warns his people not to mistreat widows, orphans, and foreigners (synonymous with the poor of their day). As theologian Daniel Groody points out, obedience to God entails making sure that social structures aid rather than oppress the poor, because God is always their defender, protector, and liberator.[3]

Unsurprisingly, then, the Hebrew Bible is replete with injunctions concerning the needy, the stranger, the orphan, and the widow. For example, when a farmer harvested grain, the farmer was instructed to leave the corners of the field unharvested. And when grapes were gathered from vineyards, harvesters were told not to come back for the grapes that were insufficiently mature the first time. In both cases, what was leftover belonged to the poor. There was also injunction against usury, taking an interest on a loan. In an agricultural society, this would have been one of the ways to oppress the poor, and farmers would seek loans in times of crop failure and other disasters that could mean the difference between life and death.[4]

The strong religious call to protect and defend the poor was justified by the experience of the Jewish people under the Egyptian boot, as recounted in the Exodus narrative. We hear this over and over again, especially in the context of taking care of the stranger. As God says, "You shall not oppress a resident alien; you well know how it feels to be an alien, since you were once aliens yourselves in the land of Egypt" (Exodus 23:9).[5] Or later in Leviticus, "You shall treat the alien who resides with you no differently than the natives born among you; you shall love the alien as yourself; for you too were once aliens in the land of Egypt" (Leviticus 19:34). This belief has modern resonance for us in terms of how we are supposed to treat migrants and refugees.

Perhaps the most well-known economic injunctions in the Hebrew Scriptures relate to the various "cycles of seven": the sabbath day, the sabbatical year, and the Jubilee. The idea of the sabbath is well-known and still honored by observing Jews—that since God rested on the seventh day, no work should be done on that day. Every seventh year was a sabbatical year, when fields were supposed to be left untilled so that the poor could feed from them. More than that, all agrarian debts were to be forgiven, and those who had sold themselves into slavery because of their debts—a common occurrence in the ancient Near East, especially in response to drought and crop failures—were to be released (notice again the theme of liberation from bondage). The most radical action of all occurred on every seventh Sabbatical, which was known as a Jubilee year. During this year, all the requirements of the sabbatical remained in place, with the addition that any land or crop rights either sold under distress or pledged to creditors since the last Jubilee were to be returned to the original owners. The justification was that the land belonged to God and that human beings only had conditional ownership of it. As Leviticus (25:23) says, "The land shall not be sold irrevocably; for the land is mine, and you are but resident aliens and under my authority."

To the modern reader, these injunctions seem radical indeed. Yet Michael Hudson argues that debt cancellations were real, commonplace, and served a valuable social purpose.⁶ He demonstrates that in Bronze Age Mesopotamia, new rulers would frequently issue "clean slate" decrees, which canceled agrarian debts, liberated those in debt bondage, and reversed land forfeitures. These actions would serve to restore economic balance and preserve a land-tenured citizenry as the source of military fighters, public labor, taxation—and social stability as a whole. Without clean slates, and given the frequency of droughts and crop failures, credit oligarchies would have ended up controlling the land, in turn posing a threat to royal officials. So clean slates reflected an element of self-interest as well as justice. Clean slates mostly occurred on the accession of new rulers; it was the ancient Hebrews that made them regular occurrences. As the centuries passed, there was a shift toward more creditor power—culminating in Roman law, which we have inherited, giving supremacy to creditor over debtor rights.

The prophets of ancient Israel, especially Amos and Isaiah, denounced the mistreatment of the poor in language that still sounds fresh and pointed today. Some examples follow:

- "They hand over the just for silver, and the poor for a pair of sandals; they trample the heads of the destitute into the dust of the earth, and force the lowly out of the way." (Amos 2:6–7)
- "I hate, I despise your feasts, I take no pleasure in your solemnities. Even though you bring me your burnt offerings and grain offerings I will not accept them; your stall-fed communion offerings, I will not look upon them. Take away from me your noisy songs; the melodies of your harps, I will not listen to them. Rather let justice surge like waters, and righteousness like an unfailing stream." (Amos 5:21–24)
- "Hear this, you who trample upon the needy and destroy the poor of the land . . . 'We will buy the destitute for silver, and the poor for a pair of sandals; even the worthless grain we will sell!' The LORD has sworn by the pride of Jacob: Never will I forget a thing they have done!" (Amos 8:4–7)
- "Ah! Those who enact unjust statutes, who write oppressive decrees, depriving the needy of judgment, robbing my people's poor of justice, making widows their plunder, and orphans their prey! What will you do on the day of punishment, when the storm comes from afar? To whom will you flee for help? Where will you leave your wealth, lest it sink beneath the captive or fall beneath the slain? For all this, his wrath is not turned back, his hand is still outstretched!" (Isaiah 10:1–4)

- "Is this not, rather, the fast that I choose: releasing those bound unjustly, untying the thongs of the yoke; setting free the oppressed, breaking off every yoke? Is it not sharing your bread with the hungry, bringing the afflicted and the homeless into your house; clothing the naked when you see them, and not turning your back on your own flesh?" (Isaiah 58:6–7).
- "Therefore they grow powerful and rich, fat and sleek. They pass over wicked deeds; justice they do not defend by advancing the claim of the orphan or judging the cause of the poor. Shall I not punish these things?—oracle of the LORD; on a nation such as this shall I not take vengeance?" (Jeremiah 5:27–29).
- "Ah! you plotters of iniquity, who work out evil on your beds! In the morning light you carry it out for it lies within your power. You covet fields, and seize them; houses, and take them; You cheat owners of their houses, people of their inheritance" (Micah 2:1–2).

Four points stand out from these passages of scripture. First, God protects and prioritizes the poor—especially the widow, the orphan, and the foreigner—promising to rain down punishment on those who oppress them and deny them their rights. This point is a matter of communal justice and societal obligation, not simply personal charity.

Second, worship and fasting are empty gestures, with no efficacy, if the poor are simultaneously mistreated. As Groody puts it, without concern for the poor, the prophets maintain that people are spiritually dead.[7] This is a strong rebuke even to those people today who say that the Church should focus on "saving souls" rather than social justice.

Third, the prophets evince a certain corruption that comes with the zealous pursuit of wealth, believing that greed and self-interest lie behind injustice. As John Donohue has noted, the prophets were writing at a time of rising material prosperity, and the disordered desire for ostentatious wealth lay behind the mistreatment of the poor.[8] This is a theme that will echo strongly among the Christian Church fathers, as we will see.

Fourth, injustice is seen as not only a moral failure, individual or communal, but as a plague that could destroy society from within. Once again, Hudson is insightful, arguing that the prophets were reacting not only to increasing prosperity but to greater power of creditors over debtors and "market forces" over land tenure rights.[9] Thus the social order became increasingly unstable. It is no accident that the prophets equate wealth worship with idol worship and a turn away from God, who protects his people from destruction.

Before leaving the Hebrew Scriptures, we need to consider one further element: the biblical injunction to care for the earth as well as the poor. As we will see in later chapters, this is central to the vision of Pope Francis. His most important text to date, *Laudato Si'* (which will be explored further in coming chapters) develops this idea in great detail. The starting point is the understanding that everything God created is good and therefore is worthy of respect and protection. God has bequeathed the earth to humankind, but we are not its owners. Instead, we are stewards of God, charged with caring for creation, making sure the needs of all are met and that the earth is fruitful and bountiful for all generations to come.

This simple idea has nonetheless proven controversial. Why? Because the book of Genesis, the first book of the Bible, states that God gave humanity "dominion over the fish of the sea, the birds of the air, the tame animals, all the wild animals, and all the creatures that crawl on the earth" (Genesis 1:26). Pope Francis explains that dominion does not mean domination, and it certainly does not mean destruction. He also argues that this passage has been abused by Christians to justify an appalling disrespect for creation and for all living things. Instead, the proper biblical mandate is to "till it and keep it." If human beings till too much and keep too little, the natural harmony and sense of interrelationship between person and creation is disrupted. As noted earlier, the earth is on loan from God and the condition of that loan is that we provide for the needs of all people and hand on the earth in good shape to those not yet born.

In this sense, the Hebrew Scriptures identify three fundamental and intertwined relationships that ground human life—with God, with our fellow human beings, and with the earth itself. The key is that when one of these relationships is ruptured, then the others are ruptured too. As Pope Francis notes, the story of Cain and Abel in the opening verses of the Bible shows this clearly. When Cain's envy led him to kill his brother, he clearly ruptured this fraternal bond of kinship. But he also ruptured his relationship with God and with the earth itself, as he was banished from the land and was no longer able to till the earth. When God questioned Cain about his brother, Cain gave a haughty and dismissive answer: "Am I my brother's keeper"? (Genesis 4:9). But in his petulance, Cain had hit on an essential truth: we are all our brother's keepers, and we are called on to "keep" the earth. Right at the beginning of the Hebrew Scriptures, we can find the basic architecture of sustainable development—the idea that we are called to respect both our fellow human beings and the rhythms of nature.

The Teachings of Jesus

Clearly, a book called *Cathonomics* will have something to say about Jesus Christ. In the Christian tradition, the understanding of who Jesus is profoundly affects how we are supposed to treat our fellow human beings. Whole books have of course been written on this. For my part, I will be content to describe briefly how the teachings of Jesus follow directly from the Hebrew Scriptures and speak to how we should understand the economy today.

The starting point is to pay close attention to how Jesus begins his public ministry. In Luke's gospel, Jesus enters the synagogue in his hometown of Nazareth and reads from the scroll of the prophet Isaiah: "The Spirit of the Lord is upon me, because he has anointed me to bring glad tidings to the poor. He has sent me to proclaim liberty to captives and recovery of sight to the blind, to let the oppressed go free, and to proclaim a year acceptable to the Lord" (Luke 4:18–19). He then turned to the congregation and announced, "Today this scripture passage is fulfilled in your hearing" (Luke 4:21). The townspeople were unimpressed with such a claim. In fact, they regarded it as blasphemous and tried to kill him, an event prefiguring the death of Jesus three years later at the hands of the Roman administrators in Jerusalem.

Pay close attention to these words from Isaiah. As Daniel Finn notes, "Jesus does not say that his mission is to bring people closer to God or to get them to be more careful in their prayers or to persuade them to attend to their liturgical responsibilities more faithfully. No, instead he says that his mission is to relieve the suffering and oppression of those most ignored, rejected, or persecuted."[10] There is a link between what Jesus preaches and the prophets of the Hebrew Scriptures. Hudson goes so far as to argue that people might have made the association between "liberty" and crippling debt and the "year of the Lord's favor" with the Jubilee of the Hebrew Scriptures. He argues that Jesus's strenuous criticism of the Jewish authorities at the time comes in the context of legalistic mechanisms they had devised to take away the strong scriptural bias in favor of debtors, aligning themselves more with the Greco-Roman legal system and its creditor oligarchies.[11]

What Jesus preached was the Kingdom of God, or what biblical scholar Gerhard Lohfink calls the "Reign of God."[12] Billions of words have been written trying to tease out what he meant by that. I will stick with the standard Catholic approach: Jesus is talking about the transformation of the world, the bending of history toward justice through the active power of God—in Lohfink's words, "God intervenes, redeems his people, and creates them anew."[13] This process has begun with the proclamation of Jesus but will not be fully accomplished until the end of time. Theologians call this the "already, but not yet" dimension of the Kingdom, one of the many paradoxes that define the Christian faith. Christians are called on to strive for justice, to seek a new kind of society that prioritizes the poor and underprivileged while at the same time recognizing that all utopian visions are fools' errands. In a sense, many of the arguments that play out within

Christianity boil down to this: should we focus on the spiritual dimension in hope of heaven or rather on building a better world in the here and now? The answer is yet another Christian paradox: it less "either/or" than "both/and."

As a perfect example of this "both/and" reasoning, consider the famous Lord's prayer—the prayer Jesus taught his disciples to pray. As laid down in the *New American Bible*, the English translation reads: "Our Father in heaven, hallowed be your name, your kingdom come, your will be done, on earth as in heaven. Give us today our daily bread; and forgive us our debts, as we forgive our debtors; and do not subject us to the final test, but deliver us from the evil one." The theologian David Bentley Hart has argued that the first part is translated correctly, calling for the coming of the Kingdom, but that the second part is more nuanced.[14] The standard Christian explanation is that Jesus is using the term "debt" as a metaphor for "sin" and is referring to the final judgment—and indeed, the anthropologist David Graeber argues that the language of sin has always been associated with the language of debt.[15] In this context, Hart favors a more literal reading of the text, claiming that debt means debt and that Jesus is talking directly about oppression by unscrupulous creditors through the law courts. Here is his translation of the second part: "Give us our bread today, in a quantity sufficient for the whole of the day. And grant us relief from our debts, to the very degree that we grant relief to those who are indebted to us. And do not bring us to court for trial, but rather rescue us from the wicked man."[16] For Hart, this is a prayer for the poor. He ties the prayers to "how often Jesus speaks of trials, of officers dragging the insolvent to jail, of men bound by or imprisoned for undischarged debts, of unmerciful creditors, of suits brought before judges to secure a coat or cloak, of the unfortunate legally despoiled by the fortunate."[17] This was all-too-real social reality, in which the poor, crippled by taxes, were frequently reduced to the status of indentured tenants following expropriation and oppressive terms of loans. In this telling, the tax collectors, loan sharks, and law courts all conspired against the poor, the people to whom Jesus preached liberty and the coming of the Kingdom. Does that mean the traditional spiritual reading of the Lord's prayer is wrong? Not at all. It's a perfect example of textured, multilayered, "both/and" reasoning.

Let me now turn to some of Jesus's concrete teachings regarding the poor and the oppressed. In the synoptic gospels—Matthew, Mark, and Luke—Jesus preaches thirty-one parables. The biblical scholar Amy-Jill Levine argues that we tend to domesticate Jesus's "provocative stories," downplaying their simple and direct messages, turning them into allegories and—worse—reading anti-Jewish tropes into them.[18] Levine notes that Jesus was deeply concerned about economic issues, including wealth management, debts, and land ownership. He chose examples he knew would resonate with his listeners. As theologian Elizabeth

Hinson-Hasty notes, nineteen of these thirty-one parables refer to indebtedness, social class, misuse of wealth, the distribution of wealth, and worker pay.[19] Levine argues that the parables teach us how to ask the right questions: "How to live in community; how to determine what ultimately matters; how to live the life that God wants us to live."[20]

In this context, one of Jesus's most famous parables is the one about the rich man and Lazarus from Luke's gospel. Lazarus was a poor man, so ignored and marginalized that he was not even given the scraps from the rich man's table. But when both died, Lazarus was taken to heaven—to the "bosom of Abraham"—while the rich man was shocked to find himself damned to an eternity of torment. The rich man, no doubt used to being heeded and obeyed, asked Abraham to send Lazarus down with a finger dipped in water to cool his tongue. Abraham said no. Next, the rich man asked Abraham to send Lazarus to warn his brothers, so they would not suffer his fate. Again, Abraham refused, on the grounds that his brothers should listen to Moses and the prophets—in other words, to the strong injunctions of the Hebrew Scriptures to prioritize the well-being of the poor and marginalized. Amy-Jill Levine stresses that we are supposed to take this parable at face value. Jesus's Jewish listeners would have expected the rich man to help Lazarus; indeed, he might have been placed at his gate for precisely that reason. But the rich man shows that he is no son of Abraham by neglecting his duties and instead living a luxurious lifestyle. Even worse, he never gets beyond seeing Lazarus as a mere slave whose job is to do his bidding. The message is clear: if we cannot see the poor person in front of us, "then we are lost."[21] Here's an interesting observation about this story: in all of Jesus's parables, he does not use names, just simple descriptions—a king, a steward, a rich man, a woman, a widow, and so on. But the poor man he calls by name, to show that Jesus is especially close to the poor.[22]

Jesus's identification with the poor suffuses the entire gospel narrative. Even before he was born, his mother, Mary, when told that she would give birth to Jesus, responded with a great prayer of thanksgiving to God that included the following lines: "He has thrown down the rulers from their thrones but lifted up the lowly. The hungry he has filled with good things; the rich he has sent away empty" (Luke 1:52–53). This subversive prayer of a poor young, pregnant woman has been adopted by the oppressed throughout history.

Jesus himself was born in the humblest of circumstances and grew up poor, learning a trade from his father. The Jesuit Fr. James Martin has made the point that although Jesus is typically described as the son of a carpenter, the word from which that derives, *tekton*, is more accurately translated as "day laborer." As he puts it, "*Tektons* were generally seen as ranking, socially and economically, below the peasantry since most didn't own a plot of land. It was probably a hardscrabble life, building doors and tables, but also likely digging ditches and building walls."[23] Nazareth was a desperately poor place full of struggling people, a backwater of the empire in the truest sense. It is no wonder then that contemporaries of Jesus would deploy the sarcastic phrase, "Can anything good come from Nazareth?" (John 1:46).

There are other examples of Jesus condemning the hoarding of wealth. In one famous passage, a rich man asks Jesus what he must do to gain eternal life. Jesus tells him to obey the Ten Commandments. He responds that he does so. Jesus then tells him to sell his possessions and give to the poor. He finds himself unable to take that final, decisive step. Jesus's conclusion would not be clearer: "How hard it is for those who have wealth to enter the kingdom of God! For it is easier for a camel to pass through the eye of a needle than for a rich person to enter the kingdom of God" (Luke 18:24–25). Jesus's point is that the pursuit of money is the pursuit of a false God. "No one can serve two masters," he says. "He will either hate one and love the other, or be devoted to one and despise the other. You cannot serve God and mammon" (Matthew 6:24). Mammon is an idol, the very antithesis of everything about the nature of God. In the words of theologians Daniel Harrington and James Keenan, Mammon "refers to money or wealth in general as something in which people place their faith or trust, and so it assumes a God-like status."[24] Groody refers to this phenomenon in its contemporary manifestation as "money-theism," which he defines as "the idolization of capital, expressed as the worship of the gods of the marketplace . . . In this system, people are measured in terms of their net worth, accumulated possessions, and incomes rather than their human worth, the quality of their character, and their spiritual depth."[25]

Perhaps the starkest characterization of Jesus's teaching about how we must treat the poor and the marginalized comes from the twenty-fifth chapter of Matthew's gospel, which talks about the Last Judgment, in which God will separate the sheep from the goats. But what criteria will he use? The answer is how we treat the "least among us" in this life. It is worth quoting in full how he addresses the "goats," those who will be damned:

Then he will say to those on his left, "Depart from me, you accursed, into the eternal fire prepared for the devil and his angels. For I was hungry and you gave me no food, I was thirsty and you gave me no drink, a stranger and you gave me no welcome, naked and you gave me no clothing, ill and in prison, and you did not care for me." Then they will answer and say, "Lord, when did we see you hungry or thirsty or a stranger or naked or ill or in prison, and not minister to your needs?" He will answer them, "Amen, I say to you, what you did not do for one of these least ones, you did not do for me." (Matthew 25:41–45)

What Jesus is saying is that he identifies personally with the poor and the victims of oppression. Christianity is a religion with a human face, the face of the poor. We are called on to see Christ in all who are suffering, excluded, mistreated, or marginalized. And if you are a believing Christian, your salvation actually depends on it.

The pinnacle of Jesus's teaching can be found in the Beatitudes from the famous Sermon on the Mount. It is worth recording them in full. Here is the version from Luke's gospel:

> Blessed are you who are poor, for the kingdom of God is yours.
> Blessed are you who are now hungry, for you will be satisfied.
> Blessed are you who are now weeping, for you will laugh.
> Blessed are you when people hate you, and when they exclude and insult
>   you, and denounce your name as evil on account of the Son of Man.
> Rejoice and leap for joy on that day! Behold, your reward will be great in
>   heaven. For their ancestors treated the prophets in the same way.
> But woe to you who are rich, for you have received your consolation.
> But woe to you who are filled now, for you will be hungry.
> Woe to you who laugh now, for you will grieve and weep.
> Woe to you when all speak well of you,
> for their ancestors treated the false prophets in this way. (Luke 6:20–26)

In Christianity, the moral imperative to respond to the needs of others with compassion and put the last first finds fullest form in these Beatitudes. Jesus is teaching that the coming of the Kingdom will turn the world upside down in favor of those currently oppressed, because, in the words of Donohue, "The Kingdom that he proclaims and enacts will confront those values and conditions that have made them marginal."[26] Or as Lohfink puts it, the hopeless, the oppressed, and the despairing are blessed because "God's intervention is about to take place and because it is especially the hopeless who will experience God's hope and salvation in a measure beyond all telling." This is not merely a claim that the miserable and the poor will enjoy a better life after death. Rather, according to Lohfink, Jesus is claiming that "this turning point is at hand. It will gather Israel anew, it will make possible a new society in which the poor have a share in the wealth of the land and the sorrowing participate in the rejoicing of the people of God."[27]

A further insight is that responding to our neighbor in need with compassion benefits not only the recipient but also the benefactor, who is given the grace of allowing him or her to see the face of Christ in the least of his brothers and sisters, and to respond accordingly. In this sense, the Beatitudes go deeper than the golden rule, the idea that a person should do unto others as she would have them do unto her—instead of an abstract view of the other, they speak of the other in his existential reality of suffering.[28]

This notion of love, mercy, and concreteness is also found in the parable of the Good Samaritan, which really answers the question, "Who is my neighbor?" This question immediately followed Jesus's description of the highest commandment as "You shall love the Lord, your God, with all your heart, with all your being, with all your strength, and with all your mind, and your neighbor as yourself" (Luke 10:27). To summarize briefly: a man on the road of Jerusalem to Jericho is robbed, beaten up, and left on the side of the road. A priest and the Levite pass him by, but a Samaritan—a member of a tribe of outcasts to the Jewish people at the time—took care of him. Thus Jesus's answer is that every single human being should be regarded as our neighbor—an antidote against insularity, xenophobia, and nationalism. This view has obvious contemporary relevance. In his own life, Jesus shocked his contemporaries by being willing to socialize and share fellowship with the despised, including sinners and tax collectors, ritual and legal outcasts of the time, those whom social structures would have placed beyond the mercy and love of God.[29]

One final point: The gospels describe exactly one time when Jesus grew angry—when he drove the money lenders from the temple. This account is described in all four gospels and shows clearly what Jesus thought about the idolatry of "money-theism." Adding some important context, Hudson notes that business contracts and oaths were sworn before the Lord in the temple, and "this oath taking sanctified the repayment of debt."[30] More than anything else, it was this subversive act that drew the attention of the authorities and set in motion the train of events that led to Jesus's torture and execution. Of course, Christians believe that out of this great evil, Christ's resurrection redeemed the whole world—perhaps the greatest of the great Christian paradoxes.

The Early Church and the Church Fathers

The New Testament describes the contours of the early Church, most notably in the Acts of the Apostles (written by the same author as the gospel of Luke) and the letters of Paul. I don't intend to spend too much time here, beyond highlighting a few pertinent points. One key point is that an ethos of economic equality permeated the nascent Christian Church. The earliest Christian communities in Jerusalem held all goods in common, forsaking private ownership.

While this radical sharing was not insisted on as the Church spread across the empire, there was nonetheless a deep concern with taking care of the weak in the community and providing financial assistance to poorer churches. As with all scriptural perspectives, this was seen not as a voluntary display of charity but a strict duty of justice. As Christian communities expanded, they encompassed more socioeconomic diversity, which brought with it the potential for socio-economic conflict. This concern was key for Paul, as he penned his letters to far-flung churches. In the words of Donohue, Paul essentially stressed that "those social distinctions between upper-class and lower-class people that are part of the fabric of the Hellenistic world would have no place in the Christian assembly."[31]

That being said, Paul did not play up some of the more radical teachings of Jesus about the allure of wealth. He left that to James, leader of the Church in Jerusalem. James lambasts those who fawn over the rich and disdain the poor. "Did not God choose those who are poor in the world to be rich in faith and heirs of the kingdom that he promised to those who love him?," he asks. He goes on to denounce the rich who hoard wealth in some of the harshest language in the Bible:

> Come now, you rich, weep and wail over your impending miseries. Your wealth has rotted away, your clothes have become moth-eaten, your gold and silver have corroded, and that corrosion will be a testimony against you; it will devour your flesh like a fire. You have stored up treasure for the last days. Behold, the wages you withheld from the workers who har-vested your fields are crying aloud, and the cries of the harvesters have reached the ears of the Lord of hosts. You have lived on earth in luxury and pleasure; you have fattened your hearts for the day of slaughter. You have condemned; you have murdered the righteous one; he offers you no resistance. (James 5:1–6)

This language sets the scene for the Church Fathers, those theologians and reli-gious leaders who wrote during the Church's early centuries, when the Roman Empire was still alive and kicking. The leading Church Fathers speaking on economic themes include Saint Basil, Saint Gregory, Saint John Chrysostom, Saint Ambrose, and Saint Augustine. These Church leaders wrote vast tomes on the topics of the stewardship of wealth and concern for the poor; my intention is only to provide a brief overview of their thought.[32] As we will see, the prophetic language about riches and injustice thundering from the Church Fathers echoes through the centuries in a way that resonates deeply today. When we peruse these ancient writings, a number of themes emerge.[33]

First, only God, as the source of all existence, satisfies our deepest yearnings. Hence we are called to seek God above all things. While everything that God created is good, created things are not the highest good and cannot provide true happiness. In particular, looking for satisfaction in wealth, possessions, and status is a form of idolatry that leads to unhappiness, disorder, and chaos.

Second, all human beings share a common bond. All have equal dignity. Social and economic distinctions mean nothing before God, who created the earth for all people. This theme points to solidarity with the poor.

Third, the goods of the earth are destined for all. This view is not so much a condemnation of private ownership but rather of hoarding wealth in the face of poverty and deprivation. While some Church Fathers looked nostalgically to the common ownership practiced in the early Church, others focused more on the obligations on the wealthy to make sure the needs of all are met. They were supposed to use their wealth to provide for basic material and social needs, not to whittle it away on frivolous luxury or vanity. As Finn puts it, the standard becomes "If I have more than I need and you have less than you need, I am obliged to share my surplus with you, because God has given the earth to humanity, and my wealth to me, to meet the needs of all."[34] It helps to hear the Church Fathers in their own words on how the goods of the earth are destined for all. Just a small flavor:

- "You are not making a gift of what is yours to the poor man, but you are giving him back what is his. You have been appropriating things that are meant to be for the common use of everyone. The earth belongs to everyone, not to the rich."—Saint Ambrose[35]
- "Not to share our wealth with the poor is theft from the poor and deprivation of their means of life; we do not possess our own wealth but theirs."—Saint John Chrysostom[36]
- "I am not constraining you to lessen your capital, not because I do not wish it, but because I see you are very recalcitrant. I am not then saying this. No. But give away the revenues; keep nothing of these. It is enough for you to have the money of your income pouring in on you as from a fountain; make the poor sharers with you, and become a good steward of the things God has given you."—Saint John Chrysostom[37]
- "Let us not usurp for ourselves what has been given to us for our brothers and sisters, who have the same needs as we do, so that we do not make wealth to be something unjust by holding on to what belongs to another."—Saint Cyril of Alexandria[38]

Fourth, God is especially close to the poor and treasures them. The rich can therefore help themselves gain eternal salvation by using their financial resources to help the poor. Indeed, some argued that God made some people rich simply so they could be given the grace of helping the poor. As time passed, and the Roman world transitioned into something more feudal, there was greater emphasis on endowing the Church itself as a means of salvation and some of the more radical teachings of the early Fathers were toned down. Part of this came from the transition in the Church itself from minority to majority religion, with all the trappings that come with wealth and power.[39] But that is another story. For my purposes, it helps to listen to the Fathers thundering against the misuse of wealth and abuse of the poor, just to see how fresh and relevant their language seems:

- "What a judgment you draw upon yourself! The people are starving, and you shut your barns; the people are groaning, and you toy with the jewel upon your finger. Unhappy man, with the power but not the will to rescue so many souls from death, when the price of a jeweled ring might save the lives of a whole populace."—Saint Ambrose[40]
- "Oh rich ones, such are your kindnesses! The less you give, the more you demand. Such is your humanity that you plunder even as you pretend to give aid! Even a poor person is for you a fruitful means of acquiring profit. In their need, you subject the poor to high interest loans, compelling them to pay what they do not have. . . . Is there anything more oppressive? The poor ask for medicine and you offer poison; they beg for bread and you stretch out a sword; they appeal for freedom and you impose servitude; they implore you to absolve them of their bondage and you twist more tightly the hideous knot of the noose."—Saint Ambrose[41]
- "The bread in your cupboard belongs to the hungry, the cloak in your wardrobe belongs to the naked, the shoes you let rot belong to the barefoot, the money in your vaults belongs to the destitute. Everyone you might help and do not—to all these you are doing wrong."—Saint Basil the Great[42]
- "Your Lord goes about hungry, and you treat yourself to luxuries—and not only this abuse, but also the fact that, in your luxury, you manage to ignore him, not that he wants much more than only a scrap of bread to alleviate his hunger. Yet, while he goes about frozen with the cold, you pay him no attention in your silken garments, and instead of showing compassion you pass by heedlessly."—Saint John Chrysostom[43]

Fifth, an attachment to wealth can corrupt the soul. This view follows from the biblical injunction in Saint Paul's letter to Timothy that "the love of money is the root of all evils, and some people in their desire for it have strayed from the faith and have pierced themselves with many pains" (1 Timothy 6:10). Or as Groody puts it, "Greed is an all-consuming god that demands unrelenting obedience."[44] This corruption manifests in disdain and mockery for the poor and excluded. It follows that a simple life, free of the snares of luxury, can be liberating. Again, the Fathers were blunt on how wealth can corrupt, ensnare, and enslave:

- "A possession ought to belong to the possessor, not the possessor to the possession. Whosoever, therefore, does not use his inheritance as a possession, who does not know how to give and distribute it to the poor, he is the servant of his wealth, not its master."—Saint Ambrose[45]
- "The swollen pride and cancerous growth of the rich have their own way of revealing themselves. These people forget their human condition and think that they are superior to nature. In the wretched state of the poor they actually find something to season their pleasures. They laugh at the poor, insult the disadvantaged, and diminish the very ones on whom any decent person would have pity."—Saint Ambrose[46]
- "How could wealth be the definition of happiness and the foundation of good fortune if it is the means by which wicked men become supercilious and puffed up, strutting through the marketplace on horseback or in carriages, despising others in so far as it is seemly for them to look down on them, wronging, grasping, appropriating what does not belong to them, coveting what is unbecoming, taking their neighbors' belongings, enjoying other people's good fortune, trading on the misfortunes of the poor, and so on?"—Theodoret of Cyrus[47]

Aristotelian Virtue Ethics

It now time to switch gears, away from the Judeo-Christian tradition toward a second major root of Catholic social teaching: the virtue ethics of Aristotle. Some are surprised by this: after all, Aristotelian virtue ethics is a branch of secular ethics, with no Christian—or indeed any other religious—connotation. Remember, though, that Christianity was birthed in the Greco-Roman world and has always been influenced by Greek philosophy. And Aristotle in particular, as we shall see, was a major influence on the thought of Saint Thomas Aquinas, the intellectual godfather of Catholic social teaching.

Aristotle lived in ancient Greece from 384 to 322 BC and made major contributions in the development of philosophy across numerous dimensions. My interest lies in what Aristotle had to say about political economy, which he saw as belonging to the domain of ethics. The main text here is the *Nicomachean Ethics*, named after his son Nichomachus.[48] Before getting to Aristotle's approach to ethics and economics, we first need to get through some preliminaries. This step is especially necessary because Aristotle's thought and reasoning can sometimes come across as odd and alien to the modern mindset. Even the word "virtue" creates some confusion, conjuring up some kind of outdated and stuffy Victorian probity. But, as we shall see, that is not what Aristotle meant by virtue at all.

First things first: Aristotle's ethical reasoning is teleological, which means that he believed everything has a final cause, an end, a propose in which it finds its perfection.[49] Hence everything is moving toward that final end, even though it can be thwarted by both external and internal impediments. When a thing, a creature, or even a person achieves an end or purpose, that thing, creature, or person is deemed to be "good" of their kind. Keep in mind how Aristotle uses the word "good"; this will turn out to be extremely important when we turn to human beings and their economic pursuits. So, for example, if the purpose of a tree is to grow and flourish and spread its seeds, a "good" tree is one that does so with maximum efficacy. If the purpose of a wolf is to run fast and hunt well, the same reasoning applies: a "bad" wolf would be one that lies around all day. Aristotle also thought this logic could be applied to inanimate objects such as rocks and fire, but that's a little bit too "out there" for us modern audiences with a greater understanding of how science works.

What about humans? What is our purpose? Aristotle believed that our purpose, our telos, what we are oriented toward, is happiness. He understood that this state could raise more questions than answers; different people might point to different factors such as wealth, fame, success, marriage, friendship. Nonetheless, Aristotle thought that all people could agree on what constituted a notion of happiness that was sought for its own sake, not merely as a means to something else.

Aristotle called this state *eudaimonia*, a term often seen as synonymous with happiness but that is really best translated as human flourishing.[50] *Eudaimonia* can be identified with living in accord with what is intrinsically worthwhile to human beings: meaning and purpose, quality relationships, good health, and the ability to make a valid contribution to society. The philosopher Martha Nussbaum defines it as "a kind of living that is active, inclusive of all that has intrinsic value, and complete, meaning lacking in nothing that would make it richer or better."[51] Another leading modern philosopher, Alasdair MacIntyre, is more succinct: *eudaimonia* to him is "the state of being well and doing well in being well."[52] For Aristotle, this entailed a lifelong quest—there was no shortcut to true happiness. He was also not naive, recognizing that bad luck (through ill health, for example) or poverty could hinder *eudaimonia*. But for the purposes of economics, he was clear that wealth was not to be pursued for its own sake: "Wealth is obviously not the good that we are seeking, because it serves only as a means; i.e. for getting something else."[53]

Let us assume we agree with Aristotle that this *eudaimonia*, this all-encompassing notion of living well, is synonymous with true happiness. Let us assume we agree that it is the telos of the human being. How do we get there? This line of thought brings us to another link in Aristotle's chain: he argues that what is distinctive about human beings is their capacity for reason. This capacity is what distinguishes us from creatures and inanimate objects. He thought that the soul was divided into parts that were common to all things, to animals, and specifically to human beings; this for him was the "rational soul." Therefore a "good" human is one who uses reason well, who puts the rational soul in the driver's seat. For him, this is the true route to *eudaimonia*.

This is where Aristotle's idea of virtue comes in. The word "virtue" derives from the Greek *arete* and is also understood as "excellence." It is taking a latent capacity and bringing it to full potential, just like the good tree and the good wolf. If you keep this in mind, you can stop your mind from thinking of Victorian moralism around the word "virtue." In my view, MacIntyre provides the best definition of "virtue" as understood in this context: "Those qualities the possession of which will enable an individual to achieve *eudaimonia*, and the lack of which will frustrate his movement toward that telos."[54] So we are driven to exercise the virtues in accord with excellence. That will make us a "good" human being and point the way toward a flourishing life well lived.

Note again the importance of the word "good." Aristotle believed in the idea of an objective good—a concept of the good that exerts a gravitational pull on human nature, common to all human beings. In this sense, the virtues can be understood as habits that orient us to act in ways that are good. And there is a dynamic element at play. It is helpful to quote MacIntyre again, who noted that exercising the virtues requires transitioning from "man-as-he-happens-to-be" to "man-as-he-could-be-if-he-realized-his-essential-nature."[55] Note what this implies: the idea that perfection is possible, that everybody is good at something, and that improvement—including moral improvement—should be our goal.

But what exactly are these virtues? One of the frustrations with Aristotle is that he fails to define them precisely, and some of the ones he mentions sound a bit odd to the modern reader. But the basic picture is clear. To start, he distinguishes between intellectual virtues such as practical reason, knowledge, and good judgment; and moral virtues such as courage, justice, generosity, friendliness, temperance, self-respect. A key virtue for Aristotle is practical wisdom, or *phronesis*, which is really about figuring the best means to achieve our ends in any given circumstance and in turn requires thoughtful, reflective deliberation, including by listening to and learning from teachers and role models.

So virtues are simply good habits that can be learned through practice. Again, "good" is crucial. A person with the capacity to be a great con artist should probably not seek to develop that capacity. But a person with the capacity to be a great musician or doctor should. As far as the moral virtues are concerned, they apply to all people. To be a good and happy person involves exercising these virtues in accord with excellence. In the words of the classicist Edith Hall, it is about "finding a purpose in order to realize your potential and working on your behavior to become the best version of yourself."[56] She notes that for Aristotle, immoral people—those who choose vice over moral virtue—are always conflicted. They strive for happiness, but deep down they know there is something missing. This conflict and misdirected purpose can lead to psychological problems. Although his knowledge of science was sorely lacking, Aristotle managed to anticipate some key insights from psychology; more of this in chapter 3.

For Aristotle, a good life is a balanced life. From this perspective, one of Aristotle's most interesting ideas is to see a virtue as the "golden mean" between two vices. For example, courage is the virtue between rashness and cowardice. Justice sits between favoritism and discrimination. Generosity balances profligacy and miserliness. Temperance is the mean between indulgence and asceticism. And so on . . . you get the picture.

Many ethical systems provide rules of behavior. Aristotle does not. His moral reasoning always depends on the context—figuring out the best course of action in concrete circumstances. In this sense, the virtues are like muscles: the more practice we get, the easier it becomes, and muscle memory gets built in. And virtuous people become role models to the rest of us, which is why ethical education is so important to classical philosophers such as Aristotle. We can learn to be good through good practice.

Before concluding with Aristotle, there is one more link in the chain we need to explore. As well as the individual good, there is something called the common good. Aristotle viewed human beings as social animals, so their happiness also has a social dimension. For Aristotle, happiness does not lie in solitude but in the context of the social life. Human beings seek not only the good life *for* themselves but the good life *with* others. This sense of mutual flourishing is embedded in the notion of the common good, which Catholic theologian David Hollenbach defines as "the good realized in the mutual relationships in and through which human beings achieve their well-being."[57] All domains of human interactions have common goods, goods that transcend the good of the individuals participating in them and which are not divisible into the sum of these individual goods. Take marriage and friendship, for example. In both cases, the good is relational, indivisible, and greater than the sum of its parts. There is a common good to be found in all of our collective activities.

This theme also holds when we turn to the political domain. For Aristotle, the good life is the telos not only of the individual but of the political community too. He believed that, through social cooperation, human beings could work out a shared understanding of what constitutes a good and dignified life, which requires reflexive political discernment.[58] As with the individual good, it is not simply about applying rules but about working out what is best in each particular context, alongside our fellow citizens. Accordingly, politics is ultimately about forming good citizens and cultivating good character, and good leaders are those who can best excel in civic virtue and deliberate for the common good.[59] And just as the body is greater than the sum of its parts, this common good is the highest good, higher than any individual good.

Especially from the modern vantage point, Aristotle can be accused of some naivete here; his view of politics seems too rosy. What might have worked for a small city-state such as Athens (which anyway did not allow women or slaves any role in political deliberation) might not work in a messy, large modern democracy, prone to partisanship and acrimony. Nonetheless, I would argue that Aristotle's notion of the common good as the telos of the political community, higher than the individual good, can act as the lodestar for democratic deliberation. The very concept of a common good is powerful yet tends to be downplayed today. As will be seen, it is central to Catholic social teaching.

This discussion brings us, finally, to economics. To be fair, economics is not central to Aristotle's thought. It is part of his political theory, which in turn is subordinated to ethics. We have already seen that Aristotle is suspicious of the pursuit of wealth for its own sake. He puts forward a useful distinction between *oikonomia* and *chrematistike*. Although typically translated as household management, what Aristotle and the ancient Greeks had in mind by *oikonomia* (the Greek root of the word "economics") were the ethical rules (*nomoi*) for governing the private and public households (*oikoi*). Economics—a branch of ethics, virtue ethics—is to be distinguished from *chrematistike*, the pursuit of wealth for its own sake, divorced from either the individual or common good.[60] Aristotle thought that *chrematistike* undermined virtue and human flourishing, enslaved people with a false view of happiness, and corrupted business practice and good workmanship. His warnings in this regard are similar to those of the Church Fathers. The ancients were of one mind, it would seem.

One caveat: Aristotle was not opposed to wealth per se. As noted, he understood that poverty would impede *eudaimonia*, no matter how virtuous the person was. The problem comes from treating wealth as an end in itself rather than as a means to the good life, which means a life of reason and virtue. Once again, it boils down to the right balance. As noted by Claus Dierksmeier, Aristotle believed that people should strive to live "temperately but liberally."[61] Unbalancing these two elements was asking for trouble. On its own, liberality would lead to luxury, which hindered virtue. Aristotle even had a word for the unwholesome and corrupting desire of wanting more than enough: *pleonexia*. Likewise, temperance on its own would lead to toil and excess hardship. The good life requires balance and a strong element of self-moderation.[62] It requires government intervention to achieve a proper balance of wealth, as otherwise social harmony is jeopardized. This account of wealth is of course alien to how we view the modern economy.

Before leaving Aristotle, though, I want to talk about a philosopher I have referenced already, MacIntyre, who wrote an influential book called *After Virtue* in 1981. In this book, MacIntyre argued that we have inherited the older language of virtue ethics but have also lost its original meaning, which leads to immense confusion over ethical matters and an inability to reach any kind of ethical consensus.

One of MacIntyre's innovations was his concept of a "practice," defined as "any coherent and complex form of socially established cooperative human activity through which goods internal to that activity are realized."[63] You can immediately see the link to Aristotle and virtue ethics. For MacIntyre, virtue is linked to the attainment of goods internal to the practice, as opposed to an external good such as wealth, fame, flattery, or power. Think of a simple example. A top tennis player can be richly rewarded with external goods, but they are ultimately motivated by the excellence of doing and being their best. For MacIntyre, all aspects of life should follow the same pattern with subordination of naturally human desires to the goods or excellences internal to your specific practice. And it entails cooperation toward a particular common good, the good of the practice. Realizing those internal goods is about the "we" rather than the "me." This is going to create problems when we turn to modern economics, which assumes that people are self-oriented, competitive rather than cooperative, and motivated to seek external goods through financial incentives. If we believe in this Aristotelian scheme, then—in the words of theologian David Cloutier—debasing internal goods in this manner will "deform us as persons, deform the activity itself, and deform the cooperation necessary for ongoing excellence in the activity."[64] I will have much more to say about this in chapter 3. For now, we can conclude that MacIntyre provides an updated version of Aristotle's virtue ethics, which is predicated on the real psychological need to excel and find meaning and purpose across all activity. Old Aristotle might have had some useful modern insights after all.

The Thought of Thomas Aquinas

Let me now turn to the great synthesis of Christianity and Aristotelian virtue ethics offered by Saint Thomas Aquinas (1225–74). By far the most important of the medieval theologians, Aquinas's theological musings are deep, highly erudite, and not always easy to follow. I am mainly interested in what he has to say about economics, though, and will endeavor to provide you with what you need to know to better understand the origins of modern Catholic social teaching.[65]

At the risk of oversimplifying, the easiest way to understand Aquinas is that he takes Aristotle's ethics and adds God. Aristotle can be appreciated without any reference to a creator. Not so Aquinas: he adopts Aristotle's teleological account of human nature, with its emphasis on living the good life through virtue, and asks where God would fit in. His answer is almost deceptively simple: that a person can find true happiness only in the highest good of all, which is God.

To delve into this, Aquinas teases out the role of the intellect and will, identified with the capacities to know and to desire. He argues that we are like God in the sense that we possess this intellect and will, which sets us above other creatures. The intellect is the capacity that allows us to know the truth and therefore inclines us to seek the truth, identified with discerning the good. The will, or what Aquinas called the rational appetite (to distinguish from the sensory appetites we share with animals) desires the good, once known, and is directed by the intellect. Both capacities need to be actualized. Happiness therefore consists in knowing and loving God, who is the ultimate good and ultimate perfection. Aquinas identifies this with the beatific vision, which must await the next life for its full unfolding. But if this union with God constitutes perfect happiness, Aquinas also recognizes "imperfect happiness" in this life. In another example of the "already but not yet" category we have seen already, happiness in this life anticipates to some extent the perfect happiness in the next life.

Another way to say the same thing is that Aquinas provides a twofold structure of happiness: the natural end, synonymous with Aristotle's *eudaimonia*, and the supernatural end, which entails union with God. And unsurprisingly, all of this entails virtue. Following Aristotle, Aquinas regards virtues as stable dispositions ordered toward good acts. On the other side of the ledger, vices are stable dispositions that incline us to act badly, in ways that are not consistent with a full unfolding of human nature. Acting on a vice leads to sin. Aquinas argued that there could be sins of the intellect, sins of passion, and sins of the will. A sin of the intellect is a sin of ignorance—choosing a disordered end, something that is not good, even if we think it is. A sin of the will is when we deliberately choose something that we know is not good for us. More technically, Aquinas describes it as choosing some lesser good over a greater good and thus blocking the actualization of our potential. Putting it simply, we go wrong when we choose something that is not good for us because we don't know any better, even if we should, and when we know what is good for us but fail to choose it.

Delving deeper, Aquinas identities seven core virtues, which perfect either the intellect or the will. The four cardinal virtues—prudence, justice, fortitude, and temperance—are habits disposing us to achieve happiness in this life. The three theological virtues—faith, hope, and charity—orient us toward our supernatural end. Just like *phronesis* for Aristotle, the virtue of prudence allows us to discern what we should do in various contexts and directs the will toward the good in question. It allows us to make sense out of messy circumstances, both in terms of choosing the end and choosing the means of attaining that end. Aquinas sees fortitude and temperance as perfecting the sensory appetites. Fortitude allows us to both overcome and respect our fears in terms of the good we are pursuing. Temperance allows us to partake in the ordinary pleasures of life without being mastered by them. Justice, on the other hand, perfects the will, or the rational appetite. This is the virtue that prompts us to give others their due and so is directed toward the common good, which Aquinas again borrows from Aristotle. Because of this, the virtue of justice, as we shall see, is extremely important in economic matters.

What about the theological virtues? As noted, these are all oriented toward union with God, our ultimate happiness and our supernatural end. Faith aligns the intellect with God, while hope and charity work on the will. Unlike the cardinal virtues, these cannot be acquired through practice. God must do some work. In Aquinas's language, these virtues are "infused" by God's grace. It would be a misinterpretation of Aquinas, however, to completely sunder the cardinal virtues ordered toward the natural end and the theological virtues ordered toward the supernatural end. There is also a feedback mechanism: the theological virtues strengthen the cardinal virtues and aid in human flourishing in this life. Nature is perfected by grace, which means the cardinal virtues are perfected by the theological virtues. In all of this, Aquinas emphasizes the "primacy of charity." He sees charity as infusing all of the moral virtues to give them an extra shot of power, as it were. It is of course up to us to choose this gift of grace. But if chosen, human nature is transformed and human capacities enhanced.

Let's now reflect a little on how Aquinas approached law. Aquinas is regarded as the preeminent natural law theologian, and his thought is often analyzed through this frame. But in reality, I would argue that Aquinas is primarily a virtue ethicist and what he says about law follows from that. The key point is that law, in tandem with virtue and grace, influences the intellect and the will. Law is about the ordering of action toward the common good.[66]

Aquinas sees four dimensions of law. First, eternal law refers to the plan of the universe in the mind of God, God's providential ordering of all creation. All other kinds of law must align with this.

Second, natural law is the participation of the human intellect in the eternal law. The basic principle of natural law is that good must be pursued and evil avoided. It is called natural law because, as rational beings, we possess the ability to undertake this moral reasoning imprinted in our nature. Putting it simply: we know right from wrong, even if this judgment can be darkened by ignorance and sin. The relationship to virtue should be clear at this point.

Third, human law applies the timeless principles of the natural law to the particular circumstances and realities of time and place. This application will require the virtue of prudence. A key point is Aquinas's argument that a human law that deviated from the natural law was no law at all and so could be disobeyed. It was precisely this reading of Aquinas that spurred Martin Luther King to refuse to obey racist laws in the United States.

Fourth, divine law is the law that God reveals directly in scripture—most especially the New Testament—where instead of being motivated to obey the law due to the threat of punishment (as in the Hebrew Scriptures), we are motivated by interior grace. The point of divine law is to correct misunderstandings and misapplications of the natural law due to sin and weakness. Note also that human law is not required to outlaw all bad acts. Such a prohibition would harm the common good; think of trying to ban lying, for example.[67]

A key point for Aquinas: the purpose of law is actually to instill and strengthen virtue. It is not just about obeying the law for external reasons—fear of punishment (the stick) or in anticipation of some reward (the carrot). Instead, we are supposed to internalize the law to become more virtuous human beings. For Aquinas, law is ultimately about strengthening dispositions toward good acts—and, ultimately, toward our end in God. It is a bit like charity, insofar as it gives a supernatural impetus to incline human nature toward its perfection. In this sense, virtue, law, and grace are all deeply intertwined with each other.

Some have argued that Aquinas's virtue ethics needs updating to account for institutions, structures, and practices. The idea is that in a modern economy or society, we can longer discuss virtue and vice solely at the level of the individual. Broader structures have the capacity to help or hinder the human good, happiness, and moral character. Theologian Daniel Daly has explored this idea, arguing in favor or what he calls structures of virtue and vice.[68] In his terminology, virtuous structures are, on one hand, those that promote the human good and human happiness. They have a moral character. But as virtues, they can also be characterized as socially rooted habits internalized by people that "consistently prescribe the human good, the common good, good moral character, and human happiness." Standing in opposition, structures of vice are those structures that impede these goods and also the internalized habits that prescribe sinful acts and produce human unhappiness. So social structures and institutions might exist independently of the person, but they influence the person's actions and shape their moral character. In this sense, Daly notes, a society with unjust institutions can induce people toward sin and vice. I will come back to this later in chapter 6 when I discuss inequality.

Let me turn now to what Aquinas has to say about economics. The first point to note is that following Aristotle, he argues that wealth cannot be an end in itself. As theologian Mary Hirschfeld puts it, "Material goods are, indeed, good. But they are purely instrumental. It is not enough to be wealthy. Happiness requires that we deploy our wealth toward the worthy end of realizing our nature as fully as possible in lives ordered to God."[69]

A key distinction for Aquinas is between natural and artificial wealth.[70] Natural wealth refers to the material bases needed to live a good life in community, things such as food and shelter. Again, natural wealth is good but is only instrumental; it is not sought for its own sake. It is about using that wealth to support a virtuous life. This view has numerous dimensions. In the first place, it entails taking care of basic bodily needs, but it goes further than that. Aquinas argued that as social creatures, we need the goods necessary to live a life becoming of our social station. Keep in mind that Aquinas lived in a highly hierarchical society with little or no social mobility. So this point appears outdated. But it nonetheless has an analogue in our own day: we need the goods necessary to be able to participate in social activities with our fellow citizens. That might require appropriate clothing. And today, it might require access to the internet and a smartphone. Another dimension is the goods needed to achieve excellence through our work—to exercise our talents to become the person we are supposed to become. For some, that means a university education. For others, it might mean practical training or music lessons.

A key point, which cannot be stressed highly enough: because Aquinas saw our needs as limited, our desire for natural wealth should also be finite. This belief is very different from how we conceive of the modern economy (much more on that in chapter 3). Aquinas regarded desire for ever more goods as the vice of covetousness. This state happens because we think, wrongly, that accumulating material goods brings happiness.

In contrast to his view of natural wealth, Aquinas saw money as artificial wealth, and he was even more suspicious of its lures. For sure, he saw that money played an important role in the economy as a medium of exchange, a store of value, and a unit of account (anybody who studied economics is surely nodding along at this point!). But money is even one step lower on the ladder of happiness: it is ordered toward natural wealth, which is in turn ordered toward the good life of virtue, and ultimately to God. As Hirschfeld puts it, money is an "instrumental good in the service of an instrumental good."[71] This makes its pursuit even more dangerous. Why? Because at least with natural wealth, there is a limit to the amount of stuff we can own—though for some people, that quantity can be large! But for money, there is no such limit. Aquinas argued that the desire for artificial wealth is infinite; that is, it becomes an end on its own, not a means to an end. Thus the pursuit of money for its own sake is disconnected from a life of virtue and the common good—Aristotle's *chrematistike* all over again. And because money is abstract, it is easier for us to pursue this false end.

Aquinas's views on the proper ordering of desires, especially when it comes to money, leads to his position on the "just price." This is a part of his theory that seems particularly alien to us, who live in a market economy where prices are supposed to be determined by supply and demand. Some have argued that Aquinas's just price was where supply meets demand in the marketplace, but this isn't quite right. For Aquinas, there should be some kind of equivalence in exchange so that the agreed price reflects the "common advantage of both parties." The price is supposed to be fair, equal to its value.[72] The seller is allowed to charge extra only if he faces a greater-than-usual loss at that particular time. So, for example, Aquinas would frown on the modern practice of price gouging: think of hotels jacking up prices in a city with a large number of conventions during a certain week of the year, a hardware store charging more for the goods needed to prepare for a major storm, or a ride-sharing company setting higher prices during congested periods. For believers in a free market, there is nothing wrong with any of these practices. But there is for Aquinas.

This is also why Aquinas was opposed to usury, charging interest on loans. Recall that the Hebrew Scriptures also condemned this practice, on the grounds that this was likely to exploit the poor. Aquinas has a somewhat more sophisticated argument, rooted in his notion of economic justice. He basically argues that usury is unjust because the lender is getting something for nothing. It is just another form of price gouging. Finn argues that Aquinas's views make more sense when we think about the difference between consumption goods, which are used up at the moment of consumption, and capital goods, which are not.[73] Aquinas argued that if you lend one item to a neighbor, you cannot ask for two items back. But if you let a neighbor use your house, you can legitimately charge rent, because the house is not "consumed" by the occupant. Aquinas regarded money as belonging to the former, not the latter category. But if we think of interest on a loan as compensation for risk or inflation, then his framework can accommodate it. Yet we still need to be careful: any interest charged above this rate would still be illegitimate.

The final issue I want to discuss relates to Aquinas's views on private property, which are highly nuanced. Like the Church Fathers, Aquinas thought that private property was legitimate but not unconditional. His argument boils down to "private ownership" and "common use." What does this mean? Starting with private ownership: even though Aquinas is predisposed to think of common ownership as the natural state, he nonetheless accepts private ownership as an addition to the natural law. Why? For very practical reasons. People are more likely to take care of things and to know who is responsible for what when property is owned privately. Think of the chaos created by communism, which experimented with communal ownership. But—and this is key—he claimed that "man ought to possess external things, not as his own, but as common, so that he is ready to communicate them to others in their need."[74] This belief reflects the logic of the Hebrew Scriptures and the Church Fathers that the goods of the earth are destined for all, and this moral injunction is not canceled simply because property is owned privately. The idea that the goods of creation are destined for all flows from the natural law, and, as we have seen, a human law that violates the natural law has no moral validity. As Aquinas says, "Hence whatever certain people have in superabundance is due, by natural law, to the purpose of succoring the poor."[75]

In the extreme case, Aquinas's position holds that even stealing can be morally justified. As he puts it, "In cases of need, all things are common property, so that there would seem to be no sin in taking another's property, for the need has made it common."[76] He goes on to explain that when a person's need is "so manifest and urgent," it becomes lawful to meet this need "by means of another's property, by taking it either openly or secretly."[77] This is sometimes known as the "Jean Valjean principle," named after the hero of Victor Hugo's *Les Misérables*, who was sentenced to twenty years' hard labor for stealing a loaf of bread to feed his family. According to Aquinas, this was not robbery or theft, and Valjean did the right thing. Some have applied this ancient principle to the modern case of a country dealing with desperate refugees fleeing for their lives; in such case, Aquinas might argue that the country is morally obligated to save their lives and meet their basic needs.[78] As with everything else in Aquinas's thought, wealth must be used to support a life of virtue and the common good, and society has the right to establish proper boundaries in this regard.

The goal of this chapter has been to show where Catholic social teaching comes from—both the biblical prescriptions centered on justice and care for the poor and Aristotelian virtue ethics centered on becoming the best versions of ourselves, especially manifested in the communal life. The genius of Aquinas is that he managed to synthesize these two different traditions, including through his emphasis on the proper ordering of money and material things. Even at this early stage, we can see that this approach to economic matters differs in fundamental ways from the contemporary understanding. The next step is to look at how modern

Catholic social teaching emerged—how this ancient tradition would be applied to the unprecedented changes in the global economy over the last few centuries. The bottom line is that while the circumstances might have changed, the principles remain enduring.

Notes

1. MacCulloch, *History of Christianity*.
2. I owe these insights to Rabbi David Rosen from the Ethics in Action initiative.
3. Groody, *Globalization, Spirituality, and Justice*.
4. For more details, see Finn, *Christian Economic Ethics*.
5. All biblical quotes are from the *New American Bible*.
6. Hudson, *. . . And Forgive Them Their Debts*.
7. Groody, *Globalization, Spirituality, and Justice*.
8. Donohue, "Bible and Catholic Social Teaching."
9. Hudson, *. . . And Forgive Them Their Debts*, ch. 23, n.p.
10. Finn, *Christian Economic Ethics*, 52.
11. Hudson, *. . . And Forgive Them Their Debts*.
12. Lohfink, *Jesus of Nazareth*, ch. 2, n.p.
13. Lohfink, 26.
14. David Bentley Hart, "Prayer for the Poor," *Church Life Journal*, June 5, 2018. https://churchlifejournal.nd.edu/articles/a-prayer-for-the-poor/.
15. Graeber, *Debt*.
16. Hart, "Prayer for the Poor," n.p.
17. Hart, n.p.
18. Levine, *Short Stories by Jesus*.
19. Hinson-Hasty, *Problem of Wealth*.
20. Levine, *Short Stories by Jesus*, 297.
21. Levine, 296.
22. I owe this observation to a homily by Father James Greenfield at St. Matthew's Cathedral in Washington, DC.
23. James Martin, "How Can You Be Christian without Caring for the Poor?," *Los Angeles Times*, December 21, 2017, https://www.latimes.com/opinion/op-ed/la-oe-martin-throwaway-holy-family-20171221-story.html.
24. Harrington and Keenan, *Jesus and Virtue Ethics*, 18.
25. Groody, *Globalization, Spirituality, and Justice*, 24.
26. Donohue, "Bible and Catholic Social Teaching," 27.
27. Lohfink, *Jesus of Nazareth*, 29.
28. I owe this insight to Bishop Marcelo Sánchez Sorondo, chancellor of the Pontifical Academies of Sciences and Social Sciences. See Sánchez Sorondo, "Church as Intrinsically a Social Movement."

29. Donohue, "Bible and Catholic Social Teaching."

30. Hudson, . . . *And Forgive Them Their Debts*, 226.

31. Donohue, "Bible and Catholic Social Teaching," 33.

32. These themes and writings reflect a particular time and place, the vastly unequal and unjust world of the Roman Empire. Some have suggested that wealth is more ethically earned today. There is a point there, but only a small one.

33. In this, I am leaning heavily on Finn, *Christian Economic Ethics*; Cloutier, *Vice of Luxury*; and Groody, *Globalization, Spirituality, and Justice*.

34. Finn, *Christian Economic Ethics*, 89.

35. Quoted in *PP*, 23.

36. Chrysostom, "Second Sermon on Lazarus and the Rich Man," 55.

37. Quoted in Finn, *Christian Economic Ethics*, 91.

38. Quoted in Groody, *Globalization, Spirituality, and Justice*, 73.

39. Brown, *Through the Eye of a Needle*; Cloutier, *Vice of Luxury*.

40. Quoted in Finn, *Christian Economic Ethics*, 90.

41. Quoted in Groody, *Globalization, Spirituality, and Justice*, 82–83.

42. Quoted in Finn, *Christian Economic Ethics*, 90.

43. Quoted in Groody, *Globalization, Spirituality, and Justice*, 81–82.

44. Groody, *Globalization, Spirituality, and Justice*, 78.

45. Quoted in Finn, *Christian Economic Ethics*, 95.

46. Quoted in Groody, *Globalization, Spirituality, and Justice*, 81.

47. Quoted in Groody, 80.

48. Aristotle, *Nicomachean Ethics*.

49. For a thorough exposition of Aristotle's ethics, see Kraut, "Aristotle's Ethics."

50. In the pre-Socratic tradition, happiness was less eudaimonia than eutychia, identified with good luck. I thank Stefano Zamagni for this observation.

51. Nussbaum, "Mill between Aristotle and Bentham," 171.

52. MacIntyre, *After Virtue*, 148.

53. Aristotle, *Nicomachean Ethics*, book 1, ch. 5, n.p.

54. MacIntyre, *After Virtue*, 174.

55. MacIntyre, 52.

56. Hall, *Aristotle's Way*, 23.

57. Hollenbach, *Common Good and Christian Social Ethics*, 82.

58. Dierksmeier, *Reframing Economic Ethics*.

59. Sandel, *Justice*.

60. I am indebted to Claus Dierksmeier for this distinction. See Dierksmeier, *Reframing Economic Ethics*; and Dierksmeier and Pirson, "Oikonomia versus Chrematistike."

61. Dierksmeier, *Reframing Economic Ethics*, 41.

62. This view leans heavily on Dierksmeier, *Reframing Economic Ethics*.

63. MacIntyre, *After Virtue*, 187.

64. Cloutier, *Vice of Luxury*, 89.

65. The main text itself is Aquinas's *Summa Theologica*. This is a mighty tome. Baumgarth and Regan, *Saint Thomas Aquinas: On Law, Morality, and Politics* provide a summary

of the relevant passages for our purposes. This section leans heavily on Pope, "Overview of the Ethics of Thomas Aquinas"; Konyndyk DeYoung, McCluskey, and Van Dyke, *Aquinas's Ethics*; Finn, *Christian Economic Ethics*; and Hirschfeld, *Aquinas and the Market*.

66. Konyndyk DeYoung, McCluskey, and Van Dyke, *Aquinas's Ethics*.

67. The example of lying comes from Finn, *Christian Economic Ethics*.

68. Daly, "Structures of Virtue and Vice."

69. Hirschfeld, *Aquinas and the Market*, 97.

70. My treatment here leans heavily on Hirschfeld.

71. Hirschfeld, 139.

72. See Finn, *Christian Economic Ethics*, ch. 9.

73. Finn, ch. 9.

74. Aquinas, *Summa Theologica*, Second Part of the Second Part, Question 66, Article 2.

75. Aquinas, Second Part of the Second Part, Question 66, Article 7.

76. Aquinas, Article 7.

77. Aquinas, Article 7.

78. I owe this point to Bishop Marcelo Sánchez Sorondo.

2

The New Stuff

Modern Catholic Social Teaching

At the turn of the nineteenth century, the English poet and mystic William Blake penned a poem titled "And Did Those Feet in Ancient Time" about an apocryphal visit of Jesus to England.[1] The poem was put to music in 1916 by Sir Hubert Parry under the title "Jerusalem." This hymn has reached anthemic levels and was even featured during the opening ceremony of the London Olympics in 2012. It is so associated with England that some have even called it an alternative national anthem. And yet the hymn, despite its airy and inspiring melody, has a dark undertone. Blake is lamenting the loss of a pastoral utopia, destroyed by what he calls the "dark satanic mills."

He is, of course, referring to the early industrial revolution. Half a century later, Charles Dickens would write a sequence of blockbuster novels about the dehumanizing effects of this revolution. A century after that, the nostalgic academic and writer J. R. R. Tolkien would echo Blake in seeing demonic forces in the technological assault on the natural world.

There is no doubt about it, the industrial revolution changed everything. The forces unleashed by it upended society. People flooded into cities to take advantage of new opportunities or because old ways of life were dying out. Traditional crafts and guilds gave way to large anonymous and oppressive factories. The benefits of technological progress accrued to a small minority, and workers were often treated abominably—forced to work for long hours, with low pay, in unsafe and unsanitary conditions, with little control over their time. New ideologies arose justifying these new conditions as fair, efficient, and natural. Unsurprising, this line of thought prompted a lot of foment and social upheaval. Theorists such as Karl Marx denounced the new overlords and predicted a day of worker liberation. Across Europe, restlessness seeped into riots and revolutions. Socialist political parties rose in popularity.

Into all of this activity was thrust the Catholic Church. Through the nineteenth century, the Church was seen as firmly on the side of traditional authority, terrified of revolution. The reactionary turn is unsurprising after the French Revolution, which unleashed its full force on a Church seen as aligned with the aristocracy. The new socialist parties also had an anticlerical fervor. Popes of this period lashed out against the rising tide of modernism, condemning not only socialism but also democracy and basic liberties such as freedom of the press. It was a period of reactionary doubling down.

But then something remarkable happened. In 1891, the reigning pope, Leo XIII, wrote an encyclical called *Rerum Novarum* (*RN*), translated as "On New Things"—the new things of the industrial revolution and its social and economic upheavals. As we saw in the last chapter, the Church had a wealth of teaching on how to order a just economy, but the circumstances were now entirely different. The time had come to address the moral questions that arose in the functioning of modern society and the modern economy. In his encyclical, Pope Leo vociferously condemned the abuses, inequities, and injustices of the new economic arrangements. While insisting that socialism was unacceptable, he nonetheless refused to baptize the emerging capitalist mode of production. Instead, he applied ancient moral principles rooted in both scripture and tradition to the new circumstances of the day, calling for just economic relationships between rich and poor, capital and labor, the powerful and the powerless.[2]

This encyclical set the stage for the next 130 years of what became known as social encyclicals. Before going further, though, let us begin with a basic question: what is an encyclical? In its traditional form, a papal encyclical is a circular letter written by the pope and addressed to the bishops of the Church. It clearly has its origins in a different time, before the advent of modern communications. Today, an encyclical is a teaching document that addresses an important matter of faith or morals, relevant to the life of the contemporary Church and the contemporary world. For Catholics, it comes with a fairly high level of teaching authority. And social encyclicals are those that address contemporary social and economic challenges, attempting to apply timeless principles to changing contexts and circumstances.

The Documents of Catholic Social Teaching

What Pope Leo XIII started, other popes continued.[3] Table 2.1 summarizes the main documents that this book will discuss. Taken together, they form the corpus of what has become known as Catholic social teaching.

I will be arguing that it is possible to distill a core set of principles from this disparate set of documents, spanning a century and a quarter. It is important to note that these encyclicals are not written as timeless documents from on high. Historical context matters. They are always written in dialogue with the world around them—the prevailing social and economic conditions and events—with a goal of offering a moral reflection on current economic reality. And they must be read that way, from Pope Leo XIII during the industrial revolution to Pope Francis in an era of runaway inequality and environmental destruction.

There is much nuance, of course. Different popes had different emphases, sometimes in subtle ways. Different times gave way to different tones and sometimes different messages. And even though the Catholic Church likes to insist that the pope is the sole author of the document, the reality is that he relies on a team of collaborators and drafters, whose makeup, too, obviously reflects times, circumstances, and personalities.

Just to give a few examples of these subtle differences: it is now acknowledged that Pope Leo XIII, the pope who started it all, had a view of private property that was stronger than that of Aquinas. As noted by Marvin Mich, Leo XIII saw private property as a natural right under the natural law rather than an addition to the natural law owing to imperfect human nature.[4] This view was corrected by his successors, reaching its apotheosis in Pope Paul VI's encyclical *Populorum Progressio* (*PP*)—*On the Development of Peoples*—in 1967, which quoted the strong language by Saint Ambrose we saw in the last chapter. Pope Francis has followed in this tradition. As a second example, Pope Pius XI—writing in the 1930s—was heavily influenced by a corporatist view of society, a rather nostalgic call for something akin to medieval guilds, whereby different industries would be run as self-governing bodies in a way that eliminated class conflict. Unfortunately for Pope Pius, even though he had no truck with totalitarianism, the corporatist model was hijacked by fascist and quasi-fascist entities, which served to—to some degree unfairly—harm its reputation. In the postwar period, popes were also influenced by the ethos of the times. For example, writing in the 1960s, Pope John XXIII had an optimistic view of the state to manage an ever-more complex economy. In this, he reflected the Keynesian consensus: the notion that technocratic management was able to limit swings of economic fortune through the business cycle. In contrast, writing after the fall of the Berlin Wall in 1991, Pope John Paul II adopted a less hostile stance toward modern capitalism than

Table 2.1. Major Documents of Catholic Social Teaching

Author	Document	Date
Pope Leo XIII	*Rerum Novarum*	1891
Pope Pius XI	*Quadragesimo Anno*	1931
Pope Pius XII	Christmas messages	1941–45
Pope John XXIII	*Mater et Magistra*	1961
Pope John XXIII	*Pacem in Terris*	1963
Second Vatican Council	*Gaudium et Spes*	1965
Pope Paul VI	*Populorum Progressio*	1967
Pope John Paul II	*Laborem Exercens*	1981
Pope John Paul II	*Sollicitudo Rei Socialis*	1987
Pope John Paul II	*Centesimus Annus*	1991
Pope Benedict XVI	*Caritas in Veritate*	2009
Pope Francis	*Laudato Si'*	2015
Pope Francis	*Fratelli Tutti*	2020

some other popes, though he always cautioned that the market must be bounded by moral concerns. (Some of his followers, incorrectly in my view, tried to align Pope John Paul with the emerging neoliberal view of economics.)

Beginning with *Rerum Novarum* in 1891, as noted, the economic context was one of capitalist domination over labor, the social context was one of upheaval and exclusion, and the political context was one of rising nationalism and revolutionary spirit.[5] Even though the encyclical was radical by the standards of the time, in many respects—especially looking back today—it comes across as a rather conservative document. Pope Leo was extremely critical and fearful of the socialist parties that competed for the allegiance of the working class. He sought social harmony rather than revolutionary zeal. To dull the edges of the socialist appeal, he argued forcefully that workers should earn a living wage and have the right to organize and bargain collectively, with the right to strike if necessary. Leo opposed the libertarian ideology that the market wage was by its nature fair and just, because it came from voluntary agreement between employer and worker. He saw, instead, that workers were too often forced to accept terrible wages and conditions because they lacked power—and this could upset the harmony between classes. He saw a role for the state in bringing about this social harmony. As noted, Leo was also a big believer in private property. Indeed, he thought that in an ideal world, all workers would be able to own some property of their own.

The second major encyclical was called *Quadragesimo Anno* (*QA*)—subtitled *On Reconstruction of the Social Order*—issued by Pope Pius XI in 1931 to mark the fortieth anniversary of *Rerum Novarum*.[6] The context is a little different, as this encyclical came out in the midst of the Great Depression, which caused a major loss of faith in the self-correcting market as the bedrock of prosperity. Pius was also dealing with the breakdown of the democratic order, as nations edged toward various totalitarian states. And he had to deal with the rise of Benito Mussolini's Fascism in his native Italy. In this sense, the encyclical walks a bit of a tightrope. While still vigorously condemning collectivist socialism, Pius also directs his ire at free market libertarianism and especially ruinous financial market power. In this, he swings the pendulum a little back to the center from Leo XIII, emphasizing more the balance between the private and social dimensions of property. Pius also introduced the now common notion of social justice into the encyclical tradition, noting that institutions needed to serve the common good. He is also concerned with income inequality, lambasting the rising disparities between rich and poor exposed by the Depression. Some of his language against mistreatment of workers and the poor by international financial capitalism is strong, sometimes harking back to the tone of the Hebrew prophets and the Church Fathers. But, as with *Rerum Novarum*, there is also a conservative strain within *Quadragesimo Anno*. This sentiment comes out especially when Pius calls for a new social order along corporatist lines—which, as mentioned, opines back to the medieval guild system. This recommendation was part of his attempt to dialogue with the various political developments at the time. Like Leo, Pius had as his goal harmonious rather than conflictual relations between the social classes. It is unfortunate and unfair to Pius that Mussolini and the Fascists were at that time giving corporatism a bad name.

Pius XII followed Pius XI. He was a wartime pope, focused intently on the situation in Europe. Despite his long pontificate (1939–58), he didn't pen a full social encyclical. Nonetheless, he gave a sequence of remarkable Christmas addresses, which not only looked back to the themes of his predecessors but forward to what a postwar society in Europe might look like.[7] In a sense, Pius XII is a hinge pope, between the prewar tradition very much rooted in the natural law of Aquinas and the postwar tradition much more comfortable with the idea of democracy and human rights. Indeed, some have argued that the notion of human rights as founded in the notion of human dignity, which is now commonplace, actually arises from Catholic debates during this period seeking a middle way between the totalitarian and libertarian options.[8] And for Pius, a core part of human dignity was the dignity of labor. Yet Pius's attempt to strike a neutral tone during the war has been understandably criticized, especially when combined with a reluctance to move from lofty principle to practical reality.

The next social encyclical was *Mater et Magistra* (*MM*)—*Mother and Teacher*, subtitled *On Christianity and Social Progress*—issued by the reforming pope

John XXIII in 1961.[9] Pope John is dialoguing with the postwar modern world and its Keynesian optimism that economic fluctuations could be successfully managed and full employment achieved. The tone of this encyclical echoes this optimism in terms of the potential for economic and social progress. Pope John's dialogue with this modern world was also more open than before, not presuming that the Church had all the answers. His dialogical method was laid out in a new methodology for relating Catholic social teaching to social problems. Instead of the high theological language of Aquinas, he instead preferred the practical scheme of what has become known as "see, judge, act." This is a threefold method of moral diagnosis: first, assess the concrete situation; second, make the moral judgments and deploy the appropriate moral principles; and third, take appropriate action on the personal and institutional levels. This methodology has stood the test of time and is still being deployed by Pope Francis. *Mater et Magistra* is favorably inclined toward government intervention in the economy to support the common good and correct economic injustice. For John, the common good was central, and he discussed many practical aspects of it, including in terms of the rights of workers, the problems of agriculture, and the need to help poorer countries. Written in the era of decolonization, *Mater et Magistra* is the first encyclical to talk about the problems of developing countries and the notion of a global common good whereby rich counties are obliged to aid their poorer neighbors, something that would become a major theme in the encyclicals that followed.

In 1963, Pope John XXIII switched gears a little, segueing from economic justice to the theme of peace. As noted by Mich, in the darkest days of the Cold War, the world was ready for a message on peace. The Korean War was a recent memory, the Berlin Wall had been built, and the Cuban missile crisis had just brought the world to the brink of nuclear war.[10] Titled *Pacem in Terris* (*PT*), this new encyclical was written in 1963, the year of the Cuban missile crisis.[11] The major theme of this encyclical is that peace is not merely negative, in the sense of the absence of conflict, but also positive, in terms of laying out the conditions that make war less likely in the first place. For Pope John, justice was the basis of peace. In this vein, he laid out the rights and duties of persons, states, and the global community. This approach sounds pretty straightforward, but it was in fact a major departure for the Catholic social tradition. The human rights tradition, with links to the rhetoric of the French Revolution and nineteenth-century anticlericalism, had been viewed with suspicion. John XXIII changed that. With this encyclical, the Church made peace with the modern human rights tradition, though John was careful to root it carefully within the Catholic tradition laid out in the first chapter. His approach to human rights very much centers on the notion of economic rights, of major interest to this book. *Pacem in Terris* also developed the idea of a universal common good that bound all nations together, a view that would form the bedrock of the Church's strong support for multilateral institutions. A final note: this document might well have been instrumental in saving the world from nuclear catastrophe. Pope John sent copies to both US president John F. Kennedy and Soviet premier Nikita Khrushchev. It had a profound effect on both men, helping them to pull back from the brink and move in the direction of peace.[12]

The next document on the list is not an encyclical. It is instead a key document of the Second Vatican Council, a great ecumenical council of bishops, called by Pope John XXIII, which sat between 1962 and 1965. It was this council, and especially the document *Gaudium et Spes* (GS)—formally known as the *Pastoral Constitution on the Church in the Modern World*—released in 1965, that witnessed an opening to the modern world in all of its messiness.[13] Because *Gaudium et Spes*—the only one of sixteen documents of the Second Vatican Council that looked out to the modern world—is a document of an ecumenical council, it is considered to have higher authority than an encyclical.[14] It is probably the most important document of Catholic social teaching of the twentieth century. In *Gaudium et Spes*, the Church was dialoguing with a world that had gone through hell—two devastating world wars, the rise of totalitarianism, economic collapse, the development of nuclear weapons, and a precarious cold war—and yet seemed in a new bright spot with rising prosperity in the west, the establishment of the United Nations, and the signing of the Universal Declaration of Human Rights. It was also an era of decolonization, which went smoother in some countries than in others. In terms of tone and themes, *Gaudium et Spes* followed the example set by Pope John XXIII in his encyclicals. It offered a positive and inviting tone, seeking genuine dialogue and cooperation with the entire human family on the social and economic issues facing the world. It relied less on the philosophical structure of the natural law and more on the insights of the human sciences.[15] At the outset, it sought to discern the "sign of the times," whereby the Church was asked to "recognize and understand the world in which we live, its explanations, its longings, and its often dramatic characteristics."[16] On the socioeconomic front, these signs included the rising gap between rich and poor, both in and between countries, in a world of great abundance. The document emphasized such themes as human dignity, the common good, solidarity, support for the poor, justice, and human rights. Yet it has been criticized as being too preoccupied with issues of concern to the developed world; this would be corrected in the documents issued after the Second Vatican Council.

The first social encyclical issued after the council was *Populorum Progressio*, written by Pope Paul VI in 1967. Paul will go down in history as the pope who deftly brought the Second Vatican Council to completion.[17] The theme of the encyclical is the development of peoples, and indeed, *Populorum Progressio* is often regarded as the Catholic charter for development. In this, Pope Paul stood in dialogue with a debate over the meaning of development in the 1960s. The Cold War was still raging, and both superpowers were trying to appeal to the developing world with different forms of assistance. Even the very definition of development was contested. For the Anglo-Saxon world in particular, development was synonymous with material conditions, especially as encapsulated by the growth of gross domestic product (GDP). And the western world was going through an unprecedented period of economic expansion at the time, which was not always shared with the developing world. Other thinkers saw development as a betterment in social conditions and human well-being; this view would eventually become the United Nations' standard. Aspects of the Francophone tradition viewed development as more "integral," including an improvement in the non-material (including the spiritual) dimension.[18] It was this tradition that Pope Paul would lean on, drawing on the humanistic vision of Catholic philosopher Jacques Maritain, one of the authors of the Universal Declaration of Human Rights. Paul saw true development as centered on human dignity and respect for the human person and so was irreducible to its material or technological components. The theme of justice is also strong in *Populorum Progressio*. One of its mantras is that development is the new name for peace. Pope Paul denounced, in often strident terms, large gaps in wealth and power between rich and poor, frustrated aspirations, and the legacy of colonialism. He was deeply suspicious of liberal capitalism and reemphasized the ancient injunction that the goods of the earth are destined for all. He also called for solidarity between peoples and nations, noting that poor countries themselves could not go it alone; they needed the help of their richer neighbors to overcome underdevelopment. All in all, *Populorum Progressio* is very much a document of the 1960s, but it nonetheless stands the test of time.

Following an all-too-brief pontificate of Pope John Paul I, Pope John Paul II reigned for almost three decades, from 1978 through to 2005. During this long pontificate, he penned three important social encyclicals. The first was *Laborem Exercens (LE)—On Human Work*—dating from 1981.[19] As the title suggests, this encyclical centers on human work. Indeed, it represents, in the words of Patricia Lamoureux, "the most comprehensive treatment of human work in the corpus of Catholic social teaching."[20] Somewhat surprisingly perhaps, this was a new departure for the Church. John Paul was focused on what work means for the human person; his emphasis is the same as Pope Paul VI's for development. In terms of how he was dialoguing with the world, John Paul had on his mind the changing world of work since the onset of the industrial revolution, especially in the context of continuous technological advancement, the increase in energy costs, and growing pressure on the earth's resources. He was undoubtedly also thinking of his native Poland, where Solidarity—Poland's independent trade union—was facing down the armed forces of the Communist government and the threat of Soviet invasion. The key insight of the encyclical is that work can reflect the innate dignity of the human being, especially in its subjective dimension (human agency). Putting it simply, the theme is that work is for the person, not the person for work. He also stressed the priority of labor over capital and elucidated a list of workers' rights, including the right to form unions and to strike. The well-being of workers was regarded as a key priority not only of the employer but for society as a whole.

John Paul's second social encyclical, issued in 1987, was called *Sollicitudo Rei Socialis (SRS)—On Social Concerns*.[21] This letter was issued on the twentieth anniversary of *Populorum Progressio* and once again took up the issue of global development. The context for the encyclical is a changing approach to development, given the rise of free market neoliberalism and globalization in the 1980s and a growing gap between rich and poor countries. Pope John Paul cast a suspicious eye of these developments and reiterated Pope Paul VI's call for an authentically humanistic vision of human development with the person at the center. But from his other eye, he was glancing nervously at communism, which few at the time predicted was in its last gasp. He expresses criticism of both market-driven liberal capitalism and authoritarian regimes that trample on freedom, human agency, and what he calls the right to economic initiative. The major theme of this encyclical is the need for greater solidarity between peoples and nations, especially in terms of putting the poor first. Echoing Pope Paul VI, he denounced the huge inequities between the global north and global south, contrasting pervasive poverty with what he called "superdevelopment." He largely blamed the rich countries for these large gaps. Borrowing from liberation theology, John Paul also introduces the idea of "structures of sin," or institutional obstacles to achieving the common good within and between nations—which he sees as arising from a thirst for power and profit. He also enunciates the idea of the preferential option for the poor, which he sees as absolutely central to the Christian tradition.

The third and final social encyclical written by Pope John Paul II is also his most ambitious. Titled *Centesimus Annus (CA)—On the Hundredth Anniversary of Rerum Novarum*—it was written in 1991 with two aims—to mark the hundred-year anniversary of Leo XIII's *Rerum Novarum* and assess the state of global affairs after the fall of the Berlin Wall and the final defeat of communism.[22] The talk at the time was of the "end of history." It was a time of optimism as the former communist countries sought to reenter the global market economy. Reflecting the new "signs of the times," John Paul gives a qualified endorsement of capitalism. But he never plays into the "end of history" optimism and cautions that a free market system can be morally justified only if it is contained within a well-defined moral boundary. In this context, he discussed the moral limits of markets and the corrupting influence of consumerism and materialism. Some commentators, particularly in the United States, claimed that *Centesimus Annus* marked a sharp discontinuity in Catholic social teaching, with the pope providing a moral seal of approval on capitalism. This simply was not the case. While John Paul is more optimistic about markets than his predecessors, reflecting the context in which he wrote, he also rings many warning bells on the corrupting influence of market ideology—bells that still sound loudly today.

What *Quadragesimo Anno* was for the Great Depression, *Caritas in Veritate—Charity in Truth*—issued in 2009—was for the global financial crisis. Conceived as a commemoration of the fortieth anniversary of *Populorum Progressio*, *Caritas in Veritate*—penned by Pope Benedict XVI—was delayed by the outbreak of this crisis, which led to the greatest economic downturn since the Great Depression. The encyclical offers its own take on the crisis, which turned out to be a rather unique one. Unlike most other takes on the global financial crisis, which emphasized economic and financial fault lines requiring technocratic fixes, *Caritas in Veritate* starts from the position that the crisis was primarily a crisis of ethics, driven by immoral behavior in the financial sector in particular. As befitting a top-class intellectual such as Pope Benedict XVI, it offers a deeply insightful view into the pathologies of the modern market economy, the defects that allowed the crisis to happen.[23] The one-line takeaway is that every economic decision is a moral decision. Springing from the Christian understanding of God, Jesus Christ, and the Trinity, Pope Benedict argues that economic life cannot be simply about profit seeking, self-interest, and accumulation. Rather, it must reflect principles of fraternity and gratuitousness, whereby people in the marketplace enter into a human relationship with one another and should be ready to give freely without expecting anything in return. Rather than being naive, the encyclical argues that this is actually how trust and social capital are cemented. For Benedict, it also reflects the nature of the human vocation. Plus, as noted by Meghan Clark, the encyclical was in dialogue with a changing perspective on development—instead of focusing only on GDP and economic growth, the United Nations had switched its emphasis toward a more holistic view of poverty, which centered on enhancing capabilities.[24] This Aristotelian approach has clear overlaps with Paul VI's call for integral human development, commemorated in this encyclical.

The penultimate encyclical on our list is *Laudato Si'*—subtitled *On Care for Our Common Home*—issued by Pope Francis in 2015.[25] This is a revolutionary document, a latter-day *Rerum Novarum*. Just as *Rerum Novarum* provided a moral diagnosis on early industrial capitalism, so *Laudato Si'* uses the "see, judge, act" methodology to provide a moral diagnosis of the great challenges of today—the intertwined social and environmental crisis that threatens our ability to flourish on a healthy planet. Pope Francis assesses the latest scientific evidence suggesting that environmental devastation, brought about by our large-scale economic activity, is threatening the health of the planet and its people. And he very explicitly seeks dialogue with all people on how to take care of our common home. If previous popes talked about development, Pope Francis talks about sustainable development—at a time when the United Nations was also shifting its focus in this direction. In one sense, Pope Francis presents a more pessimistic—and even premodern—view of progress than, say, Pope John XXIII and Pope John Paul II. He sees the roots of the crisis as a technocratic paradigm, which cannibalizes economic and political life, putting economic growth and the quest for more as its main, if not only, goal. Suffused with the deep spirituality of Saint Francis of Assisi, *Laudato Si'* calls instead for a more harmonious relationship between human beings and nature, through what Pope Francis calls an "integral ecology." This relationship requires personal transformation—what the pope calls "ecological conversation"—but also institutional transformation of political and economic structures.

The final encyclical on the list is also penned by Pope Francis. Titled *Fratelli Tutti (FT)—Brothers and Sisters All*—it is once again suffused with the spirituality of Saint Francis of Assisi. This time, Pope Francis is calling for fraternity between all peoples in a way that transcends all barriers and boundaries. The context is twofold. First, Pope Francis is reacting to the reemergence on the scene of ideologies such as nationalism, extremism, xenophobia, and polarization. He talks about how conflicts are breaking out and people are hunkering down behind barriers, forsaking an open world marked by solidarity, fraternity, and social friendship. Second, this encyclical was released during the COVID-19 pandemic, and Pope Francis is also reacting to that. He stresses that the pandemic has exposed some major fault lines in global society—a solidarity-rebuking individualism and the lack of a true sense of global community united in common purpose. It is the pope's hope that the pandemic will pave the way for a better world. In a sense, by switching from themes of economics and ecology in *Laudato Si'* to themes of peace and global fraternity in *Fratelli Tutti*, Pope Francis is making the same turn as Pope John XXIII, who also wrote two major social encyclicals. He reiterates his criticism of selfish individualism, neoliberal policies, and the technocratic paradigm. He stresses the importance of a political culture marked by dialogue and charity and denounces a globalization that benefits only powerful economic and financial interests. Instead, he calls for a new form of openness based on his model of the "polyhedron"—where all people and cultures are respected and affirmed and where the whole is greater than the parts.

Three Overarching Principles

Now that I have described the major encyclicals, I want to distill three overarching theological principles that animate modern Catholic social teaching.

The first principle is that God created the world out of nothing, and everything God created is inherently good, the precious gift of a loving creator. It follows that the appropriate response to such a magnificent gift is one of gratitude, reverence, and love. This response implies a duty to protect and sustain the earth and its bounty. Christianity also holds that God created human beings in his image and likeness, which means that humans have an inherent dignity and worth. There was a strand in early Christianity known as gnosticism that proposed a radical disunity between the creator and creation; some of these strands argued that a "spark of the divine" needs to escape an evil world and a useless body. This strand is not authentic Christianity.

Second, the doctrine of the incarnation states that the creator of the universe became a human being to bridge the gap between God and humanity. To non-Christians, this can sound crazy—as it most certainly did to the citizens of the Roman Empire in the earliest days of Christianity. But there is a certain beauty to the doctrine. It takes the claim that human beings are made in the image and likeness of God and elevates it to another level—in the words of Saint Athanasius, God became one of us so that we could become one with God. We not only benefit from the great gift of creation but also receive an invitation to share in the divine life of Christ. This theological claim has some profound implications. For Christians, God has a human face, and every human being must be regarded as another Christ. Christianity also claims that Christ redeemed not only humankind but all of creation. This claim has an almost mystical feel to it. I think it is best summed up by the poet Gerard Manley Hopkins, who wrote that "the world is charged with the grandeur of God."[26] This gives us further impetus to respect creation, stamped with the mark of the divine.

Third, if human persons mirror the life of God, then they mirror the life of the Trinity. As Clark puts it, *imago Dei*—being made in God's image—also implies *imago trinitatis*.[27] The doctrine of the Trinity states that God is absolute unity but pure relationality. Accordingly, we are relational persons; we become fully human only in relation to others. As we have seen, this doctrine echoes what philosophers such as Aristotle have to say about the social nature of the human being, but it goes further than that, suggesting that we are called to mirror the life of the Trinity, which is a life based on mutuality, reciprocal love, and equality. Christian notions of redemption entail the recovery of lost unity not only between humanity and God but between human beings themselves—a fairly radical claim, pointing to communal salvation (in the words of the great Catholic theologian Henri de Lubac).[28]

Summing up, these three doctrinal claims give us some guiding principles for action in the world, namely, every person possesses innate dignity, irrespective of wealth, position, or station; and we are all bound together in a common good with a common destiny, which entails protection of our common home. In a sense, the entirety of Catholic social teaching can be summed up in that one sentence. But let's now break this down into more concrete principles.

The Concrete Principles of Catholic Social Teaching

With such a long tradition spanning vast amounts of time, infused by the personalities of many different popes, deriving a readily agreed-on set of principles for Catholic social teaching is no easy task. I've seen many different taxonomies. For me, I would settle on the following ten principles, partly because it is a nice round (and biblical) number: (1) the common good, (2) integral human development, (3) integral ecology, (4) solidarity, (5) subsidiarity, (6) reciprocity and gratuitousness, (7) the universal destination of goods, (8) the preferential option for the poor, (9) Catholic notions of rights and duties, and (10) Catholic notions of justice. We have touched on some of these when going through the historical overview. And some of them have clear overlaps with each other. Let's now delve deeper into this decalogue of moral principles. In the next chapter, we will stack them up against the principles of neoclassical or free market economics.

The Common Good

We've already touched on the common good when discussing Aristotle and Aquinas in the last chapter. This is possibly the most important principle in Catholic social teaching—Pope Francis regards it as "a central and unifying principle of social ethics."[29] Aristotle conceived it as the highest good, greater than any individual good, just as the body is greater than any of its individual parts. Aquinas adopted and Christianized the idea of the common good, the *bonum commune*, reflecting the notion that not only are we social animals who can't flourish outside of society but that we are by our natures relational beings who mirror the inner life of the Trinity. Seeking the common good is essential to our common humanity. We don't just seek our own well-being but also the well-being of our neighbor. Each person wills the other's well-being for the other's sake, which gives rise to a true "common" good, not reducible to the good of either taken separately or summed.[30] The distinction between the individual and the person is useful. While an "individual" is defined by his or her autonomy, a "person" is always a "being in relation." The person, therefore, is intrinsically linked to the common good. As Jacques Maritain put it, "The common good is common because it is received in persons, each of whom is as a mirror of the whole."[31]

This description sounds rather technical but is a profound indictment of our modern individualistic culture—more of that in coming chapters. As Stefano Zamagni puts it, the common good is more like a geometric mean than an arithmetic mean.[32] With a geometric mean, if one person is a zero, then the product is a zero. Not so with an arithmetic mean. The person is simply excluded. I will argue that this is exactly the problem with the modern economy and its emphasis on GDP; we are numbed to the fact that we have many "zeros" who simply don't count. Theologian Hinson-Hasty makes a similar point when she notes that "the good of and for individual persons is never at odds with the good of and for the whole," which implies that "One plus One plus One equals One alone, never three."[33] Or as Pope Francis puts it, "the whole is greater than the part, but it is also greater than the sum of its parts."[34] The Christian metaphor of the Body of Christ is also useful here. Just as injury to one part of the body injures the whole body, so injury to one person or one part of society injures the whole of society.

As noted in the last chapter, every kind of human relationship gives rise to a common good—a family, a friendship, a workplace, civil society. This happens even in the economic and political sphere. Remember that Aristotle argued that we become virtuous in society by deliberating on the common good with our neighbors. He was talking about a rather limited number of people: male citizens of smallish city-states. Slaves and women certainly were not included in this common good. Christianity revolutionized everything. It said that nobody could be excluded from the common good. For sure, there are different degrees of common goods, starting with family and close friendships. But the common good expands in outward waves and ultimately encompasses the entire human race.

Pope Benedict XVI explains it well, I think: "Besides the good of the individual, there is a good that is linked to living in society: the common good. It is the good of 'all of us,' made up of individuals, families and intermediate groups who together constitute society."[35]

The "all of us" is particularly important. But this still sounds pretty amorphous. How do we define the political common good in practical terms? *Gaudium et Spes* defines it as "the sum of those conditions of social life which allow social groups and their individual members relatively thorough and ready access to their own fulfillment."[36] You will see that this has an Aristotelian feel to it; it talks about the institutions that allow each person to reach her or his fulfillment.

It is the good in and through which all can flourish. This good will include the material bases of flourishing that society must guarantee to each and every person: basic physical and economic security; basic needs such as nutrition, housing, healthcare, and education; opportunities for decent and rewarding work; and a sustainable environment. As we will see, support for the common good will be a key role for the state and sometimes even the international community.

The opposite of the common good can be identified with what Pope John Paul II called "structures of sin," institutional impediments to the common good.[37] As he puts it, structures of sin constitute "the sum total of the negative factors working against a true awareness of the universal common good, and the need to further it, gives the impression of creating, in persons and institutions, an obstacle which is difficult to overcome."[38]

This obstacle is identified with two factors in particular: "on the one hand, the all-consuming desire for profit, and on the other, the thirst for power, with the intention of imposing one's will upon others."[39] Pope Francis also speaks frequently about the need to change the rules of the socioeconomic system, to break down the structures of sin so that the common good can be supported. In the context of the Good Samaritan parable, he noted that "imitating the Good Samaritan of the Gospel is not enough. . . . It is important to act above all before the man comes across the robbers, by battling the frameworks of sin that produce robbers and victims."[40] Likewise in *Fratelli Tutti*, he argues that "it is an act of charity to assist someone suffering, but it is also an act of charity, even if we do not know that person, to work to change the social conditions that caused his or her suffering."[41] So supporting the common good and overcoming structures of sin go well beyond personal virtue and righteousness. It also means aligning our institutions with what is good for all people.

Integral Human Development

As noted already, Pope Paul VI's influential encyclical *Populorum Progressio* really centers on the idea of integral human development, which is intrinsically related to the common good. To use the language of *Populorum Progressio*, "The development We speak of here cannot be restricted to economic growth alone. To be authentic, it must be well rounded; it must foster the development of each man and of the whole man."[42] Putting this is into modern language, integral human development is defined as the fullest development of the whole person and all peoples.

This argument should have a familiar ring to it. It is not coincidental that integral human development is related to Aristotle's central idea of *eudaimonia*, or human flourishing. It calls for the fullest development of each person's potential, a vocation whereby people become active agents of their own development. Or, in the words of Pope Francis, it is a quest to "find meaning, a destiny, and to live with dignity, to 'live well,' and in that sense, worthily."[43] It is that very Catholic-Aristotelian admixture.

Accordingly, integral human development is not just about meeting people's needs but respecting their agency and dignity. It is not merely about development on an economic dimension but across all dimensions—including social, political, emotional, artistic, cultural, and religious. Integral human development warns us to avoid a narrow reduction of progress to its material dimension alone, because that fails to respect our full capacities as human beings.

From this perspective, then, integral human development is not just about "having more" but "being more." Again, this goes back to the insights of Aristotle and Aquinas, who argued that true human development and happiness entailed the subordination of lower goods toward higher goods in accord with human nature, which implies that a true vocation cannot consist in merely accumulating money, wealth, or possessions. In *Populorum Progressio*, Pope Paul VI reflects this wisdom well: "Neither individuals nor nations should regard the possession of more and more goods as the ultimate objective. . . . The exclusive pursuit of material possessions prevents man's growth as a human being and stands in opposition to his true grandeur. Avarice, in individuals and in nations, is the most obvious form of stultified moral development."[44]

For Pope Paul VI, integral human development is a call for a new humanism that rejects greed and the constant desire to "have" more. Two decades later, Pope John Paul II reflected again on this couplet of "having" and "being," noting the following paradox:

This then is the picture: there are some people—the few who possess much—who do not really succeed in "being" because, through a reversal of the hierarchy of values, they are hindered by the cult of "having"; and there are others—the many who have little or nothing—who do not succeed in realizing their basic human vocation because they are deprived of essential goods. The evil does not consist in "having" as such, but in possessing without regard for the quality and the ordered hierarchy of the goods one has. Quality and hierarchy arise from the subordination of goods and their availability to man's "being" and his true vocation.[45]

In other words, putting "having" above "being" hurts both those who have too much and those who have too little. This is a modern updating of the ancient wisdom of the Christian New Testament and the Church Fathers.

To sum up: through the principle of integral human development, human dignity forms an unbreakable couplet with the common good. It reflects the fullest development of our capacities as human beings, including the capacity to show justice, charity, and solidarity toward our neighbor. Development is therefore both personal and communal, holistic, and all inclusive.

Integral Ecology

Integral ecology is a major theme of Pope Francis's encyclical *Laudato Si'*. What does this mean, exactly? To answer that question, we need to first appreciate what *Laudato Si'* means by ecology. Its definition is pretty straightforward: "The relationship between living organisms and the environment in which they develop."[46] Integral ecology is the idea that these relationships are all interconnected, deeply intertwined, and part of a larger whole, encompassing both the human world and the natural world.

One of the basic mantras in *Laudato Si'*, repeated over and over again by Pope Francis, is that "everything is connected." At some fundamental level, the encyclical stresses, all living reality is part of a complex physical, chemical, and biological network, and human beings are embedded in this network, including by sharing a huge chunk of their genetic code with other living beings. As a result, nature is not simply "a mere setting in which we live." Rather, "We are part of nature, included in it and thus in constant interaction with it."[47]

This belief gives rise to a moral injunction: to care for and protect all of creation. In turn, this injunction has profound implications for human activity. When we disrespect or disregard the natural balance, we end up disturbing the social balance too, the lives of human beings, most especially the poor. This is integral ecology.[48] So if we degrade the earth, we in turn degrade the potential for humans to flourish, to achieve integral human development. When we harm nature, we end up harming ourselves. If we mistreat an animal, says Pope Francis, it makes it more likely that we will mistreat another person. Likewise, if we disrespect the dignity of the human person, it is more likely we will disrespect nature. As Pope Francis says clearly, if we fail to acknowledge "the worth of a poor person, a human embryo, a person with disabilities—to offer just a few examples—it becomes difficult to hear the cry of nature itself."[49]

Laudato Si' explores the theological roots of integral ecology by appealing to the three fundamental and intertwined relationships that ground human life—with God, with our fellow human beings, and with the earth itself. The key is that when one of these relationships is ruptured, then the others are ruptured too. As we saw in the last chapter, Pope Francis goes back to the story of Cain and Abel in the opening pages of the Bible to elucidate this idea. He goes on to argue that these core relationships are ruptured today, which is the theological explanation for the environmental crisis, for the appalling state of our common home. The original harmony between the Creator, humanity, and creation has been disrupted, and this disruption is brought about by human arrogance, hubris, and selfishness. As Pope Francis puts it, "Disregard for the duty to cultivate and maintain a proper relationship with my neighbor, for whose care and custody I am responsible, ruins my relationship with my own self, with others, with God, and with the earth."[50] This is integral ecology in action.

Laudato Si' goes even deeper by arguing that each creature, as a reflection of God's love, has value and significance in its own right. The great panoply of creation—in all of its complexity and variety—is part of the divine plan. Here, Pope Francis quotes Thomas Aquinas, who said that God's goodness "could not be represented fittingly by any one creature."[51] In this context, the model of the Trinity teaches us that the world exists as a web of relationships, that every living being is oriented toward other beings, and that complexity seeks harmony. God, says Pope Francis, called the universe into being, in a way that "all of us are linked by unseen bonds and together form a kind of universal family, a sublime communion which fills us with a sacred, affectionate and humble respect."[52] It follows that in some mystical sense, nature can reveal the divine to us. We can see the presence of God in every living creature and, indeed, in all of creation. This divine manifestation shows us that we are part of nature, part of something much bigger and more profound. It gives us our footing and our bearings.

Integral ecology is as broad as it is deep. The connection between humanity and the earth's systems is but one dimension of it. If we look at the relationship between people and their environments, we can identify an array of different "ecologies"—not only environmental but also economic, social, cultural, daily, and human. And these ecologies are all connected with each other. *Laudato Si'* lists some examples. Economic ecology is tied to the idea that the structure of the economy affects people and the planet, meaning that the realm of economics and economic growth cannot be considered in isolation from the environment. Social ecology relates to how the institutions of society affect the environment and the quality of human life; again, such institutions are weakened by structures of sin. Culture ecology calls for paying greater attention to how environmental problems hurt local cultures, since culture is "a living, dynamic, and participatory present reality" that affects human flourishing.[53] And, finally, there is the ecology of daily life, which calls for an urban design that respects the dignity of all inhabitants, especially the poor.

Summing up, integral ecology is a moral injunction "to hear both the cry of the earth and the cry of the poor,"[54] because that cry comes from the same source. As we will see, integral ecology is really the theology of sustainable development.

Solidarity

Solidarity is one of the most important principles of Catholic social teaching. If integral human development is most associated with Pope Paul VI, and integral ecology with Francis, it is John Paul II who really made the term "solidarity" his own. He did not invent a new principle here. Solidarity has been a constant theme of Catholic social teaching, even if it has been called by a variety of different names: Leo XIII, Pius XI, and Paul VI used the terms "friendship," "social charity," and "civilization of love," respectively to mean broadly the same thing.[55] The beauty of the word "solidarity" is that, while rooted in the Catholic ethical tradition, it can appeal across confessional divides. It is a virtue that binds.

But what exactly is solidarity? It is one of those terms that is often hard to define precisely because its usage is so commonplace. Yet in *Sollicitudo Rei Socialis*—the encyclical on solidarity—Pope John Paul II tries to give the term some flesh. Here is how he defines solidarity: "This then is not a feeling of vague compassion or shallow distress at the misfortunes of so many people, both near and far. On the contrary, it is a firm and persevering determination to commit oneself to the common good; that is to say to the good of all and of each individual, because we are all really responsible for all."[56]

Solidarity, then, is like a superhighway to the common good and is the way of avoiding those obstacles known as structures of sin. It is not just a feeling of empathy, but it must be rooted on concrete action to aid the other. In one sense, solidarity can be regarded as a moral response to the interdependence of human life, the notion that we are a single human family with responsibilities toward each other. It reflects the idea that we are not egoistic individuals following our own unique path without reference to others but that we are truly "all really responsible for all." These responsibilities apply especially to the rich and the powerful. As John Paul puts it, "Those who are more influential, because they have a greater share of goods and common services, should feel responsible for the weaker and be ready to share with them all they possess."[57]

And as the human family becomes more interdependent in the age of globalization, so solidarity must also be expanded. Solidarity becomes the moral response to global interdependence. We need solidarity among both people and nations. Otherwise, globalization will be, in the words of Pope Francis, a "globalization of indifference." Pope John Paul argues that interdependence gives rise to a common destiny, requiring solidarity as its glue, as the alternative could be conflict and violence: "At the same time, in a world divided and beset by every type of conflict, the conviction is growing of a radical interdependence and consequently of the need for a solidarity which will take up interdependence and transfer it to the moral plane. Today perhaps more than in the past, people are realizing that they are linked together by a common destiny, which is to be constructed together, if catastrophe for all is to be avoided."[58]

John Paul argues that solidarity is actually a virtue in the ancient sense of Aristotle and Aquinas. It is a Christian virtue marked by the "specifically Christian dimension of total gratuity, forgiveness and reconciliation,"[59] but it is broader than this. The full impact of solidarity as a virtue is teased out by Clark, who argues that the end of solidarity is participation by all in the universal common good.[60] From this perspective, solidarity is a virtue of both individuals and communities. It transforms institutions so that structures of sin can be turned into structures of solidarity. And in line with Aristotle's notion of virtue as the golden mean between deficiency and excess, the two vices sitting on either side of solidarity can be seen as individualism on one side and collectivism on the other.

Solidarity is also a major theme for Pope Francis, who ties it to what we owe the poor. For Pope Francis, solidarity "means thinking and acting in terms of community. It means that the lives of all are prior to the appropriation of goods by a few. It also means combatting the structural causes of poverty, inequality, the lack of work, land and housing, the denial of social and labour rights."[61]

Going further, I would argue that Francis had extended the principle of solidarity in *Laudato Si'*. He calls for a "new and universal solidarity."[62] Its use is to tackle the challenges of sustainable development, including poverty, deprivation, and environmental calamity. In the first sense, this required solidarity extends not only across space but also across time—intergenerational solidarity. "Once we start to think about the kind of world we are leaving to future generations," he says, "we look at things differently; we realize that the world is a gift which we have freely received and must share with others."[63] In the second sense, this principle incorporates a solidarity with nature, a solidarity across species. It flows from the notion that all creatures have value and worth in their own right. If everything is connected, then everything must be bonded by solidarity—a true "universal communion," to use the words of Pope Francis.[64]

Subsidiarity

Subsidiarity is often regarded as a complementary principle to solidarity. In common parlance, subsidiarity is interpreted as doing things at the level closest to the person. It has even been hardwired into the workings of the European Union. In the United States, it is often seen as synonymous with federalism or with limited government. This interpretation is prone to abuse, I would argue. We need a more precise definition. The best, in my view, comes from Clark, who defines it as the principle by which decisions are taken at the lowest level possible and the highest level necessary.[65] More formally, subsidiarity insists that higher-level communities (including the state) should assist lower-level communities but not usurp their rightful autonomy.[66] As Clark puts it, subsidiarity is an "instrument for analyzing and gauging the appropriate locus of authority for moral decisions."[67] It is about getting the balance right.

If there is one pope who is most associated with subsidiarity, it is Pius XI. For him, subsidiarity comes with a negative and a positive dimension. Here is how he describes the negative form:

> Just as it is gravely wrong to take from individuals what they can accomplish by their own initiative and industry and give it to the community, so also it is an injustice and at the same time a grave evil and disturbance of right order to assign to a greater and higher association what lesser and subordinate organizations can do. For every social activity ought of its very nature to furnish help to the members of the body social, and never destroy and absorb them.[68]

Because the important word here is "help,"—indeed, the root of the Latin word from which subsidiarity derives—it should immediately warn us that subsidiarity is no excuse for libertarianism or a laissez-faire economy. This view becomes clearer when we consider subsidiarity in its positive dimension, quoting Pius XI again: "Thereby the State will more freely, powerfully, and effectively do all those things that belong to it alone because it alone can do them: directing, watching, urging, restraining, as occasion requires and necessity demands."[69]

Pope John XXIII also discussed this theme in *Mater et Magistra*, in the context of appropriate state intervention in economic affairs. He argued that, on the basis of the principle of subsidiarity, the state's role should be "directing, stimulating, co-ordinating, supplying and integrating."[70] But it should keep the balance right and not suppress the agency or freedom of individuals or subsidiarity institutions that sit between the individual and the state. It should neither smother individual initiative nor cast people adrift on a sea of autonomy.

Indeed, it was this worry that motivated Pius XI to spell out the principle of subsidiarity in the first place. He was worried about decaying institutions of civil society, leaving only the isolated individual on one hand and an all-powerful state on the other. As he put it, "Following upon the overthrow and near extinction of that rich social life which was once highly developed through associations of various kinds, there remain virtually only individuals and the State."[71] Like solidarity, subsidiarity can also help balance the two extremes of individualism and collectivism, and it does so by fertilizing civil society and a rich associational life that stands between individual and state—groups such as families, churches, unions, cooperatives, associations, and small businesses.

As noted, subsidiarity is linked to solidarity. In fact, subsidiarity is a key method or tool for helping people live out solidarity.[72] Pope Francis echoes the importance of subsidiarity in this context, putting added stress on the responsibility of those with power. For Francis, subsidiarity "grants freedom to develop the capabilities present at every level of society, while also demanding a greater sense of responsibility for the common good from those who wield greater power."[73] Again, he stresses what he dubs the "double movement"—"from top to bottom and from bottom to top"—always respecting the agency and dignity *of* all, and the ability to participate *by* all, including the marginalized and excluded.[74] Despite the claims of some, subsidiarity is not synonymous with a hands-off state or a libertarian ideology.

Reciprocity and Gratuitousness

The themes of reciprocity and gratuitousness are most associated with Pope Benedict XVI's encyclical *Caritas in Veritate*. Reciprocity is related to solidarity in that it elevates the well-being of the other but with one crucial difference: while solidarity can be extended to all people in all corners of the world, reciprocity is a human-level principle. It says that we should care about the well-being of the person on the other side of the economic encounter because that person is a brother or sister. Market transactions are therefore mediated by interpersonal relationships, not by anonymous transactions. The principle of reciprocity implies that economic exchange and encounter are less about seeking one's own advantage or striving to maximize one's own benefit than about embedding sociability and fraternity in the marketplace. Giving freely to another person—the principle of gratuitousness—builds a stronger relationship, making it likely that the benefit will be returned and a virtuous cycle established. As defined by Pope Francis, the principle of gratuitousness refers to "the ability to do some things simply because they are good in themselves, without concern for personal gain or recompense."[75] As we will see in the next chapter, this principle is not at all how market transactions are described by the dominant economic paradigm.

We have all seen this principle of reciprocity play out in daily life. It is so obvious that we probably don't even think about it. It is how healthy families function. It forms the basis of friendship. But it also has an economic dimension. Let's say, for example, that a worker needs to take some personal time off, going beyond what is in the strict employment contract. A hard-nosed boss will say no, that it is against the rules. A boss who believes in reciprocity and gratuitousness will freely give this "gift" to the employee, trusting that the employee is asking for leave for genuine reasons and not simply taking advantage of the boss's kindness. But having done this, the employee has developed a more fraternal relationship with her boss and will be more likely to (say) work late on a project at some later date without complaint.

This is not some wishy-washy idealism. Taking reciprocity and gratuitousness to scale builds up trust in the workplace and in all areas of economic interaction, and this trust is the oil that lubricates social relationships and makes economic endeavors smoother and more collaborative—and more supportive of the common good. The basic idea is that human beings have shared needs that can be satisfied only through mutual assistance based on the spirit of fraternity and human trust.

This idea is the basis of what has become known as the civil economy paradigm, an Italian economics tradition that traces back to Antonio Genovesi, a contemporary of Adam Smith, who argued that the lodestar of economic exchange is not self-interest but rather reciprocity and sociability.[76] In this, Genovesi was inspired by Aristotle and Aquinas. As noted by Stefano Zamagni, in this tradition, market relations are based more on mutual assistance than mutual benefit. The civil economy embeds sociability within the framework of normal economic life.[77]

This civil economy paradigm had a profound influence on Pope Benedict's *Caritas in Veritate*, which imbued it with a strong theological dimension. Benedict starts from the assumption that the human being is made for gift giving, arguing that because human beings owe their very existence to God's love freely given, this fact calls for a reciprocal response in the form of fraternity, sociability, and solidarity.[78] This principle of reciprocity and gratuitousness relates once again to the notion that humans are not isolated individuals seeking their own satisfaction but always "beings-in-relation," mirroring the inner life of the Trinity.

Once again, this "high theology" is not a mere curiosity but rather has profound implications for how the economy should function. It suggests, in the logic of Benedict, that all economic behavior should be driven by logic of gift and the principle of gratuitousness. People are called on to give not only to acquire something (via the market) or out of compulsion (via the state) but simply for the sake of giving in itself. As Benedict puts it, "Authentically human social relationships of friendship, solidarity and reciprocity can also be conducted within economic activity, and not only outside it or 'after' it. . . . In *commercial relationships* the *principle of gratuitousness* and the logic of gift as an expression of fraternity can and must *find their place within normal economic activity*."[79] "The economic sphere is neither ethically neutral, nor inherently inhuman and opposed to society," he contends. "It is part and parcel of human activity and precisely because it is human, it must be structured and governed in an ethical manner." And then comes the punchline: "Every economic decision has a moral consequence."[80]

This reasoning suggests that the economy can never be a value-free zone but must always be guided by ethics and the cultivation of virtue. The market is not some arena of ethical neutrality where people transact for personal gain. Virtues such as solidarity, reciprocity, and gratuitousness belong in the very heart of the market economy. They are not merely the domain of private charity or state action. They are as central to economic flourishing as the rule of law or justice through redistribution.

Universal Destination of Goods

The universal destination of goods is a new name for one of the oldest principles in the Judeo-Christian tradition—that the goods of the earth are destined for all without exception and without exclusion. We have seen this principle in the Hebrew Scriptures, the New Testament, and Aquinas's conditional justification of private property by distinguishing between private ownership and common use.

What this principle implies is that contrary to libertarianism and free market ideology, private property is not an absolute or unconditional right. Its legitimacy is conditioned on meeting the needs of all. Pope John Paul II calls the universal destination of goods the "first principle of the whole ethical and social order."[81] In his words, "God gave the earth to the whole human race for the sustenance of all its members, without excluding or favouring anyone."[82] He further argues that private property always comes with what he calls a "social mortgage": "It is necessary to state once more the characteristic principle of Christian social doctrine: the goods of this world are originally meant for all. The right to private property is valid and necessary, but it does not nullify the value of this principle. Private property, in fact, is under a 'social mortgage'; in other words, it has an intrinsically social function, based upon and justified precisely by the principle of the universal destination of goods."[83] Pope Paul VI phrases the doctrine even more strongly, linking it to the prophetic voices of the Church Fathers:

As St. Ambrose put it: "You are not making a gift of what is yours to the poor man, but you are giving him back what is his. You have been appropriating things that are meant to be for the common use of everyone. The earth belongs to everyone, not to the rich." These words indicate that the right to private property is not absolute and unconditional. No one may appropriate surplus goods solely for his own private use when others lack the bare necessities of life. In short, "as the Fathers of the Church and other eminent theologians tell us, the right of private property may never be exercised to the detriment of the common good." When "private gain and basic community needs conflict with one another," it is for the public authorities "to seek a solution to these questions, with the active involvement of individual citizens and social groups."[84]

The implication is that the government is called on to bring private property in line with the universal destination of goods; this will have many practical applications in the chapters that follow.

Pope Francis also speaks about the universal destination of goods in strident terms, especially in terms of giving justice to the poor: "Working for a just distribution of the fruits of the earth and human labor is not mere philanthropy. It is a moral obligation. For Christians, the responsibility is even greater: it is a commandment. It is about giving to the poor and to peoples what is theirs by right. The universal destination of goods is not a figure of speech found in the Church's social teaching. It is a reality prior to private property."[85]

In *Fratelli Tutti*, Pope Francis calls the right to private property a "secondary natural right"; in one sense, this harks all the way back to how Aquinas thought private property fit with the natural law, given his distinction between private ownership and common use. In this document, Pope Francis also extends the universal destination of goods to the global stage, arguing that "each country also belongs to the foreigner, inasmuch as a territory's goods must not be denied to a needy person coming from elsewhere."[86] This view has two dimensions—extending a welcoming hand to those in need and working to improve living conditions in their native lands. I will come back to these ideas in chapter 8, in the context of an ethical globalization.

In *Laudato Si'*, Pope Francis also talks about the environment in terms of the universal destination of goods, noting that "the natural environment is a collective good, the patrimony of all humanity and the responsibility of everyone. If we make something our own, it is only to administer it for the good of all."[87] Thus we need to make sure that the fruits of the earth and its bountiful resources benefit the whole of humanity, not merely the inhabitants of rich countries. This universal destination of goods also applies across time in line with intergenerational solidarity.

Preferential Option for the Poor

As we saw in the last chapter, in Christianity, God is regarded as especially close to the poor. The Hebrew Scriptures are full of divine indignation at how the poor are mistreated, and Jesus himself especially empathized with the poor. The notion of a "preferential option for the poor" comes out of liberation theology, a theological movement that linked Christian liberation from sin with liberation of the poor from poverty and oppression.[88] It rises up from the deepest roots of Christianity—from a God who identified intimately with the poor, in whose faces we are called on to see Christ. It says that all human action and all economic policy should be judged first by how it affects the poor, the least among us, the oppressed, and the discarded. In our personal and institutional life, in our local and global endeavors, the standard of judgment must always be the promotion of the poor and the excluded.

Pope John Paul II described the preferential option for the poor as "a special form of primacy in the exercise of Christian charity, to which the whole tradition of the Church bears witness"; to him, the failure to live up to its demands is akin to the rich man ignoring Lazarus at his gate.[89]

Pope Francis links the preferential option for the poor to both the common good and solidarity. In a document called *Evangelii Gaudium* (*EG*),[90] he notes the centrality of the option for the poor in terms of what it means to be a Christian in the world today: "God's heart has a special place for the poor, so much so that he himself 'became poor.'. . . We are called to find Christ in them, to lend our voice to their causes, but also to be their friends, to listen to them, to speak for them and to embrace the mysterious wisdom which God wishes to share with us through them."[91] This belief, which lies at the heart of his oft-repeated desire for a Church that is poor and for the poor, is always a two-way street: by helping the poor, we allow them to help us. For Pope Francis, it cannot be just about delivering charity from a safe distance. It must entail going to the peripheries and getting our hands dirty.

In this document, Pope Francis also links the preferential option for the poor directly to solidarity and the universal estimation of goods. He starts by echoing Pope John Paul II on solidarity:

> The word "solidarity" is a little worn and at times poorly understood, but it refers to something more than a few sporadic acts of generosity. It presumes the creation of a new mindset which thinks in terms of community and the priority of the life of all over the appropriation of goods by a few. Solidarity is a spontaneous reaction by those who recognize that the social

function of property and the universal destination of goods are realities which come before private property. . . . Solidarity must be lived as the decision to restore to the poor what belongs to them.[92]

To sum up, then, the preferential option for the poor centers on the liberation of the poor, the powerless, the ignored, the discarded, the outcast, the excluded, the insignificant, those relegated to the margins of society. Pope Francis uses the powerful term "throwaway culture" to express an attitude in contemporary society that some people simply don't matter. The preferential option for the poor entails prioritizing the interests and elevating the dignity of these people. But it cannot center on an attitude of benevolent paternalism; the agency of the poor must always be respected.

Catholic Notions of Rights and Duties

As noted already, the Church came late to the idea of universal human rights. In the nineteenth century, it was on the side of monarchist reactionaries who denied the legitimacy of rights such as democracy, the freedom of the press, and freedom of assembly. Part of the issue is that the notion of universal human rights is distinctly modern. People and groups always claimed rights, but these rights were specific and contextual. For example, a medieval peasant might claim the right to graze his animals on common land, while a medieval landlord might claim the right to insist that tenants provide a fixed amount of free work for him each year. These were particular rights in particular circumstances. But the notion of a right that existed solely because you are a human being was not standard in premodern society. And the Church was influenced by this way of thinking for a long time.

Church thinkers, as we have seen, spoke less about rights and more about duties, especially the duty to meet the needs of all. But the Church also had the intellectual apparatus to make the shift toward universal human rights, though in a way that distinctly reflected its own intellectual tradition. This lynchpin is human dignity. Today, the notion that human rights spring from human dignity is pretty standard. But Samuel Moyn argues that this idea is actually fairly new, arising from the Catholic intellectual tradition in the 1930s and 1940s—before that, rights talk was rooted more in French revolutionary principles (which explains the Catholic nervousness about it).[93]

So what is a right? Simply put, it is a moral claim that others are obliged to accept. Rights can be divided into political and economic rights. The first are centered on things such as the right to vote and the right to free speech. In a sense, this first sense of rights relates to "negative freedom"—the duty of the state and other coercive powers not to impede people. But there are also economic rights, such as the right to food, clothing, shelter, and healthcare. This sense of rights is often seen as related to "positive freedom"—the freedom to be able to develop your capacities. You can see clearly that both senses of rights and freedoms find analogies in the Catholic tradition, but for the purposes here, I will focus on economic rights. Ironically, while political rights are now seen as baked in, economic rights are still subject to much controversy. Negative freedom—the freedom from state interference—is much more widely accepted than positive freedom, which entails the state interfering and stepping on the scales.

I would argue that the Catholic tradition has an advantage. Moyn has argued that a problem arises when rights are sundered from duties. Historically, there was far more emphasis on duties than on rights—something certainly true of the Judeo-Christian tradition, which imposed nonnegotiable duties toward the poor and the marginalized. If we forget this, and focus only on rights, Moyn argues that it becomes difficult to offer "powerful public visions of social interdependence, collective agency, or planetary responsibility."[94] We get trapped with the neoliberal values that give rise to a defective economy. Relatedly, I would argue that a right divorced from a corresponding duty does not have strong roots. A person can simply claim a right, based on a subjective individual whim. Without a root in duties, we lack the ability to judge whether that right should be affirmed or denied. Pope Francis echoes this point in *Fratelli Tutti*, calling the increasing tendency to claim "individualistic" rights that deny the social and relational nature of the human being a "misunderstanding" and a "misuse" of human rights.[95]

The pope who did the most to align Catholic social teaching with the language of rights was Pope John XXIII, as part of his opening to the modern world. But his analysis of rights is nonetheless rooted in the Catholic tradition, heavily weighted toward economic rights, and always twinned with duties. Let me quote an extended passage from *Pacem in Terris*, in which John XXIII enunciates the various rights we are obliged to endorse:

Man has the right to live. He has the right to bodily integrity and to the means necessary for the proper development of life, particularly food, clothing, shelter, medical care, rest, and, finally, the necessary social services. In consequence, he has the right to be looked after in the event of ill health; disability stemming from his work; widowhood; old age; enforced unemployment; or whenever through no fault of his own he is deprived of the means of livelihood. . . .

. . . Moreover, man has a natural right to be respected. He has a right to his good name. He has a right to freedom in investigating the truth, and—within the limits of the moral order and the common good—to freedom of speech and publication, and to freedom to pursue whatever profession he may choose. He has the right, also, to be accurately informed about public events. . . .

. . . He has the natural right to share in the benefits of culture, and hence to receive a good general education, and a technical or professional training consistent with the degree of educational development in his own country. . . .

. . . Also among man's rights is that of being able to worship God in accordance with the right dictates of his own conscience, and to profess his religion both in private and in public. . . .

. . . Human beings have also the right to choose for themselves the kind of life which appeals to them: whether it is to found a family—in the founding of which both the man and the woman enjoy equal rights and duties—or to embrace the priesthood or the religious life. . . .

. . . The family, founded upon marriage freely contracted, one and indissoluble, must be regarded as the natural, primary cell of human society. The interests of the family, therefore, must be taken very specially into consideration in social and economic affairs, as well as in the spheres of faith and morals. For all of these have to do with strengthening the family and assisting it in the fulfilment of its mission. . . .

. . . Of course, the support and education of children is a right which belongs primarily to the parents. . . .

. . . In the economic sphere, it is evident that a man has the inherent right not only to be given the opportunity to work, but also to be allowed the exercise of personal initiative in the work he does. . . .

. . . A further consequence of man's personal dignity is his right to engage in economic activities suited to his degree of responsibility. The worker is likewise entitled to a wage that is determined in accordance with the precepts of justice. This needs stressing. The amount a worker receives must be sufficient, in proportion to available funds, to allow him and his family a standard of living consistent with human dignity. . . .

. . . As a further consequence of man's nature, he has the right to the private ownership of property, including that of productive goods . . .

. . . The right to own private property entails a social obligation as well. . . .

. . . Men are by nature social, and consequently they have the right to meet together and to form associations with their fellows. . . .

. . . The founding of a great many such intermediate groups or societies for the pursuit of aims which it is not within the competence of the individual to achieve efficiently, is a matter of great urgency. . . .

. . . Every human being has the right to freedom of movement and of residence within the confines of his own State. When there are just reasons in favor of it, he must be permitted to emigrate to other countries and take up residence there. The fact that he is a citizen of a particular State does not deprive him of membership in the human family, nor of citizenship in that universal society, the common, world-wide fellowship of men. . . .

. . . Man's personal dignity involves his right to take an active part in public life, and to make his own contribution to the common welfare of his fellow citizens.[96]

A number of observations based on this (admittedly long) list: Note that the first rights listed are not political but economic—the right to food, clothing, shelter, healthcare, rest, social services, and social insurance. Obtaining these rights is going to entail an active role for the state in the pursuit of the common good. The second point to note is the emphasis on the right to participate in all aspects of the common good—in culture, in family life, in associations, in religion, in the public sphere. The language on the right to emigrate is also pretty strong, showing that the Catholic Church always regards the global common good as the highest good, higher than the good of the nation.

If you read this carefully, you will see the twinning of rights and duties. If there is a right to the basic material bases of human flourishing, there is a duty to provide these goods. If there is a right to participate in the common good, the state is obliged to respect the freedoms of individuals and subsidiary institutions. If there is a right to the opportunity to work, such opportunity must be provided. If there is a right to a just wage and working conditions, this is a duty binding on employers. The universal destination of good too can be analyzed through this lens; the right to private property is linked to a duty to provide for the needs of all. Here is how John XXIII discusses the interplay between rights and duties:

The natural rights of which We have so far been speaking are inextricably bound up with as many duties, all applying to one and the same person. . . .

. . . Thus, for example, the right to live involves the duty to preserve one's life; the right to a decent standard of living, the duty to live in a becoming fashion; the right to be free to seek out the truth, the duty to devote oneself to an ever deeper and wider search for it. Once this is admitted, it follows that in human society one man's natural right gives rise to a corresponding duty in other men; the duty, that is, of recognizing and respecting that right. . . .

. . . Hence, to claim one's rights and ignore one's duties, or only half fulfill them, is like building a house with one hand and tearing it down with the other.[97]

I want to conclude this section by reflecting on what Pope Francis says about human rights. He follows John XXIII by putting a heavy emphasis on economic rights, with special attention to the rights of the poor. He talks about the "3 L's" of land, labor, and lodging, which he uses as among the most basic human rights. On top of this, he calls for "access to education, health care, new technologies, artistic and cultural manifestations, communications, sports and recreation." He goes on:

A just economy must create the conditions for everyone to be able to enjoy a childhood without want, to develop their talents when young, to work with full rights during their active years and to enjoy a dignified retirement as they grow older. It is an economy where human beings, in harmony with nature, structure the entire system of production and distribution in such a way that the abilities and needs of each individual find suitable expression in social life.[98]

For Pope Francis, it is not just the current generation that has rights—children, workers, older people. Those not yet born also have rights, in line with intergenerational solidarity. And these rights can only be respected by leaving behind a healthy planet for future generations to enjoy. As he notes, the environment "is on loan to each generation, which must then hand it on to the next."[99] This responsibility gives rise to particular environmental rights. For example, in *Laudato Si'*, Pope Francis calls water "a scarce and indispensable resource and a fundamental right which conditions the exercise of other human rights."[100] Without this, the poor "are denied the right to a life consistent with their inalienable dignity."[101]

This reasoning leads to one of Pope Francis's most radical claims: that the environment itself has rights, for two reasons. Human beings are intimately connected to nature, and creatures have intrinsic value in their own right. In a remarkable speech to the United Nations in 2015, he said the following:

It must be stated that a true "right of the environment" does exist, for two reasons. First, because we human beings are part of the environment. We live in communion with it, since the environment itself entails ethical limits which human activity must acknowledge and respect. . . . Any harm done to the environment, therefore, is harm done to humanity. Second, because every creature, particularly a living creature, has an intrinsic value, in its existence, its life, its beauty and its interdependence with other creatures.[102]

And in one of the most poignant passages in *Laudato Si'*, Pope Francis uses the language of rights to denounce the destruction of biodiversity in what has become known as the sixth mass extinction: "Because of us, thousands of species will no longer give glory to God by their very existence, nor convey their message to us. We have no such right."[103] The bottom line is that for Pope Francis, heeding the cry of the earth and the cry of the poor means respecting the rights of the earth and the rights of the poor.

Catholic Notions of Justice

Modern Catholic social teaching retains the ancient teaching on justice, inherited from Aristotle and Aquinas. Recall that Aquinas sees justice as a cardinal virtue of the will, which is directed toward our neighbor and therefore the common good. It is about giving all persons their due, what is owed to them. But this immediately begs the question: What exactly do we owe to each other in justice? What is obligatory and not merely voluntary? Different ideologies obviously answer that question differently. For those who believe only in negative rights and freedoms, justice requires that the government stay on the sidelines as a neutral referee. But for those who believe in positive rights and freedoms, the government must assume a more active role. Its notion of justice will be different.

Against this background, Catholic social teaching sees three different dimensions to justice, again springboarding from the foundational work of Aristotle and Aquinas: commutative justice, distributive justice, and contributive justice.

Commutative justice is justice between two individuals, relating to the mutual obligations of the relationship, the notion of justice underlying contracts, agreements, and promises. As Benedict XVI wrote, it "regulates the relations of giving and receiving between parties to a transaction."[104] It would typically involve an exchange of equivalents. This notion of justice, widely understood in modern economic relationships, is the only form of justice affirmed by libertarians. But in the Catholic tradition, it is not simply reduced to market exchange. It also includes the idea of a "just wage," which is not necessarily the same as the wage arising from the free market. The bottom line is that the economy needs the trust granted by commutative justice to function well.

Distributive justice refers to the relationship of the whole to the parts, and specifically to what the community owes each individual. It asks how the fruits of the earth and economic activity are to be properly apportioned. A libertarian or a strict believer in the virtues of free markets would deny the validity of distributive justice. But in the Catholic tradition, if people have "rights" to the material bases of human flourishing—food, clothing, lodging, healthcare, education, decent work—then society as a whole has the "duty" to make sure these goods are provided. Distributive justice does not necessarily mean the government provides these goods itself; but it does mean that it should ensure that they are provided. The same applies to the intangible factors of flourishing such as participation in culture, institutions, and political life. And of course, distributive justice is closely related to the universal destination of goods and the preferential option for the poor.

If distributive justice refers to what society owes the individual, contributive justice turns this around and asks what the individual owes society. Again, it boils down to the interplay of right and responsibility—in this case, the responsibility of each individual to contribute to the common good, to look after not just your own well-being but the well-being of others, including future generations. So, for example, contributive justice would entail voting, participating in civic life, paying your taxes, and making sure that the environment is left in good shape for coming generations. Again, a libertarian would deny these strict duties in justice, arguing that this entails a form of coercion and compulsion.[105]

These dimensions of justice all come together under the banner of social justice, which refers to the institutional framework that allows each individual to participate in the common good and share in its benefits.[106] As Pope Pius XI put it, "The public institutions themselves . . . ought to make all human society conform to the needs of the common good; that is, to the norm of social justice."[107] So there is a clear role for government here. Social justice is a charter for institutional reform.

Let me end this section by borrowing a chart from Groody, which I think shows nicely how justice, rights, and duties are all related (see figure 2.1). We thus end where we began—with the common good at the top of the pyramid.

In this chapter, I tried to survey the landscape of modern Catholic social teaching. Starting with Pope Leo XIII in 1891 and culminating with Pope Francis in 2020, I went through the social encyclical tradition, focusing mainly on what this tradition has to say about economics. These encyclicals are always in dialogue with the modern world, whether it is the challenges of the industrial revolution or sustainable development. Following this, I tried to distill ten key

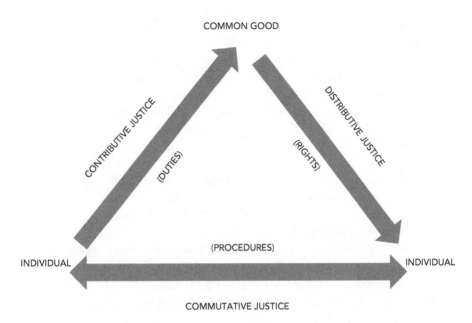

Figure 2.1. Catholic notions of justice. Reproduced by permission from Groody, *Globalization, Spirituality, and Justice.*

principles that can be used to describe and guide economic interactions—the common good, integral human development, integral ecology, solidarity, subsidiarity, reciprocity and gratuitousness, the universal destination of goods, the preferential option for the poor, Catholic notions of rights and duties, and Catholic notions of justice. In the next chapter I will argue that these principles are better placed to underpin a thriving vision of economic life than those put forth by the dominant strand of modern economics.

Notes

1. William Blake, Frank Brewer Bemis, and Lessing J. Rosenwald Collection, *Milton, a Poem in 12 [i.e. 2] Books.*

2. Annett, "Our Common Responsibility for Our Common Home."

3. In this section, I will draw on the excellent summaries and contexts of these documents found in Himes, *Modern Catholic Social Teaching;* and Mich, *Catholic Social Teaching and Movements.*

4. Mich, *Catholic Social Teaching and Movements*, ch. 1.

5. For a detailed discussion, see Shannon, "Rerum Novarum."

6. For a detailed discussion, see Firer Hinze, "Quadragesimo Anno."

7. For a detailed discussion, see Langan, "Christmas Messages of Pius XII."

8. Moyn, *Christian Human Rights*; Chappel, *Catholic Modern*.

9. For a detailed discussion, see Mich, "Mater et Magistra."

10. See Mich, *Catholic Social Teaching and Movements*, ch. 4.

11. For a detailed discussion, see Christiansen, "Pacem in Terris."

12. See Sachs, *To Move the World*.

13. For a detailed discussion, see Hollenbach, "Gaudium et Spes."

14. Mich, *Catholic Social Teaching and Movements*, ch. 5.

15. Mich, 125.

16. *GS*, 4.

17. For a detailed discussion, see Deck, "Populorum Progressio."

18. Mich, *Catholic Social Teaching and Movements*, 155.

19. For a detailed discussion, see Lamoureux, "Laborem Exercens."

20. Lamoureux, "Laborem Exercens," 403.

21. For a detailed discussion, see Curran, Himes, and Shannon, "Sollicitudo Rei Socialis."

22. For a detailed discussion, see Finn, "Centesimus Annus."

23. For a detailed discussion, see Clark, "Caritas in Veritate."

24. Clark, "Caritas in Veritate," 484–85.

25. For a detailed discussion, see Zenner Peppard, "Laudato Si'."

26. Hopkins, *"God's Grandeur" and Other Poems*.

27. Clark, *Vision of Catholic Social Thought*.

28. A side note on this: one of the participants at the Ethics in Action initiative that I described in the preface was the renowned Orthodox theologian Metropolitan John Zizioulas. He argued that human beings are not autonomous self-governing individuals but are defined by their nature as relational beings—and more than that, that Christianity entails a kind of "infinite relationality" that extends to every person in the world.

29. *LS*, 156.

30. Finnis, "Aquinas' Moral, Political, and Legal Philosophy."

31. Maritain, *Person and the Common Good*, 39.

32. Zamagni, "Catholic Social Thought, Civil Economy, and the Spirit of Capitalism."

33. Hinson-Hasty, *Problem of Wealth*, 99.

34. *EG*, 235.

35. *CIV*, 7.

36. *GS*, 26.

37. In chapter 1, I referenced Daly's elaboration of "structures of virtue and vice." Daly was influenced by this analysis of John Paul II. See Daly, "Structures of Virtue and Vice."

38. *SRS*, 36.

39. *SRS*, 37.

40. Pope Francis, "Address of His Holiness Pope Francis to Participants in the Meeting 'Economy of Communion.'"

41. *FT*, 186.

42. *PP*, 14.

43. Pope Francis, "Participation of the Second World Meeting of Popular Movements."

44. *PP*, 19.

45. *SRS*, 28.

46. *LS*, 138.

47. *LS*, 139.

48. See Annett, "Connection, Disconnection, Reconnection."

49. *LS*, 117.

50. *LS*, 70.

51. *LS*, 86.

52. *LS*, 89.

53. *LS*, 143.

54. *LS*, 49.

55. Curran, Himes, and Shannon, "Sollicitudo Rei Socialis."

56. *SRS*, 38.

57. *SRS*, 39.

58. *SRS*, 26.

59. *SRS*, 40.

60. Clark, *Vision of Catholic Social Thought*.

61. *FT*, 116.

62. *LS*, 14.

63. *LS*, 159.

64. *LS*, 76.

65. Meghan J. Clark, "Subsidiarity Is a Two-Sided Coin," *Catholic Moral Theology*, March 8, 2012.

66. This is the notion of vertical subsidiarity, favored by Catholic social teaching. There is a related concept of circular subsidiarity whereby government, market, and wider community cooperate for the common good. I thank Stefano Zamagni for this distinction.

67. Clark, "Seeking Solidarity for Development," 319.

68. *QA*, 79.

69. *QA*, 80.

70. *MM*, 53.

71. *QA*, 78.

72. I owe this insight to Meghan Clark.

73. *LS*, 196.

74. Pope Francis, General Audience, September 23, 2020.

75. *FT*, 139.

76. See Bruni and Zamagni, *Civil Economy*.

77. Zamagni, "On the Birth of Economic Science during the Italian-Scottish Enlightenment."

78. See Argandona, "'Logic of Gift' in the Business Enterprise."

79. *CIV*, 36.

80. *CIV*, 36–37.

81. *LE*, 19.

82. *CA*, 31.

83. *SRS*, 42.

84. *PP*, 23.

85. Pope Francis, "Participation of the Second World Meeting of Popular Movements."

86. *FT*, 124.

87. *LS*, 95.

88. Liberation theology arose out of Latin America in the wake of the Second Vatican Council. It reflects, in the words of Daniel Groody, in *Globalization, Spirituality, and Justice*, "a way to think about God in our contemporary world from the perspective of those left out of the benefits of the current global economy. It is also a social movement that seeks to live out what it means to be a Christian in a world of poverty. . . . Liberation then deals with God's action in history to free people from all that oppresses them right now and at the end of time" (184–85). Some aspects of liberation theology waded into controversy because they used Marxist tools of analysis. But its key principle, the preferential option for the poor, became mainstream within Catholicism.

89. *SRS*, 42.

90. This is what is known as an apostolic exhortation. Technically, it is of somewhat lower status than an encyclical, though these distinctions do not matter for our purposes here.

91. *EG*, 197.

92. *EG*, 188.

93. Moyn, *Christian Human Rights*.

94. Samuel Moyn, "Rights vs. Duties: Reclaiming Civic Balance," *Boston Review*, May 16, 2016.

95. *FT*, 111.

96. *PT*, 11–18, 20–26.

97. *PT*, 28–30.

98. Pope Francis, "Participation of the Second World Meeting of Popular Movements."

99. *LS*, 159.

100. *LS*, 185.

101. *LS*, 30.

102. Pope Francis, "Meetings with Members of the General Assembly of the United Nations Organization."

103. *LS*, 33.

104. *CIV*, 35.

105. Chapter 5 will go into more detail on why libertarianism is not compatible with the Catholic tradition.

106. See Finn, *Christian Economic Ethics*.

107. *QA*, 110.

3

Who's Right and Who's Wrong?

Catholic Social Teaching versus the Dominant Economic Paradigm

In the last chapter, I discussed the ten core principles of Catholic social teaching. In this chapter, I will stack them up against the principles of neoclassical economics and argue that the Catholic principles are better, in the sense of being more in tune with human nature and more conducive to human flourishing. This is a foundation for what comes next in the book: how the economy performs. For if we are relying on a model that gets human nature wrong, then it should come as no surprise that social and economic outcomes based on these principles will prove dysfunctional.

The principles I want to focus on here are those of neoclassical economics. Why this focus? Isn't this approach rather obscure and academic when my real interest lies with how the economy functions? I take this approach for a simple reason: over the past half century or so, the discipline of neoclassical economics has had an enormous influence over economic and social policy. It has even affected how people relate to each other and view the world. This all-encompassing worldview has been dubbed neoliberalism by some, and it springs directly from the assumptions and principles of how neoclassical economics emerged over the past century or more. Binyamin Appelbaum from the *New York Times* wrote a bestselling book on this recently called *The Economists' Hour*.[1]

A Little Bit of History

Here's how I intend to proceed. I need to start with a little history, to explore the intellectual roots of neoclassical economics, which goes back centuries. The idea is simply to show where neoclassical economics came from.[2]

The simple answer is that it came from the Enlightenment paradigm. When people hear the Enlightenment spoken of today, they think about the triumph of science and reason over medieval superstition. But this supposition is misleading. In reality, the shift was much more complicated. As I've shown, Aristotle and Aquinas developed a pretty sophisticated philosophy of human action. This worldview came to be dethroned during the Enlightenment.

I would argue that the political and economic philosophies that came out of this period had three interconnected pillars.[3]

First, there was a switch away from the Aristotle-Aquinas conception of the common good toward a greater focus on the autonomous individual. Some philosophers argue that this had its intellectual genesis in the fourteenth century with something called nominalism. Nominalism denied the reality of universals, including the notion of a universal human nature and a universal common good. Human beings therefore were no longer oriented toward the good, a good held in common, because without universals there could be no universal ends. Instead, every human being was now seen as radically individual, with their own subjective ends.[4] In the early modern period, Thomas Hobbes, John Locke, and other major thinkers promoted this notion of the autonomous individual and—in a sharp divergence from Aristotle—saw the state as no more than a voluntary social contract between these autonomous individuals.

Second, the Enlightenment shifted from balance and moderation to mastery and maximization. We have already seen that the worldview of Aristotle and Aquinas was about condemning greed, knowing when enough was enough, and finding the right balance in all areas of life. As we will see, this was replaced with the idea of maximization and the absence of an acquisitive ceiling.[5] This shift was also highly optimistic about using science to gain knowledge and control over the natural world—and in doing so, attain progress and better the lives of people. As René Descartes put it, humanity should become "masters and possessors of nature."[6] A natural consequence of this shift is the move toward limitless economic growth. As we will see in chapter 7, this change would turn out to have dire implications for the environment.

Third, the Enlightenment paradigm completely upended traditional virtue ethics by arguing that what used to be vices were now to be regarded as virtues. In the words of philosopher Vittorio Hösle, a participant in the Ethics in Action initiative I described earlier, "Some sort of behavior that was regarded as virtuous . . . leads to negative consequences, while the opposite behavior . . . can be beneficial to society at large."[7] Historian David Wootton makes a similar point, arguing that political theorists and economists began to argue that the quest for power, pleasure, and profit were the defining motivations of human beings, and these motivations could lead to favorable social outcomes. Instead of mastery of the passions, they were now seen as insatiable, things we pursue "without limit and without end."[8]

These shifts actually began in politics, not economics. Here, a key figure was the sixteenth-century Italian Niccolò Machiavelli, who argued that a good political leader should not be bound by the virtues. He should in fact jettison virtue in pursuit of power, for this would lead not only to the glory of the ruler himself but, more important, to peace and social harmony. Vice, according to Machiavelli, will lead to security and prosperity. So in practice, a ruler should display toughness rather than clemency and mercy. Likewise, the seventeenth-century British political theorist Thomas Hobbes argued that what motivated people was a quest for pleasure and power, and these appetites were insatiable. He directly opposed the notion of Aristotle and Aquinas that there was a *summum bonum*, a highest good that all people pursue. Individuals have their own priorities, but their desires are never satisfied. Because everybody acts the same way, motivated by passions, everybody is in competition with everyone else, which is bound to lead to a "war of all against all."[9] For Hobbes, the only escape was for autonomous individuals to voluntarily cede their power to an absolutist sovereign. Hobbes's contemporary John Locke was not quite as dark, but he elevated an absolutist position on property rights whereby the individual owns whatever he mixed his labor with. All of this is a far cry from Aristotle's vision of the human being as a social animal oriented toward virtue and the common good.

This turn toward the pleasure-seeking individual reached its apogee with the advent of utilitarianism in the eighteenth century. Jeremy Bentham, its founder, would argue that "nature has placed mankind under the governance of two sovereign masters, pain and pleasure. It is for them alone to point out what we ought to do, as well as to determine what we shall do."[10] So happiness is no longer *eudaimonia*; it is instead *hedonia*: pleasure and the absence of pain, without any limits. There is no common good here. As Bentham said with his trademark bluntness, "The community is a fictitious body, composed of the individual persons who are considered as constituting as it were its members. The interest of the community then is, what?—the sum of the interests of the several members who compose it."[11] For Bentham, the government should simply seek the greatest happiness of the greatest number. It is about adding up individuals' utility or happiness. You can immediately see the danger; if we are just adding up, some people can be excluded. And it is fine to ride roughshod over basic rights so as to achieve general happiness. Keep all of this in mind, as modern economics was forged in the furnace of this kind of utilitarianism.

In the eighteenth century, the philosopher David Hume was also instrumental in this turning of vice to virtue. Hume believed morality came from the passions and that reason was deployed afterward to justify the desires people have. Morality, then, was based on emotional resonance, most notably a sense of fellow feeling. But Hume argued that people took pride first and foremost in the pleasure that comes from "power, riches, beauty or personal merit" and that this pride is recognized and esteemed by others. Putting it simply, Hume thought that people looked up to wealth and looked down on the poor.[12] As David Cloutier notes, it is Hume's reflexive defense of wealth and luxury that makes his decisive turn from vice to virtue. For Hume, this was a "calm passion" that led to good social outcomes, including sociability and cooperation. Hume also famously argued that constitutions and legal regimes should assume that people are "knaves," driven only by their self-interest. Again, Hume held that that this kind of self-interest was a fairly benign passion and that virtue alone was incapable of governing a large state. Hence the legal framework should seek to harness this selfishness toward the common good.[13]

The same alchemy of turning vice to virtue took place in economics. The first mover is often regarded as Bernard Mandeville, who wrote *The Fable of the Bees* in 1714.[14] The fable is a simple morality tale, or perhaps an antimorality tale. In it, a hive of bees thrives because it is driven by selfishness, ruthless competition, pride, the love of luxury, and even fraud. Mandeville asks us to picture what would happen if the hive suddenly became virtuous and honest. He thought that the hive would collapse, as stronger enemies would attack it. His conclusion couldn't be clearer: private vice leads to public virtue. He asks the reader to choose between a decent and honest society or a powerful and wealthy society. He even gives some practical examples: without drunkenness, the sellers of alcohol would make less profits, and without thieves, locksmiths would not do business. How many times do we hear similar arguments in our own time, without really appreciating the philosophical underpinnings?

This view brings us to Adam Smith, a complicated and sometimes infuriating figure. A sophisticated moral philosopher, Smith was opposed to Mandeville's crude "in your face" moral calculus. Yet Mandeville's analysis was a huge influence on Smith's belief that people were motivated in the economic domain by self-interest rather than benevolence and generosity. As he put it, "It is not from the benevolence of the butcher, the brewer, or the baker that we expect our dinner, but from their regard to their own interest. We address ourselves, not to their humanity but to their self-love, and never talk to them of our own necessities but of their advantages."[15]

Most people are familiar with Smith's famous "invisible hand" defense of the market. They might be less aware that Smith deploys two separate invisible hand arguments. The familiar one comes from his *Wealth of Nations*, in which Smith tells the familiar story of self-interest combined with division of labor and market competition leading to rising wealth and prosperity of all. This state happens not through any deliberative intent but through the alchemy of the free market. In his *Theory of Moral Sentiments*, though, he provides a somewhat different invisible hand argument. Here, he argues that the rich miscalculate the happiness that comes from the pursuit of status and luxury, partly because they think people will look up to them and partly because their striving for more never really ends. But this very act of wealth seeking leads to more prosperity and security, which benefits all of society.[16] So in each case, self-interest and wealth seeking lead to good social outcomes—to, dare I say it, public virtue. It is Hume's "constitution for knaves" extended to the economic sphere. Like Hume, Smith believed people were motivated primarily by emotion and the passions.

Smith never completely discounted the role of virtue, though. Like Hume, he believed deeply in the power of reputation, which he saw as motivating our moral sentiments by empathy and benevolence and which also underpinned economic transactions. Mandeville's thumbs-up to fraud appalled Smith. Yet Smith's analysis of virtue was crimped. He claimed to support the virtue of prudence, for example, but in the economic sphere, he reduced it to the narrow "bourgeois virtues" of industry and frugality.[17] In this light, he was of two minds about luxury. One on hand, he recognized, as noted, that it brought about important social benefits. But he was also squeamish about it, because it went against the virtue of frugality, which he saw as necessary for investment and economic growth; this is another reason why he opposed Mandeville's love of luxury consumption.[18]

In sum, the Enlightenment paradigm presents us with a world of an autonomous individual unencumbered by social ties that are not freely chosen; seeking power, pleasure, and profit without limit; using technology to seek mastery of nature and secure ceaseless economic growth. To understand neoclassical economics, we need to understand its roots.

Principles of Neoclassical Economics versus Catholic Social Teaching

Let's now proceed with the main goal of this chapter. Table 3.1 stacks up the various assumptions of neoclassical economics and Catholic social teaching along a number of different dimensions.[19] I will talk through that table as a way of explaining things. A tip of my hand in advance, I will be arguing that

Table 3.1. Assumptions of Neoclassical Economics versus Catholic Social Teaching

	Neoclassical economics	Catholic social teaching
Understanding of the person	Autonomous individuals	Beings-in-relation
Motivation of the person	Self-interest	Solidarity, reciprocity/gratuitousness
Good of the person	Satisfaction of subjective material preferences	Integral human development
Good of society	Aggregation of subjective material preference satisfaction	The common good
Market functioning	Competition	Competition, solidarity, reciprocity/gratuitousness
Standard of judgment	Pareto efficiency, economic growth	Universal destination of goods, preferential option for the poor
Understanding of rights	Property rights	Economic rights
Norms of justice	Commutative	Commutative, distributive, contributive
Role of government	Neutral referee, correct market failures	Solidarity, subsidiarity
Treatment of nature	Extractive (in service of GDP)	Integral ecology

the assumptions of neoclassical economics are deeply flawed, so any policy advice based on them must come with a whiff of suspicion. But we need to build this argument from the bottom up.

Just as in Catholic social teaching, neoclassical economics is built on a moral or ethical framework—the Enlightenment paradigm described above. Economists don't typically think in these terms, however. Too often, they regard their discipline as scientific, rigorous, and value free. As we will see, this assumption is mistaken. Just like other ethical systems, it provides answers to some of the big questions: the nature of the human being, the purpose or goal in life, and the right course of action in different circumstances. Let's look at how.

Starting at the highest possible level, the nature of the human being, modern economics diverges distinctly from Catholic social teaching. Remember, neoclassical economics comes out of the Enlightenment paradigm that puts much more emphasis on individual freedom and autonomy than on any natural ties that bind us together. The Catholic approach, on the other hand, regards the human person always as a "being-in-relation." It takes Aristotle's idea of human beings as social animals and takes it one level higher, arguing that we are inherently relational beings. Our self-definition comes through relationship to others. We are not cast adrift on an ocean of isolation, a point important for everything that follows.

What motivates the person? In neoclassical economics, it is self-interest, a view going back to Adam Smith's claim that without self-interest, the butcher, the baker, and the brewer would not supply the goods you want. In Catholic social teaching on the other hand, the motivating virtues, as we have seen, are solidarity, reciprocity, and gratuitousness. Some might argue that this is too naive; without the self-interest described by Smith, after all, how would our needs be met? But I think Smith misses out on an important nuance. He thought that there was far too much corruption and cronyism in his day, and he was right about that. But he overreacted. His solution was an impersonal marketplace that did not rely on corrupt personal favors. As Stefano Zamagni puts it, for Smith, the market performs a civilizing function by allowing people to free themselves on the dependence of others; this marked an ethical improvement over what came before.[20] But as Luigino Bruni has argued, he is throwing the baby out with the bathwater, missing out on the relational gains from marketplace cooperation—through solidarity, reciprocity, and fraternity—which can add salt to trust and so generate even greater economic gains for all. As Bruni puts it, if you do not open yourself up to a wound, you will never receive the blessing that can come from it.[21] You won't be able to benefit from the gains that come from virtuous, not corrupt, relationships.

Neoclassical economics, though, has come a long way since Smith. It has turned into a highly rigorous and mathematical discipline based on the idea of *homo economicus*. This "economic man," as basic economics textbooks will tell you, seeks to maximize a utility function, which is merely a mathematical way of saying the person is trying to satisfy their personal preferences to the greatest extent possible. You have a bunch of goods and services that you like and want to buy and consume, but you are constrained by your income. Hence you try to consume the most you can, in line with your personal preferences, given the money you have. This logic is why I claim that for neoclassical economics, the good of the person is synonymous with the satisfaction of subjective material preferences.

Digging deeper, this view has four separate implications. First, it bakes in Smithian self-interest. This implication is actually more complicated than it seems. It is possible to put somebody else's utility in your utility function so that you are more satisfied when they get more stuff. But this is rather different from the common good; you are not willing the other's good for its own sake, or willing to sacrifice something of benefit to yourself to aid your neighbor.[22] It is still ultimately your own "jolt of satisfaction" that concerns you.

A second implication is that these preferences are subjective; you like what you like. In this light, the utilitarian roots of neoclassical economics shine through. Utility is subjective and hedonic. There is no objective individual or common good. Accordingly, there is no concept of self-perfection or ethical education. Rather, neoclassical economics starts from the premise that it is not possible to compare preferences across people, so all that matters is what they choose to buy on the market. Any questions regarding the value or worth of somebody's preferences are prohibited under the assumption that people's desires are sacrosanct.

This implication gives rise to a third one. Again, anything in theory can go into a utility function, but in practice—since we are limited to a framework based on money and material goods—good and services that can be purchased on the market are what really matter. The theory cannot really accommodate the good that comes from relationships or meaning and purpose—the core internal goods identified by Aristotle as constitutive of human flourishing. Some economists have stressed the importance of "relational goods": those goods that can be enjoyed only if shared reciprocally, are characterized by gratuitousness, and where the source of the good lies in the relationship itself.[23] The same holds for cultural goods and spiritual goods. But the neoclassical framework can't really accommodate these kinds of goods. At the same time, it holds that anything that is legal can be a valid preference—including weapons and tobacco products, luxury consumption fueled more by advertising than the desire to meet real needs, prostitution, gambling, the feeding of addictions, and like things. So clearly the satisfaction of subjective material preferences is very different from human flourishing or integral human development.

A fourth implication of the neoclassical paradigm is that wants are unbounded. Again, this view comes directly from the Enlightenment paradigm. We are supposed to maximize utility; all that stops us is inadequate income. As Hirschfeld notes, "The assumption that desires are unbounded undergirds most of economic thought. This can be best seen in the widespread assumption that, ceteris paribus (all else being equal), more economic growth is to be preferred to less."[24] But the Christian and virtue ethics tradition would argue that such an assumption is not in accord with human nature, that desires should indeed be bounded, needs should be limited, and lower goods should be subordinated to higher goods. As Hirschfeld notes, what we seek is perfection, which can in no way be seen as equivalent to maximization.[25] This assertion would cast into question the focus on endless economic growth.

Needless to say, how the two traditions view rationality could not be more different. Any economist will tell you that it is the rationality of *homo economicus* that makes economics a science. People are supposed to maximize utility, to satisfy their preferences to the best extent possible given income and market prices. But in the tradition of Aristotle, rationality has an entirely different meaning. It is about the deployment of prudence or practical reason to figure out what is good and then to choose the good actively. In the theological language of Aquinas, it is about using the intellect to understand what is good and then directing the rational will to choose that good. Neoclassical economics turns this on its head. As Hirschfeld puts it, "Rationality [in modern capitalism] comes to be identified with the irrational effort to climb a ladder of successive goods that are not coherently ordered to a well-conceived end."[26] Neoclassical economics knows no objective "good," only subjective "goods." Or, as Brad Gregory put it, the "good society" is replaced by the "goods society."[27]

Just as an individual's good differs, so does the common good. As noted, neoclassical economics has no concept of a fused interpersonal well-being that constitutes the common good. And since this economics cannot judge preferences, it cannot compare preferences across people. All it can do is add up a monetary value, which is often equated with GDP, the summation of all consumption of market goods and services in a single economy. Again, this notion comes from the utilitarian framework, which, instead of the common good, talks about the greatest happiness of the greatest number. That makes the framework additive. And with an additive standard, people can easily be zeroed out, unlike the "geometric" structure of the common good.

This brings us to the normative standard of judgment. For Catholic social teaching, this is clear: the universal destination of goods and the preferential option for the poor. For economists, on the other hand, the answer is "efficiency." People use this word all the time, but it has a fairly technical meaning in neoclassical economics. Efficiency—or more specifically, Pareto efficiency—is the point at which you maximize the satisfaction of your subjective material preferences. A market trade will take place only if it benefits both sides. Pareto efficiency is the point at which all voluntary trades that can satisfy preferences are exhausted. In other words, it is no longer possible to make somebody better off without making somebody else worse off. Economists often argue that this notion of efficiency is rational and value free, but it really just boils down to the best way to maximize your subjective preferences. Challenge that, and the whole house of cards comes tumbling down—and with it, the assumption that unbounded economic growth is always a good thing.

Pareto efficiency is simply not compatible with the universal destination of goods or the preferential option for the poor. It explicitly rules out distributional issues. It is not permitted to take a dollar from a billionaire to give to a homeless person because the billionaire is made worse off (by a dollar). Pareto efficiency is compatible with enormous inequalities of income and wealth. As Nobel Prize–winning economist and philosopher Amartya Sen put it, "A society or an economy can be Pareto optimal and still be perfectly disgusting."[28] Note that neoclassical economists might well support such monetary transfers; they would merely argue that it cannot be justified on efficiency grounds, which remains the lodestar of economic interactions. They would argue that efficiency is a scientific standard, while redistribution is merely political. As we have seen, though, this simple dichotomy carries much baggage with it.

There is one more link in the chain for neoclassical economics. As well as consumers maximizing utility, firms are supposed to maximize profits. This principle too violates Catholic social teaching, but I will wait until chapter 5 to explore the full implications of this. Neoclassical economics holds up "perfect competition" as the gold standard. What does this mean? It basically takes an extreme case, an industry whereby (1) there are many producers, so no single one of them can influence the price of the good; (2) there is a standardized good; and (3) there is free entry and exit. Under these highly rarefied and extreme conditions, we can show that the market equilibrium is efficient.

We are now getting to the case for free and unfettered markets, a case that holds such sway in neoclassical economics. As its crowning glory, neoclassical economics puts forward what are known as welfare theorems. The first of these theorems states that a perfectly competitive equilibrium leads to a Pareto efficient outcome—hence the claim that free markets are efficient. As leading economist Gregory Mankiw puts it, this theorem shows that "competitive markets with self-interested actors make the economic pie as large as possible."[29] But notice the number of hoops that economists need to jump through to reach this point, from the highly unrealistic assumptions that hardly ever hold in practice to the role of Pareto efficiency as the highest standard of judgment.

Catholic social teaching does not reject market competition outright; it recognizes that cooperation is just as (if not more) important, especially as exercised through the virtues of solidarity and reciprocity. There is no support in the tradition for central planning or for completely throwing out all price signals from markets; chapter 5 will cover this in more detail.

For now, I will just state that Catholic social teaching argues that government should intervene based on the twin principles of solidarity and subsidiarity. In neoclassical economics, as we have seen, there is a strong suspicion of government intervention. There is a basic assumption that markets are efficient, despite the ugly assumptions under the hood, and that government intervention will make things worse. This assumption is overly simplified, though: in cases of market failure, where markets demonstrably fail to live up to the lofty heights of the assumptions, economists will often argue that the government can step in to correct this market failure. Even so, the allure of the welfare theorems remains strong. Well aware of its extreme assumptions, Mankiw describes the first welfare theorem as the "crown jewel of economic theory."[30] I would argue that this jewel is a fake.

Neoclassical economics also only envisions one norm of justice: commutative justice. Along these lines, to achieve efficiency, property rights must be well defined, and all contracts well specified, complete, and respected. There is simply no role for distributive or contributive justice. Economists would argue that these forms of justice simply do not belong to the domain of economics and that they are political in nature. The exact same argument comes with the recognition of economic rights. In neoclassical economists, the only "right" is to a fair market outcome, as otherwise somebody is not being allowed to satisfy their preferences or maximize their profits in the best way possible. A precondition of this logic is strong property rights (absolute not conditional) and is why, even though neoclassical economics does not come out of the libertarian tradition, it is often aligned with it.

One final point is that neoclassical economics really has nothing to say about the environment. It employs a default mode of extractivism in the service of unlimited economic growth. Again, it betrays its Enlightenment roots. There is certainly no concept such as integral ecology in neoclassical economics. Economists will argue that if a resource is scarce, the market will simply take care of the problem by bidding up the price, a solution clearly of little help to the people and communities being walloped by environmental destruction.

Which Is More in Accord with Human Nature?

We have now assessed the principles of both Catholic social teaching and neoclassical economics. It is time to actually ask the question, Which system is more in accord with human nature: the older system, which begins with Aristotle and the Church Fathers and runs through to Pope Francis, or the newer system, which starts with Machiavelli and Hobbes; runs through Smith, Hume, and utilitarianism; and ends with the neoclassical economics taught to students all over the world? It will not surprise you that my answer is that Catholic social teaching is more in accord with human nature. I will give a number of explanations for this—including economic games, evolutionary biology, neuroscience, happiness studies, and psychology. Keep the roadmap in mind here; I am marshaling this evidence to set up what comes next in the book, the argument that an economy or a society predicated on the principles of neoclassical economics can go drastically wrong. But I need to do a little tilling before getting there.

I need to show why the principles of Catholic social teaching are both more realistic from the perspective of human nature and a healthier foundation for the global economy.

Pope Francis himself hints at this evidence. "The *homo sapiens* is deformed and becomes a species of *homo œconomicus*," he says, "a species of man that is individualistic, calculating and domineering." He goes on: "We forget that, being created in the image and likeness of God, we are social, creative and solidary beings with an immense capacity to love. We often forget this. In fact, from among all the species, we are the beings who are the most cooperative and we flourish in community."[31] The evidence I am about to marshal shows that the pope's instincts are on the mark.

Evidence from Economic Games

Let me start with the well-known idea of economic games, which involve actual interactions between people in a laboratory setting, to see how they react in different economic circumstances. The upfront conclusion is that people do not act like *homo economicus* at all. The rational economic person turns out to be a rare and endangered species.

Consider first the most famous example of this, that of the Prisoner's Dilemma. The gist goes as follows: two prisoners are being asked to confess to a crime for which there is no real evidence. The authorities already have both on a lesser charge. So if both stay quiet, they will both get a fairly light sentence, say one year in jail. But the authorities do what you have seen happen in a million TV crime programs: they tell each prisoner that if the prisoner pins the blame on the other, that person will be released and the other person will serve a steep sentence, say three years. If both pin the blame on each other, they both get an intermediate sentence, say two years. Now, it's obvious that the "rational" thing to do is to "cooperate"—both stay quiet, so both serve the minor sentence. But that is not what "rational" economic theory says at all. It says that they will not trust each other. Let's call them Zig and Zag. Zig looks at what Zag will do. If Zag stays quiet, then Zig can either stay quiet and get one year or turn on Zag and get off. Conclusion? Turn on Zag. What if Zag betrays Zig? Then Zig is looking at either staying quiet and doing three years, or turning on Zag and doing two years. Conclusion? Turn on Zag again. So no matter what, Zig will betray Zag. And Zag faces the exact same choice. The result is they both betray each other, and they both spend more time in jail than if they had opted to stay quiet. In technical terms, they choose to "defect" rather than "cooperate." And this is what neoclassical economics says they will do.

A famous version of the Prisoner's Dilemma is called the Donation Game, or the Public Goods game.[32] Here, each person can expend a cost C to give the other person a benefit B, which is greater than C. If both pay C, then both do better, as both get the bigger benefit, defined as B-C. But if one doesn't pay the cost C, but the other does, then our Zig now gets the full benefit B. The logic is the same. Neither will pay the cost C and neither receives the benefit B. Society as a whole loses. But this is what our friend *homo economicus* is supposed to do.

There are plenty of examples from real life of this game being played out. Should I pay taxes to contribute to a public good? Should my country opt to reduce the carbon emissions to fight climate change when not doing so gives it a competitive advantage? *Homo economicus* says that you should "defect"—don't pay your fair share, especially when you think there are enough people out there who will. Cheat, don't cooperate. Take advantage of the suckers.

Thankfully, things don't play out that way. When real people play this Prisoners Dilemma–style game, about half will choose to cooperate rather than defect.[33] And when players do defect, it's not because they want a bigger reward for themselves; it's that they hate the idea that somebody is taking advantage of their social nature. People don't like cheaters or free riders.

We also find this in other games. The simplest of all games is the dictator game. Here, there are again two players, and this time a "dictator" asks Zig to divide the pot between them, any way Zig likes. That's it. Rational economic theory suggests Zig gives nothing or only a token amount. But again, that's not what happens, even though there are no consequences to being selfish. Evidence suggests that most people give positive amounts, ranging from 20 to 60 percent.[34] In American studies, 95 percent of Zigs give away money, with the average offer being 40 percent. In world studies too, 30 percent offer half and 9 percent offer more than half.[35]

A more complicated version of this game is the ultimatum game. This time, being greedy has consequences. Zig is now asked to divide the pot between Zig and Zag. If Zag agrees, they each take the amount. But if Zag disagrees, they both walk away with nothing. Again, though, rational economic man says that Zig should offer the smallest amount possible, maybe a dollar out of a $100 pot. Zag calculates that a dollar is better than nothing and takes it. At this stage, you won't be surprised to learn that this is not what happens. In real-life games, the vast majority offer 40–50 percent, and offers less than 20 percent are typically rejected.[36] People really don't like being cheated or treated unfairly.

Let's look at one more game, the trust game. In this version, Zig gets the choice of a sure payout for both, say $100, or a chance to turn it over to Zag. Then Zag could either choose a payout for both that is now more for both or he could cheat Zig by keeping most of the larger sum for himself and returning a smaller amount to Zig. You will recognize this as yet another variant of the Prisoner's Dilemma. Anticipating this, Zig doesn't turn over the money. Again, they both leave money on the table because they do not trust each other. But real-life experiments don't play out like this. Instead, about two-thirds of Zigs turn the decision over to Zag, and about two-thirds of Zags reward the trust and share the pot fairly.[37] What happens when we take away the proposer's choice, so that the receiver now chooses automatically? In this case, cooperation drops from two-thirds to one-third.[38] One implication is that trust is rewarded, that prosocial behavior can have a kind of "multiplier effect."

What general lessons can we draw from these economic games? As Samuel Bowles notes, over these experiments, 40 to 66 percent of subjects engage in reciprocity, meaning that they "returned favors even when not doing so would have given them higher payoffs."[39] On the other hand, *homo economicus* is not exactly extinct, but he is in a distinct minority: 20–30 percent of people consistently choose self-interested behavior. The values displayed include altruism, fairness, and aversion to inequality. I would argue that the two big ones are solidarity and reciprocity, consistent with Catholic social teaching.

Note that this literature defines reciprocity fairly precisely. Bowles introduces a concept of "strong reciprocity," which he defines as the "propensity to cooperate and share with others similarly disposed, even at a personal cost, and a willingness to punish those who violate cooperative and other social norms, even when punishing is personally costly and cannot be expected to result in net personal gains in the future."[40] This conclusion suggests that people really dislike unfairness and are willing to punish those who are deemed to be ethical transgressors. People are willing to engage in this punishment not just to chastise the cheater but rather to "restore justice and compensate the wronged parties."[41] There is a strong sense that social norms are being violated. On the other hand, people are more than willing to return a blessing. As we will see, cooperation seems to be baked into human interaction. Score one for Catholic social teaching over neoclassical economics.

Evidence from Evolutionary Biology

Altruism exists. It is a fact of life. We all know this. Human beings are wired not only to seek their own self-interest and maximize their own personal rewards but to help people in need and to seek justice in society. This altruistic attitude manifests itself as benevolence toward others and a willingness to take care of them and meet their needs. It encompasses generosity and mutual aid.

Funnily enough, our old friend Adam Smith had quite a lot to say about this. In his *Theory of Moral Sentiments*, he stressed the importance of what he called "generosity, humanity, kindness, compassion, mutual friendship and esteem, all the social and benevolent affection" in determining how people interact with each other. For Smith, social interaction wasn't all about self-interest. Rather, he noted that "how selfish soever man may be supposed, there are evidently some principles in his nature, which interest him in the fortune of others, and render their happiness necessary to him, though he derives nothing from it except the pleasure of seeing it."[42]

It is useful to divide these altruistic tendencies into two components: empathy and compassion. These are not the same. Empathy is the ability to put oneself in another's shoes, to enter into resonance with the other in a way that dissolves the difference between the two. It causes people to feel the joy of others and the pain of others. Compassion is deeper than this. It involves not just being sensitive to the emotions of another but actually acting when a person needs help.[43] This quality need not entail empathy, even though empathy can spark compassion. But while it is possible to reach "empathy fatigue," this is not the case with compassion, which can in fact surmount fatigue.[44] In the parlance of neoclassical economics, it is possible—with some striving—to account for empathy by putting the other person's welfare in the utility function. Not so with compassion. Perhaps unsurprisingly, Adam Smith's account is more the fellow feeling of empathy than the self-sacrifice of compassion.

In a recent book, Nicholas Christakis calls these cooperative features of human interaction the "social suite." This suite includes love for partners and children, the importance of friendship, the central role played by cooperative social networks, preferences for one's own group, a sense of fairness and egalitarianism, and the prevalence of social learning and teaching.[45] He argues that this is the foundation of the good society.

But where do these tendencies all come from? A key is evolution, which becomes clear when we realize that both animals as well as babies and children can display altruistic tendencies.

Regarding animals, there is copious evidence for fellow feeling within species, especially those closest to humans on the evolutionary scale. Experiments show animals coming to the aid of others, rescuing them from danger, experiencing empathy with them, consoling them when they suffer, and mourning them when they die.[46] There is also evidence that animals are motivated by concerns of fairness and equity and—like humans—might be inclined to reject unfair payoffs. But there are limits. While animals are sometimes motivated to reduce the pain of others, we do not know if they feel that pain. They are also less inclined to help those neither related nor known to them. They also don't seem to have the ability to incur a personal loss to punish the other.

What about babies and children? The psychologist Paul Bloom has written an excellent book about this.[47] He shows that babies and toddlers can feel empathy with others they see as suffering. Babies often cry when exposed to other crying babies. In visual experiments, babies see helping acts as positive and hindering acts as negative. Reaching experiments show the same thing: infants will prefer a helper to a hinderer. The tendency to help also seems innate. Toddlers will rush to help an adult open a door when an adult not known to them pretends to have trouble doing so, without being asked. And they have tendencies to share spontaneously from a very young age. As any parent can confirm, children are strongly motivated by perceptions of fairness. They tend to have an "equality bias." Yet altruism has limits in children too. In the dictator game, they tend to give a lot less and become more amenable to sharing only as they grow older. Perhaps younger children lack the self-control to let altruism overtake self-interest. Furthermore, inequality seems to really bother children only when they are the ones who draw the short straw.

This evidence related to animals and children suggests that the roots of altruism and cooperation lie deep in the primordial soup of evolution. But this begs a further question: How exactly does evolution play a role? There are a number of competing theories, which I will describe briefly. Interestingly, leading evolutionary biologist Martin Nowak frames these evolutionary adaptations as solutions to the classic Prisoner's Dilemma. Evolution taught us how to trust and cooperate, not cheat and compete.

I will now describe three leading theories.[48] The first is called kin selection. This theory is based on the idea that altruism begins at home, with our close kin. Natural selection leads to cooperation among kin, as that is the way to pass genes across generations, an idea popularized by Richard Dawkins in *The Selfish Gene*.[49] Dawkins argued that a gene survives and reproduces when others who bear that same gene survive and reproduce. The title is a bit of a misnomer, as the "gene" actually promotes cooperation, not selfishness. A gene propagates not only by the bearer surviving but by close relatives surviving. Hence a person becomes altruistic by becoming willing to make sacrifices for family and kin. It's clear that this theory has some resonance. Think about the close bonds between children and parents, especially mothers. And human children have an especially long period of dependence in their childhood. But the very weakness of kin selection comes from the fact that we are willing to cooperate with, and meet the needs of, those who are outside of our extended family. Simply to blame that extension on some kind of "evolutionary misfire" seems to miss the broader point.

To explain the kinds of cooperation in economic games, evolutionary biologists have developed theories of reciprocal altruism, which can either be direct or indirect. The direct version refers to repeated interactions between the same small group of people, the kinds that characterized most of human history. This version manifests in the principle of give-and-take: if you are nice to me, I will be nice to you, and if you take advantage of me, I will punish you. As we have seen, people actually behave this way in economic games—in line with what Samuel Bowles calls strong reciprocity. A basic lesson from game theory is that one solution to the Prisoner's Dilemma, and indeed all trust games, is simply to play the game again. The repetition tends to encourage cooperation. Robert Trivers, the evolutionary biologist who came up with the idea of reciprocal altruism, argues that it can explain the evolution of acts and emotions such as gratitude, empathy, guilt, trust, friendship, and moral outrage.[50]

So far, we have theories explaining altruism toward kin and people with whom we are in close proximity over a long period. But that's too simple, especially today. We also cooperate with people from outside of our circles, people we don't know, and people we will never meet again. This interaction is where indirect reciprocity can play a role, at least to some extent. Indirect reciprocity relies on the power of reputation. While direct reciprocity is based on your experience with another person, indirect reciprocity is about the experiences of other people in the community. You do a good turn not to get something in return but to build a good reputation for yourself. In turn, that boosts the chance of somebody doing you a good turn sometime later. And how I treat you depends on what I know about how you treat others. You can see how this reciprocity can induce cooperation in Prisoner's Dilemma and trust games, and it also lies behind Adam Smith's analysis of morality in the *Theory of Moral Sentiments*, that we act morally because we care about our reputations and we want people to treat us well. So while the butcher, baker, and the brewer might be motivated by self-interest, this self-interest extends to developing a good reputation.

The problem with both direct and indirect reciprocity is that they can both break down as society becomes more complex. Direct reciprocity breaks down because dishonest cads can always find new victims. Indirect reciprocity breaks down because it becomes much harder to keep up with reputations. At the same time, it seems clear that some of the most important human activities take place in groups and cannot be analyzed effectively as two individuals playing some form of trust game. Think of public goods, for example.[51]

The final—and in my view most convincing—explanation of the evolution of altruism is multilevel selection. It suggests evolutionary selection not only of individuals but groups, implying that human groups that excelled at cooperating and upholding moral norms gained an advantage over other groups. In its simplest form, this idea goes all the way back to Charles Darwin himself, who argued that "there can be no doubt that a tribe including many members who . . . were always ready to give aid to each other and to sacrifice themselves for the common good, would be victorious over most other tribes; and this would be natural selection."[52]

This controversial theory was not given much credence by evolutionary biologists until the last few decades. It works as follows: defectors can gain an upper hand in a group of altruists, but a group of altruists can beat a group of defectors. So you have evolution taking place at two levels, which can explain why there are selfish and selfless people living among us. Leading evolutionary biologist E. O. Wilson puts it this way: "Selfish members win within groups, but groups of altruists best groups of selfish members."[53] For this to occur, though, requires some specific circumstances. It requires many small groups rather than a small number of large groups—which fits with the experience of most of human history, going back a quarter of a million years. But it also requires a fair amount of conflict between groups. Samuel Bowles and Herbert Gintis argued this is exactly what occurred at a formative moment in human history: in the late Pleistocene, from 10,000 to 150,000 years ago, major climatic disruptions pushed small groups of humans into more frequent conflict.[54]

The proponents of multilevel selection argue that it is much better at explaining the emergence of solidarity toward wider members of a group than is either kin selection or reciprocal altruism. I agree with that assessment. Yet I also agree with Nowak, who notes that it is the height of irony that "much of human virtue was formed in the crucible of war."[55]

Nowak's comment points to a dark side to all of this. If group selection has validity, it means that groups cooperate among themselves to beat the other group. For every "us," there is always a "them"; for every "insider," there is always an "outsider." The tendency to divide the world into "us" and "them" begins at an early age. Babies can distinguish familiar people and strangers almost immediately, and they prefer the familiar.[56] By age three or four, children can divide people by race and gender, with more negative views of the "other."[57] Evidence also shows that the barrier for forming coalitions against each other is depressingly low, sometimes even based simply on the color of a T-shirt given to a particular team.[58] We identify with our team; we want to defeat the other. In economic games, people are more trusting and cooperative with in-groups rather than out-groups. Worst of all, we are prone to dehumanizing and demonizing the other. Thinking of a "them" frequently invokes the emotion of disgust; this emotion, which many think evolved to protect us from parasites and pests, can be perverted and turned against people.[59] It is no accident that genocide often begins by referring to the demonized others as rodents or cockroaches. The bottom line is that while evolution blessed us with the altruistic heights, it also cursed us with contemptuous lows. Hold that thought for now; we'll come back to it.

Evidence from Neuroscience

This short section is closely related to the last. If we believe that evolution has shaped the emergence of cooperative and altruistic tendencies among people, we should also be able to find evidence within our brains and neural pathways. And indeed, neuroscience is increasingly able to highlight these behavioral tendencies.[60]

The starting point is to recognize that the brain is divided into two areas relevant to the topic at hand. The most ancient part, known as the limbic system, regulates our emotions. And here, the amygdala is the part responsible for fear, anxiety, and sometimes anger and aggression. For example, during the ultimatum game, it is the amygdala that activates when a player feels cheated, prompting a desire to punish, even at a personal cost. As behavioral psychologist Robert Sapolsky puts it, "the amygdala injects implicit distrust and vigilance into social decision making."[61] And yet the amygdala is also activated when we feel empathy.

The other major area of the brain is the frontal cortex, which regulates executive function—including delayed gratification, long-term planning, regulation of emotion, and reining in impulses. In the words of Sapolsky again, "the frontal cortex makes you do the harder thing when it's the right thing to do."[62] This action or inaction is especially the case with the prefrontal cortex, evolutionarily the newest zone of the brain, an area of the brain that also regulates sociability—the larger a person's social network, the larger a particular region of the prefrontal cortex. The prefrontal cortex regulates emotions by calming down the amygdala. It also helps control the desire for instant gratification, which can lead to harmful addictions.[63] It is no surprise that the prefrontal cortex is the last part of the brain to develop and is particularly underdeveloped in children and teenagers, where emotion tends to dominate reason. It is the emotional center that makes us prosocial toward in-groups but the cognitive center that inclines us toward prosociality toward out-groups.

We can also see similar types of effects when we look at hormones. Testosterone has a bad reputation, being associated with male aggressive behavior. But Sapolsky argues that it is more complicated. Testosterone prompts behaviors required to maintain status. If status is related to aggression, then testosterone fuels violence. But if status and reputation are about being virtuous, testosterone promotes prosociality—cheating less in economic games, for example. Think about the implications of this for economics: is status driven by "winning" in market competition or by being cooperative?

If testosterone has a bad reputation, oxytocin has a warm and fuzzy one. But this reputation again is overly simplistic. Oxytocin is the hormone that promotes the bond between mother and child. It is also elevated in couples engaged in a romantic relationship. Oxytocin works by inhibiting the amygdala and suppressing fear and anxiety. It activates a calmer region called the parasympathetic nervous system. Studies do indeed show that when people are given oxytocin, they become more trusting in economic games. It makes people more charitable. So far, it seems pretty warm and fuzzy. But here's the downside: these prosocial effects work only with in-groups. Oxytocin actually makes you less prosocial to those deemed an other.

When it comes to empathy, aside from the amygdala, the part of the brain known as the anterior cingular cortex turns out to be important. The activation of this region is what prompts an empathic response to the plight of another person. The prefrontal cortex also needs to get in on the act, however, especially if you haven't experienced the pain yourself and if the person in pain is from an out-group. This complexity can explain the phenomenon of "empathy fatigue"—what happens when the cognitive effort of identifying with some other just becomes too much to bear.

In this context, there is also the phenomenon of "mirror neurons": neural pathways that react to the experience of others. First discovered in the context of motor learning by observation, these neurons may allow you to take the perspective of others, feel their pain, and therefore make an empathic connection. This phenomenon remains controversial in the neuroscience literature, however.

What about moving from feeling empathy to compassion—to doing something to help another? There have been brain studies of people who underwent both empathy and compassion training. The former saw heavy amygdala activation coupled with anxiety. Not so with the latter, which instead saw activation of the prefrontal cortex. The result of this, according to Bloom, is that empathy can paralyze you from actually doing something. But it is also possible to turn empathy into compassion, and this compassion training changes the brain. In this sense, modern neuroscience affirms some ancient instincts of virtue ethics.

In sum, while the affective region of the brain can spur either self-interest or empathy, empathy can be limited and paralyzing, We need the cognitive region of the brain to actively make the harder choice—to use reason to not engage in calculating self-interest but to actively choose prosocial behavior. Maybe Aristotle, with his primitive knowledge of science, was on to something after all.

Evidence from Happiness Studies

I want to shift gears a bit at this point to ask the question, What truly makes us happy? Recall the difference between neoclassical economics and Catholic social teaching. The former argues that our appetites are insatiable, bounded only by a lack of resources, a hedonic view of happiness coming from material goods that can be purchased on the market. Accordingly, the more money we get, the happier we should be. Catholic social teaching instead adopts the framework of Aristotle and Aquinas, whereby happiness is based less on material satisfaction and more on the good life, *eudaimonia*, "being" rather than "having." Appetites are satiable, and wealth makes us happy only to the extent that it can be directed toward higher ends. Happiness comes from integral human development, the development of all capacities, intellectual and moral, to the fullest degree, in the context of community, without excluding anyone.

How can we adjudicate between these two very different moral systems? One way is to simply ask people: What makes you happy? This field of "subjective well-being" has mushroomed in recent years. The findings can be surprising. One key result, dating back to the 1960s, is known as the "Easterlin paradox." Put simply, money stops buying happiness once a certain threshold has been reached. In the context of the United States, while income per person has tripled since 1960, happiness has been flat.[64] And the threshold at which happiness stops rising has been estimated to be fairly low in the United States, tapping out at $75,000.[65]

So what does cause happiness? Two major factors: relationship and a sense of meaning and purpose in life. The importance of relationship cannot be over-emphasized. In pretty much every happiness study, human relationships predominate. In studies of so-called blue zones—pockets in which people tend to live consistently long lives—a strong sense of community seems to be a major driving factor. Conversely, people are increasingly aware that social isolation is a leading cause of early death. One of the longest running studies in human development has been tracking a group of men in the Boston area for up to eighty years. These men come from a variety of economic and social backgrounds. A main finding is that social connection and warm human relationships are vital for health and happiness. In the words of George Vaillant, the study's director, "Happiness is love. Full stop."[66] The academic literature also seems to confirm this result. One study finds that a sense of belonging to community has the same effect on life satisfaction as trebling of household income.[67] Another study shows that among fifteen activities carried out during a day, fourteen of them led to more happiness when carried out in the company of others—the exception being prayer![68]

But how do we measure happiness in this subjective manner? In two ways. The first is to ask a person about their current emotional state, either positive or

negative. The other is more substantive and asks people to grade their life satisfaction on a numerical scale of 1 to 10, known as the Cantril ladder. We can look
at these data at the country level, precisely what the *World Happiness Report* does
every year. It looks at subjective well-being across 150 or so countries and tries to
figure out the determinants. And it all boils down to six key factors: (1) income,
as measured by GDP per capita; (2) healthy life expectancy; (3) social support,
defined as the availability of people to count on in times of trouble; (4) generosity, measured by charitable donations; (5) freedom to make life choices,
based directly on a question to that effect; and (6) perceptions of corruption in
the country, for both government and business. What about the relative size of
the different effects? The most important component is social support, which
explains about a third of the total. GDP per capita explains just over a quarter
on its own.[69] This conclusion tallies with other findings. The four social and
institutional factors—social support, generosity, freedom to make life choices,
and corruption—together explain more than half of happiness differences across
countries. Social support measures quality relationships and community ties.
Generosity measures solidarity and relationality. Freedom captures meaning and
purpose, the ability to develop one's capacities. Corruption proxies for trust and
social cohesion. Which countries come out on top? It changes each year, but it
is usually the same group of Scandinavian countries that are deemed the world's
happiest.

Recent evidence also suggests that a healthy environment contributes to happiness. Researchers working on the 2020 *World Happiness Report* found that pollution and temperature extremes are negatively related, and forests are positively
related, to life satisfaction.[70] People are happy in the presence of nature, and the
majority of people around the world are willing to sacrifice GDP growth to protect and conserve the environment. Healthy natural environments contribute
to healthy people and social connectedness. So happiness studies also provide
support for integral ecology.

Summing up, it seems clear that, even though these measures of well-being
are subjective—simply asking people how they feel—they nonetheless point less
to hedonic notions of happiness and more toward *eudaimonia*. Specifically, they
identify income, health, social connectedness, and a sense of meaning and purpose. Aristotle would give these studies a thumbs-up.

Evidence from Psychology

We've touched a lot on psychological motivation, so this section will be brief.
In line with happiness studies, many psychologists also believe that people are

driven by the need for relationship on the one hand and purpose and meaning on the other.

On this topic, one of the best-selling books of all time was written by Viktor Frankl, a psychiatrist who survived the brutalities of the Nazi concentration camps. Titled *Man's Search for Meaning*, its principal argument is self-evident from the title: that what motivates the individual in the deepest recesses of the soul is a search for meaning.[71] Frankl thought that the way to survive the camps was to identify psychologically with a purpose in life. He came up with a psychiatric practice known as logotherapy, based on the idea that the quest for meaning and purpose is the great motivating force in life rather than factors such as money, pleasure, or power. In this, Frankl's theory is opposed to materialism and hedonic views of happiness. Frankl noted instead the importance of religious beliefs, communal support, and identification of clear life goals.

At around the same time as Frankl penned his compelling narrative, the American psychologist Abraham Maslow came up with a "hierarchy of needs" in a highly influential paper written in 1943.[72] Just like *Man's Search for Meaning*, this work resonated with people and entered popular consciousness. In its earliest incarnation, Maslow identified a pyramid of needs, with each building on the other. At the bottom of the pyramid lies what he calls physiological needs, identified with the basic needs of human survival: food, water, clothes, housing, rest, good health. Once that level is achieved, the next level of the pyramid is the need for safety. This level encompasses such factors as the absence of war and violence, of family trauma, and of institutionalized discrimination and demonization. But it also encompasses financial security and job security. And today, we could add a safe climate in a healthy environment. The third layer in the pyramid is the need for social belonging; once again, this points to the real human need for relationship and connection. It encompasses family, friendship, love and affection. It also encompasses the importance of belonging to various societies and groups, what Catholic social teaching identifies with subsidiarity. The fourth level is the need for esteem. This need points once again to the quest for meaning and purpose and the need to make a valid social contribution that is respected by one's peers. It encompasses esteem and self-respect. And it typically takes place within the context of vocation. The fifth and highest level of the pyramid is self-actualization, the realization of one's full potential in life. This layer aligns clearly with Aristotle's *eudaimonia* or integral human development. But notice that it remains at the level of the individual; there is no attempt to link it to the common good or to encompass all people. Later in life, Maslow added a level going even beyond the fifth one—transcendence—which he identified with going beyond oneself toward the infinite. This view is close to Aquinas's that ultimate happiness comes from knowing and loving God, the source of all being.

In recent years, the positive psychology movement has built on these foundations. Positive psychology is based on the notion that well-being is not just about the absence of trauma or negative beliefs and emotions but a positive orientation toward human flourishing identified with the good life. One of its chief proponents is American psychologist Martin Seligman, who argues that human flourishing is related to five distinct factors:[73] (1) positive emotion, which is mainly genetic but can be boosted by training; (2) engagement, which happens when a person's highest strengths match the highest challenges that come their way; (3) quality relationships; (4) meaning and purpose in life; and (5) accomplishment and achievements. Three of these five core factors support a teleological view of the structure of human psychology. And relationship, as always, is in the saddle. Once again, the positive psychology movement affirms the ancient wisdom that psychological well-being is not hedonic and not based on material or other external factors; it is, rather, about seeking what is intrinsically valuable in a human life. Relatedly, "self-determination theory" posits that three basic psychological needs are fundamental to *eudaimonia*: autonomy, competence, and relatedness.[74] Again, these needs tally with our two building blocks of human flourishing: a sense of purpose and a sense of community. We keep ending up in the same place.

Let me try to summarize this lengthy section. Marshaling different pieces of evidence, I have sought to make the case that the principles and values underlying Catholic social teaching are more in line with human nature than the principles and values underlying neoclassical economics. Let's recap a few of these findings. First, we are not merely self-interested, but we also care about the well-being of other people, especially those in our immediate circles. In other words, solidarity and reciprocity are extremely important. Indeed, reciprocity is so important that we are willing to take a personal loss simply to punish cheaters. There is such a thing as a common good. Second, and relatedly, our interactions with others are not just about competition; we are wired for cooperation. We are willing to trust people, even those we don't know well, and we reward trust. Third, happiness, or the good of the individual, is less in line with *hedonia* and the maximization of preferences and more in line with *eudaimonia* and integral human development. What matters are good-quality relationships, a sense of meaning and purpose, the degree to which we can actualize latent potential, and the ability to make a well-respected social contribution. Fourth, we are also wired for fairness, and we take great exception to cheating and a distribution of rewards that is deemed unfair. There is no evidence whatsoever that Pareto efficiency is the way we evaluate market interactions—like Sen, we would find it "perfectly disgusting."

So far so good. But we also need to get to grips with the dark side of the "social suite"—which is the tendency for in-group preferences and lingering selfishness and which requires work. Expanding our circles of solidarity requires, in the tradition of virtue ethics, ethical formation. This formation in turn requires the deployment of reason to curb emotions and gut feelings. Jeffrey Sachs has argued that modern neuroscience affirms the basic intuition of Aristotle and Aquinas that the soul is divided into a rational and a nonrational component, corresponding roughly to the frontal cortex and the limbic system.[75] From this perspective, becoming moral requires the use of reason—to control the activation of the amygdala, for example. In the eighteenth century, David Hume took the opposite perspective. He argued that morality comes from emotions and gut feelings and that reason is something we use to justify these gut feelings. In his parlance, reason is the slave of the passions. We certainly know from psychology and neuroscience that emotions do play a role in moral evaluation—about fairness, for example. But we also know that Hume didn't quite get it right, that the rational part of the brain can override the gut and help us make the harder choice, including when the harder choice is the more moral choice. Neoclassical economics claims to be rooted in rationality, but it basically assumes that people act on their desires, and so are more like animals than rational human beings. This insight comes not only from the ancient virtue ethics tradition but from the best of modern science. As Bloom puts it, "Adult morality is influenced by rational deliberation. This is what separates humans from chimpanzees and separates adults from babies. These other creatures just have sentiments; we have sentiments plus reason."[76] This is what Aristotle and Aquinas said all along. What matters is deploying this reason to identify and choose the good.

The Pernicious Effects of Neoclassical Economics

In this section, I will argue that the values promulgated by neoclassical economics actively inhibit virtuous habit formation. They make it harder to recognize and choose the good. The issue is that vices don't become virtues; they stay vices. If you tell people that they are supposed to act out of self-interest in pursuit of material goods without any acquisitive ceiling in competition with other people, then it should not be surprising that they start acting that way. If they are told to cheat and trust no one, and to take a free ride when possible because it's in their rational interest to do so, then it should not be surprising that society suffers. Values are habituated, and social norms become set. As Bowles puts it, "the policies that follow from this [*homo economicus*] paradigm sometimes make the assumption of universal amoral selfishness more nearly true than it might otherwise be."[77] In this sense, neoclassical economics cannibalizes itself—honesty, reciprocity, solidarity, and other basic virtues are undermined. Because neoclassical economics has had an exalted position among the social sciences and the policy world over the past few decades, the damage has become magnified.

There are three ways in which the values of economics can corrupt: (1) through the teaching of business and economics; (2) through the fact that the use of incentives, so central in neoclassical economics, can crowd out virtue and prosocial behavior; (3) through the increasing reach of *homo economicus* across all domains of life, whereby everything has a price and everybody becomes a cold and calculating machine of maximization.

Everything begins with education. Aristotle certainly understood this, given his notion that virtue is inculcated by training, self-discipline, and habit formation. Here's the problem: if students are taught the principles of neoclassical economics, they tend to act out these principles in real life. Copious studies show that students with exposure to neoclassical economics are more likely to be selfish, opportunistic, dishonest, and antisocial. For example, when economics students play economic games, they are far more likely to act like *homo economicus* instructs them to act—to trust less, defect more, be less generous.[78] Even worse, studies have shown that business and economics students exhibit more "dark triad traits"—narcissism, psychopathy, and Machiavellianism—as they seek power, status, and social dominance. The economist Luigi Zingales even went as far as to ask whether business schools incubated criminals, on the grounds that business education—focused on self-interest, naked competition, and profit maximization—is responsible for the spate of ethical lapses in the world of finance.[79] In all of this, the big question is the direction of causation.[80] Is it self-selection or indoctrination? Are people with these traits more attracted to economics and business, or do these disciplines teach people to act this way? There is no consensus on this in the literature, but the evidence suggests that it works both ways.

The second way in which economics corrupts is through its use of financial incentives, which can crowd out prosocial behavior and the intrinsic motivation to opt for the individual good and the common good. This was the topic of two influential books written in recent years: *What Money Can't Buy: The Moral Limits of Markets*, by philosopher Michael Sandel, and *The Moral Economy: Why Good Incentives Are No Substitute for Good Citizens*, by economist Samuel Bowles.[81] The intuition is straightforward. If you ask a neoclassical economist for the basic tenet of the discipline, they will tell you that people respond to incentives. Raise a price of a good or service, and people will buy less of it. Increase a fine for fraud, and companies will act more honestly. Give somebody a bonus, and they will work harder. Examples are legion. But as we have seen already, the Catholic social teaching tradition, with its roots in Aristotle, stresses the importance of intrinsic motivation, choosing to do something because it is the right thing to do in different circumstances. What Bowles and Sandel are arguing is that incentives can undermine and crowd out this motivation. They reduce everything to money. Three practical examples from these authors can help demonstrate this.

Example number 1: In one of the most famous results, a daycare center in Israel was facing a problem. Too many parents were showing up late to pick up their kids, inconveniencing staff who needed to go home. The daycare center decided to choose an economic solution: charge parents who showed up late. What would neoclassical economics say? People react to financial incentives. A higher price should mean less of this behavior. But guess what? The opposite happened. Late pickups actually increased. What happened here? Basically, the nature of the economic encounter changed. What was once an inconvenience now became a service that could be purchased. Parents cared less about keeping staff after hours because they were now paying for the privilege. A social norm had been corrupted by putting a price on it. Even after the center eliminated the fine after a few months, late pickups did not decline. Social norms, once corrupted, are hard to uncorrupt.[82]

Example number 2: In 1993, Switzerland was trying to find a place to store radioactive nuclear waste. One option was the small town of Wolfenschiessen. Before any decision was made, a group of economists surveyed the townspeople. What they discovered was surprising. A slim majority, 51 percent, said they would accept the nuclear waste. Then they asked a second question: What if the government offered an annual monetary contribution to each resident of the small town in compensation? Again, *homo economicus* would snatch the cash—or more accurately, would engage in a cost-benefit analysis weighing up the potential (probabilistic) costs of being exposed to nuclear waste against the compensation. But either way, this was a Pareto improvement over the no-compensation scenario, so the numbers should go up. You can probably guess what comes next. The number who said they would accept the nuclear waste fell from 51 percent to 25 percent, a huge decline. Why? Because people felt they were being bribed. They felt insulted. This bribe would crowd out an intrinsic motivation to do their civic duty as citizens. Other studies have shown that people are more likely to say yes in these situations when the compensation comes in the form of public goods that benefit the entire community, not personal wads of cash.[83]

Example number 3: In a famous study from 1970, Richard Titmuss compared blood donations in the United Kingdom, where people give blood for free, and the United States, which mixes free and bought blood. He found that freely donated blood came with both higher quantity and higher quality. More people donated, and they were more honest about their medical histories. Titmuss found that the British system worked better and that the American system was plagued by shortages, waste, and higher risk of contamination. Once again, we see financial incentives undermining the intrinsic motivation to support the common good. Titmuss argued that making blood into a market commodity diminished altruism and undermined what he called the "gift relationship"— what Catholic social teaching calls the principle of gratuitousness.[84]

The key is that extrinsic motivations (in response to an incentive) crowd out intrinsic motivation (in response to habituated or ingrained virtue), and we are worse off for it because it goes against the sociability deeply rooted in human nature.

A related point, that market goods crowd out relational goods, has been raised in the context of the Easterlin paradox: well-being stops rising after a certain income threshold, because the market is encroaching across other areas of social life. Markets are impersonal and anonymous, encouraging a distancing from all-important personal relationships and social ties. As I've noted already, Bruni argues that this was Adam Smith's big mistake.[85] Instead, as we have seen, human beings are creatures of reciprocity. We need personal ties to flourish. We are made for gift, and we value gifts. As Marcel Mauss wrote back in 1923, gift giving is a form of exchange that requires reciprocity and builds social cohesion through bonds of solidarity.[86] Anthropologist David Graeber has argued that this relationship has constituted most of human history, with the modern competitive market as an aberration.[87] *Homo economicus* doesn't understand this at all. In fact, from their perspective, gifts are not efficient. The best gift is cash so that the recipient can maximize their own subjective preferences by buying what they like. Indeed, neoclassical economist Joel Waldfogel wrote a famous article called "The Deadweight Loss of Christmas."[88] He wasn't joking.

Another peculiar argument made by neoclassical economists is that prosocial values such as love, compassion, and solidarity need to be economized. Therefore we should keep them within a narrow social arena and outsource the rest of life to the market. We should let incentives put us on autopilot so we can reserve the limited altruism we possess for where it really matters. Here's how economist Lawrence Summers puts it: "We only have so much altruism in us. Economists like me think of altruism as a valuable and rare good that needs conserving. Far better to conserve it by designing a system in which people's wants will be satisfied by individuals being selfish, and saving that altruism for our families, our friends, and the many social problems in this world that markets cannot solve."[89] This perspective is simply nonsensical. First, it assumes that economic incentives don't change the nature of the good by inhibiting virtue. Second, it wholly misunderstands virtue, which is more like a muscle that gets stronger with practice than some fixed supply of a good that is depleted with use. This is a basic insight of Aristotle, and I have argued that it is borne out by modern psychology, evolutionary biology, and neuroscience.

So this is the gist of the second form of corruption: market incentives can undermine integral human development by inhibiting virtue. But it's not all bad news. Bowles notes that if financial incentives are designed correctly, they can crowd in rather than crowd out prosocial behavior. This effect is more likely with what Bowles called "Aristotle's Legislator"—one who appeals to civic virtue to persuade the citizenry to undertake a particular act. One example he gives is Ireland's tax on plastic bags, introduced in 2002. Although the tax was minor, plastic bag usage fell by 94 percent within two short weeks.[90] In Bowles's view, the tax was subject to intensive public deliberation before it was introduced, in the context of a strong moral injunction to care for the environment by reducing plastic pollution. Perhaps a similar argument can be made for tobacco taxes; smoking falls not just because the price is higher (the extrinsic motivation) but because the price increase in itself changes social norms around smoking, inducing fewer people to use tobacco products (the intrinsic effect). But a neoclassical economist would simply not understand the power of moral messaging and appeal to civic duty.

The third form of corruption is closely related to the second—the reach of economic logic across all areas of life changes the way we think about human interactions, undermining solidarity, reciprocity, integral human development, and the common good. As many have noted, the increasing respect accorded to neoclassical economics over the past few decades has altered the way we assess whether things are right or wrong, fair or unfair, virtuous or corrupting.[91] For the sole standard of judgment remains that of efficiency; is there a monetary trade that can make most of us better off? Putting it simply, everything has a price.

Except we know that it doesn't. Throughout human history, slavery was a despicable fact of life. People could be bought and sold and were considered property. But today, we rightly find slavery abhorrent, a grievous assault on human dignity. Fine, but what about something like selling a kidney? If Zig is willing to sell his kidney to Zag, who desperately needs it, aren't both better off? Neoclassical economics, with its utilitarian calculus of costs and benefits, would say yes. Zig gets paid, and Zag gets a kidney. Both are better off. Both have freely consented to this trade. What's not to like? What about a top university selling or auctioning places? The logic of neoclassical economics might approve of this; the places go to those who value them most (and the value is always the price), and the university maximizes revenue (everybody is always maximizing something). But this logic is likely to outrage people, based both on the sheer unfairness and the fact that it would fundamentally alter the nature of a university education.[92]

Clearly, something about these examples makes us a bit queasy. We don't think like *homo economicus* in situations like these, and sometimes we're morally revolted by them. As Sandel notes, we typically have two objections. The first is fairness and coercion. We rightly ask, Are these transactions truly voluntary and consensual? A person who sells their kidney or their body often does so from extreme financial distress, and the buyer takes advantage of that. Similarly, if everything has a price, then the rich are the ones able to pay this price. But there is a second argument: the argument of corruption. Sandel's definition of corruption is pertinent: "To corrupt a good or a social practice is to degrade it," he argues, "to treat it according to a lower mode of valuation than is appropriate to it."[93] This is an argument in line with virtue ethics; should we pursue goods that contribute to the good life of human flourishing for all? Selling your kidney or your body would inhibit this goal. There is such a thing as an objective good, some goods are higher order than others, and not all preferences are equally valid. I would argue that there's a bit of a virtue ethicist in all of us.

But in spite of all of these downsides, *homo economicus* is expanding their reach into areas outside the traditional domain of economics. The most extreme example comes from the work inspired by University of Chicago economist Gary Becker. Becker believes that all aspects of life should be gauged by rational choice theory, by utility maximization and weighing up the financial costs and benefits.[94] For instance, Becker has argued that the right to immigrate should be sold on the open market. He even believes in charging refugees fleeing persecution for admission into a country. But putting a price on this good hurts those of limited financial means and degrades the duty we have to look after the least among us, which are surely refugees in dire need. For Becker, however, everything has a price and everything should be for sale, as long as the exchange is voluntary. Unsurprisingly, Becker is fine with markets for kidneys.

In one sense, Becker is merely taking the assumptions of neoclassical economics to their logical conclusion.[95] Everything in life is about maximization, everything has a price, and preferences and tastes are purely subjective and not open to question. As another example, Becker has argued that some people rationally choose to die earlier because they value immediate pleasures such as tobacco and fatty foods. This is his notion of "rational suicide." He also thinks that addictions are rational as they reflect conscious choices about lifetime utility maximization. Clearly, this notion of rationality is about as far removed from the virtue of prudence as it is possible to be.

Perhaps even more controversially, Becker believes that rational choice theory extends to marriage and human relationships. He has argued that in deciding whether to stay married or get divorced, people weigh up the expected utility of being single or finding another partner with the utility of sticking with the marriage. Missing are love, commitment, duty, or the idea that a marriage gives rise to a common good that transcends the good of each individual. Another provocative paper in this extremist rational choice field argues that a woman chooses between being a prostitute or a wife by weighing up the costs and benefits to maximize lifetime utility.[96] Something has gone very wrong; this is another example of the corruption of a genuine economic good by devaluing and degrading it.

I could write a whole book with examples from this strange literature. For example, economist Kenneth Boulding proposed "tradable procreation permits" to control population growth.[97] This behavior would be tantamount to the poor selling their children to the rich, and it degrades the act of having a child. Perhaps even worse, Richard Posner literally proposed selling children, arguing that market forces should determine which children are adopted.[98] You can imagine what would happen. The most desirable babies would be snapped up. The inalienable dignity of every human being would be fatally undermined. Along the same lines, economist Thomas Schelling even devised a way to put a price on human life, which is needed for taking cost-benefit analysis seriously. He did this by looking at two fairly identical jobs, one of which entails higher risk than the other. The argument is that people rationally calculate this risk and take the extra wage premium, so we can calculate the value the person ascribes to her own life. Of course, Catholic Social Thought objects. A person taking a highly risky job is usually not making a free choice but is driven into that role by extreme necessity. And putting a price on life clearly cheapens and degrades it. But, believe it or not, governments use these kinds of calculations when doing cost-benefit analyses, say, of new regulations, or whether to recall consumer goods that are defective and pose a risk to life.[99] So the whole activity is corrupted. Instead of being centered on promoting the common good, the good of all, regulation is seen through the prism of maximizing consumer welfare.

This approach has even cannibalized the law profession, with the rise of what has been called "law and economics." This school is predicated on the idea that law is less about justice in terms of giving a person what is owed to them than maximizing consumer welfare or wealth.[100] The intellectual genesis of this school of thought is again Posner from the University of Chicago. But this was an ideological movement, and it had traditional forms of government regulation and antitrust policy in its crosshairs. For Posner, the only way to look at antitrust policy is through the prism of economic efficiency. In practice, this legal philosophy has been deployed to defend large corporations, including monopolists, over consumer well-being and the societal common good. This application has had a huge impact on how government policy has developed over the past five decades.

What's more, the *homo economicus* model was even extended to government itself. Instead of being concerned with the common good, a locus for virtue-enhancing deliberation, government was now regarded as out for itself. According to James Buchanan, the Nobel Prize–winning developer of "public choice theory," governments, voters, and bureaucrats are all self-interested and seek to maximize their own subjective utility.[101] Governments seek power by promising things to various constituencies. And bureaucrats seek to maximize the revenues sent their way. Public choice theory has a problem explaining why people bother to vote, as the impact of a single vote is barely worth the effort extended. In this world, there is no such thing as civic virtue. Even more insidiously, the claim that governments and bureaucrats are purely selfish contributed to a political movement that sought to replace public functions with the private sector to shrink the power of what became derisively known as "big government" or the "deep state." It contributed to a general decline in trust in the public sector and across society more generally. And it helped turn politics away from sober deliberation and more toward marketing spectacle.[102]

To sum up: Neoclassical economics argues that incentives create the most efficient outcomes, the only value is financial value, and even these market values can legitimately be extended to all areas of life. But this assertion, which ends up corrupting both our view of human nature and our social interactions, is bound to create dysfunctions on the interior level (human psychology) and the exterior level (our economic and social interactions). It is bound to undermine virtue, integral human development, and the common good.

One final point: all of these neoclassical principles give rise to the myth that economics is value free, as if the very notion of Pareto efficiency itself does not embody strong values. Economics is a "science," disconnected from the question of ethics, morality, and values. But it is precisely our fear of entering the domain of values that has allowed *homo economicus* to monopolize the stage. As Sandel notes in his book's conclusion, "For fear of disagreement, we hesitate to bring our moral and spiritual convictions into the public square. But shrinking from these questions does not leave them undecided. It simply means that markets will decide them for us. This is the lesson of the last three decades."[103]

I have argued in this chapter that the ethical convictions underpinning Catholic social teaching provide a healthier, more virtuous, and more realistic basis for managing our economy than those of neoclassical economics. Let's now turn to the story of the past four decades, in which the values of neoclassical economics reigned supreme. Let's see what happened.

Notes

1. Appelbaum, *Economists' Hour*.
2. See Annett, "Human Flourishing, the Common Good, and Catholic Social Teaching."
3. See Shapiro, *Moral Foundations of Politics*; Wootton, *Power, Pleasure, and Profit*.
4. See Gillespie, *Theological Origins of Modernity*.
5. See Gregory, *Unintended Revolution*.
6. Descartes, *Discourse on Method and Meditations on First Philosophy*, 35.
7. Hösle, "Ethics and Economics."
8. Wootton, *Power, Pleasure, and Profit*, 67.
9. See Wootton, 73–74.
10. Bentham, *Introduction to the Principles of Morals and Legislation*.
11. Bentham, ch. 1.
12. Cloutier, *Vice of Luxury*, 69–70.
13. Bowles, *Moral Economy*.
14. Mandeville, *Fable of the Bees*.
15. Smith, *Inquiry into the Nature and Causes of the Wealth of Nations*.
16. See Wootton, *Power, Pleasure, and Profit*, ch. 7.
17. Wootton, 7.
18. Cloutier, *Vice of Luxury*.
19. For a preliminary version of this analysis, see Annett, "Economic Vision of Pope Francis."
20. Zamagni, "On the Birth of Economic Science during the Italian-Scottish Enlightenment."
21. Bruni, *Wound and the Blessing*.
22. For a related point, see Sen, "Rational Fools."
23. Bruni, *Wound and the Blessing*.
24. Hirschfeld, *Aquinas and the Market*, 62.
25. Hirschfeld, 116.
26. Hirschfeld, 131.
27. Gregory, *Unintended Revolution*.
28. Sen, *Collective Choice and Social Welfare*.
29. Gregory Mankiw, "CEOs Are Qualified to Make Profits, Not Lead Society," *New York Times*, July 24, 2020.
30. Mankiw.
31. Pope Francis, General Audience, August 26, 2020.
32. See Sachs, "Investing in Social Capital."

33. Bowles, *Moral Economy*.

34. Bowles, *New Economics of Inequality and Redistribution*.

35. Christakis, *Blueprint*.

36. Bowles, *New Economics of Inequality and Redistribution*.

37. Wight, *Ethics in Economics*.

38. Wight.

39. Bowles, *Moral Economy*.

40. Bowles, *New Economics of Inequality and Redistribution*, 131.

41. Christakis, *Blueprint*, 315.

42. Smith, *Theory of Moral Sentiments*.

43. Ricard, *Altruism*.

44. See Bloom, *Just Babies*; and Ricard, *Altruism*.

45. Christakis, *Blueprint*.

46. Ricard, *Altruism*.

47. Bloom, *Just Babies*.

48. I will lean on Nowak, *Super Cooperators*. See also Bloom, *Just Babies*; Ricard, *Altruism*; Sapolsky, *Behave*; and Christakis, *Blueprint*.

49. Dawkins, *Selfish Gene*.

50. Trivers, "The Evolution of Reciprocal Altruism," cited in Nowak, *Super Cooperators*, 28.

51. See Christakis, *Blueprint*.

52. Darwin, "Descent of Man and Selection in Relation to Sex," quoted in Nowak, *Super Cooperators*.

53. Wilson, *Meaning of Human Existence*.

54. Bowles and Gintis, *Cooperative Species*.

55. Nowak, *Super Cooperators*, 90.

56. Bloom, *Just Babies*.

57. Sapolsky, *Behave*.

58. Bloom, *Just Babies*.

59. Bloom.

60. For this discussion, I am relying on Sapolsky, *Behave*.

61. Sapolsky, 39.

62. Sapolsky, 45.

63. Sachs, "Addiction and Unhappiness in America."

64. Sachs, "Restoring American Happiness."

65. Kahneman and Deaton, "High Income Improves Evaluation of Life but Not Emotional Wellbeing."

66. Scott Stossel, "What Makes Us Happy Revisited: A New Look at the Famous Harvard Study of What Makes People Thrive," *Atlantic*, May 2013.

67. Helliwell, "Understanding and Improving the Social Context of Well-Being."

68. Kahneman et al., "Survey Method for Characterizing Daily Life Experience."

69. Helliwell, Huang, and Wang, "Social Foundations of World Happiness."

70. Krekel and MacKerron, "How Environmental Quality Affects Our Happiness."

71. Frankl, *Man's Search for Meaning.*

72. Maslow, "Theory of Human Motivation."

73. Seligman, *Flourish.*

74. Ryan, Huta, and Deci, "Living Well."

75. Sachs, "Addiction and Unhappiness in America."

76. Bloom, *Just Babies,* 100.

77. Bowles, *Moral Economy,* 2.

78. For a summary of the evidence, see Etzioni, "Moral Effects of Economic Teaching."

79. Luigi Zingales, "Do Business Schools Incubate Criminals?," *Bloomberg,* July 16, 2012.

80. Vedel and Thomsen, "Dark Triad across Academic Majors."

81. Sandel, *What Money Can't Buy;* Bowles, *Moral Economy.*

82. Sandel, *What Money Can't Buy,* 64–65.

83. Sandel, 114–17.

84. Sandel, 122–25.

85. See Bruni, *Wound and the Blessing;* and Tirole, *Economics for the Common Good.*

86. Mauss, *The Gift.* See also Wight, *Ethics in Economics.*

87. Graeber, *Debt.*

88. Waldfogel, "Deadweight Loss of Christmas."

89. Quoted in Sandel, *What Money Can't Buy,* 130.

90. See Aldred, *License to Be Bad,* 159; Bowles, *Moral Economy,* ch. 7.

91. Judt, *Ill Fares the Land;* Sandel, *What Money Can't Buy;* Aldred, *License to Be Bad.*

92. Although it is possible to argue that we're halfway there, with top universities reserving copious coveted spots to children of graduates ("legacy preferences") and donors.

93. Sandel, *What Money Can't Buy,* 34.

94. See, e.g., Becker, "Economic Way of Looking at Life."

95. See Aldred, *License to Be Bad,* ch. 6.

96. Edlund and Korn, "Theory of Prostitution."

97. See Boulding, *Meaning of the Twentieth Century.*

98. See Landes and Posner, "Economics of the Baby Shortage."

99. See Aldred, *License to Be Bad,* ch. 6; and Appelbaum, *Economists' Hour,* ch. 7.

100. See Aldred, *License to Be Bad,* ch. 3; and Appelbaum, *Economists' Hour,* ch. 5.

101. See Buchanan, "Constitution of Economic Policy."

102. Aldred, *License to Be Bad.*

103. Sandel, *What Money Can't Buy,* 202.

4

The Good, the Bad, and the Ugly

Practically Assessing the Global Economy

Adam Smith's ghost is alive and well. Even though there are wisps of change in the air, the dominant economic paradigm still maintains that with well-established property rights, an impartial rule of law, and a hands-off government, the free market will work its magic. This thinking has certainly been the basis of the rise of the ideology known as neoliberalism over the past few decades.

I hesitate to use the word "neoliberalism," as it is too often deployed as an ill-defined invective. But I think the term has its uses. I will define it as the extension of the values of neoclassical economics across all aspects of the economy and society, the kind of thinking highlighted in the last chapter. It is the belief that efficiency is the highest standard, that growth is the only goal as growth will trickle down, and that the private sector needs to be unshackled from the grip of government to be efficient and innovative. In turn, those factors mean privatization, deregulation, a smaller government, flexible labor markets, and free movement of capital in search of the best investment opportunities both within and between countries. There are no other standards of judgment, and we simply lost the older language of the economy as the domain of morality, imbibed with justice, solidarity, reciprocity, and like concepts.

We can see this thinking everywhere. As just one popular example of this mode of thinking, Arthur Brooks—president of the American Enterprise Institute—argues that five factors account for reductions in poverty: globalization, free trade, property rights, the rule of law, and the culture of entrepreneurship.[1] In the academic realm, one of the most influential books of the last decade was *Why Nations Fail: The Origins of Power, Prosperity and Poverty*, by Daron Acemoglu and James Robinson.[2] These authors argue that economic differences between nations boil down to institutions. In their view, countries with what they call "inclusive" institutions—the rule of law, political freedoms, equality of opportunity—do much better than countries with "extractive" institutions, where political power is concentrated, corruption is rampant, and elites protect their own position by closing the door of opportunity to others. This appealing argument, with an element of truth to it, is nonetheless too simplified. It implicitly accepts the neoliberal idea that the institutions that really matter are the ones in which free markets are allowed to do their work.

In this chapter, I will argue that success does not come simply from laissez-faire policies that prioritize the magic of the market but through a more complex confluence of factors—or a more complex confluence of institutions, if you will. The starting point is to recognize Karl Polanyi's basic intuition that we simply cannot isolate the market from the state.[3] All markets are embedded in social institutions and given shape by law and government. This fact occurs across all economic arrangements, from communism whereby the state owns the factors of production, to libertarianism, whereby the state guarantees absolute property rights and a legal apparatus that favors corporations over labor and other social stakeholders. The notion that we can simply divide the world into statist and free market outcomes is a myth. We need to get back to Polanyi's key insight.

Defects of Free Market Ideology

To explore why the simplistic neoliberal argument fails, I want to make three points. First, it is not true that when markets are fairly unencumbered, the dominant relationship between individuals and companies is a competitive one. There are plenty of examples in history in which cooperation and reciprocity dominated instead. Second, again when looking across history, it is difficult to separate trade and free markets from the exercise of political power, often brutal military power. It is rare to see "competition" without the use of force. Third, it is often the case that economic success depends on the combination of a market economy and a strong state giving it form and direction; this is the story of modern China and is the main argument against the Acemoglu-Robinson thesis.

The first point: the idea that markets are dominated by self-interest and com-petition is a fairly recent invention, thanks to the intellectual developments discussed in the last chapter. As Graeber has pointed out, throughout most of human history, exchange has taken place within the context of what he calls "human economies"—dominated by relationship, gift, honor, and duty.[4] In Italy, the so-called civil economy school of economics argues convincingly that the rise of markets in the late middle ages, especially in Tuscany, was influenced strongly by Aristotle's notion of politics and economics in the service of *eudaimonia*.[5] Members of the school call this the rise of "civic humanism" and note that it was strongly influenced by monastic culture and especially the Franciscan order in the Catholic Church. Indeed, as noted by Stefano Zamagni, the Franciscan school of economics in the middle ages laid the foundations of a civil market economy.[6] Somewhat paradoxically, the Franciscan vow of poverty meant that money management needed to be turned over to laypeople. Profit came to be seen as legitimate as long as people were treated fairly, based on the willingness of the merchant to provide a true benefit or gift to the customer. This school also laid down such economic principles as the division of labor, the allocation of income to productive investment, and the freedom of the enterprise to innovate and take on risk.

The resulting period of civic humanism reached its apogee in the second half of the fifteenth century, in the context of a remarkable economic and cultural efflorescence. For example, financial institutions called *montes pietatis* (mounts of piety) pooled charitable donations to provide cheap finance to the poor with-out any expectation of profit for the lender. This practice was an example of reciprocity in action—an economic transaction based on a personal relationship whereby the gift was intermingled with the commercial contract. Exchange took place within networks of solidarity, within a community, which bound both parties by obligation.[7] But as Luigino Bruni notes, the period of civic humanism was "as rich as it was short."[8] It was suppressed by more despotic principalities, in line with the political theories of Machiavelli.

Another example of "civil markets" comes from the Islamic middle ages, a story relayed by Graeber.[9] As he points out, for most of the middle ages, the world's economic nerve center was the Islamic world. The Islamic tradition always viewed trade more favorably than did Christianity and yet had strict injunctions against usury and taking advantage of people for the sake of profit. During this period, trade flourished on the back of credit instruments such as promissory notes. Since usury was ruled out, the dominant economic form became profit-sharing part-nerships, an entire system based on reputation and trust. It was, as Graeber notes, "a world of handshake deals and paper promises backed only by the integrity of the signer."[10] The system did not rely on state mechanisms of enforcement but on reputation and communal solidarity. And these very networks of trust and communal bonds were partly responsible for the rapid spread of Islam throughout this whole period. Notice the similarities and differences with Adam Smith. Like Smith, the Islamic world believed in the power of economic exchange to secure the common good. But unlike Smith, it was more about providing mutual aid than securing individual advantage. We see, then, that it is possible to have a "free" market—free from government interference—that does not rely mainly on self-interest and cutthroat competition.

This discussion brings me to my second point: that competition and economic exchange are rarely separate from political and military power. In the Islamic middle ages, the Indian Ocean was an ocean of tranquility. It was commonly understood that it was supposed to stay open to commercial trade, free from political rivalry. This calm all ended when the Portuguese arrived in the fifteenth century and prized open markets and trade routes through the barrel of a (very large) gun. They could do this as Europe had made a giant leap forward with military technology, especially in the use of guns and cannons.

This exploration started a dark trend. As noted by both Graeber and Sachs,[11] the European-dominated globalization that began in the early modern period and extended through the industrial revolution was extraordinarily violent and inhumane—and yet went hand-in-hand with an enormous expansion in trade, in a network that connected the entire globe for the first time ever. Although marking the genesis of what we know today as global capitalism, this period, far from being a triumph of free markets, was instead characterized by the extension of imperial power, with extractive private corporations opening markets and establishing trade privileges through force. These corporations possessed their own armed forces plus the backing of the state—sometimes implicit, sometimes explicit. The two earliest examples were the British East India Company and the Dutch East India Company, both given monopolies over trade in Asia—and empowered to do whatever was necessary to cut others out of this profitable trade.

This period was also marked by the inhumane treatment of conquered peoples in the Americas, who were forced into bonded servitude or slavery to work in the mines or plantations that sent gold, silver, and raw materials back to Europe. What's more, this brutal boot of colonialism, combined with imported diseases such as smallpox, led to the decimation of the Indigenous population of the Americas; estimates suggest a 90 percent reduction in population between 1500 and 1600. The resulting labor shortage led to the importation of enslaved people from Africa—all told, there were 36,000 slave voyages between 1514 and 1866, with about 14 million people shipped across the ocean.[12] These slaves were typically put to work in the highly profitable sugar, tobacco, and cotton plantations—which were once again sent for export to Europe.

Even after the industrial revolution, the twinning of globalization and violence did not abate. If anything, it ramped up, as military technology became more lethal. In the nineteenth century, Britain forcibly opened China to trade against its will—including a ruinous trade in opium. The British East India Company—a private corporation, remember—managed to take control over all of India, instituting a reign of terror marked by widespread famine. After a rebellion in 1857, the British government took direct control. Britain managed to suppress any competition with its own textile industry and reduced India to a mere exporter of raw materials. All told, as stressed by Atul Kohli, Britain deliberately held back development across what would become its empire, refusing to allow countries to industrialize, forcing them to buy British final products, and saddling them with debt to keep them economically subservient. It wedded the strong arm of the state to the profit interests of economic elites[13]—so much for the gains from free trade and exchange.

And in the latter half of the nineteenth century, Europe colonized most of Africa, again practically enslaving the population and turning it into a producer of raw materials for its own markets. With the rise of an oil-based economy, the imperial powers then turned to securing these supplies. As the twentieth century progressed, Britain ceded this role to the United States, which continued the pattern of linking globalization with the extension of military power—both to secure oil supplies and to put in power governments favorable to American business interests. In many cases over the course of the century—from Central America to Iran to Chile—the United States overthrew governments deemed hostile to American commercial interests. In a real sense, there is no way to separate capitalism from political power.

My third criticism of the naive neoliberal defense of free markets is that when it comes to economic success, it is fairly common to see markets combined with a strong state. This pattern again gels with Polanyi's point about how economic institutions are always embedded in wider societal norms. Acemoglu and Robinson are fond of pointing out that Britain took the economic lead because of its inclusive institutions, the checking of absolutist royal power, and the protection of property rights through a strong rule of law. As I've argued, this was happening at the exact same time as a brutal colonialist expansion. But my point here is that states and markets frequently work together, something that was extremely common across modern economic history. As Dani Rodrik notes, "the history of US economic development is one of pragmatic partnerships and close collaboration between the public and private sector" and that the government has provided investment, infrastructure, finance, education, and basic public goods that private investment needs.[14] In the postwar era, East Asian countries too went through a process of rapid industrialization guided by a strong hand of the state through industrial policy—including export subsidies, investment regulations, restrictions on the movement of capital, and directed lending.

The 800-pound gorilla here is China, which has managed to achieve tremendous economic success in recent decades through a form of state-directed capitalism. Seeing it as a major alternative to western forms of governance, Branko Milanovic calls this "political capitalism."[15] He argues, correctly in my view, that it would be a mistake to call countries like China and Vietnam communist, as they rely heavily on the price signals of markets and on private enterprise. But they are different. Milanovic argues that political capitalism has three key features: (1) a bureaucracy of technocrats seeking to generate strong economic growth; (2) a weak rule of law so that the bureaucratic elites have sufficient discretion to pursue their goals; and (3) a state pursuing the national interest, including by controlling and directing the activities of the private sector. This trifecta has been able to achieve enormous success, such as lifting hundreds of millions out of poverty in three short decades—one of the single greatest achievements in human history. It also contains some inherent contradictions, such as the tension between a competent technocracy and the high levels of corruption that exist because of a weak rule of law.

These "political capitalist" states differ from neoliberal states, but I do not believe the differences would appear so stark if we looked across the longer span of history, before the more recent advent of neoliberalism. These distinctions are a matter of degree rather than kind. The state and the market have always been entwined. One of the fallacies of neoliberalism is that the market is, in the words of Rodrik, "self-creating, self-regulating, self-stabilizing . . . self-legitimizing."[16] Polanyi was right: it is impossible to view the market without understanding the forms of governance that underpin it, which depends in turn on state institutions.

To sum up this section: I have argued that the existence of free market or neoliberal institutions—a hands-off government, a competitive market, the rule of law, and strong property rights—are neither necessary nor sufficient for economic success. I have given examples of successful market economies that relied more on cooperation than competition. I have argued that capitalist institutions cannot be divorced from political, military, and imperial power, meaning that much of the economic gain comes from force and not by mutually advantageous (or voluntary) trade. And finally, I have argued that there are capitalist systems with very different institutional underpinnings that can also enjoy considerable economic success. The case for Smithian economics is much weaker than it seems.

The Industrial Revolution

Let's now start to drill down on some more recent history. I introduced the industrial revolution in chapter 2, as it really provided the spark for the development of modern Catholic social teaching. Now I want to delve a little deeper into the economics because this is where our modern global economy begins. If you look at charts of economic growth over centuries, you will see a line that looks flat. For sure, there were periods of economic efflorescence and economic stagnation, but these look like minor blips over the long, flat centuries. In the words of leading economist John Maynard Keynes, this consistency was due to the "remarkable absence of important technical improvements and to the failure of capital to accumulate."[17] But after about 1750, everything was turned upside down. After centuries of stability, economic activity now spiked up, turning the curve from something that looked horizontal to something that looked vertical (see figure 4.1). This is the world in which we live.

But why did the industrial revolution begin in Europe in general and Britain in particular? The reality is certainly a lot more complicated than Acemoglu and Robinson's institutional argument. Indeed, historian Kenneth Pomeranz argues that on the eve of the industrial revolution, around 1800, there was little

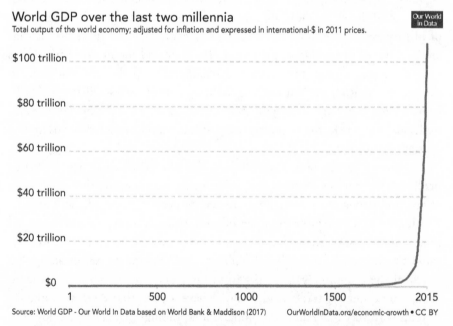

Figure 4.1. World GDP over the last two millennia. Total output of the world economy; adjusted for inflation and expressed in 2011 prices. New Maddison Project Database and World Bank, "World GDP over the Last Two Millennia."

difference between Europe, China, and India in terms of institutional quality and the spread and depth of markets.[18] What allowed Europe to take off was overseas exploitation. Specifically, Europe could import cheap food and cotton from the Americas, freeing up people to work as laborers in factories. Europe, China, and India were all facing land constraints in terms of growing food to feed a rising population; the American network solved that problem for Europe. A second factor identified by Pomeranz is the easy availability of coal reserves in Europe, especially in Britain, which gave it a first mover advantage. China had coal, but it was in more remote regions and much harder to access. So in a very real sense, the industrial revolution was powered by two forces—coal and enslaved people—two forces, two curses.

As noted by Sachs, the critical year was 1712, when Thomas Newcomen invented the steam engine. In 1776, James Watt improved the engine's design, which turned out to be, in the words of Sachs, "the most important breakthrough of the industrial era and the technological trigger of most that followed."[19] What started in England gradually spread, first to northern Europe, then to North America, and then gradually across the rest of the world. And so today, the world produces over two hundred times more than it did in 1750, on the eve of the industrial revolution. We live in a world in which endless economic growth seems normal. And yet it isn't. Most of economic history saw little economic growth. What changed with the industrial revolution was technology—in particular, wave upon wave of technological development. Each technological revolution built on the last, though all were rooted in the energy derived from burning fossil fuels. But the diffusion of the benefits of technological development were not spread evenly across the world, and they still are not.

These waves of technological advance were described well by the Russian economist Nikolai Kondratiev, dating back to 1925. As Sachs notes, his argument has been proven right and can be extended.[20] The first wave, from about 1780 to 1830, overlaps with the first industrial revolution and encompasses such developments as the steam engine and the mechanized textile industry. The second wave, from 1830 to 1880, was the age of steel and railways, which reduced transport costs dramatically. Wave number 3, lasting from 1880 through 1930, was the age of electricity and chemicals. The fourth wave, spanning 1930–70, saw the development of automobiles and mass transport, along with petrochemicals. And finally, the fifth wave, beginning in 1970, was the age of information and communications technology, unleashing the power of the digital revolution. This is the age in which we still live, marked by computers with remarkable processing power, smartphones, and the internet.

A few important points here: First, this was not a continuous process, across time or across space. Takeoffs were often followed by crashes—think of the

Great Depression of 1929 and the global financial crisis of 2008. Some regions benefited more than others, and diffusion of technological gains occurred unevenly—for many different reasons, both domestic and international.

Second, we have become accustomed to thinking of high and continuous economic growth as normal. But as I've pointed out, this mindset is a fairly recent innovation from a particular source. Modern growth comes from the waves of technological progress we have experienced over the last couple of centuries— one wave builds on the last and gradually benefits more and more countries. Nobel Prize–winning economist Robert Solow argued that about 80 percent of all economic growth is due to advances in technology.[21] Of course, there will be ups and downs in the short run, but the obsession with perpetual growth for its own sake misunderstands its roots in technological progress, which is in no way destined to continue forever.

Third, economic growth comes from innovation, as Mariana Mazzucato has demonstrated. The investments in science and technology that drive this innovation are cumulative, building on decades of work and involving collective and long-term interactions between public and private sectors.[22] Especially in recent decades, when the private entrepreneur is held on a pedestal, we tend to forget the roots of modern innovation in public-sector research. For example, Mazzucato points out that the internet, smartphone technology, and two-thirds of the most innovative drugs have their roots in government-sponsored research. Yet the private sector tends to reap a disproportionate reward from new technologies, to the detriment of the taxpayer. Worse than that, Mazzucato argues, these private-sector actors often use patents and other regulations to put money in their own pocket and actually inhibit innovation. Perhaps this profiteering can help explain the finding of economist Robert Gordon that productivity gains of the past few decades are lower than that of earlier technological waves, especially in the first half of the twentieth century.[23] Let's now turn our attention to that tumultuous century.

The Ups and Downs of the Twentieth Century

We still live in the world forged by the twentieth century, with many lessons learned and many forgotten. The first half of the century was beyond calamitous. The First World War shattered the myths that free and open markets would provide the basis for perpetual peace. Although the period prior to the war was one of high globalization with few impediments to the movement of capital, goods, and even people, it was also a period of rapacious colonialism and massive inequalities between the exalted rich and downtrodden poor—the very dysfunctions and inequities that modern Catholic social teaching rose to tackle. In this light, the war was a genuine shock to the system. And it was utterly catastrophic, deploying the new technological ingenuity toward death and destruction, with 20 million people killed and a whole generation wiped out. After the war, instead of turning to reconciliation, the victors instead opted for vengeance, imposing punitive financial terms on Germany, terms that ruined its economy and created social upheaval—in turn paving the way for the rise of Adolf Hitler.

Two people in particular saw the consequences of this: Pope Benedict XV, the pope who reigned during the war, and Keynes, the leading economist of the twentieth century. In his 1920 encyclical *Pacem, Dei Munus Pulcherrimum*, Pope Benedict XV noted that "there is no need from us of long proof to show that society would incur the risk of great loss if, while peace is signed, latent hostility and enmity were to continue among the nations."[24] Keynes, in a prophetic 1919 book titled *The Economic Consequences of the Peace*, said the following:

> If we aim deliberately at the impoverishment of Central Europe, vengeance, I dare predict, will not limp. Nothing can then delay for very long that final civil war between the forces of Reaction and the despairing convulsions of Revolution, before which the horrors of the late German war will fade into nothing, and which will destroy, whoever is victor, the civilization and the progress of our generation. Even though the result disappoint us, must we not base our actions on better expectations, and believe that the prosperity and happiness of one country promotes that of others, that the solidarity of man is not a fiction, and that nations can still afford to treat other nations as fellow-creatures?[25]

Keynes was asking for an economic and social order based on solidarity and cooperation as the foundation of a secure peace, which was not to be. Instead, the old political order was discredited, and two forces arose in its place—revolutionary socialism and xenophobic nationalism. The Communist takeover of Russia was a direct consequence of the war. And Hitler's rise in Germany came on the heels of 25 percent unemployment and a crippling foreign debt that simply could not be repaid.[26] This period also saw the world plunged into the Great Depression, discrediting the idea that capitalist economies would naturally correct themselves. The culmination of these dark forces returned the world to war—war that proved even more ruinous than before, with over 50 million dead and a continent in ruins.

Picking themselves up from the dirt-caked killing fields, the postwar leaders were determined to chart a new course. They were determined to choose cooperation rather than conflict and competition. In this, American leadership proved decisive, but the United States played a rather schizophrenic role in the postwar period. As well as being willing to deploy force to far-flung corners of the world, to topple hostile governments when needed, and to follow the old colonialist model of opening markets for its own benefit (especially oil markets), US leadership was also instrumental in laying down the framework of a cooperative international order—marked by the United Nations (UN), the World Bank, the International Monetary Fund (IMF), and what would eventually become the World Trade Organization. In stark contrast to the end of the First World War, the United States realized that rebuilding Europe was in the national and global interest. So it went big with the Marshall Plan, sending enormous financial resources across the Atlantic.

This period became, in the words of historian Tony Judt, a "social democratic moment," which encompasses the European postwar consensus, the American model predicated on Roosevelt's New Deal, and the reconstruction of Japan.[27] The old political Right was utterly discredited by war and the flirtation with fascism. And the Left had been compromised by its association with communism and the vicious Stalinist repression. Something new was needed.

Here's the interesting thing: the "social democratic moment" coincided with a "Catholic moment," especially through the rise of Christian democracy in Europe. In chapter 2, I noted that the emergence of modern human rights, rooted in the idea of human dignity and codified in the Universal Declaration of Human Rights, owed much to Catholic social teaching. The same is true of Christian democracy, which supported the idea of a "social market economy" to protect families from the vagaries of capitalism. In a recent book called *Catholic Modern*, historian James Chappel describes the intellectual evolution of Catholic thought in this period.[28] He describes a bifurcation of Catholic thought into what he calls "paternal" Catholicism, eyeing communism nervously and elevating the family as the basic unit of society, and "fraternal" Catholicism, which tended to be more left wing and more suspicious of fascism. The former gravitated toward Christian democracy and included the founding fathers of postwar Europe: Konrad Adenauer of Germany, Robert Schuman of France, and Alcide De Gasperi of Italy. The movement emphasized social harmony and the promotion of a vibrant civil life to counteract the forces of individualism and collectivism.[29] The latter strand embraced progressive forms of social democracy, especially through institutional mechanisms of worker solidarity and a strong welfare state. But especially in the early years, and especially in the realm of economics, the differences between Christian and social democrats were narrow. All supported the state's role in regulating the economy in line with the common good, providing universal social services funded by taxes and social contributions, and empowering unions as a bulwark against excessive corporate power—the kind of power that greased the wheels of fascism and Nazism. In his magisterial history of postwar Europe, Judt makes this very point, noting that "Christian Democrats of the first post-war years saw free-market liberals rather than the collectivist Left as their main opponents and were keen to demonstrate that the modern state could be adapted to non-socialist forms of benevolent intervention."[30]

The United States witnessed similar developments. Although it never had a Christian Democratic movement, Roosevelt's New Deal, which became cemented in the postwar consensus, was also influenced by Catholic social teaching—especially under the tutelage of social ethicist and Catholic priest Monsignor John A. Ryan.[31] Dubbed the "Right Reverend New Dealer," Ryan was ahead of his time, having authored the radical US bishops' Program for Social Reconstruction after the First World War in 1919; it called for a minimum wage; social insurance for illness, disability, and old age; labor's right to bargain collectively; labor participation in management; public housing; progressive taxation; the regulation of monopolies; and government control of utilities.[32] A century later, this document still has a radical feel.

Just like its postwar equivalent in Europe, the New Deal limited the excesses of the market, aimed at just and harmonious industrial relations, and protected people from various kinds of market risks. Its goals extended well into the postwar period and were widely accepted on both sides of the partisan divide. Dubbed by some the "Treaty of Detroit," this set of institutions combining high taxes on the rich, robust minimum wages, and strong collective bargaining rights helped usher in a remarkable period of industrial stability and shared prosperity.[33] The New Deal was extended by President Lydon B. Johnson's War on Poverty in the 1960s. Nonetheless, it is worth noting that the power of market ideology always remained stronger in the United States than in Europe. For example, collective bargaining coverage of workers peaked at 29 percent in 1960 but exceeded 90 percent in many European countries.[34] And European levels of social spending were higher than in the United States. But the New Deal institutions nonetheless marked a shift in a decidedly social democratic direction.

We can also see the social democratic movement at play in the restructuring of Japan. As noted by historian Walter Scheidel, Japan went, in a few short years, from one of the most unequal to one of the most equal countries on earth.[35] During the war years, incomes were compressed by government regulation, inflation, and the physical destruction of capital. But after the war too, the American occupation broke up the big business conglomerates, introduced land reforms, supported unionization, and developed a welfare state funded by high and progressive taxation. Its "Basic Directive" called for a "wide distribution of income and of the ownership of the means of production and trade."[36] The plan's goal was to prevent the kinds of alignment between big business and the militaristic state that had prompted Japan to turn to aggressive warfare. As a result, inequality in Japan, which had been at American levels at the time of the Great Depression, is now at northern European levels.

In fact, there are three explanations for this extended social democratic moment. First, the Great Depression and subsequent war utterly upended the faith in a self-correcting market. Free market economics had become intellectually bankrupt, and all accepted the need for the state to extend a guiding hand. Keynesian economics was ascendant. Second, the war itself generated an ethos of solidarity and self-sacrifice, which extended well into the postwar period and only really began to fade into the horizon when the generations shifted. Third, all politicians eyed communism nervously in the rearview mirror. In the aftermath of the war, communist parties made major gains among some large western European countries. Faced with an ideology promising an unrelenting progression toward a socialist future, those charged with managing capitalist economies needed to take the sting out of the communist tail.

In looking back at this social democratic moment, we can see defining influence of Catholic social teaching. As noted by economist Paul Collier, what made the original welfare state so successful was its notion of inbuilt reciprocity.[37] Collier's analysis stresses the importance of reciprocal obligation—with its built-in notion of fairness, shared belonging, and purposeful action—as the essence of all communal endeavors, including economics.

In this context, Collier argues that social democracy has roots in the reciprocity of the cooperative movement, which is taken to scale with the welfare state. With reciprocal obligation everyone pays in, and everyone gets taken care of in time of need—whether it is healthcare, pensions, education, or unemployment and disability insurance. Everybody pays their requisite taxes because everybody belongs to a community. Although Collier doesn't use the term, he is talking about the practical virtue of solidarity. You might be young and healthy, but you pay into health insurance, both to support the sick today and knowing that you too will be supported in times of ill health. Even if you don't have children, you pay taxes to fund schools, because education is vital to civic virtue and healthy communities. Even if you have a secure job, you contribute to unemployment and disability insurance, both to take care of the less fortunate and as insurance against your own future potential misfortune. Even if you are young, you pay into pensions—again, to support the elderly and to take care of your own future income security. Today, we are accustomed to thinking of individual insurance tied to individual risk—say, car insurance. But social insurance is different. It is not just insuring against risks in your own life, though it is that too. More fundamentally, it reflects the principles of solidarity and reciprocity.

It reflects the fact that we live in community, which comes with obligations. It links rights to these obligations—again, a major tenet of Catholic social teaching.

This linkage can go wrong when the welfare state becomes less about universal reciprocity and more about targeted charity "means-tested" for the poor. Means testing runs into three problems. First, it leads to stigma, humiliating and demeaning the dignity of the person receiving the help. Some argue that this stigma might even be legitimate, if the poor are seen as lazy and indigent; this was certainly the attitude in Victorian England as encapsulated by novels such as Charles Dickens's *Oliver Twist*. This view can still be seen today when politicians use the language of neoclassical economics to claim that the welfare state means that the poor lack "incentives" to work. Second, if tied to work status, means-tested benefits can lead to poverty traps—each dollar earned from a job is counteracted by a lost dollar in benefits, making it hardly worthwhile to work. Third, by delinking benefits from contributions, means testing makes the welfare state less politically palatable, especially among the middle class. This change is part of what we have seen over the past few decades as the welfare state has been pared back.

In some cases, the welfare state also deployed the Catholic principle of subsidiarity, something especially true in countries such as Germany, in which—in the words of Lew Daly—"the public responsibility is to authorize and finance social programs, whereas private responsibility governs the delivery of services and benefits."[38] Sometimes religiously affiliated entities are given responsibility for delivery, a good lesson in what subsidiarity is really all about. Especially in the United States, subsidiarity is sometimes seen as akin to "small government." As noted in chapter 2, this is not the case. Although the welfare state is sizable in countries like Germany, it is often administered at the local level, by subsidiary institutions, which are better able to respect the dignity and agency of the recipient. This method avoids a way in which welfare states can go wrong—becoming too large, too impersonal, too bureaucratic, and too distant.

The bottom line is that the social democratic moment was a resounding success. It delivered three solid decades of full employment, stellar economic growth, low inequality, and high upward mobility. Not only did it produce an economic boom, but one where the gains were widely shared. In Germany, it was the *Wirtschaftswunder* (the economic miracle) and in France, *les trente glorieuses* (the thirty glorious years). The United States had the Treaty of Detroit, and Britain referred to the age of affluence. Some might argue that this was a natural outcome of a low base—the destroyed infrastructure that needed to be rebuilt from scratch after the war. This fact explains some of it, yes, but not all of it. The social democratic institutions were quite specific in that they encapsulated a spirit of solidarity and shared purpose. This spirit in turn built trust and social cohesion, setting off a virtuous cycle. Also, the ethos of neoclassical economics was still at an infant stage and had not yet corrupted policies and social norms. Debates were cast not only in terms of efficiency but justice, fairness, and solidarity. As Judt notes, "There was a moralized quality to policy debates in those early postwar years."[39]

Over the past four decades or so, that world and that ethos have largely been lost. Starting in the 1970s, the postwar consensus started to fray. Judt actually traces this back to the 1960s, an era in which the communitarian impulse of social democracy started to seem a little worn, to be replaced with an ethos of individualism.[40] Matt Stoller argues that there was a major political change in the 1970s, as politicians coming of age in an affluent society identified with consumers in search of a bargain rather than with citizens seeking the common good or agents wedded to vocational good practice and the production of high-quality goods.[41] In this sense, they proved to be unwitting allies of the Chicago School, the leading intellectual agents of neoliberalism.

Throughout this decade, a series of economic crises generated by spiraling oil prices led to the worst of all worlds: high unemployment and high inflation. The old confidence that capable technocrats could successfully manage the economy and generate full employment was fatally undermined. People were looking for new answers, and those new answers turned out to be old answers—the power of an uninhibited free market to generate, via the invisible hand, growth and prosperity. Instead of a solution, government was now seen as a problem. The political apotheosis of this view was the ascent of Ronald Reagan and Margaret Thatcher in the early 1980s.

Notably, this shift back toward the free market was not inevitable; part of it resulted from the fading of the conditions that generated the social democratic moment in the first place. The war was now a distant memory, and the solidarity it generated fell by the wayside. The Great Depression was an even more distant memory, and the power of the free market seemed fresh again. Once the Soviet Union collapsed in 1989, all constraints were off—free market capitalism was seen as the only game in town, with no countervailing force to keep it honest. But part of the shift was also intellectual, a concerted effort by a group of libertarian economists to move the debate in their favor. This movement centered on the University of Chicago, led by people such as Milton Friedman and Gary Becker. It also centered on a highly influential cabal of libertarians called the Mont Pelerin Society, which mounted a successful multidecades' campaign to rally business and politicians to their side. By the 1970s, their moment had come.

So the social democratic moment gave way to the neoliberal. This ill-fated moment began in the United States and the United Kingdom, but by the 1990s, it had spread to Europe and indeed all across the world. It formed the backbone of what would become known as the Washington consensus. Its creed was simple: faith in free markets to achieve general prosperity. So governments implemented policies such as deregulation of industry, relaxed constraints on the financial sector, encouraged wide-ranging privatization, lowered taxes on capital and high-income earners, and curbed the power of unions. All of these measures were supposed to promote efficiency, innovation, and competitiveness.

But here's the problem: it didn't work. It didn't work even on its own terms. Just looking at the United States, the ground zero of neoliberalism, there is simply no evidence that these policies unleashed a wave of innovation and growth. To see this, we need to look at productivity, which I have argued is the leading driver of long-term economic growth. In his magisterial tome, *The Rise and Fall of American Growth*, economist Gordon shows that productivity, defined as output per hour worked, was an average 2.82 percent a year between 1920 and 1970—remember that this includes not only the social democratic moment but also the Great Depression and World War II.[42] This rate fell to 1.62 percent a year between 1970 and 2014, the peak years of neoliberalism. We can go one level deeper. One of the leading components of output per hour is called total factor productivity, which accounts for innovation and technological change. Here, Gordon shows that total factor productivity was three times higher in the earlier period (1920–70) than afterward. The neoliberal moment actually saw lower productivity and long-term growth. Of course, these figures do not prove that neoliberalism caused this decline, but they should give its defenders pause.

The other fact, of course, is that while overall growth slowed down under neoliberalism, the poor saw the biggest decline. As estimated by Emmanuel Saez and Gabriel Zucman, average national income per adult in the United States rose by 2 percent a year between 1946 and 1980—and remarkably, all classes and levels of society rose at this same rate.[43] The neoliberal era was vastly different. First off, echoing Gordon, Saez and Zucman show that overall growth was lower; average annual growth in national income per adult has been only 1.4 percent since 1980 and 0.8 percent since the turn of the century. And the distribution is vastly worse. Almost 90 percent of the population saw growth less than the headline number of 1.4 percent. The average pretax income of the bottom half of the population has barely budged. It is only when you get to the top 1 percent that you start seeing big rises. And the higher the bigger—the top 0.1 percent saw incomes grow by 320 percent since 1980. Again, neoliberalism failed on its own terms. It only delivered higher income growth for the extremely rich, and there was no trickle down of any benefits. In fact, even though GDP per capita is lower in France than in the United States—not because productivity is lower but because working hours are fewer—average income per adult for the bottom 50 percent of the population is higher in France than in the United States.

Of importance, this is market income—even before the state tries to equalize outcomes with taxes and transfers.[44] This inequality gave rise to grave social dysfunctions in the United States, which I will discuss later in the chapter.

The bottom line is that neoliberalism has failed on its own terms. Across all dimensions, it is inferior to the social democratic moment. And while not delivering on its own promises, the neoliberal moment gave rise to enormous dysfunctions: a widening chasm between rich and poor; rising corporate control, concentration, and corruption; and an ever more urgent environmental crisis. The destruction of virtues such as solidarity meant that neoliberalism simply lacked the tools to fix the problems it either created or inherited.

The State of the Global Economy

It's time to delve deeper into the contemporary global economy—the good, the bad, and the ugly.

The starting point is to appreciate that the economy powered by the industrial revolution has brought about enormous gains in living standards, quality of life, and human development. The global economy today amounts to about $128 trillion in international prices, over 200 times greater than at the eve of the industrial revolution, a total that gives rise to an average GDP per person of around $17,000. But of course, this is not evenly divided. Living standards are far higher in the industrialized countries, and extreme poverty remains a grim reality for hundreds of millions. Straddling each end, there are about a billion people living in high-income countries, with an average GDP of $45,000 a person and a billion people in low-income countries earning an average of $800 a person.

Yet there has also been much progress in poverty reduction. The World Bank sets its extreme poverty threshold at $1.90 a day in international prices, which is considered the bare minimum needed just to survive. If we go back to 1800, at the start of the industrial revolution, about 90 percent of the world lived in extreme poverty. Average life expectancy was only thirty-five years. Today is very different. According to the World Bank, extreme poverty fell from 2 billion in 1990 to 689 million in 2017. This is still about 10 percent of the global population. The decline was driven mainly by Asia, especially East Asia—and most especially China, which transformed from a village-based impoverished state to a middle-income country with low poverty in a matter of decades. This change is important to remember, as the defenders of neoliberalism often attribute this decline in poverty to the magic of free markets. China did indeed move away from communism and toward a market economy, but—as noted already—one more associated with political capitalism than with western-style liberal capitalism. The invisible hand of the market was guided by the visible hand of the state.

Extreme poverty remains highly concentrated in sub-Saharan Africa and South Asia, with pockets in Central America and Southeast Asia. Yet even in sub-Saharan Africa, the poorest region of the world, there is evidence of gains in poverty reduction. Again according to the World Bank, poverty rates fell from 54 percent in 1990 to 40 percent in 2017. So there has been progress, but it is much slower. Once again, though, it is hard to credit neoliberal policies. For sure, African governments have made some bad policy choices, and corruption remains a problem. But as Sachs has noted, the odds are stacked against Africa—one third of the countries are landlocked, lacking access to ports; the continent is cursed with a high infectious disease burden, especially from mosquitos; crop productivity is low; and the colonial legacy left behind lousy infrastructure and weak institutions, including a wholly inadequate educational system.[45] All of this hinders productivity, growth, and human well-being.

So what accounts for the (modest) gains? I would argue the combination of debt relief and the Millennium Development Goals. Supported by Pope John Paul II, the Jubilee campaign—named after the injunction in the Hebrew Scriptures to cancel debt periodically—led to major debt relief for the world's poorest countries, including from the IMF and World Bank, in the early 2000s. Much of the savings was ploughed back into domestic budgets to boost health, education, and social spending. And at the same time, the world community endorsed the Millennium Development Goals, described by the UN as the "most successful anti-poverty movement in history."[46] These goals, adopted in 2000, helped lift a billion people out of poverty. There were eight goals in total, mainly in the areas of health and education, which countries pledged to achieve by 2015. The goals were

1. eradicate extreme poverty and hunger
2. achieve universal primary education
3. promote gender equality and empower women
4. reduce child mortality
5. improve maternal health
6. combat HIV/AIDS, malaria, and other diseases
7. ensure environmental sustainability
8. develop a global partnership for development

The international community mobilized substantial resources, especially in the field of health, to help countries achieve these goals.

The results are certainly impressive. In an assessment in 2015, the UN documented major progress for the developing countries, and not just in poverty reduction.[47] The proportion of undernourished people fell by almost half since 1990—from 23 percent to 13 percent. Almost 2 billion people gained access to piped drinking water since 1990. Over this same period, maternal mortality was halved, with most of the decline happening since 2000. Child morality too fell by half: the number of children who died before their fifth birthday fell from 12 million a year in 1990 to 6 million a year by 2015. New HIV infections fell by about 40 percent between 2000 and 2013, and about 14 million people gained access to antiretrovirals (up from only 800,000 in 2003). Over 6 million lives were saved from malaria since 2000, owing to simple and cheap interventions such as insecticide-treated mosquito nets. Over 37 million lives were saved from tuberculosis over this same period. We can also see some strong gains in education. Primary school net enrollment rose from 83 percent in 2000 to 91 percent in 2015—with the number of primary-age children out of school declining by almost half, to 57 million. And the developing regions have eliminated gender gaps across all levels of education.

So this is the *good*. A combination of higher economic growth combined with global solidarity—in the form of debt relief and stepped-up foreign aid—led to major improvements in human development across the board. The *bad*, however, is that we still have enormous levels of poverty, deprivation, and exclusion in a world of unprecedented wealth. Extreme poverty might have fallen dramatically, but 689 million are still mired in its misery. As noted, this is almost 1 in 10 of all of the people alive today. Some have also criticized the World Bank's threshold of $1.90 a day as too low to achieve a dignified life. They note that not counting China, the numbers earning less than $2.50 a day barely changed over this period. Globally, the number living under a more dignified $5.50 has been fairly steady since 1990.[48] And looking ahead, the World Bank estimates that, as a result of the COVID-19 pandemic, up to 150 million people could be pushed into extreme poverty in 2021.[49]

The other dimensions of human well-being look equally dire. The UN notes that 820 million people still suffer from hunger, in a world where 30–40 percent of food is wasted. Because of the COVID-19 crisis, the UN World Food Program estimates that an additional 265 million people are at risk of hunger.[50] At the same time, 6 million children still die before their fifth birthday, and almost all of these lives could be saved by cheap and basic medical interventions. Over a billion people lack electricity, and almost 3 billion rely on wood and biomass for energy, which creates terrible pollution and health problems. There is a twenty-year gap in life expectancy between rich and poor countries. In terms of education, 6 out of every 10 children in primary and lower secondary across the world lack basic proficiency in reading and arithmetic. In sub-Saharan Africa, the secondary school completion rate is only 28 percent for boys and 21 percent for girls.

Thanks to neoliberalism and a pattern of globalization shaped by its values, in-equality has been rising sharply. The biggest winners of globalization are the global superrich. The world's billionaires saw their wealth doubling as a percent of global GDP since the late 1980s.[51] According to Oxfam, the world's approximately 2,200 billionaires owned more wealth than 4.6 billion people—accounting for 60 per-cent of the world's population—in 2020.[52] According to the *World Inequality Report*, the world's top 1 percent bagged twice the gains from growth as the bottom 50 percent since 1980—a sharp departure from the social democratic moment. I will talk more about the harmful effects of inequality in chapter 6.

This is the *bad*. The *ugly* side of globalization is marked by a sharp rise in corporate power, concentration, and corruption. As noted in the last chapter, the rise of neoclassical economics led to a watering down of antitrust law, as the standard moved away from concepts such as justice, fairness, and democratic accountability to the simple metric of efficiency and wealth maximization. The Chicago School also dismissed the notion of monopolies, so wedded were they to the ideology of competition. Neoliberalism also pushed the deregulation button hard, convinced that "red tape" was holding back innovation and productivity. Unsurprisingly, the last few decades witnessed the rise of giant and powerful cor-porations, with knock-on effects for democratic accountability. With little over-sight, corporate corruption and impunity skyrocketed. And with the weakening of labor rights and collective bargaining, corporate profits rose spectacularly at the expense of labor. We also saw a corporate distancing from the common good, especially the duty to pay taxes, as money stashed away in tax havens spiked.

In terms of corporate malfeasance, nothing tops the financial sector. The neo-liberal moment was also associated with massive financial deregulation, which increased the fragility of the system and made it increasingly prone to crises. During the social democratic era, regulators kept a tight lid on the financial sec-tor, limiting the risk it could take and limiting the flow of capital across borders. This regulation generated not only prosperity but also safety; there wasn't a single major financial crisis during the thirty golden years. But the brakes came off in the 1980s, with waves of deregulation starting once again in the United States and the United Kingdom and extending through competitive pressures across other regions. Once again, neoclassical economics provided the intellectual fire-power. It put forward something called the efficient market hypothesis, which said that asset prices reflect all information and so are "efficient" and can be left alone. It was an updating of the old idea that markets are self-correcting. But this policy had damaging consequences. The neoliberal era was one of massive financial fragility—from the Latin American debt crisis in the 1980s; through the financial crises in Mexico, Asia, Argentina, and Russia in the 1990s; culmi-nating in the global financial crisis of 2008, the most serious downturn since the

Great Depression until COVID-19. In each case the forces were the same: creditors seeking profit took on too many risks, leading to an economic crash and a subsequent bailout of these lenders. Sometimes they loaned to governments, sometimes to the private sector. But the results were the same. Ordinary people suffered en masse from loss of jobs, homes, savings, and livelihoods, while the lenders were bailed out. I will talk more about the role of the financial sector in the context of the common good in chapter 5.

In terms of the *bad* and the *ugly*, perhaps nothing is more important than the environmental crisis facing our planet.[53] Because of the scale of human activity, we are bumping up against some key planetary boundaries and disrupting some of the earth's core cycles of biology, chemistry, and geology.[54] While the earth's systems are resilient, the scale of change necessitates that we can no longer rule out large, abrupt changes. Instead, we are on the verge of leaving behind the "safe operating space" of the Holocene—that remarkable 10,000-year "long summer" of climatic stability that provided the ideal conditions for human flourishing—and entering the Anthropocene, a new geological epoch in which human activity is a major influence on the earth's systems, with unknown and uncertain consequences.

The surest way to abandon the Holocene is to barge through the planetary boundaries. Scientific evidence identifies at least nine such boundaries, which should be regarded as gateways to a perilous world: climate change, ocean acidification, overuse of freshwater resources, land-use changes, interference with the nitrogen and phosphorous cycles (caused mainly by fertilizers), ozone depletion, chemical pollution, atmospheric aerosol loading (airborne pollution from burning fossil fuels), and a rapid loss of biodiversity in the context of ruptured ecosystems. Scientists tell us that some of these boundaries have already been breached: most notably climate change, biodiversity loss, and the nitrogen cycle. The others are pushing dangerously against the thresholds of safety. And they are interrelated, in the sense that violating one boundary makes it more likely that others will be violated too.

The most important of these boundaries is surely climate change, caused by the burning of fossil fuels that releases carbon dioxide and other greenhouse gases into the atmosphere. We stand on the threshold of a terrifying new reality. Right now, the concentration of carbon dioxide molecules in the atmosphere is higher than at any time in the past 3 million years, a time when the environment was hotter and vastly more hostile—the planet was seven degrees warmer, sea levels were seven meters higher, and there were no humans. This existential crisis is the most serious of the twenty-first century. We face something of a paradox here. As noted, these fossil fuels powered the industrial revolution and so deserve a lot of credit for the great advances in human well-being already mentioned.

But there is a giant bug in the program. We now know that these fossil fuels are actively undermining the very potential they promise, by warming the planet on an unprecedented scale and speed. In this sense, we are sowing the seeds of our own destruction. We cannot blame neoliberal ideology for global warming. But with its utmost faith in markets, neoliberalism has proved wholly unable to grapple with and solve this problem. I will talk more about the environment crisis in chapter 7.

The bottom line is that while there has been immense progress over the past few decades, it doesn't make sense to credit neoliberalism and market ideology. Market reforms did help, but they mostly took place in the context of political rather than libertarian capitalism. The real gains in human development took the active hand of the international community rather than the invisible hand of the market—relief from crippling debt and a scaling up in aid to finance the Millennium Development Goals. Indeed, neoliberalism even fails on its own terms. It promised to unleash ingenuity and innovation but failed to do so. Instead, it brought about massive inequality, declining social cohesion, rising corporate dominance, extreme financial instability, and an inability to tackle the climate crisis. Neoliberalism is no match for the social democratic era.

In one sense, we can say that the economic juggernaut—fueled by the quest for profit and ceaseless economic growth in the context of technological innovation—overpowers the common good. One way this manifests is in an ethical misallocation of resources. In this context, the Ethics in Action initiative put together a kind of moral ledger to assess how resources are currently allocated.[55]

The first part of this ledger shows the costs of eliminating poverty, improving health and education outcomes, and solving climate change. The bottom line is that, in the context of a $128 trillion economy, these amounts are small—sometimes even miniscule. The annual cost of meeting the basic needs of all is between $300 million and $400 billion. The annual cost of saving 5 million children's lives is a mere $20 billion. Ending the AIDS epidemic by 2030 would cost $40 billion a year. The annual cost of providing universal education for low-income countries is around $40 billion. Solving climate change costs about $1 trillion a year. And the annual cost of proving clean energy to the bottom 3 billion: $200 billion. The second part of the ledger shows some of the ways in which the wealth of our economy is being ethically diverted or mismanaged. The global wealth of billionaires is $9.1 trillion. Annual military spending averages between $1.5 trillion and $2 trillion. There is $22 trillion in stranded fossil fuel assets. Annual after-tax fossil fuel subsidies amount to $540 billion. Between $20 trillion and $30 trillion is stashed away in tax havens. And the 2016 pay of top-ten-hedge-fund CEOs was around $10 billion. In contrast to the top of the table, these numbers are extremely large. They reflect an economy that does not prioritize the common good.

What does prioritize the common good is the agenda laid out by the Sustainable Development Goals, the successor to the Millennium Development Goals, intended to guide policy through 2030. Unlike the Millennium Development Goals, which applied to developing countries, the Sustainable Development Goals are for everyone. These seventeen goals challenge the dominant economic paradigm by insisting that economic progress must always go hand in hand with social inclusion and protection of nature.

The goals are as follows: [56]

1. end poverty in all its forms everywhere;
2. end hunger, achieve food security and improved nutrition, and promote sustainable agriculture;
3. ensure healthy lives and promote well-being for all at all ages;
4. ensure inclusive and equitable quality education and promote lifelong learning opportunities for all;
5. achieve gender equality and empower all women and girls;
6. ensure availability and sustainable management of water and sanitation for all;
7. ensure access to affordable, reliable, sustainable, and modern energy for all;
8. promote sustained, inclusive, and sustainable economic growth, full and productive employment, and decent work for all;
9. build resilient infrastructure, promote inclusive and sustainable industrialization, and foster innovation;
10. reduce inequality within and among countries;
11. make cities and human settlements inclusive, safe, resilient, and sustainable;
12. ensure sustainable consumption and production patterns;
13. take urgent action to combat climate change and its impacts;
14. conserve and sustainably use the oceans, seas, and marine resources for sustainable development;
15. protect, restore, and promote sustainable use of terrestrial ecosystems; sustainably manage forests, combat desertification, and halt and reverse land degradation and halt biodiversity loss;
16. promote peaceful and inclusive societies for sustainable development, provide access to justice for all, and build effective, accountable, and inclusive institutions at all levels;
17. strengthen the means of implementation, and revitalize the Global Partnership for Sustainable Development.

These goals also cohere well with the principles of Catholic social teaching. Not only do they lay down the contours of the common good motivated by the virtue of solidarity, but they also embody integral ecology and integral human development. They reflect the principle that seeking material progress for its own sake is a road to ruin, and they call instead for a more holistic sense of human flourishing. They reflect the reality that people are blocked from being or becoming who they are meant to be when they are mired in poverty; when they lack access to health care, education, nutrition, water, sanitation, social protection, and clean energy; when they are impeded from achieving a livelihood with dignity and respect, including through unjust wages and labor practices; and when they face forms of discrimination and violence, including based on gender.[57] People cannot flourish unless the planet also flourishes. So it was only fitting that Pope Francis addressed the United Nations on the day these goals were adopted in September 2015.

One caveat is that as important as they are, the Sustainable Development Goals are confined to the material realm. In this, they are more limited in scope than integral human development, which calls for the fullest development across all aspects of life, including cultural, artistic, emotional, and religious dimensions. Yet attaining the Sustainable Development Goals is a necessary condition for achieving integral human development and fully nested within it.

Wealth and Well-Being

A further issue is that our global economy is superb at producing wealth but poor at generating well-being. A key problem is that GDP and economic growth have been enthroned as the main, and even only, standards of judgment. This priority again reflects the dominance of the neoclassical economic paradigm.

One problem with GDP is that it doesn't handle inequality very well. It is a total, derived from adding up of all income, all output, or all expenditure in the economy. It is quite simply the sum of goods and services produced in an economy and as such is fairly easy to understand.[58] A high GDP growth rate could be consistent with vast amounts of poverty and exclusion. This is the old problem of utilitarianism writ large. Remember that the common good is best represented geometrically, whereby if one person is zeroed out, the whole product is zero. Exclusion is not permitted. But with GDP as the standard of economic judgment, there is simply no way to assess the common good in these terms. For example, what does a 3 percent growth rate mean? In the old social democratic era, it would likely mean that all levels in society are seeing their incomes growing by around 3 percent, so GDP could at least be seen as a measure of material well-being. But in an age of inequality, even this limited standard breaks down. It is quite possible that an average 3 percent growth rate results in a 10 percent growth rate for the rich, flat incomes for the middle class, and a decline for the poor. This scenario has indeed been happening. I've already discussed the data from Saez and Zucman showing that since 1980, only the top 1 percent have really gained from GDP growth. In the three years after the global financial crisis, nine-tenths of the growth gains went to the top 1 percent, underlining that GDP figures showing a recovery were practically useless.[59] In such a context, what does GDP growth even mean? It is perhaps no accident that GDP started to be widely used in the postwar era, when all classes did equally well, justifying the use of an average standard. GDP has far less relevance in the neoliberal era—the era that, ironically, puts it on a pedestal.

Another problem with GDP is that it fails to account for market failure. The most glaring example is of course environmental sustainability. GDP pays no attention to resource depletion or the degradation of nature. As long as an activity adds to current production, it is counted in GDP, despite the fact that it is hurting future generations—even in the narrow terms of GDP itself. More broadly, the fact that markets frequently fail means that an economy seeking to maximize the value of production is not maximizing the well-being of society. Such discrepancies include not only environmental devastation but government provision of important goods and services cheaply or for free, monopoly profits from corporate concentration, and the money spent on lobbying governments.[60] GDP has a real problem with measuring the value created by the public sector, as it implicitly assumes that government cannot add to the productivity of the economy or create value added. This devaluation of the public sector can implicitly undermine the value of government in people's eyes, laser-focused on GDP as currently measured.[61]

Another glaring flaw of GDP is that it excludes production that takes place outside of the marketplace. The most egregious example is work within the home—chiefly housework and childcare—work that is often backbreaking but not remunerated. GDP ignores unpaid care work, work typically done by women, work that is seen as "simultaneously priceless and worthless." Because this work is discounted, those who do it are rendered invisible and voiceless.[62]

This last point gets to the most fundamental problem with GDP: it doesn't account for the full extent of what accounts for a flourishing life. GDP doesn't include all "goods," and it does include some things that would be considered "bads." One way of putting it is that GDP measures wealth, and wealth is not well-being. I think this flaw was best expressed by Robert F. Kennedy. He wrote the following about GDP back in 1968:

Too much and for too long, we seemed to have surrendered personal excellence and community values in the mere accumulation of material things. Our Gross National Product, now, is over $800 billion dollars a year, but that Gross National Product—if we judge the United States of America by that—that Gross National Product counts air pollution and cigarette advertising, and ambulances to clear our highways of carnage. It counts special locks for our doors and the jails for the people who break them. It counts the destruction of the redwood and the loss of our natural wonder in chaotic sprawl. It counts napalm and counts nuclear warheads and armored cars for the police to fight the riots in our cities. It counts Whitman's rifle and Speck's knife, and the television programs which glorify violence in order to sell toys to our children. Yet the gross national product does not allow for the health of our children, the quality of their education or the joy of their play. It does not include the beauty of our poetry or the strength of our marriages, the intelligence of our public debate or the integrity of our public officials. It measures neither our wit nor our courage, neither our wisdom nor our learning, neither our compassion nor our devotion to our country, it measures everything in short, except that which makes life worthwhile.[63]

Kennedy is making an Aristotelian point—that what matters is less wealth than the goods that contribute to a flourishing life. This speech came a year after Pope Paul VI wrote *Populorum Progressio* and introduced the concept of integral human development. The problems with the focus on GDP have only been magnified in the neoliberal era, with the extension of neoclassical economics into ever more domains of life, with the belief that the only value is financial value.

There have been a number of attempts to come up with better measures of well-being: the so-called "Beyond GDP" movement. In this light, Joseph Stiglitz, Jean-Paul Fitoussi, and Martine Durand argue that no one indicator can replace GDP, and they call instead for a dashboard of indicators to account for such factors as material conditions, quality of life, inequalities, and sustainability. They call for better ways to measure factors such as economic insecurity and trust and social cohesion. The Sustainable Development Goals fit in here too, as they provide a more holistic account of societal well-being, linking economic progress, social inclusion, and protection of nature. The Organisation for Economic Co-operation and Development (OECD) has been leading the charge on the "Beyond GDP" agenda, coming up with its Better Life Initiative. This agenda constructs eleven dimensions of current well-being—income and wealth, jobs and earnings, housing, health status, work-life balance, education and skills, social connections, civic engagement and governance, environmental quality, personal security, and subjective well-being.

The fairly new area of subjective well-being is particularly important. In chapter 3, I discussed the *World Happiness Report* and how it assessed life satisfaction across countries based on six key factors: GDP per capita, health, social support, generosity, freedom to make life choices, and perceptions of corruption. I argued there that simply asking people what contributed to their well-being was revealing; it showed that social connection and a sense of meaning and purpose trumped income and GDP. Happier countries enjoy not only higher income per capita but stronger social support, higher levels of trust and generosity, and a greater ability for people to unfold capability free from impediments.[64]

Looking at the case study of the United States, Jeffrey Sachs has sought to explain the paradox of why such a rich country scores so poorly on happiness measures. While GDP per capita is still increasing, happiness is actually falling. Part of the problem is the old distributional problem—the gains in growth are accruing only to the very top. While the average income in the United States is $75,000, the average annual income of the working class—the adults in the lower half of the income distribution—is only $18,500.[65] The top 1 percent earns twice as much income as the entire working-class population. Since 1978, when neoliberalism began its ascendancy, the positions of the top 1 percent and the bottom half of the population basically switched places in terms of how income is distributed.[66] This huge disparity feeds into a broader trend; the main factors that determine happiness don't look so good in the United States. Sachs shows that a major factor has been the decline of trust and social cohesion; the all-important social and relational dimension of life is fraying around the edges.[67] Sachs's observation aligns with the decades-long work of Robert Putnam showing that social ties have been declining in recent decades, in line with both rising inequality—which creates distance between social classes—and the individualist solidarity-rebuking aspect of neoliberal ideology.[68] Sachs shows that the fall in trust maps the rise in inequality and that what plagues America is not an economic but a social crisis. As he puts it, "The United States offers a vivid portrait of a country looking for happiness in all the wrong places."[69]

The United States is also plagued by a health crisis, which has knock-on effects for happiness and well-being. Anne Case and Angus Deaton have documented that life expectancy for middle-aged white people started to reverse in the 1990s, a pattern not seen in other rich countries. Case and Deaton dub these deaths the "deaths of despair," as they can be traced back to such factors as suicides, alcoholism, and drug overdoses.[70] Jeffrey Sachs follows up on this thesis by arguing that the United States is suffering from a trio of health epidemics: obesity, substance abuse (alcohol and opioids), and mental illness (especially depression).[71] Elsewhere, he argues that Americans face an "epidemic of addictions"—not only to drugs and alcohol but to such activities as gambling, consuming unhealthy foods, shopping, digital media use, and sex.[72] All of this activity takes a toll on mental as well as physical health, and—this is crucial—happiness expert Richard Layard has argued that poor mental health is one of the leading causes of misery and unhappiness in the world.[73] Putting it bluntly, people are unhappy because they are blocked from living a thriving, flourishing life with strong community connections, and so they seek other sources of satisfaction, marked by instant gratification. The US experience here can be traced back in part to rising inequality, advertising-based consumerism whereby corporations manufacture needs and desires, and powerful corporations that profit from addictions and behavior that undermine genuine well-being.

Relatedly, psychologist Paul Verhaeghe has argued that neoliberal values foment a nexus of mass consumerism and competition for wealth and status, which in turn creates an unprecedented epidemic of stress, loneliness, and mental disorders across modern societies.[74] People who do not achieve success in the rat race are told it is their own fault, that they are dispensable. The old mediating institutions of civil society, as Robert Putnam has noted, have no real role in this world. They no longer protect people and give meaning. What ensues is a sea of increasingly disconnected and increasingly miserable people.

Michael Sandel makes a similar point about meritocracy, which he argues is the preeminent creed of the neoliberal era, on both the political Left and the political Right. The problem with this emphasis on meritocracy is that it implicitly assumes that people can rise in line with their natural talents and abilities. Value is once again reduced to market value. For the winners, this creed creates a sense of entitlement and a lack of solidarity but also the stress that comes from constant striving. For the losers, it creates a lack of self-esteem. As Sandel puts it, "The regime of merit exerts its tyranny in two directions at once. Among those who land on top, it induces anxiety, a debilitating perfectionism, and a meritocratic hubris that struggles to conceal a fragile self-esteem. Among those it leaves behind, it imposes a demoralizing, even humiliating sense of failure."[75]

If, as I have argued, neoliberal values are less in accord with human nature than are the values of Catholic social teaching, then this knock to well-being is hardly surprising. But nature abhors a vacuum, and Bruni argues that the economic system tries in vain to fill the void caused by market-generated loneliness and despair with virtual forms of community. But while real friendship matters for well-being, "virtual" friendship does not.[76] Virtual solutions to the basic human need for purpose and connection are at best unsatisfactory and, at worst, forums for the inculcation of competitive narcissism, hate, and antisocial behavior. Jean Twenge argues that a noted decline in happiness among adolescents, which is leading a bevy of mental health disorders and self-harm, can be traced to the rise in digital media.[77]

This theme was echoed by Pope Francis, who argued that digital media can lead to "addiction, isolation, and a gradual loss of contact with concrete reality, blocking the development of authentic interpersonal relationships." Even worse, "they do not really build community; instead, they tend to disguise and expand the very individualism that finds expression in xenophobia and in contempt for the vulnerable."[78]

Clearly, then, focusing on wealth and GDP misses key dimensions of what constitutes well-being. It is just the tiniest tip of the iceberg.

The Moral Diagnosis of Pope Francis

In this final section, I want to tie everything together by looking at the moral diagnosis of Pope Francis.[79] He indicts not only the modern economy but the flawed principles and faulty values on which it is based. In this, I will be quoting from *Laudato Si'*, *Evangelii Gaudium*, and *Fratelli Tutti* but also from his powerful speech to popular movements in Bolivia in 2015.[80]

The essence of the pope's diagnosis is that our global economic disorders can be traced to what he calls the technocratic paradigm in conjunction with a solidarity-rejecting individualism and faith in the magic of the free market to solve all problems. For Pope Francis, the problem can be boiled down to the "myths of a modernity grounded in a utilitarian mindset": individualism, unlimited progress, competition, consumerism, and the unregulated market.[81] This is his critique of the Enlightenment project applied to economics.

The technocratic paradigm, so dominant in our global economy today, invites people to think of all economic intervention solely in terms of utility, productivity, and efficiency—negating any inherent dignity or value either in the human person or in creation. It is the deployment of the principles of neoclassical economics to guide the economy and indeed ever-expanding domains of society. Pope Francis believes that this paradigm dominates both politics and economics. It justifies a narrow focus on economic growth, paying no heed to the limits of, or fallout from, such a strategy—even though, as Pope Francis notes, the growth fetish is too often "based on the lie that there is an infinite supply of the earth's goods."[82] And the technocratic paradigm leads businesses and financiers to believe that their only goal is to maximize profits.

This is an inherently confrontational vision, exalting human power and embracing an ethos of "possession, mastery and transformation."[83] The technocratic paradigm looks on creation as an external object to be manipulated and controlled, with no concern for its value or limits, because the only "value" it acknowledges is financial value, leading to what Pope Francis terms "modern anthropocentrism," predicated on a Promethean vision of mastery whereby human beings misunderstand their relationship to creation and their fellow human beings, thus causing them to "act against themselves."[84] This mentality prompts the pope to conclude that "immense technological development has not been accompanied by a development in human responsibility, values and conscience."[85]

When the technocratic paradigm is attached to this cult of unlimited human power, the result is a "relativism which sees everything as irrelevant unless it serves one's own immediate interests."[86] This mentality gives absolute priority to immediate convenience, driving people to treat their fellow human beings—and indeed all of creation—as mere objects to be taken advantage of. It elevates self-centeredness and self-absorption as the yardsticks of human interaction, leading to a "self-centered culture of instant gratification," which *Laudato Si'* sees as the root cause of so many social problems.[87]

This relativism has many practical manifestations in today's world. *Laudato Si'* lists some of them: forced labor, modern forms of slavery, abortion, the sexual exploitation of children, the abandonment of the elderly, human trafficking, the sale of organs, organized crime, the drug trade, and commerce in blood diamonds and endangered species. These might seem like extreme cases, but this same mindset is active in more mundane situations too. We see it, for example, in the "disordered desire to consume more than what is really necessary."[88] We see it in the mindset of those who put their full faith in "invisible forces of the market," regarding any harm done to society and to nature as acceptable collateral damage.[89]

All of this observation leads to Pope Francis's signature diagnosis: the throwaway culture, in which both people and things are used to satisfy gratification and discarded when they serve no further use. The throwaway culture gives rise to the ultimate economy of exclusion, in which "those excluded are no longer society's underside or its fringes or its disenfranchised—they are no longer even a part of it. The excluded are not the 'exploited' but the outcast, the 'leftovers.'"[90] They are merely an "afterthought . . . treated merely as collateral damage" and "frequently remain at the bottom of the pile."[91] And the same throwaway culture leads us to turn the environment into "debris, desolation and filth."[92] The throwaway culture drives a dagger through the heart of solidarity and sustainability.

In *Evangelii Gaudium*, Pope Francis asks us to say no to an economy of exclusion, the idolatry of money, a financial system that rules rather than serves, and inequality that spurns violence. He draws this out in blunt terms:

Just as the commandment "Thou shalt not kill" sets a clear limit in order to safeguard the value of human life, today we also have to say "thou shalt not" to an economy of exclusion and inequality. Such an economy kills. How can it be that it is not a news item when an elderly homeless person dies of exposure, but it is news when the stock market loses two points? . . . Today everything comes under the laws of competition and the survival of the fittest, where the powerful feed upon the powerless. As a consequence, masses of people find themselves excluded and marginalized: without work, without possibilities, without any means of escape.[93]

In Pope Francis's trenchant critique of free market ideology, his criticism centers not so much on the market itself but on this ideological baggage that weighs it down. Thus he condemns not the market but a "deified market" or a "magical conception of the market."[94] He rejects the assumption that self-interest serves the common good, seeing instead a "seedbed for collective selfishness."[95] He condemns "ideologies which defend the absolute autonomy of the marketplace and financial speculation" as a "new tyranny."[96] And he explicitly rejects the neo-liberal claims that market-spawned growth spreads to all: "In this context, some people continue to defend trickle-down theories which assume that economic growth, encouraged by a free market, will inevitably succeed in bringing about greater justice and inclusiveness in the world. This opinion, which has never been confirmed by the facts, expresses a crude and naïve trust in the goodness of those wielding economic power and in the sacralized workings of the prevailing economic system. Meanwhile, the excluded are still waiting."[97]

Pope Francis echoes this point in *Fratelli Tutti,* especially in the context of the COVID-19 pandemic:

The marketplace, by itself, cannot resolve every problem, however much we are asked to believe this dogma of neoliberal faith. Whatever the challenge, this impoverished and repetitive school of thought always offers the same recipes. Neoliberalism simply reproduces itself by resorting to the magic theories of "spillover" or "trickle"—without using the name—as the only solution to societal problems. There is little appreciation of the fact that the alleged "spillover" does not resolve the inequality that gives rise to new forms of violence threatening the fabric of society.[98]

In contrast with the much-touted "invisible hand," Pope Francis instead identifies an "invisible thread" linking all forms of exclusion—in the form of a system that "has imposed the mentality of profit at any price, with no concern for social exclusion of the destruction of nature."[99] He quotes the Church Father Saint

Basil, whom we met in chapter 1, who called money the "dung of the devil." He goes on to argue, "An unfettered pursuit of money rules. This is the 'dung of the devil.' The service of the common good is left behind. Once capital becomes an idol and guides people's decisions, once greed for money presides over the entire socioeconomic system, it ruins society, it condemns and enslaves men and women, it destroys human fraternity, it sets people against one another and, as we clearly see, it even puts at risk our common home, sister and mother earth."[100]

In another passage, he regards the zeal for money and possessions as a form of idolatry, echoing the Church Fathers: "The worship of the ancient golden calf (cf. Ex 32:1–35) has returned in a new and ruthless guise in the idolatry of money and the dictatorship of an impersonal economy lacking a truly human purpose."[101]

In his Bolivia speech, Pope Francis delivers his most searing indictment of this neoliberal ideology: "Let us say NO to an economy of exclusion and inequality, where money rules, rather than service. That economy kills. That economy excludes. That economy destroys Mother Earth."[102]

In line with what I have argued, the pope argues that these defects of neoliberal market ideology inculcate vice rather than virtue, undercutting solidarity and compassion for others, especially the poor:

> Almost without being aware of it, we end up being incapable of feeling compassion at the outcry of the poor, weeping for other people's pain, and feeling a need to help them, as though all this were someone else's responsibility and not our own. The culture of prosperity deadens us; we are thrilled if the market offers us something new to purchase. In the meantime all those lives stunted for lack of opportunity seem a mere spectacle; they fail to move us.[103]

The solution, says Pope Francis, is a different type of progress, one that is "healthier, more human, more social, more integral,"[104] escaping the confines of the technocratic paradigm and the bondage of individualism. Concretely, the pope calls for integral and sustainable human development: the combination of integral human development and an integral ecology that prizes intergenerational solidarity. It is for this reason that he endorsed the Sustainable Development Goals and called for "an integrated approach to combating poverty, restoring dignity to the excluded, and at the same time protecting nature."[105] He calls for a new "globalization of hope"; "a hope which springs up from peoples and takes root among the poor, must replace the globalization of exclusion and indifference."[106] And this shift entails what he regards as radical structural change.

In this context, Pope Francis repeatedly stresses the rights to the three "L's" of land, lodging, and labor, which he calls sacred rights. To these he adds the rights to education, healthcare, new technologies, artistic and cultural manifestations, communications, sport, and recreation; as he puts it: "No family without lodging, no rural worker without land, no laborer without rights, no people without sovereignty, no individual without dignity, no child without childhood, no young person without a future, no elderly person without a venerable old age."[107]

In this light, it is clear that change cannot entail merely technical or financial solutions. It needs to reinculcate the virtues of solidarity and gratuitousness into economic life. In the words of Pope Francis, "Many things have to change course, but it is we human beings above all who need to change. We lack an awareness of our common origin, of our mutual belonging, and of a future to be shared with everyone. This basic awareness would enable the development of new convictions, attitudes and forms of life."[108]

For this reason, Pope Francis calls for a "cultural revolution" that transforms our notion of progress and the values on which it is based.[109] Pope Francis's diagnosis of the flaws undermining the global economic model mirrors the criticisms of the spread of neoclassical economics, especially through the religion of neoliberalism. He is radical in the truest sense of the word, calling for a return to the "roots" of what economics is supposed to be about: human flourishing in the context of the common good. His analysis is proving prescient and prophetic.

To conclude this chapter, I have argued that the social democratic era was a unique period in human history. It was highly successful, and it owed much to the principles of Catholic social teaching, sometimes explicitly, sometimes implicitly. In the next chapter, I will delve more deeply into this kind of mixed economy that envisions a harmonious relationship between public and private sector, capital and labor, the real economy and the world of finance.

Notes

1. Arthur Brooks, "Confessions of a Catholic Convert to Capitalism," *America Magazine*, February 6, 2017.

2. Acemoglu and Robinson, *Why Nations Fail*.

3. Polanyi, *Great Transformation*.

4. Graeber, *Debt*.

5. See Bruni, *Civil Happiness*; Bruni and Zamagni, *Civil Economy*; and Zamagni, "Catholic Social Thought, Civil Economy, and the Spirit of Capitalism."

6. See Zamagni, "Catholic Social Thought, Civil Economy, and the Spirit of Capitalism," 61–73.

7. Zamagni, 71.

8. Bruni, *Civil Happiness*, 28.

9. Graeber, *Debt*, ch. 10.

10. Graeber, 282.

11. Graeber, ch. 11; Sachs, *Ages of Globalization*, ch. 6–7.

12. Sachs, *Ages of Globalization*, 118.

13. Kohli, *Imperialism and the Developing World*.

14. Rodrik, *Straight Talk on Trade*, 254–55.

15. Milanovic, *Capitalism Alone*, ch. 3.

16. Rodrik, *Straight Talk on Trade*, 131.

17. Keynes, "Economic Possibilities for Our Grandchildren."

18. Pomeranz, *Great Divergence*.

19. Sachs, *Age of Sustainable Development*, 76.

20. Sachs, *Age of Sustainable Development*; Sachs, *Ages of Globalization*.

21. Quoted in Mazzucato, *Value of Everything*, 192.

22. Mazzucato.

23. Gordon, *Rise and Fall of American Growth*.

24. *PDMP*, 4.

25. Keynes, *Economic Consequences of the Peace*, 268.

26. See Sachs, *Ages of Globalization*, 159.

27. Judt, *Ill Fares the Land*, 152.

28. Chappel, *Catholic Modern*.

29. See Shadle, *Interrupting Capitalism*.

30. Judt, *Postwar*.

31. See Arthur S. Meyers, "Social Justice Warrior: The Legacy of John A. Ryan," *Commonweal*, July 6, 2018.

32. US Bishops National Catholic War Council, "Program for Social Reconstruction."

33. See Levy and Temin, "Inequality and Institutions in 20th Century America."

34. Daly, "Structures of Virtue and Vice"; Shadle, *Interrupting Capitalism*.

35. Scheidel, *Great Leveler*, ch. 4.

36. Scheidel, 124.

37. Collier, *Future of Capitalism*.

38. Daly, *God's Economy*, 180.

39. Judt, *Ill Fares the Land*, 47.

40. Judt.

41. Stoller, *Goliath*.

42. Gordon, *Rise and Fall of American Growth*.

43. Saez and Zucman, *Triumph of Injustice*, ch. 8.

44. Saez and Zucman, ch. 8.

45. See Sachs, *Age of Sustainable Development*.

46. United Nations, *Millennium Development Goals Report 2015*.

47. United Nations.

48. See Alston, "Parlous State of Poverty Reduction."

49. World Bank, "Reversals of Fortune."

50. United Nations World Food Program, "COVID-19 Will Double Number of People Facing Food Crises unless Swift Action Is Taken."

51. Milanovic, *Global Inequality*.

52. Oxfam, "World's Billionaires Have More Wealth than 4.6 Billion People."

53. See Annett, "Our Common Responsibility for Our Common Home."

54. Rockström et al., "A Safe Operating Space for Humanity"; Sachs, *Age of Sustainable Development*.

55. See Annett et al., "Multireligious Consensus on the Ethics of Sustainable Development."

56. United Nations, "Transforming Our World."

57. Annett, "Ethical Actions to End Poverty."

58. There are computational complexities that we don't need to get into here.

59. Saez, "Striking It Richer."

60. See Stiglitz, Fitoussi, and Durand, *Measuring What Counts*.

61. Mazzucato, *Value of Everything*.

62. Firer Hinze, *Glass Ceilings and Dirt Floors*, 67–68.

63. Kennedy, "Remarks at the University of Kansas," n.p.

64. See Helliwell et al., *World Happiness Report 2020*.

65. Saez and Zucman, *Triumph of Injustice*, 4.

66. Saez and Zucman, ch. 1.

67. Sachs, "Restoring American Happiness."

68. See Putnam, *Bowling Alone*.

69. Sachs, "Restoring American Happiness," 183.

70. Case and Deaton, *Deaths of Despair and the Future of Capitalism*.

71. Sachs, "America's Health Crisis and the Easterlin Paradox."

72. Sachs, "Addiction and Unhappiness in America."

73. Layard, "Mental Illness Destroys Happiness and Is Costless to Treat."

74. Verhaeghe, *What about Me?*

75. Sandel, *Tyranny of Merit*, 183.

76. Luigino Bruni, "From Authenticity to Artificiality . . . and Back? Can the Market Heal the Wound It Inflicted?" *ABC Religion and Ethics*, July 2017; Helliwell and Huang, "Comparing the Happiness Effects of Real and On-line Friends."

77. Twenge, "Sad State of Happiness in the United States and the Role of Digital Media."

78. *FT*, 42.

79. This section draws heavily on Annett, "Connection, Disconnection, Reconnection"; and Annett, "Laudato Si' and Inclusive Solidarity."

80. Pope Francis, "Participation of the Second World Meeting of Popular Movements."

81. *LS*, 210.

82. *LS*, 106.

83. *LS*, 106.

84. *LS*, 115.

85. *LS*, 105.

86. *LS*, 122.

87. *LS*, 162.

88. *LS*, 123.

89. *LS*, 123.

90. *EG*, 53.

91. *LS*, 49.

92. *LS*, 161.

93. *EG*, 53.

94. *LS*, 56, 190.

95. *LS*, 204.

96. *EG*, 56.

97. *EG*, 54.

98. *FT*, 168.

99. Pope Francis, "Participation of the Second World Meeting of Popular Movements," n.p.

100. Pope Francis, "Participation," n.p.

101. *EG*, 55.

102. Pope Francis, "Participation of the Second World Meeting of Popular Movements," n.p.

103. *EG*, 54.

104. *LS*, 112.

105. *LS*, 139.

106. Pope Francis, "Participation of the Second World Meeting of Popular Movements," n.p.

107. Pope Francis, "Participation," n.p.

108. *LS*, 202.

109. *LS*, 114.

5

Who Does What?

The Roles of Government, Business, and Labor

In the last two chapters, I argued that the flawed values of neoclassical economics became ascendant over the past half century and gave rise to the political movement known as neoliberalism. Even though neoclassical economics is rooted in utilitarianism, which elevates the general welfare, it has been tempted by the siren song of libertarianism, which elevates individual freedom. This influence is rooted in strong beliefs pertaining to the ability of the unencumbered market to support the general welfare. In this chapter, I will explore the contours of an economy built on the scaffolding of Catholic social teaching. I will argue that both free market libertarianism and socialist collectivism violate the tenets of this teaching. I will then talk about what an economy centered on the common good implies for business, labor, and finance.

The Twin Rocks of Shipwreck

Back in 1931, in the encyclical *Quadragesimo Anno*, Pope Pius XI coined one of my favorite phrases in Catholic social teaching: the "twin rocks of shipwreck."[1] He was referring to the perils of libertarianism on the one hand and communism on the other. To explore the defects of both systems, he used Aquinas's twofold character of property: private ownership and common use.

For Pius, both libertarianism and communism violate the universal destination of goods, for opposite reasons. The problem with libertarian individualism is that it centers on "denying or minimizing the social and public character of the right of property," while collectivism is all about "ejecting or minimizing the private and individual character of this same right."[2] Collectivism suppresses private ownership in favor of common use, while libertarianism suppresses common use in favor of private ownership. Collectivism elevates duties and neglects rights, while libertarianism upholds rights and neglects duties. Collectivism expresses only distributive justice, while libertarianism expresses only commutative justice.

It helps to define terms. The monikers of socialism and libertarianism are frequently bandied about, often as straw men and sometimes as mere insults. For my purposes, I will define socialism or collectivism as the Soviet-style collective ownership of the means of production, something very different from the social democracy discussed and praised in the previous chapter, which is predicated on a mixed economy with distinct roles for both public and private sectors. Social democracy supports prudent redistribution and regulation but not blanket state control of industry. Libertarianism, in contrast, is a political philosophy predicated on self-ownership; you own yourself and your labor, therefore you are entitled to the fruits of your labor.[3] In one sense, the philosophy goes back to the individualistic vision of Locke, who insisted that you were entitled to what you produced when mixed with your own labor. But libertarianism is a more extreme version of this classical form of liberalism. Libertarians argue that coercion by the state amounts to violence and theft. Libertarianism elevates human freedom as the greatest good, denying the very existence of a common good. This, of course, is *negative* freedom—freedom from coercion—and not the *positive* freedom to flourish and develop your capacities in an Aristotelian sense. Libertarianism boils down to the maximum extension of individual choice, which helps explain why it fits so well with neoclassical economics, in spite of the latter's utilitarian roots.[4]

Catholic social teaching opposes the twin rocks of shipwreck because they violate its core principles. It repudiates communism because it rejects the notion of class warfare and its implicit support for violence; the suppression of individual freedom, human dignity, and agency, as well as private ownership and initiative; and the reduction of the notion of the good to the material domain. Catholic Social Thought rejects individualism because this philosophy elevates private ownership as an absolute right, competition as guiding economic life, and autonomy as divorced from the common good. Just like communist collectivism, individualism restricts well-being to the economic and social realm. Both offer a utopian vision: one from capitalism, one from the disappearance of capitalism.

Some of the strongest language against libertarianism comes from Pius XI. He refers to a "poisoned spring" and an "evil individualistic spirit." It's worth quoting him in full, as his words ring as true today as they did when he wrote almost a century ago:

> The right ordering of economic life cannot be left to a free competition of forces. For from this source, as from a poisoned spring, have originated and spread all the errors of individualist economic teaching. Destroying through forgetfulness or ignorance the social and moral character of economic life, it held that economic life must be considered and treated as altogether free from and independent of public authority, because in the market, i.e., in the free struggle of competitors, it would have a principle of self direction which governs it much more perfectly than would the intervention of any created intellect. But free competition, while justified and certainly useful provided it is kept within certain limits, clearly cannot direct economic life—a truth which the outcome of the application in practice of the tenets of this evil individualistic spirit has more than sufficiently demonstrated. Therefore, it is most necessary that economic life be again subjected to and governed by a true and effective directing principle.[5]

Pope Paul VI, writing in the late 1960s and early 1970s, detected the first inklings of the rise of neoliberalism and was disturbed by it. Here is what he has to say:

> However, certain concepts have somehow arisen out of these new conditions and insinuated themselves into the fabric of human society. These concepts present profit as the chief spur to economic progress, free competition as the guiding norm of economics, and private ownership of the means of production as an absolute right, having no limits nor concomitant social obligations. This unbridled liberalism paves the way for a particular type of tyranny, rightly condemned by Our predecessor Pius XI, for it results in the "international imperialism of money." Such improper manipulations of economic forces can never be condemned enough; let it be said once again that economics is supposed to be in the service of man.[6]

This quotation is from his 1967 encyclical, *Populorum Progressio*. In a separate document called *Octogesima Adveniens*, written in 1971, Pope Paul VI draws similar conclusions, referring to the early spring of neoliberalism as a reflection of "erroneous autonomy." The freedom of libertarianism is not true freedom, as is made clearer by quoting him in full:

We are witnessing a renewal of the liberal ideology. This current asserts itself both in the name of economic efficiency, and for the defense of the individual against the increasingly overwhelming hold of organizations, and as a reaction against the totalitarian tendencies of political powers. Certainly, personal initiative must be maintained and developed. But do not Christians who take this path tend to idealize liberalism in their turn, making it a proclamation in favor of freedom? They would like a new model, more adapted to present-day conditions, while easily forgetting that at the very root of philosophical liberalism is an erroneous affirmation of the autonomy of the individual in his activity, his motivation and the exercise of his liberty. Hence, the liberal ideology likewise calls for careful discernment on their part.[7]

Pope Francis also takes on this erroneous notion of economic freedom, noting that it is frequently a mask for economic power combined with hypocrisy: "To ensure economic freedom from which all can effectively benefit, restraints occasionally have to be imposed on those possessing greater resources and financial power. To claim economic freedom while real conditions bar many people from actual access to it, and while possibilities for employment continue to shrink, is to practise a doublespeak which brings politics into disrepute."[8]

Most popes have similarly condemned communism, that other rock of shipwreck. The most poignant analysis is surely that of Pope John Paul II in *Centesimus Annus*, penned in 1991 after the fall of the Berlin Wall and the Soviet system. He himself grew up under the communist yoke, so he was all too aware of its grave deficiencies and evils. His criticism focuses on what communism does to the human being, how it denies their agency and dignity, reducing them to a mere cog in a socioeconomic machine. Here is how the pope describes it:

Socialism considers the individual person simply as an element, a molecule within the social organism, so that the good of the individual is completely subordinated to the functioning of the socio-economic mechanism. Socialism likewise maintains that the good of the individual can be realized without reference to his free choice, to the unique and exclusive responsibility which he exercises in the face of good or evil. Man is thus reduced to a series of social relationships, and the concept of the person as the autonomous subject of moral decision disappears, the very subject whose decisions build the social order. From this mistaken conception of the person there arise both a distortion of law, which defines the sphere of the exercise of freedom, and an opposition to private property. A person who is deprived of something he can call "his own," and of the possibility of earning a living through his own initiative, comes to depend on the social machine and on those who control it. This makes it much more difficult for him to recognize his dignity as a person, and hinders progress towards the building up of an authentic human community.[9]

John Paul recognized the enticement of communism, given the mistreatment of the working classes under capitalism, but he also followed in the tradition began by Leo XIII in *Rerum Novarum* by arguing that "the remedy would prove worse than the sickness."[10]

A few points are in order. First, some Catholics have attempted to downplay the strong condemnation of libertarianism by arguing that communism was far worse. This argument has never made much sense. For a start, a rock of shipwreck is a rock of shipwreck; it serves little purpose to argue which one is bigger and more jagged. Second, this argument misses the point that the criticism of communism is inseparable from the criticism of libertarianism: both are utopian visions that promise a rosy future solely in material terms, and yet, like all utopian visions, both ultimately fail to deliver. Both conceive of the human being solely as an economic agent. And both reject the core principles of solidarity and subsidiarity.

I will be spending more time critiquing libertarianism, though, for a simple reason: while communism is largely dead and gone, libertarianism—dressed up in neoliberal policy prescriptions—is alive and kicking. So it is especially important to delve deeper into its defects.[11]

The first problem with libertarianism is that it explicitly denies the common good, challenging both "common" and "good." For libertarianism, "common" entails coercion and so must be ruled out. For libertarian philosopher Robert Nozick, anything more than a minimal state "violates persons' rights not to be forced to do certain things, and is unjustified."[12] Going further, he asserts, "There is no social entity with a good that undergoes some sacrifice for its own good. There are only individual people, different individual people, with their own individual lives. Using one of these people for the benefit of others, uses him and benefits the others. Nothing more."[13] This argument, of course, presupposes a purely negative form of freedom, not the freedom to flourish by developing the basic capacities needed for integral human development. It fails to acknowledge that people who lack these capacities are themselves frequently victims of coercion. Many libertarians argue that they are promoting nonviolence, but this argument makes little sense in light of their worldview and its implications for the well-being of people.

Likewise, libertarians take issue with the word "good." For them, freedom is the ability to do as you wish, as long as you do not violate the boundaries of another person or their property, so there can be no such thing as a good that all agree on. As libertarian economist Friedrich Hayek puts it, "Freedom granted only when it is known beforehand that its effects will be beneficial is not freedom."[14] We can see clearly why this appeals to the paradigm of neo-classical economics, given its insistence on the maximal extension of subjective individual choice. And yet in the Catholic tradition, with its roots in Aristotle and Aquinas, the freedom to choose something bad is not true freedom. This freedom is regarded as an "erroneous" form of autonomy—because it is not necessarily directed toward the common good, integral human development, or integral ecology. It does not prize virtues such as solidarity, reciprocity, and gratuitousness.

In a perceptive criticism, Pope Francis laid out the problems with this Nozick-Hayek position:

> A common feature of this fallacious paradigm is that it minimizes the common good, that is, "living well," a "good life" in the community framework, and exalts the selfish ideal that deceptively proposes a "beautiful life." If individualism affirms that it is only the individual who gives value to things and interpersonal relationships, and so it is only the individual who decides what is good and what is bad, then libertarianism, today in fashion, preaches that to establish freedom and individual responsibility, it is necessary to resort to the idea of "self-causation." Thus libertarian individualism denies the validity of the common good because on the one hand it supposes that the very idea of "common" implies the constriction of at least some individuals, and the other that the notion of "good" deprives freedom of its essence. The radicalization of individualism in libertarian and therefore anti-social terms leads to the conclusion that everyone has the "right" to expand as far as his power allows, even at the expense of the exclusion and marginalization of the most vulnerable majority.[15]

Likewise, in *Fratelli Tutti*, Pope Francis condemns this rootless individualism and the erroneous view of autonomy:

> Liberty becomes nothing more than a condition for living as we will, completely free to choose to whom or what we will belong, or simply to possess or exploit. This shallow understanding has little to do with the richness of a liberty directed above all to love. . . . Individualism does not make us more free, more equal, more fraternal. The mere sum of individual interests is not capable of generating a better world for the whole human family.

Nor can it save us from the many ills that are now increasingly globalized. Radical individualism is a virus that is extremely difficult to eliminate.[16]

Daniel Finn lists some further problems with libertarianism from the Catholic perspective: its only form of justice is commutative justice; it sees justice as a virtue only of individuals, denying problems with systems and structures of sin; it assumes absolute property ownership, denying the universal destination of goods; and it assumes markets are morally neutral, ignoring the importance of seasoning them with solidarity, reciprocity, and gratuitousness.[17]

All in all, Catholic social teaching seems a little bit schizophrenic on capitalism. It endorses a market economy within moral limits, underpinned by the appropriate virtues, and oriented toward the common good. It acknowledges a right to economic initiative.[18] But it rejects libertarianism as a philosophy, the view of human nature that underpins neoclassical economics, and many of the policy prescriptions that stem from neoliberalism. Given this, can we even say that the Catholic Church endorses capitalism? John Paul II posed that question and offered a typically nuanced answer:

> If by "capitalism" is meant an economic system which recognizes the fundamental and positive role of business, the market, private property and the resulting responsibility for the means of production, as well as free human creativity in the economic sector, then the answer is certainly in the affirmative, even though it would perhaps be more appropriate to speak of a "business economy," "market economy" or simply "free economy." But if by "capitalism" is meant a system in which freedom in the economic sector is not circumscribed within a strong juridical framework which places it at the service of human freedom in its totality, and which sees it as a particular aspect of that freedom, the core of which is ethical and religious, then the reply is certainly negative.[19]

This nuanced answer perhaps creates as many questions as answers, especially since John Paul goes on to talk about the exclusion of vast multitudes, echoing some of the criticisms I made in the last chapter. I also argued in the last chapter that social democracy owed much to, and remains compatible with, the principles of Catholic social teaching. This point is also endorsed by Pope Benedict XVI: "Democratic socialism managed to fit within the two existing models as a welcome counterweight to the radical liberal positions, which it developed and corrected. . . . In many respects, democratic socialism was and is close to Catholic social doctrine and has in any case made a remarkable contribution to the formation of a social consciousness."[20]

This discussion so far has been pretty theoretical. In the next sections, I will tease out the implications of these statements about capitalism, the market economy, and democratic socialism to explore the appropriate roles of government, business, finance, and labor.

Role of Government

For libertarianism and neoliberalism, the best government is the smallest government. From these perspectives, the boot of the state treads on individual liberty and suffocates the natural potential of the private sector to unleash innovation and growth. These traditions envisage an extremely limited role for government—to provide the basic rule of law that allows private actors to maximize wealth. Hence the support for deregulation, privatization, watering down of antitrust laws, and paring down the welfare state. To be fair, neoclassical economics is more nuanced when it comes to government's role. Since the standard is efficiency, government intervention is permitted when it enhances efficiency. Public goods are a clear example. These are goods that are nonrival and nonexcludable. Nonrival means that the good in question can be used by more than one person at the same time without diminishing it. Nonexcludable means that people who do not pay for the good cannot be prevented from using it. The private sector has a hard time providing public goods as people will free ride—they can get the benefit while having no incentive to pay for it. In these cases, public provision is justifiable. Examples of public goods include national defense, public sanitation, and scientific knowledge.

Another category of goods subject to market failure is common resources. These are goods that are rival but nonexcludable. In other words, one person using this kind of resource reduces the ability of others to benefit from it. The classic example is environmental goods such as air, water, and forests. In a free market, common resources are subject to what is known as the tragedy of the commons— people tend to overconsume as they do not take account of their activity on others. This is a classic example of what economics deems an externality, the notion that people engage in an activity that affects the well-being of others but neither pay the cost nor receive the benefit. In particular, common resources take the form of a negative externality. The market outcome turns out to be socially inefficient, as too much of the good is produced and consumed. Think of pollution or climate change. As a result, government can legitimately intervene to make sure producers pay the full cost—for example, through a tax on polluting activities.

Catholic social teaching offers a different perspective. It starts from the premise that in the words of Pope John XXIII, "As for the State, its whole raison d'être is the realization of the common good in the temporal order. It cannot, therefore, hold aloof from economic matters."[21] As John Paul II phrased it, the market should be "appropriately controlled by the forces of society and by the State, so as to guarantee that the basic needs of the whole of society are satisfied."[22] Or, as Pope Leo XIII wrote way back in 1891, "Whenever the general interest or any particular class suffers, or is threatened with harm, which can in no other way be met or prevented, the public authority must step in to deal with it."[23] The bottom line is that the common good in the economic sphere is the proper domain of government. Government is not merely the outcome of a social contract between independent agents, but a natural entity ordered to the common good. You can see the link back to Aristotle and Aquinas.

There is nuance, however. Remember that the suppression of individual initiative is condemned alongside hands-off libertarianism. In Catholic social teaching, the role of the state is both activist and circumscribed—activist, because the common good is higher than the good achieved by the individual; circumscribed, because human dignity requires that the autonomy and agency of subsidiary associations be respected. In the words of Pope John Paul II, "The State has the duty of watching over the common good and of ensuring that every sector of social life, not excluding the economic one, contributes to achieving that good, while respecting the rightful autonomy of each sector."[24]

Pope John Paul II argues that the principles of solidarity and subsidiarity ensure that the government serves the common good in the economic domain both directly (solidarity) and indirectly (subsidiarity): "Indirectly and according to the principle of subsidiarity, by creating favourable conditions for the free exercise of economic activity, which will lead to abundant opportunities for employment and sources of wealth. Directly and according to the principle of solidarity, by defending the weakest, by placing certain limits on the autonomy of the parties who determine working conditions, and by ensuring in every case the necessary minimum support for the unemployed worker."[25]

In terms of solidarity, the government is called on to ensure the provision of the basic goods necessary for integral human development, including income security, decent jobs, nutrition, healthcare, education, housing, and a sustainable environment. In other words, it is called on to implement the Sustainable Development Goals, which lay out the contours of the common good in its material dimension.

Two points are important: First, many goods cannot be provided by the market and so fall under the jurisdiction of the state to provide. Second, based on the principles of the universal destination of goods and the preferential option for the poor, the government has a special duty to look after the interest of the poor and marginalized. On the first point, Pope John Paul II says this clearly: "There are many human needs which find no place on the market. It is a strict

duty of justice and truth not to allow fundamental human needs to remain un-
satisfied, and not to allow those burdened by such needs to perish."[26] And again,
"Here we find a new limit on the market: there are collective and qualitative
needs which cannot be satisfied by market mechanisms. There are important
human needs which escape its logic. There are goods which by their very nature
cannot and must not be bought or sold."[27]

In terms of the second point, the duties toward the poor, Pope Leo XIII said
this clearly back in 1891: "The richer class have many ways of shielding themselves, and stand less in need of help from the State; whereas the mass of the poor
have no resources of their own to fall back upon, and must chiefly depend upon
the assistance of the State. And it is for this reason that wage-earners, since they
mostly belong in the mass of the needy, should be specially cared for and protected by the government."[28] So Catholic social teaching argues that the goods
necessary for human flourishing must be provided and that the poor in particular must have access to them. The state must take an active role, in line with
solidarity. Catholic teaching therefore implies a role for redistribution, which it
argues ought to be financed from progressive taxes, with the burden "propor-
tioned to the capacity of the people contributing."[29] As Pope Benedict XVI puts
it, "Grave imbalances are produced when economic action, conceived merely as
an engine for wealth creation, is detached from political action, conceived as a
means for pursuing justice through redistribution."[30]

But must the state always provide these goods directly? Not necessarily. There
are some goods I believe belong to the state—public goods, for example. But
what about vital goods like health and education? I would argue that the government must make sure these goods are provided to all, even if outsourced to the
private sector. These goods form the core of economic rights; that is, the state
has a duty to make sure they are provided. While private education certainly has
a crucial role to play, in line with subsidiarity, prudence calls for the state to take
a direct role in the provision of basic and free education at least to secondary
level. Regarding healthcare, the virtue of solidarity calls for it to be provided to
all. As Pope John Paul II put it, "Medical assistance should be easily available for
workers, and that as far as possible it should be cheap or even free of charge."[31]
He is effectively calling for universal healthcare. There are essentially two ways
to provide this. One is for the state to act as the insurer; this is the single-payer
system whereby everyone pays a contribution and everyone gets to benefit from
the healthcare system. This system is regarded as efficient, as it pools risks over
the largest number of people and doesn't need to waste money on vast amounts
of paperwork and marketing.

But there are other ways to do it. The most common is a system of universal
private insurance. Note first that an unregulated private sector will not be able

to provide healthcare for all. To maximize profits, private insurers would seek to attract only the healthiest people, leaving the old and the sick out in the cold. To make the private system work, the government needs to extend the hand of regulation, making sure that insurers cannot discriminate based on health risk. It also needs to insist that all buy into insurance, as otherwise the costs would skyrocket. And as a third pillar, government will sometimes directly subsidize the cost of healthcare for the poor. Some countries choose this route, and in the United States it forms the basic contours of the Affordable Care Act, also known as Obamacare. This route is essentially solidarity in action—young and healthy people agree to subsidize the old and the infirm (either by paying higher premiums or higher tax contributions) knowing that they will get the help they need when they fall ill. In the US debate on healthcare, we have seen a basic repudiation of this principle of solidarity. People complain about this cross-subsidization and resist the "individual mandate" to purchase health insurance on the grounds that it infringes on their freedom, libertarian "erroneous autonomy" in action. The framing of the healthcare debate has become increasingly couched in the language of consumer choice and freedom rather than in solidarity and compassionate care, a crystal-clear example of the neoclassical paradigm undercutting virtue in public life.

In this last chapter, I talked about the welfare state as it emerged in the social democratic era. I noted that it was based on the principle of reciprocal obligation, a universalism whereby everybody chipped in and everybody benefited. As I noted, the problem arises when the welfare state morphs into a way of delivering basic support to the poor, detached from this sense of universal reciprocity, leading to stigma and causing the middle classes to detach themselves from a sense of solidarity rooted in the common good. As noted by Pope John Paul II, the welfare state can also turn into a "social assistance state" marked by dependence on bureaucratic structures, erasing the agency and dignity of the recipient.[32]

This danger can be remedied by making sure that solidarity is always twinned with subsidiarity. As Pope Benedict XVI put it, "The principle of subsidiarity must remain closely linked to the principle of solidarity and vice versa, since the former without the latter gives way to social privatism, while the latter without the former gives way to paternalist social assistance that is demeaning to those in need."[33] To avoid this dependency trap, social benefits should ideally be universal and tied to individual risks, and subsidiarity should be respected by having mediating institutions that are closer to the people deliver the benefits. As I noted in the last chapter, this system is in place in countries such as Germany. The problem is that in certain circumstances, solidarity without subsidiarity can collapse on itself.

Subsidiarity, of course, refers to the notion that action should be taken at the lowest level possible and the highest level necessary. It is not about the size of government but its scope. Subsidiarity is not just about giving autonomy to lower-level institutions; it involves actively helping them develop their capacities. As Catholic social teaching notes, economic life should be "subjected to and governed by a true and effective directing principle."[34]

Subsidiarity, in other words, means the state needs to regulate the market. As Polanyi argued, all market institutions are underpinned by a wide array of rules, policies, cultural norms, and shared values. The question to ask is, Do the basic rules of the game support or impede integral development and the common good? For example, how do they deal with such questions as the reach of property rights, the degree to which market power is tolerated, the contractual determination of what can be bought and sold and on what terms, the rules governing bankruptcy, and the way rules are enforced?[35] These factors all relate to the application of subsidiarity oriented toward the common good. In this vein, subsidiarity calls for a proper balancing of the scales, with government support for what economist John Kenneth Galbraith called institutions of countervailing power—including unions, small businesses, consumer organizations, cooperatives, and regional and local banks.[36] When setting the rules of the game, therefore, government should strive to respect, assist, and promote the interests of the wider inhabitants of the civil economy.[37]

In some cases, subsidiarity calls on the government to provide the goods directly. I have already hinted at this in discussing healthcare, where solidarity insists on a hands-on approach by the government. But subsidiarity comes into play too as the government needs to either take on the role of the insurer or properly regulate private insurers so that the good in question can be attained (in this case, affordable healthcare for all).

The same argument based on subsidiarity applies to public goods like national defense and public sanitation. Most would agree that governments should ideally provide public goods as the private sector generally will not. This is an area where Catholic social teaching overlaps with neoclassical economics, but the motivation is different—for Catholic social teaching, it is based on subsidiarity, the appropriate locus of action being the state level. Likewise, neoclassical economics provides a motivation for government intervention in the area of negative externalities such as the overexploitation of common environmental resources like clean water, biodiversity, and a healthy climate. In these cases, government can legitimately intervene to make sure people pay the full social cost of their economic activities. But with neoclassical economics, there tends to be a presumption that market solutions are best. This is based on the notion that everything has a price and that the externality can be "internalized" by charging for it—for example, by taxing pollution or implementing tradable licenses to pollute.[38] But the answer, from the point of view of Catholic social teaching, is not necessarily to put a price on common resources but rather to intervene based on the principle of subsidiarity and lay down regulations to support the common good. Plus, as Samuel Bowles would put it, there is a need to make sure that economic incentives promote rather than hinder the values of good citizenship.[39]

This point gets to another dimension of government rules, regulations, and policies that neoclassical economics simply cannot envisage: whether they support or impede virtue.[40] These rules, regulations, and policies set by government can change behavior not only through financial incentives or compulsion but also by changing intrinsic motivation and social norms. Legal theorist Lynn Stout has argued that law and regulation can promote prosocial norms by signaling what conduct is appropriate, influencing the behavior of those with whom we interact and educating us on how personal choices affect others.[41] In one sense, this view of regulation harks back to Aquinas's view that the purpose of law is not merely to enforce compliance but also to help make people virtuous through force of habit. This logic can easily be extended to government policies that affect incentives. For example, a decision to look lightly on the financial sector's risk-taking, malfeasance, or even criminality might not only create incentives for more of this behavior but actually inculcate social norms suggesting that this behavior is not inappropriate. Similarly, a cut in upper-income tax rates might not only create incentives for CEOs and top business executives to award themselves higher pay but actively undermine an older social norm that regarded excessive pay gaps as imprudent and unjust.

Before concluding this section, let me ask a basic question: Does Catholic social teaching allow a direct role for the government in productive activity? The answer is yes but only in specific circumstances. As Pope John XXIII put it, public ownership of productive goods is permitted when those enterprises "carry with them a power too great to be left to private individuals without injury to the community at large."[42] Again, the consideration is based on a prudential application of the principle of subsidiarity. John Paul II also addressed this question, arguing that the state can take on a "substitute function" "when social sectors or business systems are too weak or are just getting under way, and are not equal to the task at hand."[43] Yet this intervention should be brief and tied to the exigencies of the common good.

A related question is whether the challenges of the modern era call for a larger role for government. John XXIII argued, perhaps too optimistically, that advances in scientific knowledge and technology allow the government to be better able to reduce imbalances between different parts of the economy, different regions in a country, or different countries. He also argued that it "puts into the hands of public authority a greater means for limiting fluctuations in the economy and for providing effective measures to prevent the recurrence of mass unemployment."[44] Penned in 1961, this ethos reflects that time, the optimism of the social democratic era influenced by Keynesian economic management. Perhaps we need to rekindle this sense of optimism in the ability of government to smooth out dysfunctions in the economy. Benedict XVI also argued in favor of a larger role for government in the modern era but for a more pessimistic reason: because the destabilizing forces of globalization require a firmer hand of the state at the rudder.[45] He also fretted about the "downsizing of social security systems as the price to be paid for seeking greater competitive advantage in the global market, with consequent grave danger for the rights of workers, for fundamental human rights and for the solidarity associated with the traditional forms of the social State."[46] So clearly, any diminishing role of government in the neoliberal era is met with disappointment, not praise. And looking forward, current challenges point once again to a strengthened role of government. One obvious role lies in protecting against, and responding to, public health emergencies such as the COVID-19 pandemic. And as will be discussed in chapter 7, solving the climate crisis calls for a dramatically stepped-up role for government, to shift the economy on the path of zero carbon emissions.

My main argument in this section has been that the twin principles of solidarity and subsidiarity provide a more powerful and fruitful way to assess the role of government in the economy than what is offered by neoclassical economics.

Role of Business

It should be clear by now that Catholic social teaching is not opposed to business or the market economy. Indeed, as Pope John Paul II noted, the business economy has many positive dimensions. And while Pope Francis has been trenchant in his criticism of neoliberalism and the ideology of the market, he too has positive things to say about the role of business. In *Evangelii Gaudium*, he noted that "business is a vocation, and a noble vocation, provided that those engaged in it see themselves challenged by a greater meaning in life; this will enable them truly to serve the common good by striving to increase the goods of this world and to make them more accessible to all."[47] He followed up with this point in *Laudato Si'* by noting that "business is a noble vocation, directed to producing wealth and improving our world. It can be a fruitful source of prosperity for the areas in which it operates, especially if it sees the creation of jobs as an essential part of its service to the common good."[48]

The implication is that business must always orient its activities toward the common good, not just by producing wealth but distributing it fairly. Note that this practice is antithetical to the way business is understood today. Back in 1970, Milton Friedman argued that the only role of business is to maximize profits, equated with shareholder value.[49] This view has become widely accepted, not least because it dominates the teaching in mainstream business schools. When Luigi Zingales argued that business schools incubated criminality, he was talking about the maximization of shareholder value. Because nothing else matters, business is supposed to do whatever it takes to maximize profits, and so firms will even weigh up the costs and benefits of illicit activities, figuring out if the gain in profits outweighs any potential fine from governments. Thus chemical plants will pollute with impunity, car companies will install cheat devices to feign compliance with emissions standards, and large banks will engage in all kind of crooked behavior. In each case, the fines and penalties are deemed small enough to undertake these activities. They are just the costs of doing business.

Maximizing shareholder value has been used to justify enormous compensation to CEOs and top executives, including by tying their compensation to stock prices. The result, as documented by Mariana Mazzucato, has been a decisive shift toward short-termism.[50] Instead of investing in the long-term potential of the firm, on innovation and research and development, business managers focus exclusively on short-term stock prices, using cash instead to buy back stock and increase its price. So yet again, the principle of maximizing shareholder value fails on its own terms; rather than unleashing productivity, it undermines it. Managers and shareholders engage in an "unholy alliance" to extract value from the company, hurting workers and other stakeholders.[51] As a result, business investment in the United States is at its lowest level in sixty years.[52]

It wasn't always like this. Before the ascent of Friedman and his zealous disciples, companies believed that they were beholden to a variety of different stakeholders, including workers, customers, and their communities. Mazzucato provides a useful anecdote by looking at what the presidents of IBM stated were their goals pre- and post-Friedman. In the early 2000s, the CEO declared the goal was to double earnings per share over five years, But in 1968, IBM's CEO laid out a threefold goal: respect for employees, commitment to customer service, and achieving excellence.[53] This is just one anecdote, but it symbolizes the dramatic change in mentality. Colin Mayer argues that the corporation has existed, in one form or another, for thousands of years, and has always contained an element of public purpose. It is only in the most recent years that "we have witnessed the retreat of the multi-purposed, publicly-oriented corporation into a single-focused self-interested entity."[54]

Mayer notes that the origin of the word "company" is the Latin *cum panis*, or "breaking bread together," an etymology that relates to how Catholic social teaching views the corporation—as a "community of persons" oriented toward the common good. From this perspective, all actors in society share the same common end, the mutual flourishing of all. Society deploys the virtue of prudence to deliberate on which functions belong to the public sector and which belong to the private sector. But it is always about how the common good is best served. Here is how John Paul II puts it:

> The purpose of a business firm is not simply to make a profit, but is to be found in its very existence as a community of persons who in various ways are endeavouring to satisfy their basic needs, and who form a particular group at the service of the whole of society. Profit is a regulator of the life of a business, but it is not the only one; other human and moral factors must also be considered which, in the long term, are at least equally important for the life of a business.[55]

In this vein, the Vatican produced a short document called *Vocation of the Business Leader* to tease out the implications of how business can practically serve the common good.[56] The document's starting point is that business should be seen as a community of persons that "joins together people's gifts, talents, energies and skills to serve the needs of others." The document argues that business serves the common good in three separate dimensions: *good goods, good work,* and *good wealth*—a trifecta that provides an excellent lens through which to analyze the role of business.

In terms of *good goods*, business is called on to meet human needs through the creation and development of goods and services. As the document puts it, business serves the common good by creating "goods that are truly good and services that truly serve." Thus, to be legitimate, business must produce goods with social value that contribute to human flourishing. And yet neoclassical economics is all about the maximization of subjective preferences, which should not be judged. We hear this argument from business all the time: "I am just giving the consumer what they want."

But when we think about it—and we typically don't—this position is less clear than it seems. There are plenty of activities that few people would want to flourish. Take the drug trade, for example. This is a billion-dollar industry, and yet it creates much chaos and carnage, in the supplying communities, trade networks, and in the lives of addicts. Only the most ardent libertarian supports the complete liberalization of all drugs. Most recognize that the addictive qualities of drugs such as cocaine and heroin destroy lives, families, and communities.

The same argument can be made with regard to prostitution. The neoclassical paradigm would argue that mutual needs are being satisfied, so there's no issue with prostitution. Libertarianism would say the same thing, based on freedom. But does prostitution really contribute to human flourishing and integral human development? Is it not more about degrading sexuality for the purposes of instantaneous gratification? As with the selling of kidneys, does it not often entail an element of coercion, as poor and vulnerable women are the ones most likely to be driven to sell their bodies? The same holds for pornography, another highly profitable billion-dollar industry. Again, if preferences are inviolable, then there is no problem. People are satisfying their preferences, and the economy is generating wealth. But it is difficult to make the argument that pornography contributes to human flourishing. I would argue that it degrades rather than perfects who we are as human beings. What about the arms trade, one of the most profitable in the world, and yet the cause of so much violence and misery?

We can make the same kind of argument against products that addict, including various fatty, sugary, and salty foodstuffs engineered never to satiate; casinos offering illusive gains to players but massive profits to the owners, often impoverishing addicts and destroying their families; or more mundane addictive goods such as alcohol and tobacco. Some prudence is required here. Alcohol, despite its addictive qualities and tendency to ruin lives and families, may contribute to flourishing to the extent that it facilitates social interaction. And as Aquinas recognized a long time ago, not all bads should be banned by law, as the downsides could very well exceed the benefits. A much needed but practically non-existent debate centers on precisely what goods contribute to integral human development and how. Interestingly, Frank Knight, one of the founders of neoclassical economics a century ago, understood this point well. "Ethically," he said, "the creation of the right wants is more important than want satisfaction."[57]

Once we start thinking in these terms, a lot of goods and services become compromised. Certainly, the mighty fossil fuel industry—oil, coal, and gas—claims to support human flourishing by providing needed energy but in reality is decimating the very potential for future flourishing by causing climate change. Another problematic area relates to consumerist culture and the pursuit of luxury goods. How much of our GDP is spent on advertising and marketing, an attempt to entice people to spend as much and as often as possible, even when they clearly don't need the goods and services being offered to them? Pope Francis cautions against what he dubs "extreme consumerism" that manifests in a "whirlwind of needless buying and spending."[58] This echoes Pope John Paul II, who argued against consumerism "when people are ensnared in a web of false and superficial gratifications rather than being helped to experience their personhood in an authentic and concrete way."[59]

In this vein, theologian David Cloutier, in his book *The Vice of Luxury*, argues that an attachment to luxury—seen as a disposition toward excess—inhibits human flourishing, the achievement of excellences, and the common good.[60] Cloutier's argument goes back to the Aristotelian and early Christian teaching that an attachment to wealth for its own sake corrupts the soul. As Cloutier argues, the marketing of luxury is itself almost like a religion, offering "transcendence and unique social identity."[61] Think about this today: a world where people admire luxury cars, designer handbags, yachts, private jets, and luxury apartment buildings. Do these goods contribute to genuine human flourishing? I think not. Cloutier is right; they are more likely to corrupt our social relationships and moral evaluations. This problem has become magnified in the age of social media. We now have a phenomenon known as the social media influencer: rich people who become famous simply by parading their wealth and fame in an endless cycle of vice. We have lost the ability to make moral judgments about the wealth generated by our economy.

The second major way in which business contributes to the common good and human flourishing is through *good work*. One of the themes of Catholic social teaching is the priority of labor over capital, because capital is always "the result of the historical heritage of human labour."[62] In other words, production always comes from labor's power, both physical and intellectual. As John Paul II put it, "We must emphasize and give prominence to the primacy of man in the production process, the primacy of man over things. Everything contained in the concept of capital in the strict sense is only a collection of things."[63] Work is also seen as a vocation for humanity, as human beings reach their full potential through dignified, meaningful work. Accordingly, society must prioritize access to decent work over profits. Pope John Paul II went so far as to argue that ownership of the means of production was just and legitimate only to the extent that it serves "useful work."[64]

Business therefore becomes a true noble vocation and truly serves the common good when it gives priority to the creation of decent jobs. In turn, profit cannot be the number one criterion of success, a core argument against the principle of maximizing shareholder value. As Pope John Paul put it, "Profit is a regulator of the life of a business, but it is not the only one; other human and moral factors must also be considered which, in the long term, are at least equally important for the life of a business."[65] Pope Benedict XVI also argued that profit cannot be the exclusive goal of business—more on that theme below.[66] Business should instead be oriented toward decent work, and, in doing so, it can derive some legitimate benefit for itself.

The priority of *good work* also emphasizes that business should be wary about the implications of allowing machines to supplant workers. As Pope John Paul II put it, "In some instances, technology can cease to be man's ally and become almost his enemy, as when the mechanization of work 'supplants' him, taking away all personal satisfaction and the incentive to creativity and responsibility, when it deprives many workers of their previous employment, or when, through exalting the machine, it reduces man to the status of its slave."[67] Pope Francis echoes the point that it is folly to seek to boost profits by replacing workers with machines; this serves "bad" rather than "good" work. As he puts it, "The orientation of the economy has favored a kind of technological progress in which the costs of production are reduced by laying off workers and replacing them with machines. This is yet another way in which we can end up working against ourselves. . . . To stop investing in people, in order to gain greater short-term financial gain, is bad business for society."[68]

Since work is a core dimension of human flourishing, the loss of decent work can prove devastating for human flourishing. Unemployment can undermine trust and social cohesion. Yet, over the neoliberal era, wages have taken a back seat to rising corporate profits, driven by the short-term impetus of the Friedmanite principle of maximizing shareholder value. In the United States, real median wages have been flat since the 1970s, while profits have soared—a marked departure from the shared gains of the previous era. And the jobs that do exist tend to be low paying and undervalued, with little respect for worker autonomy, agency, and dignity. It is often a case of a technocratic paradigm that treats the workers as an asset from which to squeeze value. In a highly depressing book, James Bloodworth spent six months undercover in some of the most low-paying industries in the United Kingdom.[69] He described his time as a "picker" for Amazon, one of the people who filled customer orders in giant warehouses. He documents a tyrannical regime of every movement being tracked, of workers being chastised for not picking fast enough or for taking bathroom breaks, and of their being fired for taking sick leave. As another example of how a large and powerful company cheats its workers, consider the case of retail giant Walmart. Walmart refuses to pay its workers a living wage at a time when it is earning record profits. A study calculated that raising the wages of Walmart workers to the bare minimum needed to escape poverty (simply defined as no longer being eligible for food stamps) would cost the company less than $5 billion, at a time when annual profits were $17 billion.[70] These examples are regrettably not isolated cases. "Wage theft," the act of not paying workers the full hourly wage, is a rising phenomenon in the United States. The bottom line is that work has become increasingly indecent and degrading, not the source of fulfillment and purpose. Workers lack power, and large corporations have distanced themselves from the common good. They simply put little value on good work.

The third dimension of how business supports the common good and human flourishing is through *good wealth*, creating sustainable wealth and distributing it justly. Unfortunately, modern corporations flout this ancient wisdom in many ways. Especially in a globalized world, corporations have immense power and ability to do harm, and they regularly do so. One avenue is to abuse market power through monopolies, oligopolies, and intellectual property protection. The rise of corporate concentration in recent years has proven detrimental to the common good; it harms both competition and collaboration, it hurts solidarity and subsidiarity, and it even has the potential to undermine democracy. Large and powerful technology firms also use their power to undermine privacy by exploiting personal information for profit.

One of the most egregious examples of the exploitation of market power is when pharmaceutical companies jack up the prices of lifesaving drugs to maximize profits, even when this behavior costs lives. Such a strategy directly contravenes the philosophy of Jonas Salk, the inventor of the polio vaccine, who refused to patent it on moral grounds. Today is a different story. Sachs provides an all-too-typical example: the pharmaceutical company Gilead owns the patent for Sofosbuvir, a life-saving Hepatitis C drug.[71] Even though it costs a dollar a pill to make, Gilead charges $1,000 a pill. A full course of treatment—one pill a day for eighty-four days—costs $84,000. Up to 3 million people in the United States have Hepatitis C, and most of them do not get treated. Gilead did not even do the research in developing this drug, which instead was developed in academia with government funding. This is a crystal-clear example of the point Mazzucato makes about the private sector reaping the reward of public-sector research.

Another example, particularly egregious, comes from the pharmaceutical company Valeant. Its business model was not to invest in research and development to create new drugs but to buy up existing pharmaceutical companies and jack up the prices of their drugs, which turned out to be an incredibly profitable endeavor. But people suffered and died. As one example, Valeant increased the monthly price of the drug Syprine—a life-or-death drug for people with a rare liver disorder—from $650 to over $21,000 between 2010 and 2015. (And yes, the extra zeroes are correct.)[72] At the same time, Valeant's market value grew from $2.3 billion to $78 billion. This strategy was egged on by Wall Street analysts who insisted that shareholder value be maximized. In a very real sense, the outrageously expensive price of healthcare in the United States is being driven by the callous greed of Wall Street and big pharmaceutical companies. And, of course, it was the drug companies that aggressively promoted the opioid drugs that addicted so many people in the United States—once again, for profit.

Corporations also bear much of the blame for the environmental crisis. A mere one hundred companies account for 70 percent of all greenhouse gas emissions since 1988, fossil fuel companies chief among them.[73] Multinational companies also have a dismal record of destroying the environment of developing countries to extract resources and then fighting aggressively against legal actions for restitution. Fossil fuel companies regularly spread lies and misinformation to cast doubt on the reality of climate change and the validity of climate action, in pursuit of the profits from the roughly $20 trillion of fossil fuel assets on their books that really need to stay in the ground to stop climate change from spiraling out of control.[74]

Many multinational companies also exploit globalization to avoid and evade taxes and to demand the weakest regulatory standards from host governments. Too many companies degrade human dignity across supply chains by denying workers just wages and even subjecting them to inhumane work conditions—most notoriously and shamefully through complicity in new forms of slavery.

Corporations also lobby extensively to make sure that their own interests take precedence over the common good. In the United States, lobbyists spent $3.4 billion in 2018,[75] mostly in an effort to extract value and bend policy and regulations toward their own narrow interests over the broad common good. Especially in the United States, campaign finance laws give corporations and their owners an outsize influence in policy making.

What is to be done about this? Reform must come from within (personal transformation) and without (structural change). On the one hand, reform will require role models, virtue education, and activism by consumers and civil society. On the other hand, it will also require changes to laws, regulations, and corporate governance structures. As the Ethics in Action initiative notes, "'Ethics' can never be optional, and 'corporate social responsibility' can never be an add-on, mere window-dressing, or worse—a cynical exercise in public relations."[76]

Catholic Social Thought has much to teach on how the corporations can simultaneously produce wealth and serve the common good. One key insight, especially associated with Pope Benedict XVI in *Caritas in Veritate*, is that companies should be able to make a profit and extend a social benefit at the same time. Benedict's point gets back to the principle of reciprocity and gratuitousness, that sociability and fraternity take place inside economic activity, inside business entities. This idea is controversial on both the Right and the Left. On the Right, libertarians argue that in line with Friedman, the only social function of business is to maximize profits. But modern social democrats too are often willing to overlook the lack of ethics in the market, on the grounds that the state can come in and clean up the mess. Although Catholic social teaching supports a vigorous state oriented toward the common good, it refuses to let businesses off the hook.

In this vein, Pope Benedict calls for "profoundly new way of understanding business enterprise,"[77] escaping the narrow logic of maximizing shareholder value and becoming responsible to a wider variety of stakeholders. He then goes on to argue that the hard barrier between profit-making businesses and entities that provide social benefits needs to become softer. Called for are hybrid forms of enterprise that mix profits and social benefits. As he states, "Alongside profit-oriented private enterprise and the various types of public enterprise, there must be room for commercial entities based on mutualist principles and pursuing social ends to take root and express themselves. It is from their reciprocal encounter in the marketplace that one may expect hybrid forms of commercial behaviour to emerge, and hence an attentiveness to ways of civilizing the economy."[78] Later in the same encyclical, he makes a similar point:

> It would appear that the traditionally valid distinction between profit-based companies and non-profit organizations can no longer do full justice to reality, or offer practical direction for the future. In recent decades a broad intermediate area has emerged between the two types of enterprise. It is made up of traditional companies which nonetheless subscribe to social aid agreements in support of underdeveloped countries, charitable foundations associated with individual companies, groups of companies oriented towards social welfare, and the diversified world of the so-called "civil economy" and the "economy of communion." This is not merely a matter of a "third sector," but of a broad new composite reality embracing the private and public spheres, one which does not exclude profit, but instead considers it a means for achieving human and social ends.[79]

There are plenty of antecedents for the new forms of enterprise Benedict seeks. The civil economy paradigm, which I have touched on already, is a humanized economy based on the notion of social benefit coming before private gain (the opposite of Adam Smith). In this domain, one way of tying profit to the common good is through a general sharing of risk and reward among all types of market participants: borrowers and lenders, investors and owners of enterprises, shareholders and managers, and employers and employees. It is a preference for small-scale enterprise and is vigorously opposed to concentrated industry.[80] Concrete examples include credit unions, building societies, and cooperatives for purchasing and selling. These corporate forms do not eschew profit, but they do not let it supplant social benefit either. Another example, named explicitly in *Caritas in Veritate*, is the economy of communion. This network of businesses, inspired by Catholic social teaching, divides profits in three ways: reinvestment in the business, giving to those in need, and funding the infrastructure to promote a culture of giving and reciprocity.[81] All in all, Catholic social teaching is calling for a radical reenvisioning of the role of business, whereby—whatever the institutional form—wealth should be distributed in a way that benefits broader society.

Just wealth also encompasses sustainability. Pope Francis's *Laudato Si'* is instructive in this regard. The pope identified both a negative and a positive injunction. The negative injunction relates to the injunction not to pollute, not to add to climate change beyond what is permitted by international agreements, or more generally not to contribute to environmental devastation. Profit maximization becomes perverse when these very profits come from paying only a fraction of the costs incurred. As economists would say, certain companies are not paying the full social cost of their activities for the harm they are doing to the environment. Pope Francis stresses that "the economic and social costs of using up shared environmental resources" must be "recognized with transparency and fully borne by those who incur them, not by other peoples or future generations."[82] Only when business bears the true cost of this activity, says Pope Francis, can this activity be considered truly ethical. Only then can business truly live up to its calling as a noble vocation. The implication is that a lot of profit today is improperly and unethically earned, especially when it comes to fossil fuel companies.

Laudato Si' also calls on multinational corporations to pay their "ecological debt" to developing countries, a debt "connected to commercial imbalances with effects on the environment, and the disproportionate use of natural resources by certain countries over long periods of time."[83] The pope notes that these multinational corporations treat the environment of their host countries in a way they would never treat their own homes. This is callous exploitation for profit, pure and simple.

As well as this negative injunction, Pope Francis also argues that business has a positive injunction to invest in sustainable development. *Laudato Si'* notes that "efforts to promote a sustainable use of natural resources are not a waste of money" and that "more diversified and innovative forms of production which impact less on the environment can prove very profitable."[84] Business can live up to its potential as a noble vocation by applying its creativity and ingenuity in pursuit of sustainable development solutions. In terms of the economy as a whole, this would be consistent with a shift away from a short-term focus on consumption and toward a longer-term focus on investment in efforts to resolve urgent problems facing the human family.[85] If it is good news for the planet, then it is surely good news for business—but this first requires a shift away from the short-term logic of maximizing shareholder value.

Role of Labor

In the last section, I devoted more space to *good goods* and *good wealth* than to *good work*. I intend to expand on that aspect in this section. Just as with business, Catholic social teaching also sees labor as a vocation oriented toward human fulfillment and the common good. Indeed, it is legitimate to speak of a "joint vocation" of labor and capital, oriented toward the same end.

Needless to say, this view stands in stark contrast to that of neoclassical economics. The neoclassical paradigm sees labor as a factor of production, a cost to be minimized. It argues that, in labor market equilibrium, the worker is paid in terms of what they contribute to productivity. Again, neoclassical economics finds a natural ally in libertarianism as not only is this wage efficient but it is also just, since the wage represents the outcome of free choices between worker and employer and the intersection of the supply and demand for labor. Of course, the real world is a very different place. We see corporate CEOs earning staggering salaries that are in no way connected to their productivity. Fifty years ago, for example, American CEOs earned twenty times as much as the average worker; today it is 354 times more.[86] Can that discrepancy be ascribed to rising productivity? Hardly. But it does reflect rising power. At the same time, we see powerless workers earning less and less, in more precarious positions.

Catholic social teaching recognizes these problems. It starts from the position that a worker is not a factor of production but a human being who possesses dignity and agency. From this perspective, dignified work is a path toward fulfillment and flourishing, a core dimension of integral human development. Work is not just about earning an income sufficient to support your family and enjoy a decent standard of living. It is much more than that. It's about becoming who we are meant to be. In the words of Pope John Paul II in his encyclical devoted to human labor,

> Work is a good thing for man. It is not only good in the sense that it is useful or something to enjoy; it is also good as being something worthy, that is to say, something that corresponds to man's dignity, that expresses this dignity and increases it. . . . Work is a good thing for man—a good thing for his humanity—because through work man not only transforms nature, adapting it to his own needs, but he also achieves fulfilment as a human being and indeed, in a sense, becomes "more a human being."[87]

From a theological perspective, John Paul argues that the human person, created in God's image, "shares by his work in the activity of the Creator."[88] He noted that Jesus was a worker and that early Christians dignified human labor in an empire where such work was considered by elites as demeaning, the task of slaves. The monastic movements, for example, made sure to link work and prayer. From the Christian perspective, this view of labor gives rise to a moral obligation to work.[89]

Pope Francis echoed these thoughts in *Laudato Si'*, where he argues that work is the setting for "rich personal growth, where many aspects of life enter into play: creativity, planning for the future, developing our talents, living out our values, relating to others, giving glory to God. . . . Work is a necessity, part of the meaning of life on this earth, a path to growth, human development and personal fulfillment."[90]

This approach to work and employment is also borne out in the happiness literature. The evidence shows that while one's salary certainly matters for happiness, so do numerous other factors, including working conditions, autonomy, engagement, and the social capital built from workplace relationships.[91] None of these aspects are consistent with neoclassical economics. But they are coherent with Catholic ethics.

If there is a moral obligation to work, then there must be a moral obligation for the state and business to prioritize employment, an obligation that gets back to the twinning of rights and duties in Catholic social teaching. A core priority, then, is the promotion of secure and dignified employment as a central goal of public policy. This theme has been echoed time and time again in Catholic social teaching. Pope John Paul II, for example, argued that it was essential "to act against unemployment, which in all cases is an evil, and which, when it reaches a certain level, can become a real social disaster."[92] Pope Benedict XVI argued that "being out of work or dependent on public or private assistance for a prolonged period undermines the freedom and creativity of the person and his family and social relationships, causing great psychological and spiritual suffering."[93] And, quoting Pope Benedict, Pope Francis ties entrenched unemployment to the decline in social cohesion: "The loss of jobs also has a negative impact on the economy 'through the progressive erosion of social capital: the network of relationships of trust, dependability, and respect for rules, all of which are indispensable for any form of civil coexistence.'"[94]

This diagnosis has been proven correct. Researchers have shown that prolonged unemployment is corrosive to human flourishing; not only does it lead to a loss of lifetime earnings, but it also worsens health, impedes the educational achievement of children, and depletes trust and social capital.[95] Job security is therefore vital. Accordingly, as noted by Pope Francis, while unemployment insurance to protect workers is necessary, it can never substitute for a dignified life through work. Plus, as noted by Pope John Paul II, there is a risk of a social assistance state trampling on the agency of the human being, which is most likely to happen when they are denied the ability to make a meaningful contribution to society through dignified work.

In terms of the dignity of work, the concept of the just wage is central. A key point is that the wage set by free markets for labor is not necessarily just. Catholic social teaching sees the just wage as a version of Aquinas's just price, which reflects giving both buyers and sellers what they are due, in accord with commutative and distributive justice. Libertarians argue that the market wage is in itself a just wage, as it amounts to a voluntary agreement between two parties. But this argument is folly. Workers with no bargaining power might be compelled to accept low wages because they have no choice. As Pope Paul VI wrote, "When two parties are in very unequal positions, their mutual consent alone does not guarantee a fair contract."[96] Aside from the lack of fairness, treating workers as mere factors of production and paying less than a just wage represents an assault on human dignity. Indeed, cheating a worker out of their wage is regarded as one of the most serious sins in Christianity.

It was these very concerns that drove Pope Leo XIII to condemn unfettered labor markets all the way back in 1891. In *Rerum Novarum*, he used some strong language about this: "To misuse men as though they were things in the pursuit of gain, or to value them solely for their physical powers—that is truly shameful and inhuman. . . . To defraud any one of wages that are his due is a great crime which cries to the avenging anger of Heaven."[97] Furthermore, he noted the following, which seems as true in our second Gilded Age as it was at the end of the nineteenth century:

> Hence, by degrees it has come to pass that working men have been surrendered, isolated and helpless, to the hardheartedness of employers and the greed of unchecked competition. . . . To this must be added that the hiring of labor and the conduct of trade are concentrated in the hands of comparatively few; so that a small number of very rich men have been able to lay upon the teeming masses of the laboring poor a yoke little better than that of slavery itself.[98]

He went on to argue that "if through necessity or fear of a worse evil the workman accepts harder conditions because an employer or contractor will afford him no better, he is made the victim of force and injustice."[99] These are strong words indeed.

From this Catholic perspective, the concept of a just wage arises partly from commutative justice—the outcome of a fair bargain between employer and employee. It also reflects distributive justice; the main way the person can satisfy the material bases of human flourishing, owed to them by society, is through a just wage. Along these lines, Pope Leo XIII argued that a just wage reflects "a dictate of natural justice more imperious and ancient" than the outcome of the free market.[100] A just wage also twins rights and duties, a right to a just wage with a duty to work diligently, a right to work with a duty to pay just wages. Summing it up, Pope John Paul II argued that the just wage is one of the main ways to achieve the universal destination of goods in practice. It is "the concrete means of verifying the justice of the whole socioeconomic system and, in any case, of checking that it is functioning justly."[101]

You might ask the question, What is a just wage in practice? There is no simple answer to that question. It obviously depends on context and circumstances. It can be assessed from the bottom up, seeking to cost out the basic necessities of a dignified life. Given that the emphasis is not just on material necessities but integral human development, the basic necessities would include the ability to participate in social endeavors, taking part in the life of the community.[102] Such estimates of a standard of living were common in the early twentieth century but fell into disuse with the rise of neoclassical economics and its emphasis on insatiable appetites. This approach can be complemented by a top-down approach, asking how much productivity is growing and insisting that real wages match this growth—as was the case during the social democratic era. A business should not go bankrupt, of course, but there is no case in Catholic social teaching for gains in productivity to feed into rising profits at the expense of wages, as has been the case during the neoliberal era.

Along with just wages, Catholic social teaching recognizes an array of rights due to the worker in line with justice and dignity. As laid down by Pope John Paul II in *Laborem Exercens*, these include pensions; unemployment benefits; affordable or even free healthcare; family support; adequate rest and vacation time; and work environments that do not impede health, safety, and moral integrity. Catholic teaching also respects the right to strike, as long as this is not exploited.

Pope John Paul II once again argued that unemployment benefits, just like wages, are justified based on the principle of the universal destination of goods: "The obligation to provide unemployment benefits, that is to say, the duty to make suitable grants indispensable for the subsistence of unemployed workers and their families, is a duty springing from the fundamental principle of the moral order in this sphere, namely the principle of the common use of goods or, to put it in another and still simpler way, the right to life and subsistence."[103]

But he also cautioned about excess reliance on unemployment benefits, which ran the risk of disconnecting the recipient from the common good. This risk can be overcome both by prioritizing employment as a priority goal and deploying the principles of subsidiarity and reciprocal obligation throughout the welfare state.

Catholic social teaching also strongly supports the rights of workers to form and join unions and to bargain collectively, one of the strongest and most consistent elements of its labor market ethics. There are two justifications: one based on subsidiarity, one based on solidarity. In terms of the subsidiarity argument, Pope John Paul II argued that unions form an "indispensable element of social life." They exist as a core dimension of civil society, through which the relational life is firmed up. As some concrete examples, unions can help workers foster friendships, further their education, take care of each other in times of need, or help integrate migrants and refugees into the workforce.

In terms of solidarity, unions allow workers to "protect their just rights vis-à-vis the entrepreneurs and the owners of the means of production" and act as a "mouthpiece for the struggle for social justice."[104] For Pope Francis, unions play a prophetic role in society: "Unions are born and reborn each time that, like the biblical prophets, they give a voice to those who have none, denounce those who would 'sell the needy for a pair of sandals' (cf. Amos 2:6), unmask the powerful who trample the rights of the most vulnerable workers, defend the cause of foreigners, the least, the rejected."[105]

In this vein, unions are perhaps the prime example of what the economist Galbraith refers to as countervailing institutions. It seems beyond dispute that had unions not been reduced in power in the United States in the neoliberal era, the economic and social dysfunctions I have documented could have been diminished or even halted.

The Catholic praise for unions is not uncritical, however. Pope Benedict XVI argued that they should not only focus on the interests of their own membership but also broaden solidarity to account for non-union members as well as workers in developing countries (where labor rights are often violated).[106] In the words of Pope Francis, a union rooted in solidarity also "guards and protects those who are outside the walls," including "those who do not yet have rights, those who are excluded from work and who are also excluded from rights and from democracy."[107] Pope John Paul II argued that while unions' concern for the common good compels them to get involved in the political sphere, he cautions them not to act like political parties.[108] Pope Francis reiterates that same point.

Yet Pope Benedict XVI also argued that unions must "be honoured today even more than in the past."[109] This is because governments increasingly tend to limit the freedoms and negotiating power of unions in response to the competitive pressures of globalization. Putting it bluntly, globalization dramatically increases the power of corporations; unions must keep up.

One final aspect of the vocation of labor from Catholic social teaching worth making is the idea that workers should be able to share in both the profits and the management of the firm. In this view, such an arrangement would break down any conflictual relationship between capital and labor, uniting them in common purpose and joint vocation. It also would allow workers to exercise appropriate agency in line with subsidiarity. It is an example of the civil economy in action, whereby human relationships and mutual sharing of risks and returns take precedence over profit maximization in a context that treats labor as a cog in the machine.

This is a fairly central aspect of Catholic social teaching, even if its practical application has been limited. Pope Pius XI called for workers to "become sharers in ownership or management or participate in some fashion in the profits received." He suggested that a work contract be replaced by what he called a "partnership contract."[110] As noted in chapter 2, Pius proposed a corporatist industrial order, built around councils of industry and labor representatives that would replace competition with bargaining and coordination.[111]

After World War II, Pope John XXIII also called for workers to share in the ownership of their companies.[112] He believed this shared ownership would allow workers to better participate in the shared community that is the corporation.[113] Pope John Paul II agreed, affirming the "joint ownership of the means of work, sharing by the workers in the management and/or profits of businesses, so-called shareholding by labour."[114] Rather than the collectivization of the means of production, he called for its "socialization" so that "on the basis of his work each person is fully entitled to consider himself a part-owner of the great workbench at which he is working with everyone else."[115]

Especially in an era of large and dominant corporations, including in the technology sector, combined with ever more precarious employment contracts with low pay and few protections, some are arguing that cooperatives—whereby workers own the enterprise—represent a viable way forward. Nathan Schneider, for example, argues that cooperatives are not just utopian dreams; they can be competitive and efficient, support democracy, and often arise to overcome moments of crisis.[116] Nowhere is this principle clearer than with the Mondragon Corporation, a worker cooperative founded by a Catholic priest in 1956 and which is now the tenth-largest company in Spain. Mondragon has branches in finance, retail, industry, and education. It operates on mutualist principles, and the salaries of managers are capped at nine times those of the lowest-paid workers.[117] In assessing the success of Mondragon, John Medaille argues that it actually enjoys a competitive advantage over more traditional enterprises and that there is no contradiction between justice and running a business.[118]

Another live debate centers on codetermination, the model whereby workers are given a say in running the enterprise. This concept is associated with the German model of industrial relations in particular—worker representation on boards, work councils at the level of the enterprise that give employees a stake in decision making, and wage negotiation at the regional or sectoral level underpinned by strong unions. German law states that corporations with more than two thousand workers are required to have half of the members on their board of directors chosen by workers; smaller companies (with between five hundred and two hundred workers) need a third. Another example is Sweden, which reserves a third of board seats for workers in firms with more than twenty-five employees. Other countries adopting codetermination include Austria, Denmark, and Norway. The evidence suggests that codetermination works. German industrial relations, for example, are famously harmonious. Codetermination seems to make firms place less weight on the interests of shareholders, including by avoiding major restructurings or mass layoffs.[119] It leads to higher productivity, lower wage inequality, and smaller compensation packages for senior executives. In the words of Thomas Piketty, "co-management has been one of the most highly developed and durable means of institutionalizing the new balance of power between workers and capital."[120]

In Germany, codetermination is complemented by self-governing vocational institutions that regulate labor market entry, including by enforcing training and ethical practices within the sector. These practices give rise to a virtuous cycle of not only decent wages but also a sense of vocation, good practice, and democratic participation.[121] This system solidifies the countervailing institutions that serve as a check on corporate power and represents the active legacy of Catholic social teaching in Germany and central Europe, arising out of a postwar Christian democratic and social democratic consensus that sought a middle way between the free market and state domination.

Neoliberalism, in contrast, places a high premium on what it calls flexible labor markets. The logic is simple: if wages are the outcomes of free labor markets, any interference in the labor market would hinder efficiency and only generate unemployment. This view harks back to the old idea, heavily criticized by Keynes in the context of the Great Depression, that markets would naturally return to equilibrium, with entrenched unemployment impossible. And so neoliberalism opposes what it sees as excessive interference in labor markets—including minimum wages, protections against workers getting fired, welfare states, and unions.

But this set of ideas is misplaced. As Keynes showed, it is possible to have prolonged unemployment even with flexible labor markets. And because workers lack power and options, flexible labor markets tend to generate jobs that are low paying and insecure, most recently in the gig economy. In this system, flexibility is synonymous with insecurity, inequity, disengagement, and a decline in workplace trust and social capital. This toxic admixture of a massive power imbalance and low trust can lead to ever more coercive control of workers by employers, which undermines agency, initiative, and engagement—and this can in turn lead to lower productivity.[122] This labor insecurity is certainly a poor substitute for genuine workplace democracy in the context of cooperative bargaining between employers and unions, which can be productive, competitive, and equitable. As Maurice Glasman puts it, "Germany has successfully exported its goods, but not the virtues of its economic system."[123] We should not forget that the German system is the legacy of Catholic social teaching.

Role of Finance

The triumvirate of goals—*good goods, good work, good wealth*—applies to finance too. But finance is a special case, not least because it is the ground zero of poor ethics. Society certainly needs finance. Finance allows people and businesses to save for the future. It gives loans to people who cannot afford a large down-payment, mortgages being a key example. And it brings together savers and borrowers, so investments can be financed. The old model of finance is best encapsulated by the sentimental movie *It's a Wonderful Life*, in which the main protagonist runs a small-town bank. He serves the needs of his customers because he knows them. He knows their needs, their ability to pay, their character. If they need to miss a payment because they fall on hard times, he will be flexible. And in turn he will ask them not to withdraw too much money at once and risk a bank run. This old model is an example of the civil economy in action—a human economy seeded with fraternity, gratuitousness, and solidarity.

Sadly, that system is a relic of the past. Finance today is a behemoth that serves its own interests rather than the real economy. Especially in the neoliberal era, egged on by deregulation and hands-off supervision, there has been a dramatic shift from relationship-based finance to more impersonal and anonymous transaction-based finance in tandem with a dizzying degree of financial innovation, causing the stock of financial assets and the volume of financial transactions to dwarf global GDP.[124] In the United States, finance's share of value added doubled between 1960 and 2014, from 3.7 percent to 8.4 percent, while manufacturing fell by half from 25 percent to 12 percent.[125] This gives rise to what Nicholas Shaxson dubs the "finance curse":[126] as finance grew, the real economy contracted. The share of finance in corporate profits was stable at around 10–15 percent in the United States during the social democratic era; it is now over 20 percent.[127] In the process, the sector has become increasingly self-referential, striving for short-term financial gain by engaging in what Lord Adair Turner—former chairman of the UK Financial Services Authority—called "socially useless activity" and hence becoming increasingly divorced from any obligation to the common good.[128] Mazzucato documents that only 15 percent of the funds managed by the financial industry go to businesses in the real economy.[129] Finance is out for itself, not to serve others.

At no time was this clearer than during the global financial crisis. The crisis came on the back of increasingly complex financial engineering, creating murky and opaque financial instruments, an explosion of capital flows across borders, and heightened pressures for "light touch" regulation and bank supervision.[130] Financial actors sought the largest profit possible, believing that markets were efficient and that if things went south, the government would always bail them out. Instead of serving the real economy, banks turned toward trading from their own accounts, seeking to make a profit from what amounted to gambling rather than providing a genuine social benefit.

Instead of the old model of making loans based on personal relationships, loans were securitized—multiple loans packaged into a single security and sold off to investors. This practice gave rise to many problems: The banks no longer had an incentive to care about whether people could pay back their loans, as they now just sold them off in return for a fee. And investors demanded higher returns, thus demanding riskier loans. They convinced themselves that markets were efficient and that if some mortgage holders defaulted on their loans, there were enough diversified loans in the securitized package to guarantee safety.

Thus was born the subprime crisis, as unscrupulous lenders issued mortgages with little due diligence—sometimes not even asking for documentation of the borrower's income. These mortgages proved deceptive. The early payments were low but soon magnified. The goal was to hoodwink the borrower—offer an attractive teaser rate, and then bury a substantial adjustment a few years down the line in confusing legalistic language. This was a classic example of the usury condemned for thousands of years, preying on the poor for a profit. Modern debt peonage resulted in the poor losing their houses and their livelihoods. In the United States, the ground zero of the financial crisis, people lost over $20 trillion in wealth, and more than 9 million families lost their homes.[131] Unemployment rose to levels last seen during the Great Depression.

Some people wanted to cast the blame on the borrower for taking out loans they could not afford—this reaction was the spark that lit the Tea Party movement in the United States. But it misses the point that it takes two to tango and that laws can be structured to favor either creditors or debtors. Catholic social teaching stress that debtors must come first; this is an example of the preferential option for the poor. The Tea Party critique also misses the point that in a world of stagnating real wages, the only option available for many to maintain living standards—especially the kinds of living standards enjoyed in the social democratic era—was to take out debt.

But after the crisis, households were left to sink, while the big banks and financial institutions were bailed out to the tune of trillions of dollars. The lenders anticipated this would happen. The argument enunciated by governments was that letting big financial institutions fail could have a catastrophic effect on the real economy. And indeed, the bankruptcy of Lehman Brothers was the spark that lit the full-scale financial crisis. So there is some merit to this argument. But anticipating this, banks felt free to take on huge risks, assured that they would keep the profits on the upside and be bailed out on the downside—the so-called privatization of gains and socialization of losses. As Robert Reich put it, these institutions and their top executives were "too big to fail, jail, or curtail."[132] This finance-first argument missed the point that the ensuing economic crisis was driven not so much by a failure of financial intermediation as by a massive slump in the real economy—unemployment and lower purchasing power.[133] Since many of the crisis fighters hailed from the world of financiers, they tended to share their worldview and take their side. This tendency would have grave implications for politics going forward.

In many respects, the crisis of 2008 should be seen as a crisis of ethics. It was driven by greed, by the ruthless search for ever-higher profit, returns, and bonuses by banks and investors. It was the principle of maximizing shareholder profits on steroids. If Aristotle dubbed greed divorced from the common good as *chrematistike*, then surely this was peak *chrematistike*. In the wake of the crisis, a survey of five hundred senior financial executives in the United States and the United Kingdom found that a quarter believed that people in the industry needed to cut ethical corners to be successful.[134] And experiments found that bankers were more likely to act dishonestly when primed to think of their professional role rather than their broader social role.[135]

Documenting the ethical lapses of the financial sector would take a whole book in itself. But to paint a clearer picture of the kind of duplicity that underlay the financial crisis, it helps to look at some examples. As documented by Sachs, one of the most egregious was the crooked bargain between hedge fund manager John Paulson and investment bank Goldman Sachs.[136] Goldman deliberately bundled a security full of bad mortgages that it peddled to investors as a good bet, in this case to German banks. Paulson bet against the security and made a billion dollars—the amount that the investors lost. Goldman was forced to pay a minor fine, but Paulson walked away scot free with his reputation intact. Goldman was not the only villain; other banks such as Deutsche Bank and JP Morgan were also failing to disclose the toxicity of their securitized subprime mortgage bundles and sometimes betting on their downfall. After US regulators started to crack down on some of this most egregious behavior, Goldman Sachs urged its traders to try their luck in Asia, which retained a more "wild west" feel. This is how Goldman got entangled in one of the most outrageous heists of all time—the looting of a sovereign wealth fund in Malaysia by a crook named Jho Low, who stole billions from the Malaysian people and used the proceeds to fund a lavish and luxurious lifestyle, courting Hollywood elites. Goldman Sachs made massive fees on these fraudulent bond sales.[137] Low got away with it because he was able to use secretive offshore accounts to hide his filthy lucre.

Since the crisis, the ethics of finance has not improved much. Although regulation is a little tighter, not much has changed. We still see scandal after scandal involving the major banks, which are larger and more powerful than ever: massive amounts of speculative trading, falsifying documents to push through foreclosures, money laundering for mafiosi and drug kingpins, aiding with tax evasion, rigging prices in key financial markets, falsely opening accounts for customers who don't ask for them. And of course, payday lenders still operate with impunity, preying on the weak and vulnerable by charging misleading and usurious rates of interest. *Chrematistike* remains near its peak.

It is also not just the banks. One of the most egregious business models lies in the so-called leveraged buyout private equity industry.[138] In this model, the firm's owners invite contributions to a pool of capital, which is used to buy up companies with a view to restructuring them and making or increasing profits. Under neoliberalism, this is the magic of the market—smart and gutsy investors take hold of an ailing company and turn it around, unleashing productivity and growth. But the reality is rather different. As Shaxson documents, private equity is less about creating value than extracting value; it's more of a heist than a helping hand. The way it works is that investors seek to extract as much cash from a company as possible and then use that to borrow more money, which boosts profits for them; debt typically amounts to 60–80 percent of the cost of an acquisition.[139] How does the company extract the initial cash? It's not hard to figure out—firing people, cutting wages, stopping investment, reneging on pension promises. And since the debt taken out is saddled on the company, the private equity firm is not burdened by any potential bankruptcy. The partners put little of their own money in but take out a lot in management fees and profit shares. And if the company fails, they just walk away from the hulking ruin. Once again, it's a case of heads-I-win-tails-you-lose. It's maximizing shareholder returns on steroids, with everyone else losing, including the long-term viability of the company itself. As Mariana Mazzucato puts it, "PE [private equity] is MSV [maximizing shareholder value] turbo-charged."[140] It's the ultimate form of short-termism disconnected from the common good.

Another dark player of the financial world is the so-called vulture fund. Vulture funds are the bottom-feeders of the hedge fund world. Their strategy is to buy up cheap sovereign debt, usually from countries whose debt is not sustainable and unlikely to be repaid. In such cases, the debt costs less than face value, because the risk of default is high. But then vulture funds try to find a complaint court to rule that the amount must be repaid in full; a debt is a debt after all. If private equity is shareholder value on steroids, vulture funds represent the fullest form of creditor primacy. Oftentimes, these debts are from some of the poorest countries of the world, and with repayment governments cut back on health, education, and social services. But it is a lucrative strategy for the big vulture funds. Vulture funds also throw a wrench into the works of shared solidarity and global cooperation. Often, countries with distressed debt try to work out a restructuring with their creditors to them get back on their feet. Vulture funds will typically hold out—in the classic style of the defector in Prisoner's Dilemma games. But in this case, defection has devastating real-world implications.

Unsurprisingly, some of the strongest statements against the dysfunctions, depredations, and depravities of the financial sector in Catholic social teaching come from the encyclicals written in the wake of the Great Depression (*Quadragesimo Anno*) and the global financial crisis (*Caritas in Veritate* and *Laudato Si'*). Back in 1931, Pope Pius XI railed against an "economic dictatorship" that was upending the economy and destroying social and political bonds. It is worth quoting him in full because it's still so relevant:

> Not only is wealth concentrated in our times but an immense power and despotic economic dictatorship is consolidated in the hands of a few, who often are not owners but only the trustees and managing directors of invested funds which they administer according to their own arbitrary will and pleasure. This dictatorship is being most forcibly exercised by those who, since they hold the money and completely control it, control credit also and rule the lending of money. Hence they regulate the flow, so to speak, of the life-blood whereby the entire economic system lives, and have so firmly in their grasp the soul, as it were, of economic life that no one can breathe against their will. This concentration of power and might, the characteristic mark, as it were, of contemporary economic life, is the fruit that the unlimited freedom of struggle among competitors has of its own nature produced, and which lets only the strongest survive; and this is often the same as saying, those who fight the most violently, those who give least heed to their conscience . . . Free competition has destroyed itself; economic dictatorship has supplanted the free market; unbridled ambition for power has likewise succeeded greed for gain; all economic life has become tragically hard, inexorable, and cruel.[141]

John Paul II also argued that speculation divorced from the real economy is an act of economic sabotage: "The spread of improper sources of growing rich and of easy profits deriving from illegal or purely speculative activities, constitutes one of the chief obstacles to development and to the economic order."[142] He argued that speculation is one of the activities, along with economic exploitation and breaking solidarity of working people, that makes ownership of the means of production illegitimate.[143]

Writing on the heels of the global financial crisis of 2008, Pope Benedict XVI also inveighed against speculation and a self-referential financial sector that puts its own interests over the common good:

> Finance, therefore—through the renewed structures and operating methods that have to be designed after its misuse, which wreaked such havoc on the real economy—now needs to go back to being an instrument directed towards improved wealth creation and development. Insofar as they are instruments, the entire economy and finance, not just certain sectors, must be used in an ethical way so as to create suitable conditions for human development and for the development of peoples. . . . Financiers must rediscover the genuinely ethical foundation of their activity, so as not to abuse the sophisticated instruments which can serve to betray the interests of savers.[144]

And again,

> In recent years a new cosmopolitan class of managers has emerged, who are often answerable only to the shareholders generally consisting of anonymous funds which de facto determine their remuneration. . . . What should be avoided is a speculative use of financial resources that yields to the temptation of seeking only short-term profit, without regard for the long-term sustainability of the enterprise, its benefit to the real economy and attention to the advancement, in suitable and appropriate ways, of further economic initiatives in countries in need of development.[145]

Pope Francis too is well aware of the problems of finance, and he notes that while the crisis provided an opportunity for reform, this opportunity was lost:

> Saving banks at any cost, making the public pay the price, foregoing a firm commitment to reviewing and reforming the entire system, only re-affirms the absolute power of a financial system, a power which has no future and will only give rise to new crises after a slow, costly and only

apparent recovery. The financial crisis of 2007–08 provided an opportunity to develop a new economy, more attentive to ethical principles, and new ways of regulating speculative financial practices and virtual wealth. But the response to the crisis did not include rethinking the outdated criteria which continue to rule the world.[146]

In turn, Pope Francis argues that this lack of reform makes it harder to grapple with the environmental crisis: "Finance overwhelms the real economy. The lessons of the global financial crisis have not been assimilated, and we are learning all too slowly the lessons of environmental deterioration."[147] On the contrary, he argues that "economic powers continue to justify the current global system where priority tends to be given to speculation and the pursuit of financial gain, which fail to take the context into account, let alone the effects on human dignity and the natural environment."[148]

In sum, Pope Francis asks us to say "no to a financial system which rules rather than serves."[149] This rejection of the current financial system is bound to involve much tighter regulation of all aspects of the financial sector, to curb the greed and reckless risk-taking behavior, the opacity of financial instruments, the anonymity and scale of financial transactions, the continued dominance of oversized "too big to fail" institutions, the unquenching thirst for financial value in the shortest of short runs, the extension of financialization across so many areas of the economy, the shameless resort to usurious interest rates, the use of tax havens and secrecy jurisdictions to hide murky and dubious behavior, and—last but not least—the outright fraud and dishonesty that are still prevalent across the industry. It will require getting past the neoliberal insistence that no amount of finance is bad for the economy, that financial markets are efficient, and that cross-border flows of capital are always beneficial. Restoring ethics to finance will allow it once again to serve the common good.

Notes

1. *QA*, 46.
2. *QA*, 46.
3. See Sandel, *Justice*.
4. Libertarian arguments, by the way, transcend the political spectrum. People on the Left appeal to self-ownership to defend the right to abortion, for example, while those on the Right appeal to the exact same principle to justify a minimal state in the economic sphere. I would argue that much political incoherence today boils down to this failure to appreciate the reach and the defects of libertarian arguments.
5. *QA*, 88.

6. *PP*, 26.

7. *OA*, 35.

8. *LS*, 129.

9. *CA*, 13.

10. *CA*, 12.

11. See Finn, "Nine Libertarian Heresies Tempting Neoconservative Catholics to Stray from Catholic Social Thought," for the myriad ways in which libertarianism is incompatible with Catholic social teaching.

12. Nozick, *Anarchy, State, and Utopia*, ix.

13. Nozick, 32–33.

14. Hayek, *Constitution of Liberty*.

15. Pope Francis, "Message from the Holy Father to the Participants in the Plenary Session of the Pontifical Academy of Social Sciences."

16. *FT*, 103–5.

17. Finn, "Nine Libertarian Heresies Tempting Neoconservative Catholics to Stray from Catholic Social Thought."

18. *SRS*, 42.

19. *CA*, 42.

20. Pope Benedict XVI, "Europe and Its Discontents," *First Things*, January 2006.

21. *MM*, 20.

22. *CA*, 35.

23. *RN*, 36.

24. *CA*, 11.

25. *CA*, 15.

26. *CA*, 34.

27. *CA*, 40.

28. *RN*, 37.

29. *MM*, 132.

30. *CIV*, 36.

31. *LE*, 19.

32. *CA*, 48.

33. *CIV*, 58.

34. *QA*, 88.

35. For an exposition, see Reich, *Saving Capitalism*.

36. Galbraith, *American Capitalism*.

37. See Annett, "Economía de la virtud y desafíos económicos actuales."

38. These tradable licenses set the overall level of pollution and allow firms to buy and sell licenses to emit pollution within this limit on the market.

39. Bowles, *Moral Economy*.

40. See Annett, "Economía de la virtud y desafíos económicos actuales."

41. Stout, *Cultivating Conscience*.

42. *MM*, 116.

43. *CA*, 48.

44. *MM*, 54.

45. *CIV*, 41.

46. *CIV*, 25.

47. *EG*, 203.

48. *LS*, 129.

49. Milton Friedman, "A Friedman Doctrine—The Social Responsibility of Business Is to Increase Its Profits," *New York Times*, September 13, 1970, https://www.nytimes .com/1970/09/13/archives/a-friedman-doctrine-the-social-responsibility-of-business-is -to.html.

50. Mazzucato, *Value of Everything*, ch. 6.

51. Mazzucato, 174.

52. Mazzucato, 180.

53. Mazzucato, 179.

54. Mayer, *Prosperity*, 15–16.

55. *CA*, 35.

56. Dicastery for Promoting Integral Human Development, *Vocation of the Business Leader*.

57. Quoted in Sandel, *Tyranny of Merit*, 140.

58. *LS*, 203.

59. *CA*, 41.

60. Cloutier, *Vice of Luxury*.

61. Cloutier, 177.

62. *LE*, 12.

63. *LE*, 12.

64. *CA*, 43.

65. *CA*, 35.

66. *CIV*, 21.

67. *LE*, 5.

68. *LS*, 128.

69. Bloodworth, *Hired*.

70. Bryce Covert, "Walmart Prices Would Rise by Pennies if It Paid Workers More than Poverty Wages," *Think Progress*, April 11, 2014.

71. Jeffrey D. Sachs, "The Cure for Gilead," *Huffington Post*, August 3, 2015.

72. See Katie Thomas, "Patients Eagerly Awaited a Generic Drug. Then They Saw the Price," *New York Times*, February 23, 2018, https://www.nytimes.com/2018/02/23 /health/valeant-drug-price-syprine.html.

73. Carbon Majors Database, *Carbon Majors Report, 2017*.

74. See Oreskes and Conway, *Merchants Of Doubt*; Mayer, *Dark Money*; Bill McKibben, "Global Warming's Terrifying New Math," *Rolling Stone*, July 19, 2012.

75. Evers-Hillstrom, "Lobbying Spending Reaches $3.4 Billion in 2018."

76. Annett et al., *Ethics in Action for Sustainable Development*.

77. *CIV*, 40.

78. *CIV*, 38.

79. *CIV*, 46.

80. See Milbank and Pabst, *Politics of Virtue*.

81. See Gold, *New Financial Horizons*.

82. *LS*, 195.

83. *LS*, 51.

84. *LS*, 191.

85. *LS*, 192.

86. See Aldred, *License to Be Bad*, 216.

87. *LE*, 9.

88. *LE*, 25.

89. *LE*, 16.

90. *LS*, 127–28.

91. See De Neve and Ward, "Happiness and Work."

92. *LE*, 18.

93. *CIV*, 25.

94. *LS*, 128.

95. See Dao and Loungani, "Human Cost of Recessions."

96. *PP*, 59.

97. *RN*, 20.

98. *RN*, 3.

99. *RN*, 45.

100. *RN*, 45.

101. *LE*, 19.

102. See Cloutier, *Vice of Luxury*, ch. 7.

103. *LE*, 18.

104. *LS*, 20.

105. Pope Francis, "Address of His Holiness Pope Francis to Delegates from the Italian Confederation of Workers' Unions (CISL)."

106. *CIV*, 64.

107. Pope Francis, "Address of His Holiness Pope Francis to Delegates from the Italian Confederation of Workers' Unions (CISL)."

108. *LE*, 20.

109. *CIV*, 25.

110. *QA*, 65.

111. For a deep dive into this kind of Catholic corporatism, see Daly, "Church of Labor."

112. *MM*, 77.

113. See Shadle, *Interrupting Capitalism*, ch. 7.

114. *LE*, 14.

115. *LE*, 14.

116. Schneider, *Everything for Everyone*.

117. Hinson-Hasty, *Problem of Wealth*, 179.

118. Medaille, *Vocation of Business*.

119. See Matt Mazewski, "Bringing the Workers on Board: The Catholic Roots of Codetermination," *Commonweal*, March 14, 2019; Glasman, "Politics of Employment"; Piketty, *Capital and Ideology*.

120. Piketty, *Capital and Ideology*, 500.

121. Milbank and Pabst, *Politics of Virtue*.

122. See Bowles, *New Economics of Inequality and Redistribution*; Anderson, *Private Government*.

123. Glasman, "Politics of Employment."

124. See Dembinski, "Fecundity vs. Efficiency."

125. Mazzucato, *Value of Everything*, 138.

126. Shaxson, *Finance Curse*.

127. Mazzucato, *Value of Everything*, 139.

128. Jill Treanor, "FSA Boss Lord Turner Attacks CBI Chief over 'Socially Useless' City Behaviour," *Guardian*, November 23, 2009.

129. Mazzucato, *Value of Everything*, 136.

130. Tooze, *Crashed*.

131. Tooze.

132. Reich, *Saving Capitalism*.

133. Mian and Sufi, *House of Debt*.

134. Labaton Sucharow, "Wall Street, Main Street, Fleet Street."

135. Cohn, Fehr, and Marechal, "Business Culture and Dishonesty in the Banking Industry."

136. Jeffrey D Sachs, "The Harvard IKB School of Engineering," *Huffington Post*, June 5, 2015.

137. This sordid tale is documented in Wright and Hope, *Billion Dollar Whale*.

138. See Shaxson, *Finance Curse*, ch. 9.

139. Mazzucato, *Value of Everything*, 157.

140. Mazzucato, 167.

141. *QA*, 105–9.

142. *CA*, 48.

143. *CA*, 43.

144. *CIV*, 65.

145. *CIV*, 40.

146. *LS*, 189.

147. *LS*, 109.

148. *LS*, 56.

149. *EG*, 57–58.

6

Inequality

The Root of Social Ills

The title of this chapter comes from a Pope Francis quote in *Evangelii Gaudium*.[1] It marks the culmination of long-running concern in Catholic social teaching that a skewed distribution of income and wealth is not only inherently unjust but can result in a host of economic and social dysfunctions. Inequality has in recent years justifiably risen to the top of the political agenda. Economists, long schooled in a neoclassical tradition that pays little heed to distributional issues, are once again starting to take inequality seriously. Inequality is also reflected in an employment crisis, given the increasing prevalence of poor pay, unstable work, and few protections for workers.

Back in 1936, Keynes concluded his magnum opus, *The General Theory of Employment, Interest, and Money*, with the claim that "the outstanding faults of the economic society in which we live are its failure to provide for full employment and its arbitrary and inequitable distribution of wealth and incomes."[2] The same failure is true today, possibly even more so. And once again, the corpus of Catholic social teaching has been ahead of the curve in warning about these dysfunctions.

Inequality in Catholic Social Teaching

Catholic social teaching has condemned both inequality within and between countries. The concern with inequality within countries goes all the way back to

Pope Leo XIII in *Rerum Novarum*, when he railed against the rich being able to "lay upon the teeming masses of the laboring poor a yoke little better than that of slavery itself."[3] The concern in these early encyclicals is that such treatment of the poor and the working class harms social harmony. Not only is inequality unjust in itself—by violating the principles of commutative, distributive, and social justice—but it could lead to social upheaval and a strengthening of support for socialist collectivism, a specter that has always haunted the Church.

Pope Pius XI stated the position clearly in *Quadragesimo Anno*:

> Therefore, the riches that economic-social developments constantly increase ought to be so distributed among individual persons and classes that the common advantage of all. . . . By this law of social justice, one class is forbidden to exclude the other from sharing in the benefits. . . .
>
> . . . To each, therefore, must be given his own share of goods, and the distribution of created goods, which, as every discerning person knows, is laboring today under the gravest evils due to the huge disparity between the few exceedingly rich and the unnumbered propertyless, must be effectively called back to and brought into conformity with the norms of the common good, that is, social justice.[4]

Pius sees a role for the state in bringing the distribution of income into conformity with the common good. Pope John XXIII took up this theme in *Mater et Magistra*, arguing that justice called for full participation in the economic and social life of the community, which meant that inequalities had to be kept in check.

> Economic progress must be accompanied by a corresponding social progress, so that all classes of citizens can participate in the increased productivity. The utmost vigilance and effort is needed to ensure that social inequalities, so far from increasing, are reduced to a minimum. . . .
>
> . . . From this it follows that the economic prosperity of a nation is not so much its total assets in terms of wealth and property, as the equitable division and distribution of this wealth.[5]

This is a strong claim. Pope John is essentially denying that true prosperity can be achieved when inequality is too high. What matters is the distribution. Remember that GDP is a sum, and a sum can simply zero people out. Pope John XXIII follows up with this theme: "Increase in production and productive efficiency is, of course, sound policy, and indeed a vital necessity. However, it is no less necessary—and justice itself demands—that the riches produced be distributed fairly among all members of the political community."[6]

All of this teaching is summed up succinctly in the important Vatican II document *Gaudium et Spes*: "Excessive economic and social differences between the members of the one human family or population groups cause scandal, and militate against social justice, equity, the dignity of the human person, as well as social and international peace."[7]

As I've noted already, there was a notable shift in Catholic social teaching from this period onward from a unique focus on justice between classes in industrial countries to the plight of undeveloped nations, including in terms of inequalities between countries. Pope Paul VI in *Populorum Progressio*, for example, notes a widening gap between rich and poor nations combined with social unrest spreading throughout the world. He traces this condition to the fact that "there are the flagrant inequalities not merely in the enjoyment of possessions, but even more in the exercise of power."[8]

Likewise in *Sollicitudo Rei Socialis*, Pope John Paul II denounced the gap between rich and poor across the world: "One of the greatest injustices in the contemporary world consists precisely in this: that the ones who possess much are relatively few and those who possess almost nothing are many. It is the injustice of the poor distribution of the goods and services originally intended for all."[9]

Pope John Paul argues that this sorry state of affairs hurts not only the excluded but also the rich, who put possessions over what truly matters for happiness in the sense of integral human development—the focus on "being" rather than "having." It is in this context that he condemns the stark juxtaposition of underdevelopment and "superdevelopment."[10]

We can see that this view prefigures Pope Francis's strong critique of the economy of exclusion and the throwaway culture in *Laudato Si'*. Before we get there, though, to respect the chronology, we need to look at what Pope Benedict XVI had to say in *Caritas in Veritate*. Like his predecessors, Benedict was alarmed by the growing disparities of income and wealth—not only by the exclusion of those on the bottom but on the misplaced priorities of those on the top. Again, he contrasts deprivation and superdevelopment: "The world's wealth is growing in absolute terms, but inequalities are on the increase. In rich countries, new sectors of society are succumbing to poverty and new forms of poverty are emerging. In poorer areas some groups enjoy a sort of 'superdevelopment' of a wasteful and consumerist kind which forms an unacceptable contrast with the ongoing situations of dehumanizing deprivation. 'The scandal of glaring inequalities' continues."[11]

In a useful insight, Pope Benedict also links growing inequality to the undermining of trust and social capital, which could have knock-on effects for stability, cohesion, and even democracy. In this situation, he clearly sees inequality as the enemy of the principles of solidarity, reciprocity, and gratuitousness:

> The dignity of the individual and the demands of justice require, particularly today, that economic choices do not cause disparities in wealth to increase in an excessive and morally unacceptable manner, and that we continue to prioritize the goal of access to steady employment for everyone. . . . Through the systemic increase of social inequality, both within a single country and between the populations of different countries (i.e. the massive increase in relative poverty), not only does social cohesion suffer, thereby placing democracy at risk, but so too does the economy, through the progressive erosion of "social capital": the network of relationships of trust, dependability, and respect for rules, all of which are indispensable for any form of civil coexistence.[12]

Pope Francis follows on from this observation, explicitly linking inequality to instability and violence: "Until exclusion and inequality in society and between peoples are reversed, it will be impossible to eliminate violence. . . . This is not the case simply because inequality provokes a violent reaction from those excluded from the system, but because the socioeconomic system is unjust at its root."[13]

Leading from this assertion he declares that inequality is the root of social ills and that we must accordingly reject and repudiate an economy of exclusion and inequality—which, in his view, is intricately connected to free market ideology and the subservience of the economy to finance. He explicitly condemns a "winner takes all" economy: "This vision of 'might is right' has engendered immense inequality, injustice and acts of violence against the majority of humanity, since resources end up in the hands of the first comer or the most powerful: the winner takes all."[14] For Pope Francis, the same attitudes that are used to defend and perpetuate inequality also lead to destruction of the environment—the same "might is right" attitude in the context of hyperconsumption of the few juxtaposed against the exclusion of the many. Thus inequality is not just a social condition; it is the result of an interior corruption of who we are supposed to be as human beings.

The Scope of Inequality

This rise in inequality is certainly a defining economic narrative of our era. While income inequality between countries has narrowed over the past few decades, inequality within countries has widened sharply[15]—so much so that in countries like the United States and the United Kingdom, the distribution of income is back to where it was during the Gilded Age. The reduction of between-country inequality reflects a laudable process of convergence, driven by rapid economic growth and poverty alleviation in countries such as China and India. Some have argued that this convergence indicates that overall inequality in the world is not as bad as it seems and that we can safely ignore rising inequality within countries. But this assertion makes little sense. It would involve telling a working-class person in the United States to accept their lot in life because their compatriots in China are doing better. This is clearly not a sustainable argument, politically or economically. And the locus for policies that affect inequality tends to be at the level of the nation-state. There's nothing fateful about rising inequality; it boils down to policy decisions.

In 2020, the United Nations documented the widespread nature of inequality across the world. It noted that, over the past three decades—as the neoliberal era entered full throttle—income inequality increased in most rich countries and in some middle-income countries, including China and India. These countries represent over 70 percent of the world's population. Over this period, the share of income accruing to the top 1 percent jumped in forty-six out of fifty-seven countries for which data are available.[16]

This pattern is also borne out in the *World Inequality Report*, published in 2018. The authors, leading experts in inequality research, show again that income inequality has increased in all world regions, though at different speeds.[17] It is lowest in Europe and highest in the Middle East; other regions with high inequality include Latin America, South Asia, and sub-Saharan Africa. It is especially instructive to look at the differences between western Europe and the United States (see figure 6.1).

In 1980, inequality was similar between these regions; the top 1 percent gained about 10 percent of all income. By 2016, this figure had nudged up to 12 percent in western Europe. But in the United States, it hit 20 percent. As for the bottom 50 percent's share of the wealth, it has held steady in western Europe but fallen in the United States from over 20 percent to barely 12 percent—a mirror image of the top 1 percent. In fact, the gains of the top 1 percent are as large as the losses of the bottom 50 percent.[18] As Emmanuel Saez and Gabriel Zucman point out, the top 1 percent earns twice as much as the entire working-class population—the half of the US population getting by on an average income of $18,500. This group is fifty times larger than the top 1 percent. It's actually worse for wealth than for income; the top 1 percent's share of total wealth rose from 22 percent to 39 percent since 1980.[19] The comparisons with Europe show clearly that inequality is not predetermined by economic

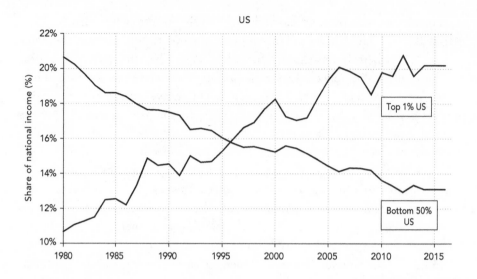

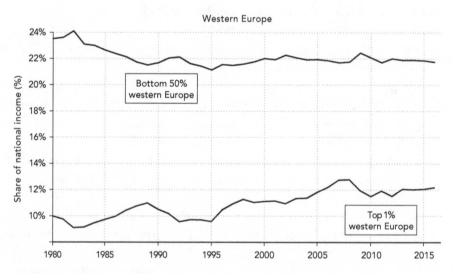

Figure 6.1. Top 1 percent versus bottom 50 percent of national income shares in the United States and western Europe, 1980–2016: diverging income inequality trajectories. (a) In 2016, 12 percent of national income was received by the top 1 percent in western Europe, compared to 20 percent in the United States. In 1980, 10 percent of national income was received by the top 1 percent in western Europe, compared to 11 percent in the United States. (b) In 2016, 22 percent of national income was received by the bottom 50 percent in western Europe. Reproduced by permission from Alvaredo et al., *World Inequality Report 2018*. See wir2018.wid.world for data series and notes.

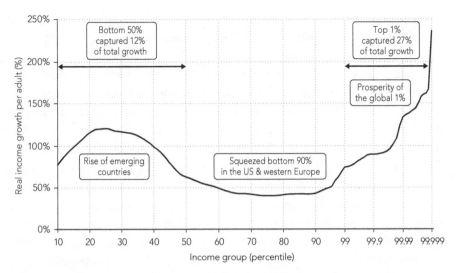

Figure 6.2. The "elephant curve," showing global inequality and growth, 1980–2016. On the horizontal axis, the world's population is divided into a hundred groups of equal population size and sorted in ascending order from left to right, according to each group's income level. The top 1 percent group is divided into ten groups, the richest of these groups is also divided into ten groups, and the very top group is again divided into ten groups of equal population size. The vertical axis shows the total income growth of an average individual in each group between 1980 and 2016. Income estimates account for differences in the cost of living between countries. Values are net of inflation. Reproduced by permission from Alvaredo et al., *World Inequality Report 2018.* See wir2018. wid.world for data series and notes.

laws but instead responds to economic policies and social norms. It is no accident that the United States, the ground zero of neoliberalism, has witnessed the sharpest spike in inequality since 1980.

Across the world, as noted in chapter 4, the top 1 percent captured twice as much of the wealth as the bottom half since 1980. Yet at the global level, the bottom half saw income gains, largely from high growth in China and India. This pattern gives rise to the famous "elephant curve"—some gains at the bottom, thanks to growth in rising Asia; very large gains at the top; and a squeezed middle, representing the working and middle classes in the United States and western Europe (the bottom 90 percent); see figure 6.2. The really big winners over the past three decades were the global plutocrats, especially the cadre of billionaires whose wealth more than doubled as a share of global GDP over this period.[20] This chart alone can explain so much of the political dynamics of inequality: the increasing distance of the wealthy from the common good, combined with rising social and political tensions among the working classes in the United States and Europe.

What accounts for this rising inequality? The standard economic reason is a combination of technological change and globalization.[21] The technology argument essentially says that the nature of technological progress over the past few decades has boosted the productivity of high-skilled workers over low-skilled workers. Proponents of this argument call the extra wages a "skill premium" and argue that it is justifiably earned because the workers have invested in the education needed to do well in this modern economy. This argument is one reason why neoliberalism puts so much of its faith in education; if people get enough education, then the skill premium should fall, perhaps even to zero. The globalization argument is also one based on fate. It says that countries that face more competition from places with lower wages lose out, especially lower-skilled workers in those countries. Politicians often blame immigration for the downward pressure on wages, as immigrants compete for low-wage jobs. But this argument is more about the free movement of capital. Firms can easily outsource and shift business to—or use supply chains from—countries offering lower wages, lower labor protections and other regulations, and lower taxes. Outsourcing is again expected to lead to a wage premium of high-skilled over low-skilled workers, as the latter are competing with workers in developing countries. And the answer, once again, is deemed to be investment in education.

These economic factors have a lot of validity. They certainly can help explain the "hollowing out" of the working class in communities across the United States and Europe, as those without the right skills to function in today's economy find themselves left out in the cold. But this explanation is by no means the whole story. As Thomas Piketty has noted correctly, this story ignores the role of capital.[22] While economists were debating the skills premium between different kinds of workers, Piketty argued that they should be taking one step back and looking at the distribution between capital and labor itself, a leading concern of economics before neoclassical economists insisted on playing down these differences. Also, this neglect might have been justified by the stability of the labor and capital shares of national income; people assumed this was some kind of iron law that could never change. But change it did. In the United States, the labor share of national income, which was around 67 percent in the late 1970s, has fallen by 4–5 percentage points since then, and the capital share of national income has risen accordingly. As noted by Branko Milanovic, this change increases inequality for two reasons: first, people who rely a lot on capital income are genuinely rich, so the rich are getting richer, and second, capital ownership is highly concentrated.[23] He presents some numbers to back this up. For example, in the United States, the top 1 percent hold half of all stocks and mutual funds, 55 percent of securities, 63 percent of shares in business, and 65 percent of financial trusts. Overall, the top 10 percent control more than 90 percent of financial assets.[24] These figures should be borne in mind the next time financial markets are put forward as indicators of economic health and well-being. At the same time, the kinds of capital held by the rich generate higher returns. In 2013, 20 percent of American households had zero or negative net wealth, while two-thirds of the wealth of the middle 60 percent consisted of housing and pension funds. For the top 20 percent, the picture is very different. These people hold much more wealth in equity and financial instruments—three-quarters for the top 1 percent. Why does this matter? Because the rich win not only in levels but in composition. From 1983 to 2013, the average real rate of return on financial assets was 6.3 percent. For housing it was a mere 0.6 percent.[25]

Based on all of this, Piketty proposed a new "iron law": as countries get richer, the capital share will increase, causing inequality to increase. He argued that the relatively low level of inequality in the social democratic era was the exception rather than the rule, driven both by the destruction of capital in war and the sense of solidarity generated by the war.

What can help explain the rise in capital ratios during the neoliberal era? In addition to the twin forces of technological change and globalization, one key seems to be the reduced bargaining power of labor; quite simply, capital gained the ability to capture a larger share of the pie for itself. As Anthony Atkinson notes, this unbalanced bargaining power can shred basic norms of prudence and fairness in terms of the distribution between wages and profits; in older parlance, virtue can be undermined.[26]

It seems clear that differences in unionization rates across both space and time can account for different patterns of capital and labor shares of national income. In the United States, the number of workers covered by collective-bargaining agreements reached 29 percent of all workers at its peak in 1960. But even then, European collective-bargaining rates often exceeded 90 percent, with effectively the entire economy under the auspices of unions. By the early 2000s, collective-bargaining coverage in the United States had fallen to 13 percent—and less than 8 percent in the private sector.[27] Japan too manages to keep inequality low with high unionization rates. While unionization rates in Japan were under 10 percent before the war, they had risen to 60 percent by 1949—part of the American occupation's plan to reduce inequality and support democratization of Japanese economic institutions.[28]

A further factor in explaining inequality is the scaling back of progressive taxation and the welfare state. All across the world, thanks in part to globalization, corporate taxes have fallen substantially over this period, while the tax burden on wages has barely changed. These patterns are stark, especially in the United States. Saez and Zucman show that when we account for all taxes, the US tax system looks like a giant flat tax whereby all social groups pay an average 25–30 percent of their incomes—except for the superrich, who pay only a bare 20 percent. Indeed, they find that billionaires now pay lower tax rates than the working class.[29] Why do the poor pay so much? Because they pay both payroll taxes and consumption taxes, both of which are regressive. The reduction in tax progressivity has a couple of effects. The direct effect is straightforward; it allows the rich to keep more of every extra dollar earned, with everybody else either paying more or enjoying lower levels of public services (which can in turn increase inequality). The indirect effect works by encouraging companies and executives to seek higher capital income and executive pay, as each extra dollar faces a lower tax rate—thus perpetuating the cycle of inequality. Lower transfers in turn fail to protect people from the effects of market inequality as they did in the social democratic era. That era managed to keep inequality in check both because it kept market incomes from getting too dispersed and because the welfare state could even out the market distribution. In the neoliberal era, we are losing out on both fronts.

From this recent historical evidence, it seems clear that high inequality is not destiny. Piketty is too pessimistic when he calls it endemic to capitalist modes of production, on the basis that the financial return on wealth tends to exceed the rate of economic growth over long periods of time. He is surely right that inequality can become entrenched and self-perpetuating, leading to what he calls "patrimonial capitalism," marked by rising shares of capital in national income. But whether we allow these forces to emerge in this way is a conscious choice.

It is similarly misguided to claim that the twin forces of technology and globalization lead to natural increases in inequality. As noted, both the United States and western Europe faced the same economic forces but with vastly different trajectories for inequality. I think Milanovic says it best: inequality with roots in economics tends to be reinforced by politics as the increasing power of elites allows them to bend policy toward their will, allowing it to become long lasting and self-perpetuating.[30] Indeed, this outcome is what seems to have happened: during the two great waves of inequality—the long one that began at the beginning of the industrial revolution and only ended in the 1930s, and the more recent one that began around 1980—the driving forces might have been technological change and globalization, but these forces were reinforced in each case by various packages of pro-rich policies, such as cuts in upper income and capital taxes, curbs on the bargaining power of labor, a rollback of social protections, greater tolerance for monopoly power, and looser restraints on financial innovation.

The bottom line is that the state of inequality boils down to political will. Yes, there are forces that drive inequality up, but will these be fed or fought? The problem today is that it is becoming increasingly difficult to slow down the juggernaut. Especially in the United States, the plutocratic forces of large corporations and the superrich now dominate politics and bend policies toward their will like never before, in part due to loose campaign finance regulations and a cavalcade of money in politics. As noted by Milanovic, a tiny sliver of the superrich—the top 1 percent of the top 1 percent—contributed 40 percent of campaign contributions in the United States in 2016.[31] No wonder that some have argued that the United States is now a functioning plutocracy and that politicians cater almost exclusively to the interests of the wealthy.[32]

A further political economy effect comes from one of the unique features of the neoliberal era: the people who own a lot of capital today also earn high wages from labor. This was certainly not true during the first Gilded Age, when a true leisure class earned income solely from capital—think of Downton Abbey. Today, the owners of capital work and draw high salaries—think of investment bankers. In 1980, only 15 percent of the top decile in capital income were also in the top decile of labor income; this figure has doubled since then.[33] This change means that it is hard to put together a coalition against plutocracy, as it is bound to overlap with wage earners.

Both globalization and technological change are also hurting the power of labor to organize. Globalization essentially boosts the power of capital over labor, and a globalization of financialization—with free movements of capital jetting across borders seeking the highest short-term return—makes matters worse. Indeed, a major IMF study (spanning 149 countries over four decades) demonstrates that financial globalization directly increases inequality for two reasons.[34] First, financial globalization is more likely to lead to financial crises in the form of boom-bust cycles—money flooding in, and money flooding back out on the slightest hint of bad news. These financial crises make inequality worse. Second, capital mobility boosts the power of capital over labor, again making inequality worse. What effects has technology had? Some have argued that the favoring of high-skilled over low-skilled workers breaks labor solidarity, making it harder for workers to find common cause.[35] These lower-skilled workers tend to conglomerate in corners of the economy that are just harder to unionize as they don't rely on the old plant-based industrial model—the services sector and the gig economy, for example. Given all of this, it is no surprise that labor protections have been stripped away over the past few decades and that this has been shown to feed into rising inequality.[36]

It is certainly true that over the long haul of history, inequality has tended to be the norm. In perhaps one of the most ambitious books ever written on the subject, historian Scheidel looked at patterns of inequality over the broad span of human history, from ancient Mesopotamia to the present day.[37] He shows that inequality almost never falls for benign reasons; its decline is almost always due to malign factors such as mass-mobilization warfare, revolutions, state collapse, or major pandemics. Piketty's focus is on much more recent history, but he would surely agree with this—hardly a cheerful conclusion. Branko Milanovic, while focusing on more recent centuries, also notes that high inequality eventually reaches a breaking point, but it usually does not fall on its own; it risks, instead, generating processes such as wars, revolutions, and massive social disruption that ultimately bring it down. He is thinking here about the two world wars and the calamitous first half of the last century, which he saw as partly due to inequality collapsing under its own weight.

From this historical perspective, then, the social democratic era was clearly abnormal. It showed that inequality could be kept low for benign rather than malign reasons. For sure, there were some unique factors—the legacy of destruction by war, an ethos of solidarity that extended across three decades, a collapse of faith in free markets, and a fear of communist gains. These factors all came together to produce policies that resisted any natural tendencies toward an inequality spiral: high and progressive taxes, robust welfare states based on universal transfers, strong unions and high levels of collective bargaining, restraints on monopoly power, and strong financial regulations and limited movement of capital across borders. At the same time, education expanded dramatically as secondary education became free and more and more children were able to attend university for the first time. So yes, this was a unique period. But it also gives us hope, showing that it is possible to reduce inequality with the right level of social cohesion and political determination. Fighting the plutocratic forces that lead to self-perpetuating inequality might be difficult, but it is not impossible. The policies needed to reduce inequality today might not be the same as during the social democratic era, given that the challenges and constraints are somewhat different. But we can take comfort from the fact that an ethos of solidarity is capable of delivering great benefits. This is what Catholic social teaching has been saying all along.

Why Inequality Matters

I have been assuming so far that keeping inequality low is a worthy goal, in line with the insights of Catholic social teaching. But is it? Neoclassical economics, remember, puts inequality on the back footing. It argues that the focus should be on Pareto efficiency, the point at which it is no longer possible to make somebody better off without making somebody else worse off. Pareto efficiency, recall, is compatible with vast amounts of inequality, and it pretty much rules out income redistribution. Neoclassical economists will argue that this does not necessarily mean that inequality is unimportant, just that it belongs to the domain of politics, not economics. And neoclassical economics believes there will be trade-offs; if you want lower inequality, you will need to sacrifice growth, as the policies to achieve this lower inequality lead to reduced incentives to work, save, and invest. And if all factors of production are paid their marginal product, then market outcomes are fair too and should not be interfered with. All told, there has been a strong bias against any concern for inequality in neoclassical economics.

There is a second argument against a focus on inequality. This one says that, yes, distributional concerns matter as well as efficiency but that we should focus on the bottom of the pile, not the entire distribution. In other words, focus on poverty, not inequality. Make sure people have enough resources to live a dignified life, and don't pay any attention to vast amounts of wealth at the very top. There's certainly some logic to this. The preferential option for the poor tells us that the bottom of the pile should be top of our concerns. Some Catholic theologians, such as Finn, have argued that Catholic social teaching focuses primarily on meeting the needs of all and less on large fortunes at the top.[38] Of course, one counterargument is that providing all with the resources to achieve integral human development requires some leveling at the top. But the deeper question still holds: Is there anything wrong per se with a concentration of income and wealth at the top?

Let me take these two objections in turn. The first is the notion that there is a trade-off between equity and economic growth, a standard argument of neoclassical economics. The evidence suggests that this argument does not apply in recent times. In a number of groundbreaking studies, the IMF has shown that inequality is associated with lower and less durable economic growth and that growth trickles up from the poor and middle classes, not down from the rich.[39] Specifically, if the income share of the top 20 percent rises, economic growth declines over the medium term; but if the income share of the bottom 20 percent rises, then so does medium-term economic growth. This phenomenon gels with the postwar evidence of lower growth and productivity in the neoliberal era, marked by high and rising inequality, than in the social democratic era, as documented by Gordon.[40]

Why might inequality lead to lower growth? I can think of at least six reasons.

First, since the rich tend to save a greater proportion of their income than the poor or middle class, then aggregate demand is lower in more unequal societies, and aggregate demand drives growth at least in the short run. This argument goes back to Keynes and was made in more recent times by Nobel Prize–winning economist Joseph Stiglitz in the context of inequality.[41]

Second, getting back to the insights of Pope Benedict and Pope Francis, inequality has been shown to undermine trust and social capital.[42] Since trust is the lubricant that makes economic interactions work smoothly, this lack of trust in turn reduces economic efficiency and growth. In extreme cases, it can lead to instability and violence. Take the example of Latin America, for example, one of the world's most unequal regions.[43] Here, the pattern tends to be a seesaw between oligarchic dominance and populist backlashes, a pattern that is bad both for growth and the common good. As inequality in the United States inches toward Latin American levels, it could end up gravitating toward this political economy model; indeed, recent evidence points in that direction.

Third, inequality of outcomes is associated with inequality of opportunities, denoting the waste of skills and talents, undermining productivity and growth. Evidence suggests that advantage today tends to be transmitted across generations more than in the past, in the sense that there is a stronger correlation between parents' and children's incomes. Indeed, what Alan Krueger dubbed the "Great Gatsby Curve" shows that upward mobility across generations is negatively correlated with inequality within countries.[44] And within the United States, researchers have shown that regions with higher social mobility have lower inequality and higher social capital.[45] The fabled "American Dream" seems to be in abeyance. Richard Reeves referred to this phenomenon as "dream hoarding," whereby the wealthy monopolize advantages for the own children—the combination of better education, superior social advantages, and stronger social connections.[46] Inequality magnifies the social advantages of the rich, but the rich are not necessarily the most productive.

Fourth, inequality is in part due to financialization of the real economy and financial-sector dominance. There are a number of reasons why a large financial sector can lower growth. For a start, financialization can create bubbles, and bubbles burst, leading to damaging financial crises. We saw this most starkly during the 2008 global financial crisis. Another reason is that financialization leads to a misallocation of talent, as the best and brightest join an industry that basically amounts to high-tech gambling, rather than devoting their talents to the development of the real economy.[47] Another issue is that the financial sector extracts value from the economy and makes corporations focus too much on the short term. During the neoliberal era, the focus shifted away from producing quality goods and services towards a model of financialization focused on gimmicks to boost stock prices—mergers, stock buybacks, corporate raiders saddling a company with debt. A major IMF study encompassing 128 countries from 1980 to 2013 showed that the effect of financial-sector development on productivity and growth was bell shaped, starting out as positive but eventually turning negative—and that the United States was over the hump in terms of having too much finance.[48] Another study from the Roosevelt Institute tries to estimate the overall costs of excess finance for the United States, coming up with a price tag of somewhere between $12.9 trillion and $22.7 trillion since 1990—between $40,000 and $70,000 for every man, woman, and child in the United States.[49] The "finance curse" identified by Nicholas Shaxson comes from the costs of the global financial crisis combined with the costs of misallocation of resources and value extraction.[50]

Fifth, and relatedly, inequality tends to be accompanied by rent seeking, which stifles innovation and healthy competition.[51] Rent seeking is the name for the tendency to extract rather than create wealth, and it is driven by such factors as monopoly power, corporate concentration, and weak corporate governance. While the lid was kept on corporate power during the social democratic era, this lid has largely been lifted in the neoliberal era.[52] The IMF has argued that market power is rising, which could hurt investment and innovation as well as lower the labor shares of national income, pointing once again to both low growth and high inequality.[53] Rent seeking is particularly marked in the financial sector— the Roosevelt Institute study estimated a $3.6 trillion–$4.2 trillion cost of rent seeking in this sector since 1990, driven by such factors as anticompetitive practices, government subsidies such as bailouts, fraudulent activities, and excess pay of bankers and financial sector executives.[54]

Sixth, inequality reduces the will and resources to make the investments needed to drive long-term growth, especially in areas such as infrastructure, health, education, and research and development. In unequal societies, the rich tend to gravitate to separate enclaves, and so tend to have little contact with the nonrich. They feel little inclination to fund the basic public goods that support integral human development and the common good. Instead, they seek to cut their own taxes so they can meet their own needs privately. But without public funding of these basic activities, long-term economic growth is bound to suffer.

I now want to address the second objection opposed to a focus on a skewed income distribution—that we should care more about poverty than inequality, that as long as the poor are taken care of, large disparities of income are not worth worrying about. I want to argue that inequality itself undermines solidarity and human flourishing and thus can also hurt the rich as well as the poor.

In its essence, as hinted at already, inequality severs the sense of shared purpose necessary for the realization of the common good.[55] The rich shrink into circles of social similarity, with greater distance from, and care for, their fellow citizens. As proximity diminishes, so does solidarity, and this distancing also relates to what Sandel dubs the "tyranny of merit," the notion that people are responsible for their own fate and get what they deserve from the market.[56] Hence trust, cohesion, and social capital are all diminished. Note that this breakdown feeds into the market ideology of neoliberalism; as the rich distance themselves from the common good, they become more inclined to view their success as earned by themselves, and this mindset in turn shreds solidarity even further. Thus we can see a vicious cycle: neoliberalism, which downplays solidarity, boosts inequality, and this in turn further undermines solidarity, which increases the traction of neoliberal prescriptions.

This critique of inequality, though, is far older than neoliberalism. Plato called inequality "the greatest of all plagues" because the rich felt free to eschew the norms of social cooperation.[57] He argued that society should avoid both extreme poverty and excess wealth. Likewise, Aristotle held that the ability of the political community to promote the common good would be impeded by large gaps between rich and poor—because the poor are too poor to embrace civic duty, while the rich are more attached to their wealth than to civic obligations. The founding fathers of the United States fretted over similar concerns of oligarchic control of politics in the face of high inequality.[58] If anything, this predicament is magnified by neoliberalism, which insists that wealth seeking is the main purpose in life.

Our old friend Adam Smith also offered some useful insights. Smith saw morality as driven by fellow feeling: the innate tendency to form an empathic connection with our fellow human beings by imaginatively placing ourselves in their shoes. He believed happiness flows from giving and receiving this "sympathy." Yet Smith argues that this impulse can misfire in the sense that we are more inclined to sympathize with the rich than the poor. In his words, this "disposition to admire, and almost to worship, the rich and the powerful, and to despise, or, at least, to neglect persons of poor and mean condition" is "the great and most universal cause of the corruption of our moral sentiments."[59] Thus, as noted by political scientist Dennis Rasmussen, Smith's framework suggests that inequality has the potential to undermine virtue among rich and poor alike.[60] Why? Because the rich can gain social approval without needing to act morally, and others seek to emulate the unworthy rich—undermining moral norms more generally. In turn, this corruption in moral sentiments reduces happiness and well-being; it leads people to obsess over wealth, and it deprives the poor of crucial bonds of sympathy. Inequality, therefore, hurts both the rich and the poor.

The economist Thorstein Veblen made a somewhat similar point in a book he wrote back in 1899 called *The Theory of the Leisure Class*. In this book, Veblen described the kinds of inequality during the first Gilded Age—whereby the rich lived, Downton Abbey style, from capital income and enjoyed a life of leisure and conspicuous consumption. He argued that greed ensnared people, and the plutocrats sought more and more, even if they did not contribute to the common good.[61] As with Smith, Veblen thought that the poor were collateral damage in this moral corruption, as they sought to emulate the rich. Today, as noted above, we do not have this kind of leisure class as the owners of capital also tend to work.[62] But the analysis still holds: the "lifestyles of the rich and famous" still entice, and people still seek to emulate them.

In the Christian tradition, of course, this wealth seeking is regarded as a form of moral corruption. Recall from chapter 1 that the Church Fathers felt strongly that the greed animating an idolatry of wealth hurts the rich as well as the poor. Aquinas agreed, arguing that the preoccupation with wealth accumulation that underpins income inequality is disordered, as it fails to recognize that wealth is only a means to an end and should not be sought for its own sake. Recently, theologian Kate Ward has focused explicitly on the link between virtue ethics and inequality, drawing a link between the distribution of income and the degradation of virtues such as justice, solidarity, and humility. She argues that this association is due to such factors as the segregation associated with inequality, whereby the rich and poor live nonoverlapping lives, and the tendency for the rich to enjoy outsize economic and political power, which tends to corrupt.[63]

Moreover, it is not surprising that researchers have found that inequality lies behind a host of social dysfunctions. In a landmark book called *The Spirit Level*, social epidemiologists Richard Wilkinson and Kate Pickett have demonstrated that inequality reduced empathy and trust across the board.[64] Their analysis linked a skewed income distribution to a litany of social ills, including high unemployment and economic insecurity; high personal indebtedness; poor nutrition; low life expectancy; high infant mortality; poor physical and mental health; more prevalent drug abuse; weak educational attainment; limited social mobility; more crime, violence, and imprisonment; and higher levels of obesity, more teenage pregnancies, and poor child well-being. And while the poor suffer most, outcomes tend to be weaker even for the better off in more unequal societies. The problem is that inequality undermines social cohesion, with lower levels of civic engagement and greater social distance between people. Inequality fosters a lack of trust and solidarity, causing the common good to rip apart. It is this lack of trust that accounts for the results relating to violence and health. These relationships show that we are truly social animals bound to a common good, and when this falls apart, all hell breaks loose.

In a follow-up book called *The Inner Level*, Wilkinson and Pickett drill down into the psychological dimension of the social dysfunctions wrought by inequality.[65] They argue that different social structures promote different psychological responses. In more egalitarian societies, social strategies are based on friendship, reciprocity, and cooperation. Hence in highly unequal societies, things tend to go wrong at the psychological level. Wilkinson and Pickett argue that status becomes more important in these societies, which in turn leads to status anxiety. This phenomenon can become evident in two different ways. First, people can be over-come with thoughts of inadequacy, self-doubt, low self-esteem, and depression. Second, on the opposite end of the scale, they can gravitate toward narcissism and self-aggrandizement that serves as a mask for self-doubt. Wilkinson and Pickett show that mental disorders such as depression, anxiety, schizophrenia, and psychosis are more common diagnoses in more unequal societies. Depression seems to come from the combination of low social capital and high status anxiety. People participate less in community life because social contact becomes more stressful. They deal with stress by resorting to disordered goods such as alcohol, drugs, comfort eating, and shopping. None of these activities buys real happiness. Narcissism is also more elevated in more unequal societies. The authors also note that those born later, coming of age in the neoliberal years, ranked wealth, image, and fame over self-acceptance, affiliation, and community. These outcomes reflect the symbiosis between the reality of inequality and the ideology of neoliberalism.

In tandem with these findings, psychological studies have shown that higher social class predicts more unethical and antisocial behavior. Across a variety of different experiments, richer people displayed less empathy, proved to be less generous, and were more likely to lie or cheat.[66] To explain these stark find-ings, the researchers suggested that the combination of increased resources and a degree of independence from others led the wealthy to view self-interest and greed as virtuous. Other studies find that the rich evade their taxes more than any other class; Emmanuel Saez and Gabriel Zucman show that the fraction of taxes owed but unpaid in the United States is about 10 percent across the income scale but 25 percent for the superrich.[67] Again, they feel they are merely keeping their just deserts from the prying hands of government. Again, the sym-biosis of inequality and market ideology proves toxic.

It shouldn't be surprising, then, that the countries scoring best in the annual *World Happiness Report* are the most equal countries in the world. The Nordic countries always top the list. These are the countries, after all, that enjoy not only high incomes and good health but high levels of trust and social support. Happiness researchers have also found that people are less satisfied with life in societies characterized by large gaps between rich and poor.[68]

We are now in a position to sum up why inequality is damaging to integral human development. First, because the rich have distanced themselves from the general welfare, ordinary people—especially the poor—lack the basic resources necessary for human flourishing and participation in the common good. Second, people are blocked from fulfilling their potential, becoming who they are sup-posed to be, because opportunity is choked off in more unequal societies. The rich get ahead based on advantage and connections, not on ability. Third, in-equality pushes people to seek the wrong kinds of goods, rooted especially in excessive consumerism—"having" rather than "being." In older language, inequality undermines virtue—the virtue of those who benefit materially from inequality and those who seek to emulate them. Fourth, inequality promotes a cavalcade of mental health disorders due to status anxiety and a deep feeling of unfairness pervading the economy.

In sum, inequality causes the sense of an all-encompassing common good, of being cojoined to a common purpose, to evaporate—making it much harder to reach consensus on collective problems. Inequality undermines integral human development, reinforcing a social norm centered less on inclusive solidarity and more on acquisitive self-interest. And it undermines GDP and material prosperity, hitting the negative trifecta. In this view, historian Tony Judt is right to say that "inequality is corrosive. It rots societies from within" and that "it illustrates and exacerbates the loss of social cohesion . . . [it is] the pathology of the age and the greatest threat to the health of any democracy."[69] And it is why Pope Francis is right to call inequality "the root of social ills."[70]

Inequality and the Future of Work

Let me turn now to employment and the future of work, which is related to the discussion on inequality. As noted already, the labor share of national income has been on the decline for decades, and work is increasingly low paying and fragile, lacking protections, lacking dignity. Up until the beginning of the neoliberal era, the growth of real wages matched productivity. But then this started to diverge widely; real wages stagnated, while productivity kept on growing.

Globalization is a key factor, given competition from low-wage countries in a world of open borders. And corporations find it easy to outsource to locations with low pay, weak labor protections, and limited taxation. In the United States, as the tradable sector is badly damaged by competition, nearly all of the employment growth over the past few decades has come from the nontraded sector, which tends to have lower productivity, lower wages, and fewer labor protections.[71] Related to this change, there has been a sharp rise in "alternative work arrangements"—identified with temporary help agency workers, on-call workers, contract workers, and independent contractors and freelancers. One striking estimate is that 94 percent of net employment growth in the United States from 2005 to 2015 came from these alternative work arrangements.[72] Work has become increasingly precarious and cruel, lacking security and dignity. Think of the life of the Amazon "picker" I described in the last chapter.

The other existential issue facing workers is that the rise of robots and artificial intelligence has led to the replacement of more and more jobs—including in nontraded sectors shielded from globalization. In some senses, this is an old problem in a modern wrapping; workers have looked nervously at technological change since the onset of the industrial revolution two and a half centuries ago. Economist Carl Frey has explored how technological change has affected workers since the beginning of the industrial revolution.[73] He argues that some changes are labor replacing and some are labor enabling. Labor-replacing technologies make jobs and skills redundant, as machines can do the work. Labor-enabling technologies, on the other hand, make people more productive in their existing roles or create entirely new jobs. Frey argues that the technologies of the early industrial revolution were labor replacing, as craft workers lost out to factory machines.[74] Yet he argues that the technological waves of the twentieth century were more labor enabling—the development of technologies such as electricity and the internal combustion engine led to widespread prosperity, paving the way for the admixture of high growth and low inequality of the social democratic era. And these advances were bolstered by welfare institutions that protected workers from harsh swings of fortune.

But Frey's analysis is ultimately pessimistic; he argues that the era of artificial intelligence is another labor-replacing era. In his view, this technological revolution, despite the wonders it can produce, will look more like the early industrial revolution than like the twentieth century. It will boost inequality, both by rewarding the owners of capital and lowering the wages of low-skilled workers.[75] Frey shows that the number of robots produced in the United States rose by 50 percent between 2008 and 2016, with each of them replacing 3.3 jobs. Other researchers argue that one additional robot causes seven workers to lose their jobs.[76] Frey and his colleague Michael Osborne argue that 47 percent of US jobs are at risk from automation, especially low-income jobs that do not require a high level of education.[77] Building on this figure, the US Council of Economic Advisors predicted that 83 percent of workers in jobs paying less than $20 an hour were at risk from automation, as opposed to only 4 percent of workers making more than $40 an hour.[78]

These trends could easily provoke a backlash, just as in the early phases of the industrial revolution. Indeed, we are already seeing some of this political backlash as low-wage workers rail against what they regard as a fundamental unfairness. So far, this backlash is directed at trade and immigration rather than automation. Many economists—accustomed to thinking of trade as bringing net benefits to the economy and appreciating that technological change bears more of the blame for job displacement—are puzzled by the emphasis on trade, especially in the United States. Yet economist Dani Rodrik argues that this is not mysterious insofar as globalization-induced job displacement provokes a visceral psychological response in a way that technological change does not.[79] Why?

Because people look differently on companies gaining a competitive advantage through innovation versus relocating to a regime with lower labor, environmental, and safety standards. The latter is seen as a violation of basic social norms. Yet if Frey is right, we should expect more of the backlash to be directed against technology in the future. This reaction could take longer to emerge, as the effects are less obvious and visceral, but as more and more jobs are replaced, the negative response is bound to come—unless policies are put in place to share the benefits more fairly.

So far I have talked largely about developed countries. But these challenges related to the dignity of work also apply to the developing world. To appreciate this, we need to acknowledge that the old model of rapid development—moving from low-productivity agriculture to high-productivity manufacturing—might now be off limits to the developing world. This was the model deployed by East Asia, most recently China, with enormous success. But the combination of technology and pressures from globalization seems to be closing off this avenue, leading to what Dani Rodrik dubs "premature industrialization."[80] The worst-hit regions seem to be Latin America and Africa. With few opportunities in manufacturing, workers are instead drawn toward the services sector, which tends to have lower productivity, lower wages, and fewer protections. It is much harder for countries to develop and it is also much harder for individuals to develop in the service sector, marked as it is by the informality of the work available. According to this trend, inequality will be higher and opportunities for workers to organize and protect themselves more limited.

As noted in the last chapter, work is central to human flourishing. Catholic social teaching argues that it is a vocation, a source of meaning, purpose, dignity, and identity. The issue is not just the lack of jobs; it is that so many of the jobs on offer are offensive to human dignity. One result of this sorry state of affairs is that people just give up and leave the labor force, making unemployment statistics rosier than they seem. Nicholas Eberstadt has argued that based on current trends in the United States, a quarter of prime-age men will be out of work by 2050.[81]

The COVID-19 pandemic has also been disastrous for work. According to the International Labor Organization (ILO), the world lost 114 million jobs in 2020.[82] The picture is even starker if we look at working hour reductions, which fell by the equivalent of 255 million full-time jobs.[83] Recall again from the last chapter that unemployment and underemployment are leading causes of unhappiness and create a host of social problems, including poor health, low educational attainment, and lower trust and social cohesion.

We should note once again that none of this is destiny. Many dignified forms of work should be immune to replacement—including in the areas of care, creativity, and complex interpersonal communications. In other words, the jobs that most fully reflect our humanity will continue to exist, and they must be amply rewarded. Technology also gives us the scope to pursue fulfilling activities outside of the workplace. Back in 1930, Keynes wrote a tract called "The Economic Possibilities for Our Grandchildren," in which he argued that—in the long run—technology would solve the economic problem and people would only need to work fifteen-hour weeks.[84] Obviously, it hasn't panned out that way. But the economic problem has indeed been solved. Technology, if managed correctly, can provide scope for the pursuit of rewarding leisure—relational goods, cultural goods, spiritual goods, goods that are vital to human flourishing and yet are not included in GDP. Technology can give people the freedom to pursue the all-important nonpecuniary aspects of integral human development.

But we are a long way from that vision. The increasingly precarious nature of employment and wages portends poorly for happiness and flourishing, which depends crucially on people making a social contribution through dignified, decent, and secure jobs. Specifically, the crisis of work could undermine (1) integral human development, reflected in the diminished ability to unfold capability and achieve the intrinsic rewards of pursuing a vocation; (2) the common good, especially in the context of diminishing social capital, of less faith in social institutions, and of a decline in the associational life that used to take root in the occupational or vocational context (including unions); and (3) material prosperity, especially for lower-income, lower-skilled workers.

How to Reduce Inequality

What do these circumstances signify in terms of policies? Many experts in inequality—including Atkinson, Milanovic, Piketty, and Saez and Zucman[85]—have offered a wide variety of policy proposals to reduce inequality. I will assess some of these proposals from the point of view of the principles of Catholic social teaching.

The starting point is fiscal policy: taxes, government expenditure, and transfers. The evidence shows clearly that market inequality can be lessened by government transfers financed by progressive taxation. Many of the European countries with low inequality have fairly high market inequality; it is the tax and transfers system that knocks it down to manageable levels. The German system, for example, of offsetting rising market income inequality since the 1980s with large social transfers financed by progressive taxation, has not been echoed in the United States.[86] The prime example of this model seems to be the Scandinavian experience, where high and progressive taxation used to finance universal social benefits can lead to a society that is simultaneously prosperous, equitable, cohesive, and happy.

As noted in the last chapter, the function of government is to promote the common good, including in the economic life of the nation. Making sure that all people have access to the material bases of a dignified life allows them to participate in the life of their communities—including food and water, education, healthcare, housing, and employment. These are all considered basic human rights in Catholic social teaching. The state also needs to make sure that people have adequate insurance against the risks that come with any market economy—chiefly unemployment, ill health, and old age.

Regarding education, many economists attribute the economic success of the United States in the twentieth century to its early adoption of public education for all through the secondary level. Economists Claudia Goldin and Lawrence Katz have argued that in the race between technology and education, education won for a large part of the twentieth century, allowing for high prosperity in the context of low inequality.[87] Piketty argues that the United States had a fifty-year head start on Europe in terms of universal secondary education, which explains high productivity in the postwar period—an advantage that eroded over the latter decades of the last century.[88] Milanovic similarly argues that the extension of free secondary education was one of the factors that kept inequality in check in the postwar west.[89] But he also suggests that free education runs up against a natural limit in terms of the number of school years, so further gains are unlikely to materialize. Yet there is one policy he does not consider: the extension of free education to the university level. Given that the artificial intelligence revolution signifies that technology is winning the race against education, leading to greater inequality in wages, perhaps we need to consider some form of free public third-level education that would be this century's version of free secondary education and would serve the same purpose in a different context. As Piketty notes, though, no country has yet made the leap from a revolution in primary and secondary education to a revolution in tertiary education.[90] Perhaps the time has come for such a revolution. Not only would it teach technical skills but it would also reanimate the humanities—to better emphasize critical thinking, creativity, and empathy.

A key problem is the still huge differences in the quality of education received, especially in the United States. The children of the poor usually receive inferior education. Solving this problem calls for a massive investment in education for all, which would equalize the quality of education across schools and end education's dependence on parental resources. This solution requires the equalization of teaching standards, giving the poor the same chances as the rich.[91] A guaranteed right to early childhood education is also in order, as evidence shows that inequality of education begins at the earliest age. Neuroscience indicates that most brain development occurs from the prenatal period to age three years and that the three-year-old brain is twice as active as an adult brain. If we do not invest heavily in universal childcare and early childhood education, the race could be over before it has even begun.

The same argument can be made at the university level. As noted by Milanovic, among the top thirty-eight American universities, there are more students from the top 1 percent than the bottom 60 percent of the income distribution. Piketty notes that in the United States, access to higher education is largely determined by parental income; in the mid-2010s, only 20–30 percent of the children of the poorest households went to college, rising to 90 percent for children of the richest parents.[92] This phenomenon reflects both financial and nonfinancial resources available to the children of the rich plus the skyrocketing cost of university education. Even in countries where a university education is free or nearly free, the rich still have an advantage, as they have better secondary education and better access to the social capital needed to thrive in a university setting.

In perhaps the greatest educational injustice of all, "legacy" admissions, students accepted because family attended the particular school, account for between a tenth and a quarter of students in the top one hundred universities in the United States.[93] Likewise, many top colleges reserve places for the children of large donors. At the same time in the United States, the cost of private higher education has increased several times faster than the cost of living, putting it out of reach of the middle class, let alone the working class.[94] Increasingly, top universities are playgrounds for the rich.

This educational advantage might end at college, but it begins at the earliest stage. As noted by Daniel Markovits, the extra education of the rich over the middle class is equivalent to an inheritance of between $5 and $10 million.[95] Like Sandel, Markovits thus argues that meritocracy is a sham, a cover for the intergenerational propagation of wealth and privilege. Markovits suggests tying tax-exempt status for private universities to their admitting at least half of students from the bottom two-thirds of the income scale.[96] Sandel suggests a "lottery of the qualified" for top universities—setting a minimum threshold of qualification and then choosing students at random.[97] In tandem with ratcheting up resources devoted to public education, policies such as these should help reduce educational inequalities—inequalities so severe, according to Thomas Piketty, that the solidarity underpinning social democracy is undermined.

One important caveat: a push for greater access to third-level education should not denigrate the dignity of those who do not go to college. Since a sense of vocational attainment is so important to integral human development, any investment in traditional university education must be matched by investments in vocational training. Even if a college education is more important than in the past, there are still numerous routes to dignified work that makes a purposeful social contribution. We need to avoid Sandel's "tyranny of merit," which causes the educated to look down their noses at those who do not have a college degree. Sandel notes that as well as distributive justice—which, recall, is what the community owes the individual—there is a need to emphasize contributive justice, whereby workers can take pride in the social contribution that comes from producing goods and services valued by others.[98] This perspective lies at the heart of the Catholic insistence on the dignity of work.

Let's talk about taxes. It has become an article of faith in the neoliberal era that tax cuts, especially on corporations and the rich, unleash a wave of productivity and innovation. As I argued in chapter 4, this never happened. Instead, I would argue that high and progressive taxes are needed to fund the universal public goods and services that keep inequality in check, support the common good, and allow people to achieve integral human development. There is another reason for high progressive taxes on the rich, though. As argued persuasively by Saez and Zucman, taxing the rich at punitive rates stops the concentration of income and wealth that proves harmful to democracy. Putting it in the language of Catholic social teaching, it would support the common good, the sense of purpose that binds all citizens together. It might also inculcate virtue, given the evidence of less solidarity, generosity, and empathy among the rich in more unequal societies.

Saez and Zucman appeal to the American past to make their argument. They note that from 1930 to 1980, the top marginal tax rate averaged 78 percent and reached 91 percent from 1951 to 1963. Large bequests were also taxed at extremely high rates—80 percent for the wealthiest Americans from 1941 to 1976.[99] The high progressive tax emerged as an American phenomenon not so much to raise revenue but to avoid the kinds of oligarchic control of politics and economics that Americans then associated with Europe. The United Kingdom adopted similarly high marginal tax rates over this period, but Continental Europe did not.[100] The situations are now reversed, of course.

Indeed, President Franklin Delano Roosevelt, the author of the New Deal in the 1930s, went so far as to argue that there should be a limit on top incomes. To accomplish that, he implemented a confiscatory top marginal tax rate of 94 percent, which only applied to the superrich, those who made more than the equivalent of $6 million today. Those earning more than the equivalent of $1.2 million paid marginal rates between 72 percent and 94 percent. Below that, rates were no different than they are today. But the rich—defined as the top 0.1 percent—still paid more than half of their total incomes in taxes from the 1930s through the 1970s, three times more than the bottom 90 percent.[101] People actually paid these rates, and tax dodging was limited. As Saez and Zucman put it, "The United States, for almost half a century, came as close as any democratic country ever has to imposing a legal maximum income."[102]

Catholic social teaching certainly has a case for this kind of taxation, given that the tradition has always decried the virtue-reducing role that riches can play. It has argued that wealth corrupts and that one role of law and policy is to promote virtue. So it is valid to argue that there is both a moral floor and a moral ceiling to a person's income. And Roosevelt did indeed couch his argument in moral terms, which might explain why it was accepted. The United States took a similar tack with the occupation of Japan after the war, imposing tax rates that were deemed confiscatory, to break the power of the oligarchs that were aligned with the militaristic state during the war. As Scheidel has noted, between 1946 and 1951, a massive and progressive wealth tax was introduced in Japan, with a top marginal rate of 90 percent. This measure went hand in hand with the breaking up of industrial conglomerates and the compulsory purchase of land from absentee and large landlords.[103] These policies, combined with inflation, led to a decline in the real value of the top 1 percent of estates in Japan between 1936 and 1949.[104]

Today, the moral floor argument on income is ethically uncontroversial, except maybe for libertarians. But the moral ceiling argument supported by confiscatory taxation would probably be associated with communism. It should not be. As seen in both the United States and Japan, such a system is about protecting the common good from plutocratic capture and supporting social solidarity. And it is about inculcating the virtue needed for integral human development.

The counterargument, of course, is that a confiscatory top rate is fundamentally unfair as it penalizes effort and hard work. But this argument contains the tacit assumption that, in line with neoclassical economics, we are paid our marginal productivity. But this is fallacious reasoning. Did the productivity of CEOs rise from twenty times the median worker to 354 times the median worker over the space of half a century? Hardly.

Nobel Prize–winning economist Herbert Simon argues that we probably truly "earn" no more than a fifth of our income:

> If we are very generous with ourselves, I suppose we might claim that we "earned" as much as one fifth of it. The rest is patrimony associated with being a member of an enormously productive social system, which has accumulated a vast store of physical capital, and an even larger store of intellectual capital—including knowledge, skills, and organizational know-how held by all of us—so that interaction with our equally talented

fellow citizens rubs off on us both much of this knowledge and this generous allotment of unearned income.[105]

Putting this in the language of Catholic social teaching, Simon is saying we are all part of the common good, and we all benefit from the common good in a way that transcends our individual efforts and contributions. As Sandel puts it, the community has a legitimate moral claim on part of this money, perhaps a large part.[106] Paying back in taxes is a matter of contributive justice, just as meeting peoples' needs from that tax revenue is part of distributive justice. But I believe Roosevelt was right that the purpose of taxation is not merely to raise this revenue; it is to help instill social norms and virtues about how much is enough.

In terms of reform going forward, Saez and Zucman propose an average tax rate of 60 percent on the top 1 percent, which translates into a 75 percent marginal tax rate on incomes over $500,000. They derive this rate from what they think would maximize revenue. They argue that all income should face this marginal rate without loopholes—wages, dividends, interest, rents, and business profits. This approach would both reduce inequality—the top 1 percent income share would fall from 20 percent to 16 percent—and raise about four percentage points of GDP in revenue, to pay for important social investments.[107]

Especially today, with the concentration and wealth, Saez and Zucman argue that any higher progressive tax on income must be bolstered by a tax on wealth. Their point is that many among the superrich have a lot of wealth but little taxable income; a wealth tax better gets at their ability to pay. The authors suggest doubling estate taxes and imposing a wealth tax of 2 percent above $50 million in wealth and 3.3 percent above a billion.[108] This could raise a further 1.2 percent of national income in revenue. Overall, it would create a system that would once again look like the 1950s in terms of progressiveness.

But what about a return to confiscatory tax rates? It would certainly be possible to return to top marginal income tax rates of 90 percent-plus above a certain threshold. Saez and Zucman argue, though, that this wouldn't really matter to many billionaires. Instead, they suggest a much larger wealth tax: 10 percent on wealth over $1 billion. This tax, they argue, would reduce the number of multibillionaires. This is undoubtedly true, but I think they downplay the moral resonance of Roosevelt's argument for a top income—even if set at a very high level, such as $5 million a year.

There is also the issue, fairly alien to economics, of using tax policy to inculcate virtue and more prosocial norms. For example, just as lower marginal tax rates on higher income helped make large pay gaps more socially acceptable, so a reversal of this policy might restore the older social norm that looked askance at such pay gaps, with minimal effect on economic incentives. This solidarity-enhancing effect might be magnified with confiscatory tax rates above a certain high level. We could also consider ways to overhaul the corporate tax code to better align incentives with virtuous behavior. For example, corporate tax rates could be tuned to such factors as ratio of CEO to median worker pay.[109] Once we start thinking of tax policy as a way to inculcate better norms of behavior, many doors can be opened.

Supporting the common good and integral human development also calls for a significant inheritance tax. To reiterate Piketty's key point, the transmission of privilege across generations can lead to a self-perpetuating cycle as wealth accumulates across generations, resulting in "patrimonial capitalism."[110] And while some regard this as more of a European problem, generations in the making, the United States happens to be on the cusp of the largest intergenerational transfer of wealth in history—with an expected $36 trillion set to be passed on to heirs over the next four decades.[111] An inheritance tax can help cut this self-perpetuation across generations and level the playing field in the present. Such a tax is fair and just because it taxes wealth that has not been earned. And it aids democracy by clamping down on plutocratic capture by elites.

Inheritance and wealth taxes only go part of the way in evening out capital inequality, however. Both Atkinson and Milanovic have argued that an inheritance tax should be used to fund a capital endowment for all adults, a concept based on the idea that redistribution should encompass not only income but assets too. Accordingly, Atkinson recommends a capital endowment, a minimum inheritance, paid to all upon attaining adulthood.[112] Piketty makes a similar proposal, funded by a progressive wealth tax; in his view, such an endowment would ensure a permanent circulation of wealth.[113]

When we talk about sharing capital more equitably, we stand on the intersection of redistribution and predistribution. Fiscal policy mainly deals with the former, which takes market income as given and seeks to even it out using progressive taxes and transfers. Predistribution seeks a more equitable distribution of market income itself. There is some overlap. With confiscatory tax policies, the benefit of higher incomes above a certain level will be taxed away, meaning that market incomes themselves will trend lower. Similarly, inheritance taxes used to fund capital endowments can change the market distribution of wealth. But the importance of predistribution policies will rise in years to come. Why? Because as inequality inches ever higher, there are limits to what fiscal policy can do, including in terms of political economy. And even if the effects are exaggerated, globalization can still reduce the ability of high taxes and large transfers to smooth out the distribution of income.

Catholic social teaching is pretty rich when it comes to predistribution policies because of its basic assumption that market outcomes are not necessarily fair and its appeal for a more harmonious relationship between capital and labor. We discussed many of these options in chapter 5. The key priority of resetting the bargaining power between capital and labor, so that labor can capture its fair share of national income, calls for institutional recognition of the rights of labor to organize and bargain collectively across all levels.

I would argue that a level playing field for wage bargaining is an institutionally more effective means of delivering fair and just wages than is the blunt instrument of a minimum wage. Genuine collective bargaining allows compensation to reflect specific conditions and can take account of how wages affect overall unemployment. It honors not only solidarity but also subsidiarity. This collaboration can be broadened to encompass a social partnership framework, whereby all relevant stakeholders come together to reap the benefits of a coordinated and harmonious rather than a decentralized and conflictual approach.

This is not to say that the minimum wage is unimportant. In fact, a legislated minimum wage can help set societal standards on acceptable levels of wages. Ideally, it would be bolstered by a voluntary code of practice that would help restore the virtues of justice and prudence to wage determination, including in terms of maximum pay gaps within a corporation.[114] Minimum wages could also be extended to the informal economy, where workers tend to fall through the margins and lack access to basic forms of social protections, especially those funded by social insurance. In these cases, Pope Francis has argued that workers deserve what he calls a "universal basic wage" to bolster their meager earnings, which would be provided by the government.[115] According to the ILO, 4 billion people across the world lack access to basic social protections, lacking health and income security.[116] A universal basic wage would help reach these marginalized people.

We should also consider profit-sharing arrangements that give workers an ownership stake in the means of production; not only would this tilt the balance away from capital and toward labor but it would support integral human development by giving each worker greater agency and ability to develop capabilities. I would argue that with a corporate structure more horizontal than vertical, where the workers already own much of the capital, elements of the sharing economy lend themselves naturally to cooperative enterprise. Yet corporate practices typically don't play out that way. As noted in the last chapter, the sharing economy has in too many instances become a locus of low wages and paltry labor protections, especially when workers are conveniently classified as independent contractors. In a sense, this model links the newest advances in information technology with the oldest forms of labor exploitation. Another form of Catholic mutualism discussed in the last chapter centers on giving workers a voice in management and on boards—the codetermination model, which would reduce inequality by making sure that capital and labor more fairly share the gains of material progress, including by inhibiting excessive CEO pay and shareholder returns.

Relatedly, if one of the problems is outsize power by large corporations and institutions, then it is also necessary to design rules, institutions, and policies to correct this imbalance directly. As suggested in the last chapter, a priority would be to provide the legal and regulatory basis for a corporate governance structure predicated less on maximizing short-term shareholder value and more on a fiduciary duty to a wider array of stakeholders. Such governance reform would encourage the melding of profit-making and social functions, as supported by Catholic social teaching. This reform would both boost countervailing power and have the potential to mold more prosocial norms.

Another priority in this area is a more vigorous competition and antitrust policy, which would focus not only on economic efficiency and "consumer welfare" but also on the negative effects on small businesses and fair competition, the reduced bargaining power of workers, and the harm to the common good (and even democracy) from corporate dominance over political processes and countervailing institutions. Antitrust policy has special relevance in the modern era, given the ease with which technology companies such as Facebook, Google, and Amazon can control networks and platforms—setting prices, dictating terms, destroying competitors. Such an antitrust strategy would prioritize breaking up monopolies and undoing mergers in sectors and industries with demonstrable evidence of harm, loosening intellectual property protections that act as little more than sources of rents, and regulating the new platform monopolies like old-style utilities. Once again, this reform is about making markets work for the benefit of the common good. Catholic social teaching has always preached the virtue of smallness, in line with subsidiarity and the importance of human relationships in economic life.

The financial sector is in a class of its own, making reform essential. The current financial system undermines the common good and actively promotes values at odds with human flourishing, chiefly an insatiable appetite for wealth at all costs. For financial reform, an obvious place to start is to impose greater capital and leverage requirements on large financial institutions, which would reduce risk taking by forcing them to make risky bets using their own money rather than borrowed funds. Given that much of the problem stems from the increasing magnitude, speed, complexity, and opaqueness of trading, the judicious application of a financial transactions tax could reduce the size and profitability of the sector without harming the real economy.[117]

Another priority is to end the implicit subsidy given to the largest banks on account of their being too big, too complex, and too interconnected to fail.

Since the crisis, banks are only getting bigger and more concentrated, in viola-tion of the principle of subsidiarity. By 2014, America's largest banks accounted for 45 percent of all banking assets, up from 25 percent in 2000.[118] These banks are still tempted to take dangerous risks, as their very size means that their failure would have calamitous effects on the economy—with the possibility of bailouts yet again. Because of their position, these banks enjoy a subsidy in terms of being able to fund themselves on cheaper and easier terms than small banks—surely a violation of subsidiarity. This implicit subsidy remains substantial; the IMF estimated that it amounted to about $70 billion in the United States and $300 billion in the Euro Area in the years immediately following the crisis.[119] With-out this subsidy, these banks would not be able to earn such large profits. And with it, they stifle competition from the kinds of small relationship-based banks favored by Catholic social teaching. One solution would be to break up these megabanks along antitrust lines so that no single bank can hold more than a cer-tain percentage of total banking assets.[120] As well as reducing the power of large banks, policy makers could be urged to support regional and sectoral banks that are restricted to lending within their specific region or area of specialization; this is another aspect of the much-touted German industrial model. Along similar lines, governments could actively encourage more mutualized forms of bank-ing, including credit unions, mutual associations, and building societies.[121] This strategy would help foster more broad-based development based on subsidiarity and reciprocity—the bedrock of a virtuous economy and the antidote to finan-cial sector *chrematistike*.

I also wanted to say a few words about debt in the context of inequality. New research by economists Atif Mian, Ludwig Straub, and Amir Sufi shows that the high savings by the rich in the age of inequality did not feed through to higher investment—the main reason why neoclassical economics posits a positive re-lationship between inequality and growth—but rather into higher debt of the poor and middle class.[122] Specifically, the savings of the top 1 percent are chan-neled into rising debt of the bottom 90 percent. In other words, the rich lend money to the poor and the middle class, and this borrowing is the only way to keep up consumption. But this lending occurs in a highly precarious way, as the financial crisis teaches us.

We saw this outcome most clearly with the global financial crisis. During the financial sector deregulation of the neoliberal era, governments often set aside antiusury laws that set upper limits on interest rates. Today, people are saddled by debt from a variety of sources: credit cards, student loans, medical bills, even payday loans. As wages remain flat in an era of prosperity, debt is often the only recourse of the poor—an eerie parallel with the ancient world, which gave rise to biblical calls for freedom from debt bondage. The problem is that bankruptcy laws remain creditor friendly. As noted in the last chapter, while creditors and bankers were bailed out during the financial crisis, debtors were left to fend for themselves—and millions lost their homes, their savings, their livelihoods. In the United States, laws were tightened to make it harder for ordinary citizens to declare bankruptcy, another example of procreditor legislation. Thus when it comes to fighting inequality, a good case can be made for periodic debt relief. For example, as many college graduates cannot find decent work, student loans weigh down on them; these loans account for 10 percent of all debt in the United States.[123] Student loans are surely a good candidate for debt relief—for both economic and justice reasons.

So far, I have discussed ways to reduce the inequality crisis. I would argue that many of these fixes also work for the related employment crisis, especially since the factors driving both crises are so similar. But, given employment's centrality to a full vision of human flourishing as elaborated by Catholic social teaching, it is worth considering some options to protect workers from unemployment directly.

A first priority would be a recommitment to the goal of full employment. This goal fell out of favor in the 1970s, following the macroeconomic errors associated with stagflation, but it remains essential. And here, a good place to start would be to make central banks responsible for employment as well as price stability, as is the case for the US Federal Reserve. There is also merit in going further and considering Atkinson's proposal for governments to adopt an explicit unemployment target, underpinned by a promise to provide guaranteed public employment at the minimum wage.[124] Such employment-of-last-resort could help deliver vital public services such as childcare, elderly care, and preschool education as well as upgrades in vital public infrastructure. Building an economy on a foundation of secure, dignified work also calls for stepped-up public investment in infrastructure, research and development, and in greening the economy—investments that can be both relatively labor intensive and needed to halt the coming slowdown in economic dynamism and shift the global economy toward climate safety. As Atkinson notes, technology is not destiny; government policy can encourage innovation that increases the employability of workers, including by how it finances research and sets the rules by which the rewards from technological advances are distributed.[125]

In dealing with unemployment, temporary financial help for the unemployed, while vitally important, can never truly substitute for fulfilling work. This is another insight from Catholic social teaching. For this reason, governments should invest in job search assistance, job-training schemes, employment subsidies, and public-sector job creation (including the already noted employer-of-last resort proposal). They should especially consider short-term work programs, such as the German *Kurzarbeit*. These are cooperative programs, embodying both solidarity and subsidiarity, whereby workers agree to voluntary reductions in hours, employers agree not to lay people off, and governments agree to subsidize some portion of the wage bill. In a startling example of success, the German *Kurzarbeit* program helped make sure that the unemployment rate in Germany did not increase during the global financial crisis, even though output fell commensurate with other advanced economies. The program is demonstrating its value again during the COVID-19 crisis, across a wider array of countries. This program, of course, requires government funding to subsidize wages. But given the importance of work to human flourishing, solidarity calls for shared sacrifice. It calls for keeping workers on the payroll, even if that leads to lower profits and higher taxpayer subsidies. Neoliberalism's mantra of "protect the worker, not the job," from the point of view of Catholic social teaching on the dignity of work, gets it exactly backward.

In-work benefits, such as the earned income tax credit in the United State, are also frequently offered as a solution to low living standards. These benefits have major advantages; they supplement wages in a way that reduces poverty without creating disincentives to work caused by poverty traps. But they can encourage businesses to shirk their responsibility to pay a living wage and use a taxpayer subsidy to boost profits instead. In such a case, a key ethical obligation is outsourced to government, which could easily settle into a negative social norm. These kinds of in-work benefits can certainly play an important role but ideally in the context of a comprehensive industrial relations policy.

What about the much-touted universal basic income (UBI), which is gaining currency as a response to the displacement of work by technology? In its most basic form, a UBI is a payment to all, regardless of income or labor market status, financed by general taxation. Such a program has clear advantages. Like in-work benefits, UBI can reduce poverty while avoiding both poverty traps and stigma effects. Some critics of basic income argue that it undermines the incentive to work and so inculcates negative norms. But if this is true, then the recipients of capital income would face similar temptations and should face similar opprobrium. A universal basic income would avoid the problems of in-work benefits letting employers take advantage of a taxpayer subsidy to get away with paying paltry wages. In reality, the recipient would have the freedom to walk away from demeaning work, which should bid up wages and the attractiveness of jobs. It would also give people the freedom and security to further their integral human development, to invest in nonmarket goods, and to engage in underpaid but socially meaningful activities.

Despite these benefits, I am not sold on the idea of a universal basic income as a panacea. Perhaps it reflects my suspicion of a policy gaining support from both libertarians and Silicon Valley elites. For a start, a UBI sufficient to meet peoples' basic needs could prove prohibitively expensive. The real problem with the UBI, though, is that it narrows the issue to one of income security rather than the broader ability to make a genuine social contribution as embodied in integral human development and the common good. A universal basic income would not prevent a growing disconnect between ordinary people with precarious employment prospects and the fortunate few who gain from technological advances. A better solution would be to support policies and institutions that allow workers to share fairly in the creation of wealth and to complement these policies and institutions with the provision of universal benefits that underpin human flourishing, such as healthcare, education, and child support.

Let me try to sum up: In this chapter, I have argued that inequality today is the preeminent economic problem; the wealthy have dramatically increased their income and wealth over the past four decades at the expense of everyone else. In turn, this concentration leads to lower overall prosperity plus an undermined common good and crimped sense of integral human development, including in the sense of the dignity of work. Accordingly, reducing inequality should be a major policy goal.

Let me end with a list of fifteen concrete proposals that I believe would simultaneously reduce inequality, support integral human development, and further the common good:

1. Provide universal access to the material bases of human flourishing such as healthcare, education, housing, and social protection, funded by progressive taxes.
2. Invest heavily in public education and vocational training. Consider making early childhood development and some forms of public third-level education free of charge.
3. Raise taxes on the rich from all sources of income. High taxes on wealth are also essential, especially for billionaires. Consider confiscatory taxes rates above a certain high income level.
4. Raise inheritance taxes substantially to fund a capital endowment to all citizens upon reaching the age of majority.
5. Introduce a publicly funded basic minimum wage for workers in the informal economy.
6. Support public investment in labor-intensive technological change, including in terms of moving toward an economy powered by renewable energy.
7. Ensure that unions are sufficiently strong to enable collective bargaining for just wages, benefits, and working conditions.

8. Support worker participation in boards of governance and management of enterprises.

9. Support ways for workers to share in the profits, such as worker cooperatives.

10. Change corporate governance laws and regulations to ensure that corporations are responsible to a wider variety of stakeholders than just shareholders. Consider also institutional support for hybrid firms that mix profits and social benefits.

11. Enforce antitrust laws to break up monopolies, including in the technology sector, and reduce intellectual property protection.

12. Make full employment a policy goal, including for central banks. Consider offering guaranteed public employment-of-last-resort at the minimum wage.

13. Support keeping workers on the books during downturns through wage subsidies and reduced work hours.

14. Restructure the financial sector by breaking up too-big-to-fail firms, introducing a financial transactions tax, prohibiting stock buybacks, and supporting credit unions and small and regional banks.

15. Reinstate antiusury laws, ban payday lending, and instigate periodic debt write-downs.

Notes

1. *EG*, 202.
2. Keynes, *General Theory of Employment, Interest and Money*, ch. 24.
3. *RN*, 3.
4. *QA*, 57–58.
5. *MM*, 73–74.
6. *MM*, 168.
7. *GS*, 29.
8. *PP*, 9.
9. *SRS*, 28.
10. *SRS*, 28.
11. *CIV*, 22.
12. *CIV*, 32.
13. *EG*, 59–60.
14. *LS*, 82.
15. See Milanovic, *Global Inequality*.
16. United Nations, *World Social Report 2020*.
17. Alvaredo et al., *World Inequality Report 2018*.
18. Saez and Zucman, *Triumph of Injustice*.

19. Alvaredo et al., *World Inequality Report 2018*, 16.

20. Milanovic, *Global Inequality*.

21. See Atkinson, *Inequality*; and Milanovic, *Global Inequality*.

22. Piketty, *Capital in the Twenty-First Century*.

23. Milanovic, *Capitalism Alone*.

24. Milanovic, 26.

25. Milanovic, 31–32.

26. Atkinson, *Inequality*, 91.

27. Daly, "Church of Labor."

28. Scheidel, *Great Leveler*, 127.

29. Saez and Zucman, *Triumph of Injustice*, ch. 1.

30. Milanovic, *Global Inequality*.

31. Milanovic, *Capitalism Alone*, 57.

32. Gilens and Page, "Testing Theories of American Politics."

33. Milanovic, *Capitalism Alone*, 34.

34. Furceri and Loungani, "Capital Account Liberalization and Inequality."

35. Atkinson, *Inequality*, 94.

36. Jaumotte and Buitron, "Inequality and Labor Market Institutions."

37. Scheidel, *Great Leveler*.

38. Finn, *Christian Economic Ethics*.

39. Ostry, Berg, and Tsangarides, "Redistribution, Inequality, and Growth"; Dabla-Norris et al., "Causes and Consequences of Income Inequality."

40. Gordon, *Rise and Fall of American Growth*.

41. Stiglitz, *Price of Inequality*.

42. Gould and Hijzen, "Growing Apart, Losing Trust?"

43. See Sachs, "Social Conflict and Populist Policies in Latin America."

44. Corak, "Income Inequality, Equality of Opportunity, and Intergenerational Mobility"; Alan B. Krueger, "The Great Utility of the Great Gatsby Curve," *Brookings*, May 15, 2015, https://www.brookings.edu/blog/social-mobility-memos/2015/05/19/the-great-utility-of-the-great-gatsby-curve/.

45. Chetty et al., "Where Is the Land of Opportunity?"

46. Reeves, *Dream Hoarders*.

47. See Cecchetti and Kharroubi, "Reassessing the Impact of Finance on Growth."

48. Sahay et al., "Rethinking Financial Deepening."

49. Epstein and Montecino, "Overcharged."

50. Shaxson, *Finance Curse*.

51. Stiglitz, *Price of Inequality*.

52. See Stoller, *Goliath*.

53. International Monetary Fund, "Rise of Corporate Market Power and Its Macroeconomic Effects."

54. Epstein and Montecino, "Overcharged."

55. The following draws heavily on Annett, "Laudato Si' and Inclusive Solidarity"; and Annett, "Economía de la virtud y desafíos económicos actuales."

56. Sandel, *Tyranny of Merit.*

57. See David Lay Williams, "Tackling Poverty Isn't Enough. Inequality Is a Serious Problem, Too," *Washington Post*, September 13, 2016, https://www.washingtonpost.com/news/monkey-cage/wp/2016/09/13/tackling-poverty-isnt-enough-inequality-is-a-serious-problem-too/.

58. Mayville, *John Adams and the Fear of American Oligarchy.*

59. Smith, *Theory of Moral Sentiments*, ch. 3.

60. Rasmussen, "Adam Smith on What Is Wrong with Economic Inequality."

61. Veblen, *Theory of the Leisure Class.*

62. Milanovic, *Capitalism Alone.*

63. Ward, "Wealth, Poverty and Inequality."

64. Wilkinson and Pickett, *Spirit Level.*

65. Wilkinson and Pickett, *Inner Level.*

66. Piff et al., "Higher Social Class Predicts Increased Unethical Behavior."

67. Saez and Zucman, *Triumph of Injustice*, 60–61.

68. Burkhauser, de Neve, and Powdthavee, "Top Incomes and Human Well-Being around the World."

69. Judt, *Ill Fares the Land*, 21, 185.

70. *EG*, 202.

71. Spence and Hlatshwayo, "Evolving Structure of the American Economy and the Employment Challenge."

72. Katz and Krueger, "Rise and Nature of Alternative Work Arrangements in the United States, 1995–2015."

73. Frey, *Technology Trap.*

74. This provoked a backlash, but this backlash was suppressed by the strong arm of the state—at the same time as Britain was using force and violence to extend its trading empire across the globe. But the backlash was more limited, and social disorder more contained, in the parts of England where welfare provisions for the poor were more generous. See Frey, *Technology Trap*, 344.

75. See Berg, Buffie, and Zanna, "Robots, Growth, and Inequality."

76. Acemoglu and Restrepo, "Robots and Jobs."

77. Frey and Osborne, "Future of Employment."

78. Quoted in Frey, *Technology Trap*, 322.

79. Rodrik, "Populism and the Economics of Globalization."

80. Rodrik, *Straight Talk on Trade*, ch. 4.

81. Eberstadt, *Men without Work*, quoted in Frey, *Technology Trap*, 346.

82. International Labor Organization, "COVID-19 and the World of Work."

83. International Labor Organization.

84. Keynes, "Economic Possibilities for Our Grandchildren."

85. Atkinson, *Inequality*; Milanovic, *Capitalism Alone*; Piketty, *Capital in the Twenty-First Century*; Saez and Zucman, *Triumph of Injustice.*

86. Milanovic, *Capitalism Alone*, 45.

87. Goldin and Katz, *Race between Education and Technology.*

88. Piketty, *Capital and Ideology*, 546.

89. Milanovic, *Capitalism Alone*.

90. Piketty, *Capital and Ideology*, 513.

91. Milanovic, *Capitalism Alone*, 50.

92. Piketty, *Capital and Ideology*, 535.

93. Milanovic, *Capitalism Alone*, 59–60.

94. Milanovic, 59.

95. Markovits, *Meritocracy Trap*.

96. Markovits, 276–77.

97. Sandel, *Tyranny of Merit*, 184–88.

98. Sandel, 206.

99. Saez and Zucman, *Triumph of Injustice*, ch. 2.

100. Piketty, *Capital and Ideology*, 31.

101. Saez and Zucman, *Triumph of Injustice*, 41.

102. Saez and Zucman, 37.

103. Scheidel, *Great Leveler*, 123–29.

104. Scheidel, 115.

105. Simon, "Public Administration in Today's World of Organizations and Markets."

106. Sandel, *Tyranny of Merit*, 130.

107. Saez and Zucman, *Triumph of Injustice*, ch. 7.

108. Saez and Zucman, ch. 7.

109. See Reich, *Saving Capitalism*.

110. Piketty, *Capital in the Twenty-First Century*.

111. Reich, *Saving Capitalism*, 144.

112. Atkinson, *Inequality*, ch. 6.

113. Piketty, *Capital and Ideology*, ch. 17.

114. Atkinson, *Inequality*.

115. Pope Francis, "Letter of His Holiness Pope Francis to the Popular Movements."

116. International Labor Organization, "World Social Protection Report 2017–19."

117. See Baker, *Rigged*.

118. Reich, *Saving Capitalism*, ch. 12.

119. International Monetary Fund, "How Big Is the Implicit Subsidy for Banks Considered Too Important to Fail?"

120. See Johnson and Kwak, *Thirteen Bankers*.

121. See Milbank and Pabst, *Politics of Virtue*.

122. Mian, Straub, and Sufi, "Saving Glut of the Rich and the Rise in Household Debt."

123. See Reich, *Saving Capitalism*, ch. 7.

124. Atkinson, *Inequality*, ch. 5.

125. Atkinson, ch. 4.

7

Care for Our
Common Home

According to veteran environmental activist Bill McKibben, the most important document about climate change over the past decade was Pope Francis's encyclical *Laudato Si': On Care for Our Common Home.*[1] This encyclical not only provides an accurate and sophisticated analysis of the current environmental crisis, but it also explores the roots of the crisis in the technocratic paradigm and a misguided libertarianism and offers both individual and collective solutions.

All the way back in chapter 2, I introduced the principle of integral ecology. This is one of the ten basic principles of Catholic social teaching and yet the most recent, fleshed out in *Laudato Si'* in 2015. Integral ecology is about the relationships between the human and the natural world. It states that these relationships are all interconnected, deeply intertwined, and part of a larger whole. So if we hurt creation, we hurt our fellow human beings, especially the poor and vulnerable. Pope Francis has argued that each creature has value and significance in its own right, not merely as utility to human beings, and so deserves care and respect. The pope's view differs from neoclassical economics, which promotes an extractivist vision whereby nature is merely raw material to be manipulated in the service of efficiency and productivity. Pope Francis condemns this attitude, blaming it for the current environmental crisis.

The Spiritual Vision of *Laudato Si'*

Laudato Si' is suffused with the spirituality of Saint Francis of Assisi. The title of the encyclical comes from its opening line, "Laudato Si', mi Signore"—"Praise be to you, my Lord"—which comes from Saint Francis's beloved "Canticle of the Sun." Pope Francis appeals to his namesake because—as he says at the beginning of the encyclical—"Saint Francis of Assisi reminds us that our common home is a like a sister with whom we share our life and a beautiful mother who opens her arms to embrace us."[2] It is worth reminding ourselves of this beautiful poem:

> Praised be you, my Lord, with all your creatures,
> especially Sir Brother Sun,
> who is the day and through whom you give us light.
> And he is beautiful and radiant with great splendour;
> and bears a likeness of you, Most High.
> Praised be you, my Lord, through Sister Moon and the stars,
> in heaven you formed them clear and precious and beautiful.
> Praised be you, my Lord, through Brother Wind,
> and through the air, cloudy and serene, and every kind of weather
> through whom you give sustenance to your creatures.
> Praised be you, my Lord, through Sister Water,
> who is very useful and humble and precious and chaste.
> Praised be you, my Lord, through Brother Fire,
> through whom you light the night,
> and he is beautiful and playful and robust and strong.[3]

But who was Saint Francis exactly? Francis of Assisi was born toward the end of the twelfth century, the son of a wealthy merchant. He gradually became disillusioned with the worldly life, especially the lure of wealth. Instead, he embraced "Lady Poverty" and was deeply inspired by the example of Jesus, who urged his followers to go out and proclaim the good news while carrying no money or possessions with them. In 1209, Francis was given permission by Pope Innocent III to found a new order of mendicant preachers, which became the Franciscan Order. To this day, Saint Francis is one of the most popular and revered saints, even among non-Christians.

In his namesake, Pope Francis sees a man who "loved, and was deeply loved for his joy, his generous self-giving, his openheartedness." He sees a man who "lived in simplicity and in wonderful harmony with God, with others, with nature, and with himself"; a man who knew how "inseparable the bond is between concern for nature, justice for the poor, commitment to society, and interior peace."[4] Saint Francis loved all creation, and he communed with all creation. He didn't just look at the world with "intellectual appreciation of economic calculus."[5] No, he approached nature with awe and wonder and regarded all creatures as his brothers and sisters. Pope Francis is so taken with the example of his namesake that he also appeals to him in his next encyclical, *Fratelli Tutti*, which uses the example of Saint Francis to promote universal fraternity.

In *Laudato Si'* the pope invokes the example of Saint Francis because we are mistreating our common home. We are mistreating our sister, our mother. Pope Francis begins *Laudato Si'* with this impassioned plea:

> This sister now cries out to us because of the harm we have inflicted on her by our irresponsible use and abuse of the goods with which God has endowed her. We have come to see ourselves as her lords and masters, entitled to plunder her at will. The violence present in our hearts, wounded by sin, is also reflected in the symptoms of sickness evident in the soil, in the water, in the air and in all forms of life. This is why the earth herself, burdened and laid waste, is among the most abandoned and maltreated of our poor; she "groans in travail" (Rom 8:22). We have forgotten that we ourselves are dust of the earth (cf. Gen 2:7); our very bodies are made up of her elements, we breathe her air and we receive life and refreshment from her waters.[6]

Theologically speaking, Pope Francis argues that such mistreatment of our common home constitutes sin, manifested in a rupture with God, our fellow human beings, and the earth itself. For Pope Francis, the root of this sin lies in a disordered relationship between humanity and creation. The original biblical mandate is that God gave humanity dominion over all of creation. But *Laudato Si'* identifies what it regards as a basic misconception of the creation narrative, the notion that humanity's "dominion" over the earth is a warrant to exploit nature without any kind of restraint. Pope Francis calls this a "distorted anthropocentrism," the idea that we can use nature as we see fit. Dominion does not imply domination, and it certainly does not imply destruction. Yet too many Christians over the centuries have followed this misguided approach, which partly explains the current state of affairs. The original harmony between the Creator, humanity, and creation has been ruptured, and this disruption is brought about by human arrogance, hubris, and selfishness.

The proper biblical mandate is instead to "till it and keep it."[7] As Pope Francis notes, "Tilling refers to cultivating, ploughing, or working, while keeping means caring, protecting, overseeing, and preserving." If humanity tills too much and keeps too little, then the natural harmony is disrupted. In reality, the charge to "till it and keep it" leads to a "relationship of mutual responsibility between human beings and nature."[8] As *Laudato Si'* emphasizes, "Each community can take from the bounty of the earth whatever it needs for subsistence, but it also has the duty to protect the earth and to ensure its fruitfulness for coming generations."[9] In other words, the earth is not merely a legacy from the past but also a loan from the future. This intergenerational stewardship is another manifestation of the universal destination of goods—the fact that the needs of future generations must also be met—and of solidarity and justice.

The bottom line is that while human beings certainly occupy a privileged place in the order of creation, they must also respect the essential truth that each creature has its own value, purpose, and destiny. "If we approach nature and the environment without this openness to awe and wonder, if we no longer speak the language of fraternity and beauty in our relationship with the world," says Pope Francis, "our attitude will be that of masters, consumers, ruthless exploiters, unable to set limits on their immediate needs."[10]

To understand the point the pope is making, it helps to go back once again to the essential message of creation—that it is good, the precious gift of a loving God. In the created world, we can see both the intelligence and benevolence of the creator. As Pope Francis puts it, "Creation can only be understood as a gift from the outstretched hand of the Father of all, and as a reality illuminated by the love which calls us together into universal communion."[11] In another passage, he writes that "the entire material universe speaks of God's love, his boundless affection for us. Soil, water, mountains: everything is, as it were, a caress of God."[12] And in another: "The universe unfolds in God, who fills it completely."[13] He also writes, "Every creature is thus the object of the Father's tenderness . . . even the fleeting life of the least of beings is the object of his love, and in its few seconds of existence, God enfolds it with his affection."[14] This spirituality is all an echo of that of Saint Francis of Assisi, a person who lived out virtues of integral ecology—a deep love of nature, a deep kinship with the poor, a deep reverence for sustainability, and a deep commitment to peace.

In one of the most beautiful passages of the encyclical, Pope Francis invokes the imagery of Saint Francis of Assisi to paint a picture of this universal communion: "Everything is related, and we human beings are united as brothers and sisters on a wonderful pilgrimage, woven together by the love God has for each of his creatures and which also unites us in fond affection with brother sun, sister moon, brother river and mother earth."[15]

A key implication of this deeply sacramental view of the world is that no part of existence remains untouched by God's grace and presence. The great Jesuit poet Gerard Manley Hopkins put it beautifully when he wrote that "the world is charged with the grandeur of God."[16] This attitude allows us to truly see God in all things. That all aspects of the material universe are in some sense touched by divine love—human beings and all living creatures—really gets to the deep roots of integral ecology. It is why Pope Francis can detect a "mystical meaning to be found in a leaf, in a mountain trail, in a dewdrop, in a poor person's face."[17]

And because our connection runs so deep, it is possible to feel the pain of creation under stress. On this point, Pope Francis reiterates a passage from his earlier document *Evangelii Gaudium*: "God has joined us so closely to the world around us that we can feel the desertification of the soil almost as a physical ailment, and the extinction of a species as a painful disfigurement."[18]

It is to these aliments and disfigurements that we now turn.

The Practical Vision of *Laudato Si'*

Back in chapter 4, I talked about the planetary boundaries that define the limits of a hospitable habitat, suitable for human flourishing.[19] To recap, there are nine. The first is climate change, caused by the emission of carbon dioxide and other greenhouse gases. This is the most important boundary, and I will discuss it in greater detail in the next section.

The second boundary is ocean acidification. This is closely related to the first and is caused by carbon dioxide dissolving in the oceans, producing carbonic acid. Rising acidity undermines the delicate ecosystem of the oceans, threatening all kinds of marine life—including corals, shellfish, and plankton. There has already been a 26 percent increase in the acidity of the oceans, and it is poised to get worse.

The third boundary is marked by the overuse of freshwater resources. As noted by Jeffrey Sachs, 70 percent of all freshwater is used for agriculture and 20 percent for industry, leaving just 10 percent for human needs. More water is now being extracted than refilled by rainfall. Climate change, by causing droughts, will only make this scarcity worse in the decades to come. As early as 2030, global water demand is expected to exceed supply by 40 percent.[20]

The fourth boundary is land-use changes. Human beings are clearing more and more land for agriculture, timber, and expanding cities. The chief problem here is deforestation, which adds to carbon emissions, destroys ecosystems, and upsets the delicate balance of nature.

The fifth boundary is the interference with the nitrogen and phosphorus cycles, caused mainly by use of fertilizers. This is a tricky issue. Without fertilizer, as noted by Sachs, crop yields would be less than a ton per hectare, rather than three to five tons with fertilizers. These fertilizers feed an estimated 4 billion people. Yet they also poison our groundwater and rivers.

The sixth boundary is ozone depletion caused by industrial chemicals eroding a protecting barrier in the upper atmosphere. Back in the 1980s, scientists found a huge hole in the ozone layer caused by these chemicals—chlorofluorocarbons. This is one area where the world has made progress, but the threat remains.

The seventh boundary is chemical pollution, where industries such as steel, petrochemicals, and mining despoil local environments, which can harm human health as well as the vitality of ecosystems and other species.

The eighth boundary is called aerosol loading. This is a fancy term for airborne pollution caused by burning fossil fuels. These small particles called aerosols are particularly harmful to the lungs. Many cities, including in China and India, suffer greatly from this form of pollution. Millions die each year.

The ninth and final boundary is a rapid loss of biodiversity in the context of ruptured ecosystems. As noted by Sachs, the earth is home to between 10 and 100 million different species, most of which have not even been discovered. This biodiversity is not merely a source of joy and wonder but forms ecosystems that come with enormous practical benefits. Ecosystems provide directly for human needs—including food, water, wood, and biomass. They serve humanity by making sure that agriculture delivers needed food supplies, including through the cycling of nutrients and formation of healthy soil. They play an important regulating role, including by forming a crucial first line of defense against floods. They protect us from pathogens and pests. Ecosystems also regulate the climate. Biodiversity is important because it promotes the health, vitality, and productivity of these ecosystems. Yet the other planetary boundaries tend to unite to ravage this vital biodiversity—so much so that we are going through the sixth great extinction, the only one caused by human rather than natural forces.

As I noted in chapter 4, the planetary boundaries are in one sense the result of scale. The footprint of humanity on the natural world has become enormous, as we disrupt some of the earth's cycles of biology, chemistry, and geology. The problem is that if we trespass these boundaries, we step into the great unknown. We step out of the Holocene—the 10,000-year period of balance, stability, and fecundity that laid the groundwork for human civilization—and into the Anthropocene, a new geological epoch in which human activity is a major influence on the earth's systems. What lies ahead is unknown, but we can be certain that it is a harsher and more unpredictable realm, far less conducive to human flourishing.

The planetary boundaries analysis is cutting-edge science. What makes *Laudato Si'* so remarkable is that although Pope Francis does not use the term "planetary boundaries," he discusses all of these issues, including their complex interrelationship and how they feed on each other. *Laudato Si'* is a deep spiritual reflection combined with hard scientific rigor.[21]

Laudato Si' begins its analysis on the state of our common home by discussing pollution in remarkably blunt terms, noting that "the earth, our home, is beginning to look more and more like an immense pile of filth."[22] It refers to atmospheric pollution that causes health hazards, especially for the poor, as well as pollution caused by fertilizers, insecticides, fungicides, herbicides, and agro-toxins. And it references the problems caused by the acidification of the soil and water.

Turning to climate change, the most dangerous planetary boundary of all, *Laudato Si'* affirms the "solid scientific consensus" that the earth is warming and that this is due to the concentration of greenhouse gases in the atmosphere, mainly as a result of human activity.[23] Pope Francis assigns the blame where it belongs, on a model of development based on the intensive use of fossil fuels. He also singles out land-use changes, principally deforestation. And he points to various tipping points and feedback loops that come with climate change, including changes in the carbon cycle, a destruction of biodiversity and the loss of vital ecosystems, an increase in ocean acidification, and the potential release of methane from the melting of the ice caps.

Laudato Si' correctly regards climate change as a problem of utmost urgency, one with severe environmental, social, economic, political, and distributional implications.[24] It notes that the poor live in areas most affected by climate change and rely on livelihoods most vulnerable to climate change. Accordingly, the poor will feel the earliest and worst effects from ever more severe floods, droughts, and other natural disasters. At the same time, they lack the resources and support systems to cope with such disruption. *Laudato Si'* warns that this vulnerability of the poor could lead to greater patterns of migration and ever more climate refugees. And it could lead to greater instability, conflict, and war in the years ahead.

Laudato Si' also discusses the issue of access to freshwater, another of the planetary boundaries. Pope Francis insists that "access to safe drinkable water is a basic and universal human right, since it is essential to human survival and, as such, is a condition for the exercise of other human rights."[25] Yet, he points out, correctly, that water demand frequently exceeds sustainable supply and that water poverty is a major problem in places such as Africa, where people lack access to safe drinking water and live in areas prone to droughts that hurt agricultural productivity. *Laudato Si'* talks about water quality as well as quantity, noting that unsafe water leads to disease and that underground water sources are being despoiled by mining, farming, and industrial activity. Overall, the encyclical stresses that severe water shortage is a looming reality that could affect billions of people and that control of water supply by multinationals could become a major source of conflict.

Finally, *Laudato Si'* addresses one of the other major planetary boundaries: the loss of biodiversity, the destruction of the web of life that sustains our planet. Interestingly, the encyclical devotes more ink to this issue than to climate change. At his most passionate, Pope Francis claims that "because of us, thousands of species will no longer give glory to God by their very existence, nor convey their message to us. We have no such right."[26] Once again, *Laudato Si'* acknowledges the science, highlighting the important role played by ecosystems in sustaining the planet and human well-being. And it notes that these ecosystems require biodiversity for their productivity and healthy functioning. The encyclical talks about the great tropical forests, at risk from rampant deforestation, as well as the aquifers and glaciers. It talks about the oceans, where marine life is under threat from overfishing, ocean warming, and acidification. It talks about the destruction of the coral reefs, second only to the rainforests in terms of biodiversity. Ultimately, *Laudato Si'* appreciates that biodiversity is interdependence in action. As Pope Francis puts it, "Because all creatures are connected, each must be cherished with love and respect, for all of us as living creatures are dependent on one another."[27] He takes a scientific reality and endows it with moral meaning.

The Challenge of Climate Change

As environmental challenges go, climate change is surely at the top of the list. In this section, I will delve deeper on this challenge, describing both the causes and consequences of climate change.[28] In this, I will reference a number of books on climate change, especially aimed at the nonscientific reader—including those by Sachs, Mark Lynas, Bill McKibben, David Wallace-Wells, and Gernot Wagner and Martin Weitzman.[29]

I suppose we should start at the beginning. Over its long history, our planet has cycled through immense gyrations of climate, driven by an array of complex and interconnected factors. Over the past 2.5 million years, it has cycled in and out of ice ages. The ebb and flow of glaciers are due to slight changes in the earth's orbit around the sun; these "wobbles" change the amount of sunlight reaching earth and hence can change the climate. For the last 800,000 years, the cycles averaged 100,000 years, with ice building up over about 80,000 years, followed by rapid deglaciation, and an interglacial period lasting about 10,000 years.

In this context, the Holocene is actually an interglacial period following the waning of the ice sheets at the end of the last ice age. This period has lasted about 10,000 years. It gave rise to the "long summer" of human civilization, producing ideal conditions for human flourishing.[30] Even within the Holocene, however, climatic shifts have occurred. But these have typically been limited and localized. For example, the so-called Rome Climate Optimum may have paved the way for the expansion and thriving of the late Roman Republic and the early Roman Empire. The most recent example of this is the "medieval warm period" and ensuing "Little Ice Age." But these were rather small blips over the very long term.

So while the climate is always in flux, large changes have played out over vast expanses of time. But this is no longer true. Today, the planet is warming rapidly at an unprecedented pace, and there is nothing natural about it. Today, we are in grave danger of exiting the safety and security of the Holocene for the Anthropocene, caused by the speed and scale of the human impact on the climatic system.

Let's explore this a little. To understand this dynamic, we need to look at the link between the concentrations of greenhouse gases in the atmosphere and global temperatures. Scientists can measure the concentration of carbon dioxide, the main greenhouse gas in the atmosphere, over the past 800,000 years. We measure this concentration as "parts per million," or the number of molecules of carbon dioxide for every million molecules in the atmosphere.

Here's the rub: scientists have shown a clear link between this concentration of carbon dioxide in the atmosphere and global temperatures. When the concentration was high, the planet was warm, and when the concentration was low, the planet was cold. Carbon and temperature move together. This finding is not new. Back in 1896, the Swedish scientist Svante Arrhenius accurately calculated the effects on temperature from a doubling of carbon dioxide—long before the era of advanced computer modeling. He just couldn't fathom that it would happen so quickly. We can see this relationship clearly in figure 7.1. For me, this is the strongest evidence against climate change deniers. It shows clearly that global temperatures map carbon emissions in the atmosphere almost perfectly.

How does this work? Science says that these gases warm the earth by creating a "greenhouse" effect—hence, greenhouse gases. The major greenhouse gases include carbon dioxide, methane, and nitrous oxide. Greenhouse gases make our earth hospitable. They provide a comfortable security blanket for humanity to flourish. Without them, the earth would be a vastly colder and more desolate place.

But there is such a thing as too much of a good thing. Since the onset of the industrial revolution in the eighteenth century, the massive burning of fossil fuels—coal, oil, and gas—has released enormous amounts of greenhouse gases into the atmosphere. The security blanket is becoming too heavy, and it is now smothering the planet.

We are now clearly in the danger zone. The concentration of carbon dioxide has now hit 420 parts per million, represented by a giant spike over the past 150 years, a mere blink of an eye in planetary history. This level is higher than at any time in the past 800,000 years. Indeed, the last time the level of carbon dioxide was so high was probably 3 million years ago, when the earth was a hotter and more hostile place, devoid of humans.

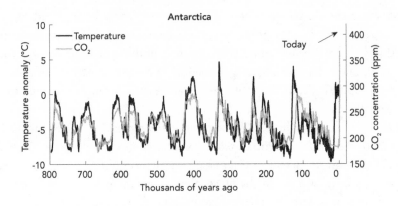

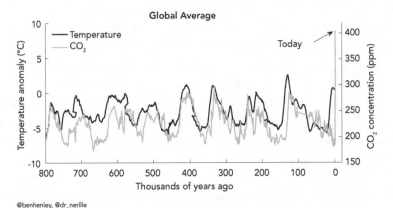

Figure 7.1. Temperature and carbon dioxide concentration over the last 800,000 years. Reprinted by permission from Ben Henley and Nerilie Abram, "The Three-Minute Story of 800,000 Years of Climate Change with a Sting in the Tail," *Conversation*, June 12, 2017. Data from Parrenin et al. 2013; Snyder 2016; Bereiter et al. 2015.

The speed of increase is unprecedented. As McKibben puts it, "There are perhaps four other episodes in Earth's 4.5-billion-year history where carbon dioxide has poured into the atmosphere in greater volumes, but never at greater speeds. . . . Even during the dramatic moments at the end of the Permian Age, when most life went extinct, the carbon dioxide content of the atmosphere grew at perhaps one-tenth the current pace."[31]

The emission of greenhouse gases shows no sign of abating, reflecting the growth of our energy-intensive global economy. We are already at 420 parts per million, and this level is increasing by about 2 parts per million each year. If this pace continues, we could easily exceed 500 parts per million in just fifty years. Yet if the global economy grows faster, so could carbon emissions. A prudent estimate suggests that the global economy could increase threefold by midcentury; this is based on continued economic convergence alongside forecast population growth. Such a tripling of the global economy by 2050 would cause carbon concentrations to increase by over six parts per million a year (assuming the energy intensity of the global economy is unchanged).[32] This path is extremely perilous. Indeed, without any action, it could lead to atmospheric concentrations greater than 1,000 parts per million by 2100.[33]

What does this carbon output mean for temperatures? It all depends on how much effort is taken by countries to reduce emissions, of course. So far, human activity has caused global average temperatures to rise by more than 1 degree Celsius above preindustrial levels. According to the scientific consensus represented by the Intergovernmental Panel on Climate Change (IPCC), without any action, global average temperatures would increase between 3.7 degrees and 4.8 degrees this century. Warming is more likely than not to exceed 4 degrees Celsius above preindustrial levels.[34] This increase would be catastrophic. Even worse, there is about a 10 percent chance that global average temperatures would exceed 6 percent. This would be "game over" for human civilization. Luckily, the latest estimates from the IPCC are not quite so dire, because countries have plans in place to reduce emissions. If countries do what they promise over the next decade, warming would increase by 3 degrees Celsius by the end of the century. But this assumes they will do what they promise, and there is not much evidence of this so far. And even 3 degrees would still be a disaster.

Where should we be? The international consensus encapsulated by the Paris Agreement on Climate Change (more on this soon) calls for limiting warming to under 2 degrees, or ideally 1.5 degrees. The IPCC argues that 1.5 degrees is far safer than 2 degrees.[35] For a realistic chance of staying under 1.5 degrees, global emissions would have to decline by 45 percent from 2010 levels by 2030 and hit net zero by 2050. To stay below 2 degrees, the numbers are 25 percent by 2030 and net zero by 2070. The first path is clearly far more ambitious, given that we have already warmed by more than 1 degree Celsius.

What about the consequences of climate change? As emissions keep growing, global temperatures keep rising. We have just lived through the hottest decade ever recorded, and the past five years have been the hottest on record.[36] In its 2014 report, the IPCC pointed out that the previous thirty years were the warmest of the last 1,400 years in the Northern Hemisphere.

Sea levels are also on the rise, especially as the Arctic and Antarctic ice sheets melt. The latest estimates from leading climate scientist James Hansen are that we are looking at a sea level rise of several meters over the next 50 to 150 years. And this change is only with a 2-degree rise in temperatures.[37] By 2100, if we don't act, 5 percent of the world's population could be flooded every single year.[38]

Although temperatures have risen by just over 1 degree so far, we can already see the consequences. We are witnessing more severe droughts, flooding, forest fires, heat waves, and storms. Scientists have shown that across the world, the incidence of heat waves has increased dramatically since the 1950s—instead of 1 or 2 times per thousand days, they now occur at 50–100 times per thousand days.[39] And severe weather events are on the rise; the warmer oceans make storms more powerful, and rising sea levels make them more harmful when they make landfall. With just 1 degree of warming, there has been a 25 to 30 percent increase in category-four and -five storms.[40] Over the past few years, flooding in places such as China, Thailand, and Indonesia hurt the global economy and human well-being. In 2012, New York City was devastated by the powerful superstorm Sandy, and the rising sea level made the flooding associated with this storm a lot worse. A year later, a typhoon devastated the Philippines, claiming thousands of lives. Meanwhile, places such as Australia and Russia suffered record heat waves. Africa was hit by drought-induced famine. South Asia was hit by one of the worst heat waves in history. Temperatures in cities in Iran and Pakistan reached the highest ever recorded. The western United States suffered from catastrophic forest fires, threatening the homes of millions of people. The litany gets longer with every passing year.

Some of the worst impacts of climate change so far are being felt in already fragile areas such as the Sahel region, a dry zone in Africa between the desert and the tropics. Even with a 1-degree Celsius increase in global temperatures, the impact in this region is elevated. What was once savannah and scrubland has turned into full-blown desert, and Lake Chad—a great lake that used to cover 50,000 square miles—has now practically dried up. Other parts of the world that are highly vulnerable to drought include the US Southwest and the entire Mediterranean region—including southern Europe, North Africa, and eastern Mediterranean countries such as Turkey, Syria, Israel, and Jordan.

Climate change is also likely to produce water shortages. Right now, half of the world's population depends on seasonal melt from high-elevation snow and ice.[41] Climate change puts this in peril. The United Nations estimates that 5 billion people would have their access to freshwater jeopardized by 2050.

Climate change has devastating effects on human health. In 2015, the *Lancet*—one of the world's most prestigious medical journals—dubbed climate change the greatest global health issue of the twenty-first century.[42] This effect is especially true for the poor, who already have inadequate access to basic healthcare. Direct and grave threats to life and health will come from greater exposure to heat, storms, and flooding. Life and health will also be endangered by drought and flooding, which will lead to widespread food insecurity—and the threat of severe famine will always be lurking. Ecological harm and loss of biodiversity will reduce protection against the adverse effects of nature. Rising temperatures will bring an increased risk of disease. Air pollution will also get worse, with particular problems for cardiovascular and respiratory health. Also, as emissions rise, cognitive ability declines; one estimate is that at a thousand parts per million, cognitive ability falls by a fifth.[43] Climate change and pollution are also responsible for mental health problems. One estimate is that climate change is already responsible for 59,000 suicides, many of them poor farmers in India.[44]

On the whole, estimating the death toll from climate change is no easy task. One study estimated that climate change is responsible for 400,000 deaths a year and that this death toll could rise to 700,000 by 2030. This number includes deaths from illnesses, hunger, and disease that primarily affect children. But if we add premature deaths from the pollution caused by burning fossil fuels, then this number increases dramatically to 5 million people a year, rising to 6 million by 2030. More than 90 percent of these deaths will be in developing countries.[45] And these figures are projected through 2030. The results would be dramatically worse with a trajectory of warming by three degrees or more by the end of the century. Globally, one estimate is that one out of six deaths is caused by air pollution.[46] There would also be a dramatic difference between whether we manage to stick to 1.5 degrees or 2 degrees; the difference has been estimated at 150 million people dying from air pollution over the course of the century.[47]

The effects of climate change on GDP are also difficult to pin down. But they will be substantial. A current estimate suggests that climate change is costing the world $1.2 trillion each year, or about 1.6 percent of GDP.[48] As the planet warms, these costs will get dramatically worse over the course of the century. The *Stern Review*, a major work issued by the United Kingdom government under the direction of economist Nicholas Stern—published in 2006 but still relevant—argues that the economic effects of climate change will exceed the costs of the two world wars and the Great Depression combined.[49] Another study suggests that climate change could reduce global output by 23 percent by the end of the century. Climate change would also widen inequality and hit the poor hardest.[50] And another study says even 3.7 degrees of warming could lead to damages of $551 trillion by the end of the century.[51] Channels of economic disruption include lower productivity, lower agricultural output, reduced capital accumulation, and worse health outcomes.

A recent World Bank study suggests that climate change could force 100 million people into extreme poverty by 2030.[52] The United Nations has estimated that the number of hungry people is on the rise again, increasing by 38 million, largely due to climate change.[53] A good rule of thumb is that for every degree of warming, crop yields decline by 10 percent. By the end of the century, we might have 50 percent more people to feed and 50 percent less grain with which to feed them.[54]

This is a common theme: as climate change advances, the poor will be on the front lines. They will suffer most from droughts, floods, diseases, and severe weather events. And these are the very people least responsible for climate change. As noted by climate scientist Veerabhadran Ramanathan, the poorest 3 billion people account for a mere 6 percent of the cumulative carbon emissions that threaten the health and vitality of our planet. In contrast, 85 percent of emissions come from 2.5 billion people in upper- and middle-income countries.[55] A mere fifteen countries account for over 70 percent of the emissions. The United States seems to be a particular culprit here in terms of its carbon-lavish lifestyle. The average American emits seventeen tons of carbon dioxide a year, while the average citizen of the European Union emits just seven tons. And while China is the biggest emitter today, the United States amounts for about a quarter of all cumulative carbon emissions.[56]

Climate change will also lead to population displacement, as climate refugees flee from places that are increasingly inhospitable, offer little in the way of livelihoods, or suffer from climate-related conflict. These effects are hard to estimate, but the consensus is that they will be large. The International Organization for Migration is predicting a staggering 200 million climate refugees by 2050 alone, with a high estimate of a billion.[57] About 1.5 billion, a fifth of humanity, live in regions that could become inhabitable for human beings, as temperature and humidity reach chronic levels. These areas include some of the world's most densely populated and politically volatile regions such as South Asia and the Middle East.[58]

How bad could it get? The consensus is: very bad. Remember, the effects we have seen so far have come from a mere rise of 1 degree Celsius over preindustrial levels. As noted, the IPCC is predicting 3 degrees by the end of the century even if countries do what they have promised. But without action at all, warming will likely exceed 4 degrees. Back in 2008, Lynas wrote an interesting book looking at what would happen as temperatures sequentially rise, degree by degree.[59]

At 2 degrees Celsius, the Arctic ice could tip over into an irreversible melt, and we could see millions displaced by torrential monsoons in places such as Bangladesh. Meanwhile, countries such as Peru, Ecuador, and Bolivia could face grave water shortages. At 3 degrees Celsius, we could expect to see chronic drought, water shortages and agricultural devastation in places such as southern Africa, Central America, Pakistan, and Australia. Most of the Arctic sea ice will vanish, and land ice caps and glaciers will be retreating rapidly. Disastrously for the global ecosystem, the Amazon basin could even dry up. This scenario is where we are headed based on current policy promises. With a 4-degree Celsius increase in temperatures, we could face a worldwide agricultural drought, including in areas that were once breadbaskets. Crop yields would collapse across the world, and Africa would be especially devastated, with yields down by 50 percent. Sea levels would rise dramatically. And the Antarctic ice, once thought impregnable, would start to chip away. With temperatures jumping by 5 degrees Celsius or more, the world will be a very different place. The last time the earth was this warm, sea levels were several meters higher. This rise in sea levels would be enough to inundate New York, London, Shanghai, Tokyo, Hong Kong, and other major coastal cities. The world's deserts will all have expanded, and new deserts will have arisen in places such as the Amazon, as the rainforests disappear. In inland areas, temperatures would be up to 10 degrees warmer than now. All in all, human flourishing will only be possible in ever-shrinking habitable zones near the poles.

This step-by-step analysis is clever but also deceptively simple. There are also nonlinear effects, as we hit various tipping points and feedback loops; rising temperatures could set in train a vicious cycle and accelerate the process of global warming. These effects are what really alarm climate scientists.

Take the melting of the ice sheets, for example. The disappearance of the polar ice caps would darken the surface of the earth, making it easier to absorb sunlight, which warms the planet even more. If the planet warms by 4 degrees Celsius or more, up to 500 billion tons of trapped carbon could be released from the previously frozen arctic soils—either as carbon dioxide or as methane.

We can find similar feedback risks coming from the rainforests. If the Amazon dried out due to climate change, or disappears due to deforestation, global warming would be magnified. A major feedback loop could come from a potential reversing of the carbon cycle. Right now, the rainforests act as the lungs of the planet, absorbing carbon dioxide. But as the soil warms, the stored carbon could be released back into the atmosphere. This tipping point would trigger the collapse of the Amazon and add dramatically to climate change.

Further feedback loops come from the world's oceans. The combination of ocean warming and acidification is killing ocean life, especially the all-important plankton. Since marine creatures absorb a huge chunk of carbon dioxide, their destruction could initiate a vicious cycle of accelerating climate change.

The main takeaway from these tipping points and feedback loops is that global warming could become a runaway process. Once warming hits 3 degrees, it might not take much for it to jump to 5 or 6 degrees. And at that point, there is very little we can do about it.

Let me end this section with a discussion of climate change and conflict. As climate change progresses, economic opportunities are likely to diminish, and conflict for precious resources such as water is likely to increase. People are likely to migrate to more hospitable areas. A fallout of this could be greater violence, societal breakdown, and war. One study found that almost a quarter of conflict in ethnically diverse regions had roots in weather disasters.[60]

We can see this in some of the world's driest zones, including the eastern Mediterranean and the Sahel region of Africa. Across the Sahel, drought is driving conflict between pastoralists and farmers, fomenting religious division, and pushing vulnerable people into the arms of terrorists, traffickers, and other criminal elements. And although we've heard a lot about the Syrian Civil War, we've heard little of its links to climate change. Yet Syria suffered its worst drought and most severe crop failure in recorded history from 2006 to 2010. The drought affected 1.3 million people, with herders losing 85 percent of their livestock and 75 percent of farmers experiencing crop failure.[61] The ensuing civil war caused 800,000 to lose their livelihoods and pushed 80 percent of the population into poverty.[62] While it would be too simplistic to say that climate change caused the civil war, which can instead be traced to neighboring wars and geopolitical rivalry, it certainly fanned the flames. And as climate change wreaks havoc in more and more regions, conflicts like this could be the shape of things to come.

History can also teach us valuable lessons in this regard. Evidence shows that sustained shifts in climate tend to lead to greater conflict, societal disruption, and even collapse. For instance, a long-lasting drought about four thousand years ago is associated with the collapse of numerous nascent civilizations in Egypt, Mesopotamia, India, and China.[63] Another widespread drought about a thousand years later may have contributed to the collapse of the world's first network of globalization during the Bronze Age—affecting the Hittites, the Mycenaeans, the Egyptians, the Assyrians, and the Babylonians.[64] Recent research also suggests the possibility that the fall of the Roman Empire was due to climatic disruption following the end of the Rome Climate Optimum—a warm, wet, and predicable climate uniquely favorable to the empire's key agricultural crops.[65] Furthermore, the collapse of the once great Mayan empire is commonly linked to severe ecological pressures. In more recent times, a comprehensive study traced the huge jump in violence in the seventeenth century—fifty revolts, revolutions, and civil wars between 1618 and 1688—to the deep chill at the nadir of the Little Ice Age.[66] Climate change also influences religious conflict; one scholar traced the dramatic deterioration in relations between Christians, Muslims, and Jews in the fourteenth century to climatic effects across Eurasia.[67]

While these historical analyses relate mainly to the effects of cooling, recent evidence suggests that the propensity for conflict is actually greater when the climate is warming,[68] both because of the economic effects and noneconomic impacts; psychological evidence suggests that individuals are more aggressive in higher temperatures, possibly because warming leads to lower serotonin levels as the body regulates its temperature. The decline in cognitive ability could also increase violence. Pollution is known to lead to cognitive impairment and trauma too. In light of these effects, numerous studies find that advancing climate change could unleash large-scale violence. For example, researchers find that for every half degree of warming, there would be between a 10 and 20 percent increase in the likelihood of armed conflict.[69] Another study, which estimates that global warming will increase armed conflict by 54 percent in the next few decades, leading to 393,000 extra deaths by 2030, doesn't even account for the destabilization and political backlashes in host countries that will surely follow mass migrations.

Without an integral ecology, we will see a diminution of integral human development, as people will no longer be able to exercise their capacities owing to poor health, cognitive impairment, and all forms of climatic disruption that prohibit them from attaining the material bases of human flourishing. The common good will likewise be undermined by climatic disruption, which will be magnified by political instability and rising conflict.

We can also see that climate change violates solidarity, distributive justice, and the preferential option for the poor, given that the poor suffer the most from climate change while bearing the least fault. I will end this section with a quote from Cardinal Charles Bo of Yangon, Myanmar, who uttered these prophetic words at a Vatican event on climate change in 2016: "Unless rich countries agree to reduce the global warming, more people will die. This to me is a criminal genocide, when the poor and the weak are exposed [to] violent nature created by unrestricted use of fossil fuels by rich countries."[70] Strong words, indeed, yet apt words. But what are we going to do about it?

Climate Change Solutions

In *Laudato Si'*, Pope Francis argues that solving the climate crisis calls for both individual and institutional conversion. Essentially, he calls for an "ecological conversion" to break free of the stranglehold of consumerism, individualism, self-centeredness, and self-absorption. He argues that this kind of conversion is essential if we are to care for our brothers and sisters and the natural environment.[71]

In this regard, *Laudato Si'* is calling for a new "ecological citizenship" infused with new ecological virtues.[72] This commitment goes far deeper than merely enacting and respecting laws and regulations. Rather, in line with the ancient wisdom of Aristotle and Aquinas, it centers on inculcating the intrinsic motivation to live in a certain way. A virtue, remember, is simply a good habit that can be perfected only by practice. These efforts can be small, as Pope Francis notes, but they are nonetheless worthwhile; they allow people to live more fulfilled lives, and they "call forth a goodness which, albeit unseen, inevitably tends to spread."[73] The message here is that virtue can be infectious; the good habits of one person can encourage good habits in others, which can in turn mold better social norms.

Pope Francis gives examples of "little daily actions" that can inculcate virtue and hopefully change social norms. They include "avoiding the use of plastic and paper, reducing water consumption, separating refuse, cooking only what can reasonably be consumed, showing care for other living beings, using public transport or car-pooling, planting trees, turning off unnecessary lights or any number of other practices."[74]

He goes on to argue that the inculcation of ecological virtue is not optional for a Christian: "Living our vocation to be protectors of God's handiwork is essential to a life of virtue; it is not an optional or a secondary aspect of our Christian experience."[75]

Theologian Daniel DiLeo argues that we can apply the four cardinal virtues toward ecological ethics. He argues that prudence helps us appreciate the interconnectedness of all creation, which sets the stage for the inculcation of the other virtues. Justice then inspires sustainable action by giving each what is their due, including those not yet born. Fortitude allows people to fight obstacles to environmental sustainability and emboldens them to shed ecologically harmful attitudes. Finally, temperance can help moderate consumerism and help people enjoy material goods in a balanced way, consistent with true happiness.[76] Another environmental theologian, Joshtrom Kureethadam, takes a somewhat different tack, identifying a new set of environmental virtues. His close read of *Laudato Si'* yields the following virtues: praise, gratitude, care, justice, work, sobriety, and humility.[77] In this, he argues that humility is "the mother of all ecological virtues."[78] In a similar vein, a group of Catholic ethicists devised seven principles of energy ethics: (1) cherishing and protecting life as a gift from God, (2) accepting an appropriate share of responsibility for the welfare of creation, (3) living in solidarity with others for the common good, (4) striving for justice in society, (5) giving special attention to the needs of the poor and members of minority groups, (6) widespread participation in decision-making processes, and (7) employing technological prudence.[79]

We can see that, in line with Catholic social teaching, these virtues and principles do not belong to the domain of the individual alone. They also have a communal dimension. Indeed, *Laudato Si'* makes clear that individual initiative alone is not enough, as uncoordinated actions cannot solve complex social problems. As Pope Francis puts it, "Self-improvement on the part of individuals will not by itself remedy the extremely complex situation facing our world today."[80] The ability of disconnected individuals to solve collective problems is even more limited in modern globalized economies, where power is increasingly concentrated in corporate and bureaucratic structures. So to be truly effective, individuals must band together in a coordinated communal endeavor. Ecological conversion entails not only individual conversion but also community conversion.

The starting point for any solution must be a global commitment at the institutional and political level to reduce carbon emissions, which essentially means moving from high-carbon to low-carbon forms of energy. *Laudato Si'* states that "technology based on the use of highly polluting fossil fuels—especially coal, but also oil and, to a lesser degree, gas—needs to be progressively replaced without delay."[81] Yet it decries the slow pace of change, the refusal of polluting countries to take the lead in reducing emissions, plus the tendency of business to prioritize short-term profits over the common good and of governments to prioritize national interests above the global common good. All of this is a "failure of conscience and responsibility."[82]

Since climate and other environmental problems do not respect international borders, *Laudato Si'* argues, "interdependence obliges us to think of one world with a common plan."[83] Until recently, such common plans were lacking. Yet in December 2015, after the release of *Laudato Si'* and on the back of the UN Sustainable Development Goals, 196 nations signed the Paris Agreement on Climate Change. In Paris, the nations of the world committed to taking action to stay beneath the 2-degree Celsius limit. In fact, they stepped up the level of ambition, promising to pursue efforts to contain global warming to 1.5 degrees Celsius—in recognition of new scientific evidence on fast-rising sea levels. The backbone of the agreement is that countries commit to peaking global emissions as soon as possible, with the goal of reaching net-zero greenhouse gas emissions in the second half of the century. Yet, as we have seen, the cumulative effect of these climate plans, which are in many cases merely aspirational, points to a 3-degree Celsius increase.

The primary way to achieve the Paris goal is through a profound transformation of the energy system, through what is known as "deep decarbonization."[84] Decarbonization has three key strands. The first of these strands is improving energy efficiency. There are a lot of possibilities here—including more fuel-efficient vehicles, smarter urban design that upgrades public transportation and minimizes commuting distances, and more energy-efficient buildings to reduce heating, cooling, and ventilation. This shift will entail an upfront cost but ultimately should save money by lowering energy costs, especially important for the poor.

The second strand of decarbonization involves making electricity carbon free. This would replace electricity generated by fossil fuels (coal, oil, gas) with electricity generated by renewables (hydro, wind, solar, geothermal). Such "clean" energy does not emit greenhouse gases into the atmosphere.

The third strand is fuel switching. This strand means shifting from the direct use of fossil fuels for energy to electricity that is generated by clean sources. For example, furnaces and boilers to heat buildings can be replaced by heat pumps that are powered by electricity. Internal combustion engines in cars can be replaced by electric motors. And low-carbon fuels can be used for things that cannot easily be electrified, such as airplanes and large trucks.

All in all, decarbonization presents a momentous challenge on scientific, economic, and financial fronts. Yet we have the technological ability to decarbonize without any real deterioration in the quality of life. Recent technological advances include large reductions in the cost of wind and solar energy as well as improvements in batteries for electric vehicles, smarter power grids, and far more efficient building design. Thanks to technological improvements, the cost of clean fuels is competitive with fossil fuels. Moreover, as technology advances, and as we become more efficient in our use of energy, these costs will only fall further. Indeed, as climate scientist Michael Mann has noted, existing renewable energy technologies can be scaled up to meet 80 percent of global energy demand by 2030 and a hundred percent by 2050.[85]

What about the overall costs of this energy transition? According to the International Energy Authority, about $40 trillion in additional investment is needed to transition to a low-carbon energy system consistent with staying under the 2-degree limit.[86] This investment amounts to less than 1 percent of cumulative global GDP through midcentury. Similarly, the Deep Decarbonization Pathways Project calculates that investment in low-carbon technology must rise to about 1.25 percent of GDP a year.[87]

The key is that this transition is affordable in an extremely wealthy global economy. Plus, according to the IMF, fossil fuel subsidies amount to a whopping 6.5 percent of global GDP, largely because polluters are not paying the full social costs of their activities.[88] So it is less a matter of resources than of priorities. And not only is this additional investment affordable but it also pays for itself many times over; the International Energy Authority calculates that the eventual fuel cost savings will be three times the additional investment. This investment is a small price to pay to avoid catastrophic consequences. This small transition cost needs to be assessed against a possible reduction in GDP by a quarter by end of century if we do not change course.

What is the best way of getting from here to there? Economists typically coalesce around the idea of carbon pricing. This idea, which has a lot of merit, says that the prices of fossil fuels do not account for the costs they impose on society, so these prices need to rise. As noted in chapter 5, neoclassical economists dub this a negative externality. To deal with it, they have made "getting the prices right" a mantra for fighting climate change. In practice, there are a number of ways to do this. The simplest is a tax on carbon, where the tax attempts to approximate the social cost of carbon emissions. This tax raises the cost of oil, coal, and gas relative to wind, solar, nuclear, and other low-carbon options. Another way is to issue tradable emissions permits. To be allowed to emit carbon, people would need to purchase a permit on the open market, and such permits are limited to make sure that emissions are capped—hence "cap-and-trade."

The IMF has a made a strong argument for carbon pricing, especially carbon taxation, as the main strategy to reduce carbon emissions.[89] The idea is that carbon pricing provides across-the-board incentives to reduce energy consumption, use cleaner fuels, and mobilize private finance. It can induce decarbonization along all dimensions: energy efficiency, shift to renewable electricity generation, and fuel switching. In terms of actual prices, the IMF estimates that a carbon price of around $35 per ton would be enough to meet the pledges for the G20 countries, which together account for four-fifths of global emissions. But remember these pledges are only consistent with 3 degrees of warming. To stay below 2 degrees, these countries would need a global carbon price twice as high as this, around $70 a ton. To realize the scale of this problem, note that the current global average carbon price is only $2 a ton.

A deeper problem, harking back to the critique of neoclassical economics laid out in chapter 3, is that economists across the ideological spectrum tend to rally around carbon pricing because they believe everything must have a price, people respond to incentives, and the market can work its magic. There's no concept of ecological virtue—doing the right thing for its own sake. In fact, in line with the arguments of Samuel Bowles and Michael Sandel, putting a price on carbon might undermine the virtues of ecological citizenship because people might regard the payment as a license to pollute. This outcome is more likely with cap-and-trade than straight-up carbon taxation, if people think they can simply purchase the right to pollute.

What's more, carbon pricing can backfire dramatically. All over the world, rising fuel prices cause social upheaval and unrest, even violence—something true in poor and rich countries alike. Consider the recent riots in France by the discontented "yellow vests," spurred by a rise in fuel prices. Neoclassical economists will argue that in some vague sense, the "losers" can be compensated—but this compensation tends to be more theoretical than practical and usually does little to reduce economic hardship. For this reason, Sachs has argued that carbon pricing hits the wrong target: existing capital rather than new investment.[90] Take the example of cars. A carbon price raises fuel prices for people already driving cars. But what we need to do is make sure that only electric vehicles are sold after a certain date. This kind of change is the province of regulation, not taxation. And because it does not tax existing capital or penalize existing car owners, such regulation is much less likely to provoke a backlash. The same argument holds that all new electricity generation must be sourced from renewable energy after a certain date. From this perspective, carbon pricing can act as a reinforcement, used to tax really old capital, such as cars older than fifteen years or coal plants older than forty years. But to go beyond fossil fuels, it is better to choose a direct rather than a market-based mechanism.

To get a feel for what such a strategy might look like, consider Sachs's ten bright line rules for reducing carbon emissions:[91]

1. stop new coal plants,
2. stop new oil and gas exploration,
3. stop new fracking,
4. stop new oil and gas pipelines,
5. stop new deforestation,
6. shift to battery electric vehicles by 2030,
7. reduce beef eating,
8. interconnect renewables,
9. divest from greenhouse gas companies and projects,
10. restrain oil companies and procarbon governments.

These bright lines focus largely on the regulatory and legal mechanisms and are what is required today to keep temperatures in the relatively safe zone in the future. By being clear and straightforward, they also reduce uncertainty for business going forward.

Sachs's bright lines mix technical solutions with efforts to instill virtue and combat the power of the fossil fuel lobby. This power is immense, by the way. Fossil fuel companies are some of the largest and most politically connected entities on the planet. According to the Fortune 500, seven of the ten largest companies in the world are in the energy sector. And as noted already, a hundred companies account for 70 percent of all greenhouse gas emissions since 1988, fossil fuel companies chief among them.[92] Their continued profits depend on extracting and burning as much oil, coal, and gas as possible. One study suggested that if all known fossil fuel reserves are extracted and burned, global temperatures could rise by almost 10 degrees Celsius, well beyond even the worst-case scenario of the IPCC.[93] As environmental activist McKibben has argued—using the math of carbon budgets—80 percent of oil, coal, and gas reserves on the books of fossil fuel companies need to be kept in the ground if we are to have any chance of staying under 2 degrees Celsius.[94] But these reserves amount to about $20 trillion in assets, so we can see why fossil fuel companies fight to delay or block the energy transition, including by suppressing evidence about the harmful effects of fossil fuels and funding climate change denialism. In these efforts, these companies have a natural ally in libertarians, who are naturally suspicious of any government attempt to suppress the "freedom" of people to choose the lifestyles they wish. For example, as McKibben notes, between 2012 and 2016, Rupert Murdoch's *Wall Street Journal* published over three hundred op-eds, columns, and editorials on climate change—95 percent of which promoted climate change denialism.[95]

Laudato Si' is well aware of these problems. "There are too many special interests," says Pope Francis, "and economic interests easily end up trumping the common good and manipulating information so that their own plans will not be affected."[96] He notes that "many of those who possess more resources and economic or political power seem mostly to be concerned with masking the problems or concealing their symptoms."[97] As well as this narrowness of vision, Pope Francis condemns a certain shallowness of vision. In this, he criticizes "superficial rhetoric, sporadic acts of philanthropy and perfunctory expressions of concern for the environment" without any serious efforts to change things.[98] Likewise, he calls out "a false or superficial ecology which bolsters complacency and a cheerful recklessness." "Such evasiveness," he says, "serves as a licence to carrying on with our present lifestyles and models of production and consumption."[99] Taking on the superficial attempts of business to come to grips with the environmental crisis, Pope Francis also argues that "the social and environmental responsibility of businesses often gets reduced to a series of marketing and image-enhancing measures."[100] This practice too is an example of shallowness of vision, stuck in the language of finance and technocracy rather than true ecological conversion.

In 2018, Pope Francis addressed a gathering of oil company executives at the Vatican. His topic was precisely the power of special interests and the gap between what is happening and what is needed. He did not hold back:

> If we are to eliminate poverty and hunger, as called for by the United Nations Sustainable Development Goals, the more than one billion people without electricity today need to gain access to it. But that energy should also be clean, by a reduction in the systematic use of fossil fuels. Our desire to ensure energy for all must not lead to the undesired effect of a spiral of extreme climate changes due to a catastrophic rise in global temperatures, harsher environments and increased levels of poverty. As you know, in December 2015, 196 Nations negotiated and adopted the Paris Agreement, with a firm resolve to limit the growth in global warming to below 2° centigrade, based on preindustrial levels, and, if possible, to below

1.5° centigrade. Some two-and-a-half years later, carbon dioxide emissions and atmospheric concentrations of greenhouse gases remain very high. This is disturbing and a cause for real concern. Yet even more worrying is the continued search for new fossil fuel reserves, whereas the Paris Agreement clearly urged keeping most fossil fuels underground. This is why we need to talk together—industry, investors, researchers and consumers—about transition and the search for alternatives. Civilization requires energy, but energy use must not destroy civilization![101]

Practical solutions must include holding fossil fuel companies to account, including suing them in court for the harm they have wrought, especially since they knew at an early stage what their emissions were doing to the environment and yet covered it up, funding all kinds of climate change denialism and obfuscation. Another strategy here is economic and political action. In this sense, civil society and religious groups have an important role to play. The true power of civil society comes from its ability to influence politics and economics, to counteract the forces of inertia and ideology that inhibit virtuous action.[102] Pope Francis himself is explicit on this point, praising international agencies and civil society organizations that "draw public attention to these issues and offer critical cooperation, employing legitimate means of pressure, to ensure that each government carries out its proper and inalienable responsibility to preserve its country's environment and natural resources, without capitulating to spurious local or international interests."[103]

In recent years, the greatest signs of hope for the climate movement are coming from young people who understand that they will be coming of age in a barely habitable world if no action is taken to decarbonize the economy. An unlikely leader has emerged in Greta Thunberg, a teenage Swedish climate activist who began a one-person "school strike for climate," which unleashed a global movement and prompted millions of similar actions by students across the world. This is our hope.

Another strategy is fossil fuel divestment. We can see some support for this in *Laudato Si'*, whereby Pope Francis praises consumer movements that boycott certain products. This kind of boycott can, he claims, change the way businesses operate, "forcing them to consider their environmental footprint and their patterns of production."[104] This logic could be extended to the burgeoning movement to divest from investments in fossil fuels. As noted by Bill McKibben, more than $8 trillion has already been committed to fossil fuel divestment. Both a practical and moral case arises: the practical case is that these assets are "stranded assets" and thus represent a lousy business investment as the world transitions to clean energy. And as the divestment movement grows, this risk becomes ever greater. But there is also a clear moral case. As a group of Catholic ethicists have written, the goal is to morally stigmatize fossil fuel companies so that politicians stop doing their bidding and taking their financial contributions.[105] As the American Civil Rights and the South African Anti-Apartheid Movements demonstrate, financial boycotts can make a real difference in terms of changing the politics. But divestment alone is not enough. Ideally, we need divestment twinned with reinvestment so that these resources can be deployed toward renewable energy to further the energy transition.

Shifting the economy toward one powered by renewable energy is going to require stepped-up public investment. This would both provide dignified employment and support decarbonization, the most urgent priority in the world today. Great need exists for green industrial policies, for state-directed investment in the green technologies. This industrial policy could also take the form of subsidies that would do two things: (1) nudge the private sector to make big, risky investments and (2) counter the effects of subsidies enjoyed by fossil fuels, including from not being priced correctly.[106] In this vein, politicians across the world are talking about a "Green New Deal" that would solve the climate crisis in a way that generates much needed investment and jobs. In this context, there is ample evidence that decarbonization is pretty labor intensive. For the United States, one estimate is that the investments to achieve zero emissions between 2020 and 2050 could generate 2.5 million jobs each year directly; this figure rises to 4 million if we include "indirect jobs" from the extra demand created.[107] There is simply no excuse not to make these investments, especially at a time when interest rates are at record lows.

To sum up: I have argued that decarbonization by midcentury is technologically and financially possible. We have the means to do it. The missing link is the political will and the translation of this will into concrete and courageous action, partly because of the power of the fossil fuel industry complex. The moral imperative required makes leaders such as Pope Francis all the more important.

Beloved Amazon

I want to end this chapter by discussing a very practical application of *Laudato Si'*. In 2019, Pope Francis sought to put this encyclical into action by convening a meeting of bishops—called a synod—at the Vatican on the particular challenges facing the Amazon region. Before this meeting, the Vatican engaged in a deep consultation with those who live in the region, including Indigenous people, who tend to be the most marginal and dispossessed. Overall, 87,000 individuals were consulted from across the nine countries spread across the region.[108]

Before this synod, in *Laudato Si'*, Pope Francis expressed concern for the destruction of cultures taking place through the leveling of globalization and consumerism. "The disappearance of a culture," he says, "can be just as serious, or even more serious, than the disappearance of a species of plant or animal." He avers, "the imposition of a dominant lifestyle linked to a single form of production can be just as harmful as the altering of ecosystems."[109]

This comment has special resonance when it comes to Indigenous people. Here is what the pope writes in *Laudato Si'*:

> In this sense, it is essential to show special care for indigenous communities and their cultural traditions. They are not merely one minority among others, but should be the principal dialogue partners, especially when large projects affecting their land are proposed. For them, land is not a commodity but rather a gift from God and from their ancestors who rest there, a sacred space with which they need to interact if they are to maintain their identity and values. When they remain on their land, they themselves care for it best. Nevertheless, in various parts of the world, pressure is being put on them to abandon their homelands to make room for agricultural or mining projects which are undertaken without regard for the degradation of nature and culture.[110]

After the Amazon synod, Pope Francis penned a document, an apostolic exhortation called *Querida Amazonia*, "Beloved Amazon." In it, he attempts to summarize the themes of the synod, including the social and ecological oppression of the inhabitants of the region by the forces of big business and an extractivist mentality. He begins his reflection with four dreams for the Amazon:

> I dream of an Amazon region that fights for the rights of the poor, the original peoples and the least of our brothers and sisters, where their voices can be heard and their dignity advanced. I dream of an Amazon region that can preserve its distinctive cultural riches, where the beauty of our humanity shines forth in so many varied ways. I dream of an Amazon region that can jealously preserve its overwhelming natural beauty and the superabundant life teeming in its rivers and forests. I dream of Christian communities capable of generous commitment, incarnate in the Amazon region, and giving the Church new faces with Amazonian features.[111]

This document is really integral ecology in action, on the front lines of both social exclusion and environmental devastation. It notes that the Amazon is facing an ecological disaster as both legal and illegal "colonizing interests" are expanding timber and mining industries, expelling or marginalizing Indigenous peoples.[112] This disaster comes from an attitude whereby the Amazon region "has been presented as an enormous empty space to be filled, a source of raw resources to be developed, a wild expanse to be domesticated." In consequence, "none of this recognizes the rights of the original peoples; it simply ignores them as if they did not exist, or acts as if the lands on which they live do not belong to them."[113] Forced to migrate to cities, these Indigenous peoples find "the worst forms of enslavement, subjection, and poverty," including "xenophobia, sexual exploitation, and human trafficking."[114] Echoing the strong language of *Rerum Novarum* during the industrial revolution, Pope Francis argues that the Indigenous people are victims of crime and injustice by powerful corporations: "The businesses, national or international, which harm the Amazon and fail to respect the right of the original peoples to the land and its boundaries, and to self-determination and prior consent, should be called for what they are: *injustice and crime*."[115] When this happens, *Querida Amazonia* argues, globalization becomes a "new version of colonialism." It points the finger at business out for a quick profit that appropriates lands, razes forests, pollutes the environment, or privatizes potable water. Indigenous people who protest these projects are frequently harassed and sometimes even murdered. It is clear that colonialism has not ended but instead has been "changed, disguised, and concealed."[116] "The land has blood, and it is bleeding," says Pope Francis. "The multinationals have cut the veins of our mother Earth."[117] This lament relates to what *Laudato Si'* calls an "ecological debt," as multinationals—especially mining and energy companies—housed in rich jurisdictions befoul the environments and destroy communities in regions like the Amazon.[118]

In contrast to the consumerist mentality exported by globalization, *Querida Amazonia* praises the strong sense of community among the Indigenous inhabitants of the Amazon region. It notes that "everything is shared; private areas—typical of modernity—are minimal. Life is a communal journey where tasks and responsibilities are apportioned and shared on the basis of the common good. There is no room for the notion of an individual detached from the community or from the land."[119]

These cultures are worth preserving, Pope Francis proclaims, so that the people can enjoy "good living" as well as purpose and meaning in the context of community and the common good. In this sense, we can learn from Indigenous peoples in terms of correcting the defects of our own societies and cultures: "Factors like consumerism, individualism, discrimination, inequality, and any number of others represent the weaker side of supposedly more developed cultures. The ethnic groups that, in interaction with nature, developed a cultural treasure marked by a strong sense of community, readily notice our darker aspects, which we do not recognize in the midst of our alleged progress. Consequently, it will prove beneficial to listen to their experience of life."[120]

Pope Francis also addresses the ecological importance of the Amazon, where the great rallying cry of *Laudato Si'* that "everything is connected" has special resonance. It turns out that the Amazon is vitally important to the health of the entire planet, given its amazing biodiversity and the fact that it serves as a carbon sink. Yet Pope Francis sounds a warning note: if the forest is eliminated, it will not be replaced. The great carbon sink will be gone forever, as will the vital eco-systems and precious biodiversity of the region. And the waters, vital for human flourishing, are suffering terribly from pollution. Once again, it comes back to a deformed economic vision. "The interest of a few powerful industries should not be considered more important than the good of the Amazon region and of humanity as a whole," says Pope Francis.[121]

Instead, we need to protect the Amazon region with a mix of ancestral wisdom and contemporary technical knowledge[122]—as always in Catholic social teaching, merging the best of the old with the best of the new. We need a greater sense of responsibility by both governments and business. The solution is deceptively simple: with respect to the Amazon, "we can love it, not simply use it. . . . Even more, we can feel intimately a part of it and not only defend it; then the Amazon region will once more become like a mother to us."[123] Harking back to *Laudato Si'*, Pope Francis argues we need to conquer our "self-destructive vices."[124] He implores us to instead develop a sense of ecological virtue—"new habits" that are "less greedy and more serene, more respectful and less anxious, more fraternal."[125]

In sum, *Querida Amazonia* is a fitting follow-up to *Laudato Si'*, a practical petri dish for the application of integral ecology. In fact, the combined social, economic, and environmental challenges of this region touch on all of the core principles of Catholic social teaching: the common good, integral human development, inte-gral ecology, solidarity, subsidiarity, reciprocity and gratuitousness, the universal destination of goods, the preferential option for the poor, rights, and justice. What matters in the Amazon therefore matters for all of us, and not just because of its centrality to the environment and to climate.

Notes

1. Whitney Bauck, "'The Dominant Theological Issue': Environmentalist Bill Mc-Kibben Wants Your Pastor at the Global Climate Strike," *Washington Post*, September 19, 2019.

2. *LS*, 1.

3. Quoted in *LS*, 87.

4. *LS*, 10.

5. *LS*, 11.

6. *LS*, 1.

7. *LS*, 67.

8. *LS*, 67.

9. *LS*, 67.

10. *LS*, 11.

11. *LS*, 76.

12. *LS*, 84.

13. *LS*, 233.

14. *LS*, 77.

15. *LS*, 92.

16. Hopkins, *"God's Grandeur" and Other Poems*.

17. *LS*, 233.

18. *LS*, 89.

19. This section leans on Sachs, *Age of Sustainable Development*, ch. 6.

20. Wallace-Wells, *Uninhabitable Earth*, 87.

21. The following is based heavily on Annett, "Our Common Responsibility for Our Common Home."

22. *LS*, 21.

23. *LS*, 23.

24. *LS*, 25.

25. *LS*, 30.

26. *LS*, 33.

27. *LS*, 42.

28. This section leans heavily on Annett, *Resource Guide on Climate Change for Religious Communities*, a publication I wrote for the Religions for Peace, a remarkable group committed to multireligious dialogue.

29. Lynas, *Six Degrees*; Sachs, *Age of Sustainable Development*; Wagner and Weitzman, *Climate Shock*; McKibben, *Falter*; Wallace-Wells, *Uninhabitable Earth*.

30. See Fagan, *Long Summer*.

31. McKibben, *Falter*, 22.

32. Sachs, *Age of Sustainable Development*, ch. 12.

33. Intergovernmental Panel on Climate Change, "AR5 Synthesis Report."

34. Intergovernmental Panel on Climate Change.

35. Intergovernmental Panel on Climate Change, "Global Warming of 1.5 Degrees C."

36. Climate Central, "10 Warmest Years on Record."

37. McKibben, *Falter*, 40; Wallace-Wells, *Uninhabitable Earth*, 51.

38. Wallace-Wells, 60.

39. Sachs, *Age of Sustainable Development*.

40. Wallace-Wells, *Uninhabitable Earth*, 81.

41. Wallace-Wells, 87–88.

42. Lancet Commissions, "Health and Climate Change."

43. McKibben, *Falter*, 35.

44. Wallace-Wells, *Uninhabitable Earth*, 138.

45. Development Assistance Research Associates and the Climate Vulnerable Forum, *Climate Vulnerability Monitor*.

46. Wallace-Wells, *Uninhabitable Earth*, 104.

47. Wallace-Wells, 28.

48. McKibben, *Falter*, 28.

49. Stern, *Economics of Climate Change*.

50. Burke, Hsiang, and Miguel, "Global Non-linear Effect of Temperature on Economic Production."

51. See Wallace-Wells, *Uninhabitable Earth*, 122.

52. Hallegatte et al., *Shock Waves*.

53. McKibben, *Falter*, 29.

54. Wallace-Wells, *Uninhabitable Earth*, 49.

55. Ramanathan, "Two Worlds Approach for Mitigating Air Pollution and Climate Change."

56. Hannah Ritchie and Max Roser, "CO_2 and Greenhouse Gas Emissions," *Our World in Data*, May 11, 2017, https://ourworldindata.org/co2-and-other-greenhouse-gas-emissions#citation.

57. McKibben, *Falter*, 42.

58. McKibben, 59–60.

59. Lynas, *Six Degrees*.

60. Wallace-Wells, *Uninhabitable Earth*, 126–27.

61. Femia and Werrell, "Syria."

62. Kelley et al., "Climate Change in the Fertile Crescent and Implications of the Recent Syrian Drought."

63. See Fagan, *Long Summer*.

64. See Cline, *1177 BC*.

65. Harper, *Fate of Rome*.

66. Parker, *Global Crisis*.

67. Philip Jenkins, "Burning at the Stake," *New Republic*, December, 2007.

68. Burke, Hsiang, and Miguel, "Climate and Conflict."

69. Burke, Hsiang, and Miguel; Wallace-Wells, *Uninhabitable Earth*, 125.

70. Bo, "Submission by Charles Cardinal Maung Bo."

71. *LS*, 208.

72. *LS*, 211.

73. *LS*, 212.

74. *LS*, 211.

75. *LS*, 217.

76. DiLeo, "Creation Care through Consumption and Life Choices," 220–21.

77. Kureethadam, *Ten Green Commandments of Laudato Si'*.

78. Kureethadam, 206.

79. Lothes Biviano et al., "Catholic Moral Traditions and Energy Ethics for the Twenty-First Century."

80. *LS*, 219.

81. *LS*, 165.

82. *LS*, 169.

83. *LS*, 164.

84. See Sustainable Development Solutions Network and Institute for Sustainable Development and International Relations, "Pathways to Deep Decarbonization."

85. Mann, *New Climate War*, 171.

86. International Energy Agency, *Energy Technology Perspectives 2015*.

87. Sustainable Development Solutions Network and Institute for Sustainable Development and International Relations, "Pathways to Deep Decarbonization."

88. Coady et al., "Global Fossil Fuel Subsidies Remain Large."

89. International Monetary Fund, "How to Mitigate Climate Change."

90. Sachs made this argument in a presentation at a Vatican meeting on climate change on May 27, 2019.

91. Sachs, "Climate Change and New Evidence from Science, Engineering, and Policy."

92. Carbon Majors Database, *Carbon Majors Report*.

93. Tokarska et al., "Climate Response to Five Trillion Tonnes of Carbon."

94. Bill McKibben, "Global Warming's Terrifying New Math," *Rolling Stone*, July 19, 2012.

95. McKibben, *Falter*, 119–20.

96. *LS*, 54.

97. *LS*, 26.

98. *LS*, 54.

99. *LS*, 59.

100. *LS*, 194.

101. Pope Francis, "Address of His Holiness Pope Francis to Participants at the Meeting for Executives of the Main Companies in the Oil and Natural Gas Sectors, and Other Energy Related Businesses."

102. See Annett, "Our Common Responsibility for Our Common Home."

103. *LS*, 38.

104. *LS*, 206.

105. Erin Lothes Biviano, Daniel DiLeo, Cristina Richie, and Tobias Winright, "Is Fossil Fuel Investment a Sin?," *Health Care Ethics USA*, Winter 2018.

106. Rodrik, *Straight Talk on Trade*, ch. 11.

107. Sustainable Development Solutions Network, "America's Zero Carbon Action Plan."

108. Vatican, *Final Document of the Synod on the Amazon*.

109. *LS*, 145.

110. *LS*, 146.

111. *QAm*, 7.

112. *QAm*, 8–9.

113. *QAm*, 12.

114. *QAm*, 10.
115. *QAm*, 14.
116. *QAm*, 16.
117. *QAm*, 42.
118. *LS*, 51.
119. *QAm*, 20.
120. *QAm*, 36.
121. *QAm*, 48.
122. *QAm*, 51.
123. *QAm*, 55.
124. *QAm*, 53.
125. *QAm*, 58.

8

Expanding Our Circles

The Global Dimension

In some circles today, globalism has become a dirty word, but not in Catholic social teaching. Perhaps this is not too surprising, given that the Catholic Church is the quintessential global institution. Catholic social teaching holds that some problems should be solved at the global level, through international coordination and cooperation among countries.[1] Of course, enlightened self-interest can play a role too, as supporting the global common good is often the best way to support the national common good. Note that this is not a call for a new cosmopolitanism to take precedence over preexisting communities, local and national. Rather, it is about recognizing the common humanity of all inhabitants of our common home, sharing a common human dignity, and bonded together in common purpose. It is about making sure that all can participate in the interdependent good of an interdependent world.[2]

The case for solving some problems at the multilateral level is once again based on the twin principles of solidarity and subsidiarity. The argument based on solidarity is fairly straightforward. Solidarity, the notion that all are responsible for all, extends to all peoples. It can be seen as a moral response to increasing interdependence, to the fact that we are all, now more than ever, linked by a common destiny. The argument based on subsidiarity might appear stranger. After all, the principle of subsidiarity is usually deployed to justify decision making at the lowest possible level, to better reflect the dignity and agency of the human being. But subsidiarity is more complicated than that; it is about making decisions at the lowest level possible and the highest level necessary. Sometimes that level is the global level. Subsidiarity operates upward as well as downward. Why is this? Because so many problems today are global problems that cannot readily be solved at the national level. A powerful example is the environmental crisis—the climate does not respect borders, after all—but it is also true of many features of modern globalization.

There is a long tradition in Catholic social teaching arguing in favor of global solutions. Pope John XXIII, in *Pacem in Terris* in 1963, praises the United Nations and the Universal Declaration of Human Rights as the basis for "the establishment of a juridical and political ordering of the world community."[3] As he puts it,

> The United Nations Organization has the special aim of maintaining and strengthening peace between nations, and of encouraging and assisting friendly relations between them, based on the principles of equality, mutual respect, and extensive cooperation in every field of human endeavor.
>
> A clear proof of the farsightedness of this organization is provided by the Universal Declaration of Human Rights passed by the United Nations General Assembly on December 10, 1948. The preamble of this declaration affirms that the genuine recognition and complete observance of all the rights and freedoms outlined in the declaration is a goal to be sought by all peoples and all nations. . . .
>
> . . . The document should be considered a step in the right direction, an approach toward the establishment of a juridical and political ordering of the world community. It is a solemn recognition of the personal dignity of every human being; an assertion of everyone's right to be free to seek out the truth, to follow moral principles, discharge the duties imposed by justice and lead a fully human life. . . .
>
> . . . It is therefore Our earnest wish that the United Nations Organization may be able progressively to adapt its structure and methods of operation to the magnitude and nobility of its tasks. May the day be not long delayed when every human being can find in this organization an effective safeguard of his personal rights; those rights, that is, which derive directly from his dignity as a human person, and which are therefore universal, inviolable and inalienable.[4]

This optimism about the family of nations bound by the UN Charter and the Universal Declaration of Human Rights permeates Catholic social teaching and influences its approach to global cooperation in the postwar period. Pope John XXIII was chiefly concerned with peace between nations during the darkest days of the Cold War. Future popes moved into a more explicitly economic justification for global cooperation. This focus began with Pope Paul VI in *Populorum Progressio*, in which he argued that development was the "new name for peace," given that "extreme disparity between nations in economic, social and educational levels provokes jealousy and discord, often putting peace in jeopardy."[5] He went on to argue for a global approach because "nations are the architects of their own development, and they must bear the burden of this work; but they cannot accomplish it if they live in isolation from others."[6] Accordingly, Pope Paul calls for an "effective world authority": "Such international collaboration among the nations of the world certainly calls for institutions that will promote, coordinate and direct it, until a new juridical order is firmly established and fully ratified. We give willing and wholehearted support to those public organizations that have already joined in promoting the development of nations, and We ardently hope that they will enjoy ever growing authority."[7]

In concrete terms, linking peace to economic development, Pope Paul calls for a "world fund" whereby nations would "set aside part of their military expenditures . . . to relieve the needs of impoverished peoples." For, he contends, "only a concerted effort on the part of all nations, embodied in and carried out by this world fund, will stop these senseless rivalries and promote fruitful, friendly dialogue between nations."[8] Pope Francis takes up this call anew in *Fratelli Tutti*.[9]

Pope John Paul II was also a supporter of global cooperation, including through the power and agency of international organizations. He argued that globalization ought not to be left to the whims of the market but should be given direction by the international community—a globalization of solidarity, as it were. He was also concerned that these venues should not be dominated by powerful countries; rather, they should represent the interests of all nations. Here is how he puts it in *Centesimus Annus*, from 1991:

> Today we are facing the so-called "globalization" of the economy, a phenomenon which is not to be dismissed, since it can create unusual opportunities for greater prosperity. There is a growing feeling, however, that this increasing internationalization of the economy ought to be accompanied by effective international agencies which will oversee and direct the economy to the common good, something that an individual State, even if it were the most powerful on earth, would not be in a position to do. In order to achieve this result, it is necessary that there be increased coordination among the more powerful countries, and that in international agencies the interests of the whole human family be equally represented. It is also necessary that in evaluating the consequences of their decisions, these agencies always give sufficient consideration to peoples and countries which have

little weight in the international market, but which are burdened by the most acute and desperate needs, and are thus more dependent on support for their development. Much remains to be done in this area.[10]

Writing from the depths of the global financial crisis, Pope Benedict XVI also saw merits in global cooperation to solve the dysfunctions of financial globalization—the kinds of dysfunctions that gave rise to the crisis in the first place. He puts forward a rather bold proposal for a "world political authority": "This seems necessary in order to arrive at a political, juridical and economic order which can increase and give direction to international cooperation for the development of all peoples in solidarity. To manage the global economy; to revive economies hit by the crisis; to avoid any deterioration of the present crisis and the greater imbalances that would result; to bring about integral and timely disarmament, food security and peace; to guarantee the protection of the environment and to regulate migration."[11]

Rather than set up a new organization afresh, Benedict is instead calling for "a reform of the United Nations Organization, and likewise of economic institutions and international finance, so that the concept of the family of nations can acquire real teeth . . . in the face of the unrelenting growth of global interdependence."[12] He notes, "The integral development of peoples and international cooperation require the establishment of a greater degree of international ordering, marked by subsidiarity, for the management of globalization."[13]

In *Laudato Si'*, Pope Francis extends this theme, especially in the context of environmental action. As he puts it, "Interdependence obliges us to think of one world with a common plan."[14] He goes on to argue that "a global consensus is essential for confronting the deeper problems, which cannot be resolved by unilateral actions on the part of individual countries. Such a consensus could lead, for example, to planning a sustainable and diversified agriculture, developing renewable and less polluting forms of energy, encouraging a more efficient use of energy, promoting a better management of marine and forest resources, and ensuring universal access to drinking water."[15]

In this light, Pope Francis gives strong support to the UN Sustainable Development Goals and the Paris Agreement on Climate Change. He calls for enforceable international agreements to govern all aspects of the global commons. According to the pope, "Enforceable international agreements are urgently needed, since local authorities are not always capable of effective intervention. Relations between states must be respectful of each other's sovereignty, but must also lay down mutually agreed means of averting regional disasters which would eventually affect everyone. Global regulatory norms are needed to impose obligations and prevent unacceptable actions, for example, when powerful companies or countries dump contaminated waste or offshore polluting industries in other countries."[16]

Pope Francis also criticizes the lack of action on commitments made at the Rio Earth Summit in 1992 on greenhouse gas emissions and also the lack of progress on commitments on biodiversity and desertification. He states that "recent World Summits on the environment have not lived up to expectations because, due to lack of political will, they were unable to reach truly meaningful and effective global agreements on the environment."[17] He attributes this lack of progress to the fact that "international negotiations cannot make significant progress due to positions taken by countries which place their national interests above the global common good."[18] In response to this failure that continues to block action, because narrow national interests continue to hinder wider global concerns, *Laudato Si'* calls for strengthened international agreements and institutions:

> A more responsible overall approach is needed to deal with both problems: the reduction of pollution and the development of poorer countries and regions. The twenty-first century, while maintaining systems of governance inherited from the past, is witnessing a weakening of the power of nation states, chiefly because the economic and financial sectors, being transnational, tends [*sic*] to prevail over the political. Given this situation, it is essential to devise stronger and more efficiently organized international institutions, with functionaries who are appointed fairly by agreement among national governments, and empowered to impose sanctions.[19]

In this same light, Pope Francis notes the need for richer countries to help the poorer ones in a spirit of global solidarity. This help will require "the establishment of mechanisms and subsidies which allow developing countries access to technology transfer, technical assistance and financial resources."[20] To achieve these aims, he calls for a "new and universal solidarity."

Pope Francis develops these themes in *Fratelli Tutti*, appealing for an ethical globalization marked by strong international institutions. He condemns a form of globalism that "has been co-opted by the economic and financial sector" and that "strengthens the identity of the most powerful."[21] He repeats the plea for a "world authority," tying it to "stronger and more efficiently organized international institutions" that are "equipped with the power to provide for the global common good, the elimination of hunger and poverty and the sure defence of fundamental human rights."[22] He has in mind a reform of the United Nations oriented toward justice and universal fraternity instead of being co-opted by the powerful.

Elements of an Ethical Globalization

Based on the principles of Catholic social teaching, I will now look at seven distinct elements of what an ethical globalization might look like: in the areas of the global commons, tax havens, financing the Sustainable Development Goals, debt relief, globalization and finance, globalization and trade, and globalization and people.

The Global Commons

It seems appropriate to start with the global commons, in light of its importance in *Laudato Si'*. When discussing policies that belong to the multilateral level, economist and globalization expert Dani Rodrik hones in on two: the global commons, whereby outcomes depend on what happens at the global rather than the national level, and what he calls "beggar-thy-neighbor" polices whereby a country extracts a gain by imposing a cost on another.[23] Rodrik, a globalization skeptic, deliberately seeks to limit the scope of binding international agreements, which he fears will be tilted toward powerful interests and restrict the legitimate authority of the nation-state. He is in effect making an argument based on subsidiarity.

The clearest example of a global commons is of course climate change and the other environment challenges that delineate the planetary boundaries. Here, efforts to come up with a "common plan" for the world date back to 1992, to the Rio Earth Summit. That summit gave rise to the United Nations Framework Convention on Climate Change (UNFCCC), in which all parties pledged to achieve the "stabilization of greenhouse gas concentrations in the atmosphere at a level that would prevent dangerous anthropogenic interference with the climate system."[24] It also gave rise to two other enormously important international environment agreements: the Convention on Biological Diversity and Convention to Combat Desertification. Twenty years later, in 2012, the world went back to Rio to assess progress on these three treaties. The results painted a dismal picture. As argued by Sachs, the grade given for implementing these treaties should be an F.[25] Pope Francis shares this pessimism in *Laudato Si'*.

Part of the problem was that no country wanted to take responsibility for the global common good, fearful that other countries wouldn't act—the *homo economicus* free-rider problem at the global level. Major countries were also unwilling or unable to resist the immense pressure coming from the fossil fuel industries for access to continued profits, or to reject the technocratic paradigm of economic governance, which proved incapable of understanding "value" outside of narrow financial terms.

In terms of climate change, almost a quarter of a century passed without any real action. The UNFCCC treaty parties met each year yet seemed incapable of halting the continuous rise in emissions. With the 1997 Kyoto Protocol, richer countries pledged to reduce emissions by 20 percent in 2012 compared with 1990. This pact was a failure, in part because it excluded major developing countries such as China, a key source of new emissions. In Durban, South Africa, in 2011, the parties agreed that they would finally reach an agreement in 2015, in which all countries—not just the rich ones—would make binding commitments to reduce emissions. And in Copenhagen in 2009, the parties to the UNFCCC agreed that richer countries would mobilize $100 billion a year by 2020 to support climate action in developing countries.

This history forms the backdrop to the Paris Agreement on Climate Change, signed by 196 countries in December 2015. As noted in chapter 7, with this agreement, the nations of the world committed finally to taking action to stay beneath the 2-degree Celsius limit. In fact, they stepped up the level of ambition, promising to pursue efforts to contain global warming to 1.5 degrees Celsius. This commitment is backed up by a bottom-up approach; each country is called on to come up with a climate plan. The backbone of the agreement is that countries commit to peaking global emissions as soon as possible, with the goal of reaching net-zero greenhouse gas emissions in the second half of the century.

The Paris Agreement is a dynamic, ever-evolving process. Every five years, countries are required to come back with updated climate plans; the aim is to increase the ambition of national climate plans. And as green technology improves, and as wind energy and solar energy get progressively cheaper relative to fossil fuels, we might expect greater ambition in the years ahead. But this change is also going to require what Pope Francis calls a new and universal solidarity, including a changing mindset.

Speaking of global solidarity, the Paris Agreement also reaffirms the commitment that developed countries will provide $100 billion a year to developing countries to help them cope with climate change by 2020. After 2025, governments will adopt a higher goal, with the $100 billion regarded as a floor. It is deemed important to not only help countries decarbonize but also to help them cope with the effects of climate change that are already built in. This latter idea is known as adaptation. It reflects the fact that climate change is especially harmful to poorer countries. For example, the economic losses from some of the hurricanes that battered small Caribbean island nations in recent years exceeded 200 percent of their GDP. Going forward, countries are going to need to invest in upgrading infrastructure, irrigation systems, early warning systems, and building codes. These countries are going to need financing, and they are going to need social protection systems to deal with climate disruption. The IMF estimates that the costs of adaptation in developing countries are between $56 and $73 billion right now, which is two-to-three times higher than available financing, a cost that will rise to $140–$300 billion by 2030.[26] Clearly, the international financial solidarity built into Paris is vital and urgent.

On the whole, the Paris Agreement is strong. By aligning all countries toward a single goal, it is truly transformative. Yet the hard work lies ahead. One way to boost each country's commitment is to dedicate an international organization to monitoring the implementation of the Paris Agreement at the country level. This arrangement could follow the example of the IMF. How? Each year, the IMF gives each member country an "annual health checkup" to assess macroeconomic performance in the country and ensure that there is global consistency in the sense of supporting global economic stability. The same evaluation could be performed for climate change, with each country assessed each year in terms of Paris commitments and recommendations made in terms of strengthening commitments.

Another important area that belongs to the global commons has come to the fore in the wake of the COVID-19 crisis: public health systems. As Rodrik notes, pandemics, just like climate change, do not respect national borders. Dealing with them requires global cooperation through the World Health Organization. This cooperation would encompass such issues as an advance warning system, a common information base, large and coordinated budgets for medical research and vaccine development, coordinated strategies for fighting emergencies, financing for poor countries, and prohibitions on attempts by one country to benefit over others.[27] To Rodrik's list I would add preventing private-sector pharmaceutical countries benefiting from extended patent protection in a way that puts their profits over the lives of people. This too is a core component of an ethical globalization.

Tax Havens

The second area that Rodrik would consign to the multinational arena concerns beggar-thy-neighbor policies, whereby one country benefits from imposing a cost on another country. In today's global economy, the main example of this policy is tax havens, which Shaxson defines simply as "to escape rules you don't like, you take your money elsewhere, offshore, across borders."[28] Offshore entities offer a variety of advantages to multinational corporations and wealthy individuals—chiefly low taxes but also fewer financial regulations, secrecy, and even a blind eye to criminality.

Estimates suggest that between $20 trillion and $30 trillion are stashed away in tax havens; this is between 16 and 24 percent of the entire global GDP.[29] Not surprisingly, the tax revenue lost is equally astronomical. As noted by Shaxson, tax havens cost governments between $500 billion and $600 billion a year; this figure includes $200 billion for low-income countries, desperate for revenue to implement the Sustainable Development Goals. Note that this cost is greater than the official aid low-income countries receive each year, which amounts to $150 billion.[30]

Tax havens therefore act as "reverse Robin Hoods," taking from the poor to give to the rich. Many of the transactions involved are perfectly legal, but owing to the murkiness and secrecy that characterize many tax havens, a lot of them are not. Tax havens, enemies of the common good, support corporate power and concentration by helping multinationals and large financial institutions over small and medium-sized enterprises.

In chapter 6, I talked about the decline in corporate taxation over the past few decades. Tax havens have a lot to do with this. As more countries compete for business by offering lower tax rates, we see a race to the bottom. Taxpayer loss tends to be multinationals' gain, further boosting their power in this unethical form of globalization. This tax competition has seen corporate tax rates fall by half over the neoliberal era; average corporate tax rates fell from 49 percent in 1985 to 24 percent today.[31] As some economists have noted, if the current trend continues, the global average corporate tax rate will hit zero by midcentury.[32] Thanks to globalization, the future of corporate tax itself is in jeopardy.

A big problem is that multinationals are easily able to book their profits in low-tax jurisdictions. Thanks to the way accounting principles work, subsidiaries of multinationals are treated as separate entities for tax purposes. This murkiness is especially pronounced in the technology sector, where assets tend to be intangible. So, for example, major American companies such as Apple and Google can book profits in low-tax jurisdictions such as Ireland or zero-tax jurisdictions such as Bermuda, while it is clear to every observer that the real economic value is not being produced in these jurisdictions. Today, as reported by Saez and Zucman, 40 percent of all multinational profits are shifted to tax havens; this rises to 60 percent for US multinationals.[33] These are purely paper profits—not factories, offices, or workers. In fact, about 95 percent of all workers employed by American multinationals live and work in countries with fairly high tax rates, not the tax havens. Likewise, the equivalent figure for capital stock—plants, equipment, offices, and so on—is 82 percent.[34]

The financial flows into tax havens certainly benefit the financial sector but not necessarily the economy as a whole. As noted in chapter 6, finance causes a brain drain from productive sectors, leads to unproductive rent-seeking, heightens inequality and corruption, and increases the likelihood of financial crises.[35] So as well as hurting other countries directly, they are also hurting themselves indirectly.

So what can be done? This area surely warrants international action, as taxpayers from most countries are losing out big time. And there has been some action. For example, countries have stepped up efforts to exchange financial information across borders to help tax authorities track tax evasion. Thanks to this coordinated action, the OECD noted that 90 countries had shared information on 47 million accounts worth almost $5 trillion.

To be more ambitious, Saez and Zucman recommend a four-part plan.[36] They call these four pillars exemplarity, coordination, defensive measures, and sanctions against free riders.

"Exemplarity" signifies that countries should police their own multinationals. Thanks to the OECD, multinationals are now required to report their taxes and profits in each country in which they operate. So countries could make sure that multinationals are paying a minimum corporate tax rate, something around 25 percent. But countries would still have an incentive to compete with each other on taxes. This is where the second component comes in—coordination, which would include agreement among major countries on a common minimum corporate tax. The risk, of course, is that multinationals would just move their corporate headquarters to tax havens, escaping the clutches of their home countries. But Saez and Zucman think this threat is exaggerated, as very few large multinationals are headquartered in tax havens. Of the two thousand largest companies in the world, half are headquartered in the United States and the European Union.[37] So even with a small number of countries involved, a lot of tax dodging could be stopped. The third pillar, "defensive measures" against countries that refuse to participate in international coordination, is quite simple: collect the taxes that the scofflaws refuse to collect. Do this by apportioning profits to the countries where sales take place. So each country can look at the percentage of sales of each multinational in its country and assume that the sales proxies profits and tax accordingly. This sales-based formula, which is actually how US states collect corporate tax revenue, is viable as this information on profits, sales, and taxes already exists. The fourth pillar is "sanctions against free riders." For the small number of countries whose main business is to attract foreign capital via low taxes or secrecy, a tax on financial transactions could be imposed.

The key point is that there are few practical impediments to cracking down on these reverse Robin Hoods, save for political will in light of the intense wealth and lobbying power of these financial behemoths. But it ultimately serves both the national and global common good to crack down on tax havens. Atkinson even believed that the creation of a "world tax administration" to coordinate global taxation is not infeasible.[38] This too would serve the global common good.

Financing the Sustainable Development Goals

So far I have focused on the two areas whereby economists would argue for multilateral solutions—issues relating to the global commons such as climate change and beggar-thy-neighbor polices like tax havens. The third area I want to focus on, financing the Sustainable Development Goals in developing countries, is an issue of global solidarity that does not easily find a place in the framework of neoclassical economics. Yet it is central to Catholic social teaching. The argument is based on both solidarity and subsidiarity. Solidarity calls for global responsibility to further the integral development of all members of the human family. The seventeen UN Sustainable Development Goals (SDGs) form the contours of the global common good, the bedrock of human flourishing in the material dimension. It is no accident that Pope Francis addressed the United Nations on that fateful morning in September 2015 when the nations of the world endorsed these goals. But the argument is also based on subsidiarity. Why? Because even though the normal locus for development lies at the domestic level, the cost of implementing the SDGs is simply beyond the capacity of the poorest countries. Therefore the proper locus for financing the Sustainable Development Goals is the global level.

Overall, the cost of financing the Sustainable Development Goals as a whole, probably around $3 to $4 trillion a year—around 3 to 4 percent of global GDP—is not insignificant but is certainly manageable for the world as a whole. And it includes the cost of the energy transition.

But the challenge is of course particularly acute in developing countries. Here, let me appeal to some important work conducted by the IMF.[39] Its researchers looked at the costs of implementing a number of key SDGs—health, education, roads, electricity, and water and sanitation—in both emerging markets and low-income countries. They found that these costs would reach $2 trillion a year by 2030 for emerging markets and half a trillion dollars a year for low-income countries. Even though the figure is much larger for the former group, the costs are more manageable—because these countries are richer. Subsidiarity certainly calls for ownership to take place at the national level. And here, the IMF found that emerging markets could do it. In this group, average additional spending is about 4 percentage points of GDP. Not trivial, but manageable.

But in the poorer group of low-income countries, the average additional spending reaches about fifteen percentage points of their GDP. This cost is simply not politically or economically feasible at a national level, and so both solidarity and subsidiarity call for additional international support.

Again, though, subsidiarity requires domestic efforts to take pride in place. Plans for financing and implementing the Sustainable Development Goals must be domestically owned and tailored to local conditions; they cannot be imposed externally. The first question to ask is how much revenue low-income countries could realistically raise on their own. The IMF argues that they could possibly raise an additional five percentage points of GDP in extra domestic revenue through raising taxes and improving revenue efficiency, but that is ambitious. They could also try to make spending more efficient. But even if countries do all of this, there is still going be a gap—which the IMF estimates at $350 billion a year. Again, this is a large number, but this additional spending amounts to only 0.3 percent of global GDP—a small cost for meeting a major ethical imperative. We should note that the IMF estimates refer to only a subset of the Sustainable Development Goals and that the real costs will be higher.

How can these goals be financed then? This topic was discussed by Ethics in Action in terms of the actions needed to end extreme poverty.[40] The first place to start is Official Development Assistance—donor funds. Developed countries have long committed to deploying 0.7 percent of gross national income toward foreign aid to help the world's poorest countries. Rich countries are a long way from that, however. Today, the average Official Development Assistance is a mere 0.3 percent of GDP, with only a handful of countries reaching 0.7 percent. But if countries lived up to these promises, it would be possible to raise another $230 billion a year, according to the IMF. That revenue would go a long way to filling the gap.

Another option discussed by Ethics in Action is to ask the world's approximately 2,200 billionaires—with a combined net worth of $9.1 trillion—to donate a mere 1 percent of their net worth every year toward meeting the Sustainable Development Goals. A global "billionaire tax" along these lines would raise about $90 billion a year. Again, this additional funding would help fulfill the basic needs of some of the poorest people in the world. According to the Sustainable Development Solutions Network, this "tax" could be complemented by a voluntary "giving pledge" by billionaires. Right now, fewer than 10 percent of the world's billionaires have signed this pledge to give away at least half of their wealth through philanthropy over their lifetimes. The Sustainable Development Solutions Network proposes a campaign for the giving pledge signatories to direct at least half of their giving toward the Sustainable Development Goals. The network estimates that this could raise a further $30 billion on top of the wealth tax.[41]

A related option is to use some of the proceeds from cracking down on tax havens, through international tax reforms, for financing the Sustainable Development Goals. The Sustainable Development Solutions Network estimates that a global effort to crack down on the abuse of tax havens could raise $36 billion a year, while a policy of raising corporate tax rates and phasing out tax havens would raise $50 billion.[42] They also estimate that a global financial transactions tax, as recommended in chapter 6, could raise a further $50 billion.

Another option suggested by Ethics in Action is to divert 10 percent of current global military spending to finance the SDGs. This idea follows directly from the call of Pope Paul VI in *Populorum Progressio* to establish a world fund that would set aside a portion of military expenditures to fight poverty. Such a fund could be dubbed the "Pope Paul VI Fund" and could raise between $150 billion and $200 billion a year.

The private sector also has a role to play. It has a coresponsibility for the common good with the government and should not abandon its responsibilities. This is also the argument made by Pope Francis in *Laudato Si'*—business is a "noble vocation" only to the extent that it supports the common good. And there is no better way to do this than to support the SDGs. Private business and finance have a particularly important role to play in building infrastructure and financing the development of renewable energy. Such action would require a strong partnership between governments and the private sector. We need investors and corporations to take a risk on sustainable development, to focus more on building long-term value and less on short-term profits.

Within the private sector, the financial industry is of particular importance for sustainable development. The industry must channel trillions of additional dollars of public and private investment into low-carbon energy, infrastructure, agriculture, and other critical sectors. At the same time, the industry must essentially stop providing finance to entire sectors, including the fossil fuel industry, which remains stubbornly large despite the Paris Climate Agreement; since 2016, thirty-five private banks have funded fossil fuels to the tune of $2.7 trillion.[43] As noted by Aniket Shah, development banks can play a particularly important role in the channeling of public and private capital for sustainable finance.[44] There are currently over 450 development banks globally with total assets of over $11 trillion. These development banks, as state-owned entities that intermediate private capital, embody the needed partnership between public and private sectors for the achievement of the SDGs.

Once funds are raised for the SDGs, they could be managed through global funds. Global funds are a tried-and-tested strategy and have shown amazing success in the area of public health. Thanks to the initiative of people such as Sachs, funds such as the Global Fund to Fight AIDS, Tuberculosis and Malaria were instrumental in improving health outcomes in the world's poorest countries. These global funds have clear advantages. They pool resources in a way that avoids overlap and duplication. They are based on clear metrics, clear evaluation, independent reviews, and good governance structures. And they respect subsidiarity by basing funding on homegrown plans, local knowledge, and local circumstances. In this context, Ethics in Action also proposed a "global fund for education" to mobilize $40 billion a year to provide universal education to secondary level to all children in low-income countries. In the scheme of things, this is a tiny investment. And yet it would deliver incalculable returns.

Debt Relief

The theme of relieving the poor from the crushing burden of debt runs through Catholic social teaching. Both commutative justice and distributive justice call for an equitable sharing of the burden in times of economic strife. This idea of justice applies not only at the level of the individual but at the country level too. When a country falls into an economic crisis, the burden of debt repayments often grows, with governments needing to choose between paying back creditors and meeting obligations to their own citizens in areas such as health, education, and social protection. If debt contracts are seen as inviolable, why are common good "contracts" seen as negotiable? Why should the poor take a hit to bail out creditors? Sharing the burden between debtors and creditors is surely connected to the universal destination of goods and the preferential option for the poor.

Yet we live in a world where creditor rights take precedence, a far cry from biblical norms of justice. A country that fails to repay its debts is regarded as a moral failure, an international scofflaw that has violated a basic promise. But it wasn't always that way. In an insightful book, Jerome Roos argues that before the neoliberal era, default on government debt was a standard response to financial crises. This is no longer true. Instead, since 1982, developing countries have transferred $4.2 trillion in interest payments to creditors in Europe and North America, an amount that far exceeds official aid over this period.[45] In the neoliberal era, characterized by free flows of capital, not only are financial crises more common but debt defaults are far less common. What this status denotes in practice is that countries are forced into crippling austerity, whereby the poor pay the price of paying back creditors—exactly what the injunctions of the Hebrew Scriptures were designed to protect against.

The idea that debt must always be repaid actually makes little economic sense, but this notion is seldom questioned. To understand why, we need to understand the basic link between risk and return. If you buy a US government bond, the interest rate paid to you is pretty low because you're not taking much risk. The American government is unlikely to default. But investors like higher returns. So they are enticed by governments and other borrowers that offer higher returns on their bonds. These entities need to offer a higher rate because their debt is riskier, in the sense that it has a higher risk of default. Investors know this. But in the neoliberal era, investors want to have their cake and eat it. They lap up the higher yields, but they also insist that debt contracts are inviolable; they must get paid in full no matter what. This is a simple insight, and yet it is lost on supposedly sophisticated investors, bringing to mind the classic quote of Upton Sinclair—"It is difficult to get a man to understand something, when his salary depends on his not understanding it"[46]—his salary or in this case his interest rate.

Why did debt norms change in the neoliberal era? Roos argues that the shift is due to the increasing power of globalized finance over the past four decades, the ability to deny countries short-term credit unless they play by the rules of investors.[47] He notes that something similar happened in the age of imperialism when creditor states began to intervene to defend bondholder interests and credit contracts. Strikingly, he estimates that noncompliant borrowers faced a 30 percent chance of being at the mercy of force in the form of invasion or gunboat diplomacy at that time. The neoliberal era, of course, does not rely on outright force, but it still manages to enforce the will of creditors. The social democratic era, with its capital controls and the tight lid on finance, managed to avoid a major financial crisis. But the neoliberal era is plagued by them; financial crises have become twice as frequent since the 1970s as during the first age of globalization before the First World War. Yet sovereign defaults have become extremely rare because, Roos claims, of the power of finance—the ability to withhold short-term credit lines from governments, businesses, and households. This stranglehold shifts the international balance of power toward creditors and financial institutions, and the domestic balance of power toward financial elites.[48]

Where does this power come from? Roos points to a number of factors. First is the growing concentration and centralization of credit markets, meaning that borrowers are dealing with a smaller circle of large and powerful banks and financial institutions. Second, because these banks and financial firms are so large and powerful, they are "too big to fail"; failure would lead to financial crisis in creditor countries. Hence the international community, led by the IMF, has taken the lead in providing "lender of last resort" financial assistance but often by insisting on a clean bill of fiscal health, which in turn makes it more likely that creditors can get paid. Third, financial globalization and deregulation make states more dependent than ever on private credit, which shifts the balance of power toward the creditors and financial elites. Taken together, all of these factors lead to a situation whereby creditor rights are given pride of place, and debtor countries are forced to prioritize interest payments in times of crisis.

The need for reform today is urgent, especially in the midst of the COVID-19 crisis. Even before the crisis, the IMF estimated that half of all low-income countries were at high risk of, or already in, debt distress, facing higher interest payments. The UN agency United Nations Conference on Trade and Development (UNCTAD) notes that the developing countries will face a wall of debt service payments over the next decade. In 2020 and 2021 alone, it estimates that repayments on developing countries' public external debt will be between US$2.6 trillion and US$3.4 trillion.[49] To deal with the pandemic, the IMF and UNCTAD have estimated that these developing countries will need about $2.5 trillion in financing. Accordingly, UNCTAD has called for burden sharing between debtors and creditors, suggesting a $1 trillion debt write-off—a modern day "clean slate" to deal with one of the biggest economic crises ever faced by the global community. This write-off would be considered as part of financing the SDGs, the implementation of which is becoming increasingly challenging in the era of COVID-19.

Among the many precedents for this, perhaps the most famous example is the London Debt Agreement of 1953, which wrote off half of West Germany's external debt and refinanced the rest on highly favorable terms. This relief paved the way for a remarkable recovery. More recently, the Jubilee 2000 campaign— an umbrella group of religious campaigners supported by Pope John Paul II— helped shift the needle on debt relief for poor countries, ultimately leading to $76 billion in debt reduction for heavily indebted poor countries (amounting to two-thirds of their debts), spearheaded by the IMF and World Bank.[50] This relief paved the way for poverty reduction and a dramatic improvement in health outcomes in the world's poorest countries, under the auspices of the Millennium Development Goals.

Yet we need more than stopgap measures; we need something for ordinary as well as extraordinary times. To fully restore the logic of Jubilee, and to shift the balance of power between creditors and debtors, we need a bankruptcy regime policed at the multilateral level.[51] Lack of such a regime remains one of the most significant gaps in the international architecture. In the early 2000s, the IMF proposed a sovereign debt-restructuring mechanism at the global level, but this idea did not survive the ferocious lobbying of Wall Street and creditor interests. Without such a regime, debt restructurings are ad hoc and voluntary, with clear incentives to hold out in the hope of getting more money. As noted in chapter 5, the worst villains in this game are the vulture funds. Their business model is to buy cheap debt, cheap because it is at high risk of default, and use the courts to try to get paid in full. This is the notion of creditors, rights taken to the maximum, as courts often grant their right to be fully repaid, even though the debt is trading on the free market at a discount. These "vultures" prey on some of the world's poorest and most vulnerable countries.

What would a global sovereign bankruptcy regime look like? UNCTAD has put together some proposals in this regard.[52] They begin by stressing the weaknesses of the current system: (1) fragmentation and a lack of coordination, creating uncertain and legal incoherence; (2) a lack of fairness, most notably when some creditors (such as vulture funds) seek their own maximum advantage both over other creditors and debtor states; (3) the fact that debt restructurings come "too little too late," as creditors refuse to take early losses, even though this hurts not only the country but also creditors themselves in the long run.

To fix this, UNCTAD proposes a new organization—a sovereign debt workout institution—that would facilitate an inclusive dialogue between creditors and debtors, aiming at a consensual debt workout. It is important that any restructuring achieves the support of a supermajority of creditors, both to ensure fairness toward earnest creditors and as a way to stop holdouts such as vulture funds. This outcome could be achieved either by direct negotiation or through a mediator, which would be binding on all parties.

Such a new organization would be justified in terms of both solidarity and subsidiarity. Solidarity would prioritize the interests of debtors and poorer countries over those of creditors, richer countries, and powerful financial institutions. Subsidiarity would provide a multilateral locus of deliberation for coordination between creditors and debtors, another example of the global common good in action.

Globalization and Finance

In the final three subsections of this chapter, I will talk about three core dimensions of globalization: the free movement of finance, goods, and people. Let me start with finance, as financial globalization is emblematic of our current model in terms of the free movement of both physical and financial capital across borders. There are prudential differences, of course. Most would argue, justifiably, that foreign direct investment—investment in the productivity capacity of the economy—is better than investment in financial instruments, which tend to be about garnering quick and easy returns. Yet in the neoliberal era, it has become an article of faith that financial capital should be free to move across borders, on the grounds of economic efficiency; that is, foreign capital always benefits the recipient country. I want to argue that this form of globalization has gone too far, with two key arguments: one based on corporate power and one based on instability.

The first argument is that financial globalization confers an inordinate amount of power on large corporations and financial institutions, violating subsidiarity and undermining the common good. We have already seen aspects of this in the previous sections. Financial globalization is largely responsible for the proliferation of tax havens and secrecy jurisdictions across the world, in effect stealing resources from governments. It is also responsible for an unhealthy race-to-the-bottom in terms of corporate tax rates, as large corporations are able to hop across borders to lower tax jurisdictions. This argument goes beyond taxes. Countries that seek to strongly regulate their financial systems to avoid crises—for example, through strong capital and liquidity requirements, regulation of derivatives, financial transactions taxes, and efforts to clamp down on too-big-to-fail financial firms—could see their efforts undermined by jurisdiction hopping. Once again, this activity could lead to a race to the bottom. In the run-up to the global financial crisis, for example, the United Kingdom deliberately implemented a light-touch regulatory regime to encourage global banks and financial institutions to move to London—with disastrous consequences. Relatedly, as noted above, the power and concentration of global finance turned out to be decisive in shifting the bargaining power from debtor toward creditor states in the neoliberal era.

This outsize corporate power also has implications for the welfare state. If taxes are too high, the argument goes, then capital and rich individuals will just hop across borders to a jurisdiction with lower taxes, undermining the tax base and the efficacy of the welfare system. Pope Benedict XVI made this argument in *Caritas in Veritate*. Yet even so, globalization does not necessarily sound the death knell of the welfare state. Atkinson notes that the welfare state was actually born during the first wave of globalization in the late nineteenth century, to protect people from the vagaries of global markets. In his view, the argument that globalization hurts welfare states is overblown because companies take many factors into consideration, not just taxes, and because it is possible to reach international agreements to prevent the worst aspects of tax avoidance and tax competition.[53] I think he is right. Reports of the death of the welfare state in an era of globalization have been greatly exaggerated, though this is still an argument for reining in the excesses of financial globalization.

The second argument against excessive financial globalization is that it too often leads to financial crises. It is worth looking at some history here. In the first wave of globalization before the First World War, the tight regime of the gold standard resulted in a global financial system plagued by instability and crises. This lack of stability was simply seen as a cost of globalization, but things were very different in the social democratic era. After the Second World War, the Bretton Woods system set up a global financial regime that encouraged trade but discouraged the free movement of capital. It allowed for capital controls to block speculative capital, which had the effect of allowing countries to use domestic policies to stabilize their economies and build their welfare states. Countries were no longer at the whim of global finance.[54] As noted many times, the social democratic era was one of rising economic growth, shared prosperity, and financial stability. And the neoliberal era marked in many respects a return to the past of the first age of globalization. From the 1980s on, free capital mobility was once again the name of the game. The result was crisis after crisis—Latin America in the 1980s and Mexico, Asia, Russia, and Argentina in the late 1990s and early 2000s, culminating in the global financial crisis of 2008. As noted already, financial crises, eagerly absent in the social democratic era, were twice as frequent in the neoliberal era as during the first age of globalization before the First World War. Plus, the most successful developing countries over the past four decades were countries such as China that showed a great wariness about financial liberalization.[55]

One reason for this enhanced instability is that the money flooding into developing countries tends to boost consumption rather than investment. As noted already, capital is motivated primarily by high and fast returns; there is no patience for the kinds of long-term investment in infrastructure, decarbonization, and other things that would benefit the recipient country. Instead, the inflows are short term—get in fast, make money, get out fast. This mentality fuels euphoric bubbles that leave countries overindebted, leading to mass capital outflows and economic collapse. External finance does little to help growth in developing countries, because growth tends to be constrained less by a shortage of savings and more by a reluctance to invest.[56] So capital inflows go toward a consumption binge. The resulting appreciation of the currency hurts tradable industries and lowers investment even more.

All in all, there is a good case to be made for a return to a Bretton Woods system of capital controls, at least for short-term financial flows. In developing countries, the focus should be on real investment in needed sectors, most notably connected to the SDGs. To these ends, the evidence suggests that the public sector has a leading role to play, including through the use of development banks to leverage private capital. This is the best way for global finance to marshal its resources to aid developing countries instead of the perennial quest for the quick and easy return.

Globalization and Trade

The other major aspect of globalization is the belief in free trade, the idea that free movement of goods (and sometimes services) across borders benefits the liberalizing country. This belief stems from one of the most basic and enduring insights of neoclassical economics, that of comparative advantage. In a nutshell, comparative advantage says that countries should specialize in what they produce relatively well, which leads to gains in both countries. In the parlance of neoclassical economics, opening up to trade by reducing impediments such as tariffs and quotas is a Pareto improvement, though this is an extremely simplified version of the case for free trade, and—to be fair to neoclassical economists—they recognize much more nuance and complexity. But there is nonetheless a default assumption that trade is good, even if it is well known that some can lose from trade—because the increase in the overall pie is regarded as big enough for those who benefit to compensate those who do not.

In the real world, of course, that kind of compensation tends to be more theoretical than practical. It is no accident, though, that the countries most open to trade are those countries with the most extensive welfare states.[57] To really benefit from free trade, countries need strong systems of social and labor protection. Such conditions do not exist in the United States, for example, which might explain why the backlash against trade is most pronounced there. Another issue is that the general benefits of free trade are often small, while specific costs can be large. For example, Dani Rodrik points to research showing that the benefits of the North American Free Trade Agreement (NAFTA) to the United States were minimal, with an aggregate boost to the US economy of as little as 0.1 percent of GDP. But at the same time, NAFTA led to slower wage growth, by 8 percent, for those without high school degrees in regions affected by this trade agreement over 1990–2000.[58] Combined with the lack of a robust safety net, these free trade deals—alongside technological progress—are clearly contributing to the populist backlash in the United States.

So is there a case for free trade, or is protectionism to be preferred? There is no black-and-white answer to this question. Answering it will require old-fashioned democratic deliberation on the common good, asking questions such as, Does trade contribute to peaceful cooperation between nations? How much economic and social disruption will trade bring about? How will the poor and vulnerable fare? What are the net effects on jobs? Are welfare states strong enough to protect people? Should trade be treated differently than technology in terms of its distributional implications? Are trading partners adequately respecting environmental standards? What about key labor rights such as fair wages, collective bargaining, and bans on child labor? Is the trade fair, or are corporations in either country gaining an advantage based on their power? Is there a case for sheltering industries from foreign competition at an early stage of development? These are all important questions, the answers to which will depend on specific contexts and circumstances. But there is no general presumption that free trade must always be enforced through international agreements and multilateral mechanisms.

On this point, a key issue is that modern trade deals tend to be more about extending corporate power than seeking the mutual benefits of trade. Pope Paul VI was prescient back in 1967 when he wrote that "trade relations can no longer be based solely on the principle of free, unchecked competition, for it very often creates an economic dictatorship."[59] What are often referred to as "free trade" agreements are in effect not about free trade at all but about exploiting unequal power relations. When this happens, it is a violation of justice and subsidiarity.

Once again, it is Rodrik who reveals those aspects of modern trade agreements that are more about entrenching corporate power rather than reducing the price of imports.[60] One example is intellectual property protection, which benefits large multinational industries, especially in the pharmaceutical industry. With this advantage on the corporations' side, people in developing countries pay more for medicines and other goods, while the multinationals soak up monopoly rents. A second area is the liberalization of capital flows, which have nothing to do with trade and yet are now standard in trade agreements. This one benefits the rents of the financial sector. The third problematic area is the so-called harmonization of regulatory standards. The idea is to lay down a level playing field, but it leans in a neoliberal direction when it comes to regulation. The fourth problem relates to what are called "investor-state dispute settlement" procedures, which allow multinationals and foreign investors to sue governments in special arbitration tribunals when host country governments enact policies that reduce the investors' actual or expected profits. These mechanisms are especially pernicious. As documented by researchers at Columbia University, they have been used to undermine environmental action by nations. For example, corporations have taken cases against governments that seek to combat climate change by rejecting new pipelines and fossil fuel infrastructure or by shutting down coal-fired power plants by a certain date—because future profits are on the line. Similarly, investors have challenged the ability to protect water from contamination and pollution and ensure that water is accessible and affordable to all.[61] These agreements give investors and multinationals far greater rights than other stakeholders, especially the poor and the Indigenous. They represent a major violation of environmental justice and show disdain for the notion of an "ecological debt" as described by *Laudato Si'*.

The bottom line when discussing modern trade agreements is that we need to rebalance power relationships. In trade and indeed in globalization more generally, there should be a shift from the interests of capital to the interests of labor, and from the interests of large corporations to the interests of the global common good, including the environment. And as with finance, this is one area where globalization has probably gone too far, especially through the instruments that boost the power of capital. An application of the principle of subsidiarity might appreciate that trade can benefit countries while also respecting the ability of the nation-state to impose limits when necessary for the common good, both domestic and global.

Globalization and People

So far, I've looked at globalization in terms of the free movement of capital and the free movement of goods and services. What about the third dimension, the free movement of people? Immigration has become an extremely fraught issue, especially in the United States and Europe, for both economic and cultural reasons. At the economic level, people fear that immigrants will take scarce jobs and bid down wages even further at a time of increasing economic precariousness. And at the cultural level, they feel that immigrants don't really "fit" into their countries, thus undermining social cohesion.

There are no easy answers to this conundrum. Prudentially, it would be really difficult to make the case for fully open borders. Yet we need to recognize that a lot of the blame directed at immigration—for loss of jobs, low wages, undermining basic social bargains—should be directed at corporations and the free movement of capital. At the same time, Catholic social teaching is highly sensitive to the rights of immigrants, because immigrants—unlike corporations and capital—are people, endowed with rights and possessing human dignity. Pope John XXIII, in *Pacem in Terris*, recognized this. "When there are just reasons in favor of it," he argued, "[every human being] must be permitted to emigrate to other countries and take up residence there."[62] The question, of course, is what constitutes "just reasons." On the issue of refugees, he uses even stronger language:

> Refugees are persons and all their rights as persons must be recognized. Refugees cannot lose these rights simply because they are deprived of citizenship of their own States. And among man's personal rights we must include his right to enter a country in which he hopes to be able to provide more fittingly for himself and his dependents. It is therefore the duty of State officials to accept such immigrants and—so far as the good of their own community, rightly understood, permits—to further the aims of those who may wish to become members of a new society.[63]

The question boils down to what "so far as the good of their own community, rightly understood" means in practice. But there is a general presumption that doors must be opened to refugees, who are fleeing their homelands because of war or other calamities.

In this context, I think it is useful to discern what Pope Francis has written on the plight of migrants and refugees.[64] Noting that there are 250 million migrants worldwide, of which 22.5 million are refugees, he notes that "we are obliged to respect the right of all individuals to find a place that meets their basic needs and those of their families, and where they can find personal fulfillment."[65] Concretely, he calls on government leaders to deploy the virtue of prudence to welcome, promote, protect, and integrate migrants and refugees in line with the common good. What do these measures entail? By "welcome," he calls for expanded legal pathways for entry and avoiding any arbitrary expulsion of migrants and refugees, an appeal based on the virtue of solidarity and on the principle of the universal destination of goods. By "protect," he is talking about the duty rooted in justice to defend the dignity of those who flee real danger in search of security and peace and making sure they do not fall prey to exploitation, forced labor, and human trafficking. This is the principle of respect for human rights, which in turn flows from the inherent dignity of every human being. By "promote," he means supporting the integral human development of migrants and refugees in their countries of origin, transit, and destination, including by ensuring access to education and healthcare. The goal is to allow migrants to develop their capacities in a way that contributes to their host countries. And by "integrate," he means allowing migrants and refugees to fully participate in society, "as part of a process of mutual enrichment and fruitful cooperation in the service of integral human development." He notes that openness to other cultures can bring about reciprocal gifts as both sides benefit from the exchange and encounter.[66] He also deploys the principle of gratuitousness, noting that this "makes it possible for us to welcome the stranger, even though this brings us no immediate tangible benefit."[67] As we can see, he is deploying the broad swath of the principles of Catholic social teaching to defend migrants and refugees.

In assessing the requirements of the common good, there is, of course, a distinction to be made between refugees and migrants. Refugees are not merely seeking a better life; they are seeking to protect their lives. Such forced displacement has its roots in war, violence, persecution, and human rights violations. A key problem is that these conflicts are becoming increasingly complicated and protracted, with no clear end in sight. And as noted in the last chapter, the looming environmental crisis is creating millions of climate refugees. To repeat an important point: the International Organization for Migration is predicting a staggering 200 million climate refugees by 2050 alone, with a high estimate of a billion.[68] These people will be fleeing from both increasingly uninhabitable regions and from the wars and societal collapse that will inevitably result from environmental stress. The mass influx of migrants into Europe and the United States over the past decade should be seen as merely the opening gambit.

Accepting refugees, then, can be regarded as a strict duty rooted in justice. In this, countries implicated in the harm that spurs population displacement have a specific moral obligation to accept refugees, including former colonial powers, countries that intervene in unjust wars that destabilize other countries and regions, and countries responsible for the greatest carbon emissions and environmental carnage. Indeed, the universal destination of goods is especially relevant. Aquinas's dictum that "in case of need all things are common property" can be applied to the situation of refugees.[69]

The situation of economic migrants is somewhat different. Unlike with refugees, countries accept economic migrants based on mutual need, which puts economic migration into a separate moral category.[70] Still, with the climate crisis in particular, the boundaries are increasingly blurred. The primary obligation is to support sustainable development in home countries—by financing the SDGs. As noted by the Ethics in Action initiative, people are attached to their "homes" as loci of culture and civic identity. They migrate mainly because they lack opportunities at home. They have a right to remain in their home countries.

An oft-noted problem with an influx of migrants is the pressure it puts on welfare states. Milanovic, for example, argues that if people can move freely, they will flock to countries with the most generous welfare states, which in turn creates a political base for curbing the generosity of these welfare states.[71] There is certainly a point here, but—as noted already—the welfare state is already being undermined by the free movement of capital.

To thread the needle on this thorny topic, avoiding political backlashes while allowing both migrants and home countries to mutually benefit from migration, Milanovic and others proposed a kind of tiered citizenship whereby migrants do not enjoy all the benefits of full citizenship. These arrangements are common across the world; think of guest worker and permanent residency programs. Yet if countries go this route, they must not deny the fourfold requirement to welcome, protect, promote, and integrate. There is a stronger moral case for protecting the rights of people who cross borders over capital and corporations. The duty to "welcome the stranger" cannot simply be ignored. There is also a strong moral case for an international agreement on migrants and refugees; as Pope Francis notes, nation-states are not able to implement adequate solutions on their own.[72] The strongest moral case of all, though, is for financing the SDGs in developing countries.

In conclusion, I have argued in this chapter that Catholic social teaching can help map out the contours of an ethical globalization, deploying principles such as solidarity and subsidiarity to identify the proper locus of moral decision-making in an increasingly interconnected world. I have identified seven key topics of particular relevance to the global economy today: supporting the global commons, curbing tax havens, relieving sovereign debt, and financing sustainable development, as well as reflecting on the movement across borders of goods and services, capital, and people from an ethical perspective. If badly managed, globalization can prompt various kinds of populist backlashes. We know this not just from recent political developments but from the history of the twentieth century too. As this book draws to a close, the time has come to deploy some of these lessons of history to help us reach the shores of a more stable future. I will take this up in the conclusion.

Notes

1. See Hollenbach, *Common Good and Christian Social Ethics*.
2. Annett, "Human Flourishing, the Common Good, and Catholic Social Teaching."
3. *PT*, 144.
4. *PT*, 142–45.
5. *PP*, 76.
6. *PP*, 77.
7. *PP*, 78.
8. *PP*, 51.
9. *FT*, 262.
10. *CA*, 58.
11. *CIV*, 67.
12. *CIV*, 67.
13. *CIV*, 67.
14. *LS*, 164.
15. *LS*, 164.
16. *LS*, 173.
17. *LS*, 166.
18. *LS*, 169.
19. *LS*, 175.
20. *LS*, 172.
21. *FT*, 12.
22. *FT*, 172.

23. Dani Rodrik, "Globalisation after Covid-19: My Plan for a Rewired Planet," *Prospect*, May 4, 2020.

24. Quoted in Sachs, *Age of Sustainable Development*, 441.

25. Sachs.

26. Zhang, "Opening Remarks by Deputy Managing Director Tao Zhang at the 2019 Seminar on Climate Resilience for Small Islands States."

27. Rodrik, "Globalisation after Covid-19."

28. Shaxson, "Tackling Tax Havens."

29. Reuters, "Super Rich Hold $32 Trillion in Offshore Havens," *Reuters*, July 22, 2012, https://www.reuters.com/article/us-offshore-wealth/super-rich-hold-32-trillion-in -offshore-havens-idUSBRE86L03U20120722.

30. Shaxson, "Tackling Tax Havens."

31. Shaxson.

32. Saez and Zucman, *Triumph of Injustice*, 87.

33. Saez and Zucman, 76.

34. Saez and Zucman, 79–80.

35. Shaxson, *Finance Curse*; Shaxson, "Tackling Tax Havens."

36. See Saez and Zucman, *Triumph of Injustice*, ch. 6.

37. Saez and Zucman, 120.

38. Atkinson, *Inequality*.

39. Gaspar et al., "Fiscal Policy and Development."

40. See Annett, "Ethical Actions to End Poverty."

41. Sustainable Development Solutions Network, *SDG Costing and Financing for Low-Income Developing Countries*.

42. Sustainable Development Solutions Network.

43. Rainforest Action Network, *Banking on Climate Change*.

44. Shah, "Foundations of Development Banking."

45. Roos, *Why Not Default?*, 2.

46. Sinclair, *I, Candidate for Governor: And How I Got Licked*, 109.

47. Roos, *Why Not Default?*, 2.

48. Roos, 11.

49. United Nations Conference on Trade and Development, "From the Great Lockdown to the Great Meltdown."

50. See Roos, *Why Not Default?*, 304.

51. Eric LeCompte, "The World's Poor Are Drowning in Debt: Here's How to Help Them," *Barrons*, May 8, 2020, https://www.barrons.com/articles/the-worlds-poor-are -drowning-in-debt-heres-how-to-help-them-51588896716.

52. United Nations Conference on Trade and Development, "Roadmap toward Sustainable Sovereign Debt Workouts."

53. Atkinson, *Inequality*, ch. 10.

54. See Rodrik, "Globalisation after Covid-19."

55. Rodrik, *Straight Talk on Trade*, 30.

56. See Rodrik, ch. 9.

57. Rodrik, 204.

58. Dani Rodrik, "The Trouble with Globalization," *Milken Institute Review*, Milken Institute, October 20, 2017, https://www.milkenreview.org/articles/the-trouble-with -globalization?IssueID=26; Rodrik, "Globalisation after Covid-19."

59. *PP*, 59.

60. See Rodrik, "What Do Trade Agreements Really Do?"

61. Sachs, Johnson, and Merrill, "Environmental Injustice."

62. *PT*, 25.

63. *PT*, 105–6.

64. Pope Francis, "Message of His Holiness Pope Francis for the Celebration of the 51st World Day of Peace."

65. *FT*, 129.

66. *FT*, 133.

67. *FT*, 139.

68. McKibben, *Falter*, 42.

69. I owe this insight to Bishop Marcelo Sánchez Sorondo.

70. I owe this insight to Vittorio Hösle of the Ethics in Action initiative.

71. Milanovic, *Capitalism Alone*, 50–55.

72. *FT*, 132.

Conclusion

As I write this conclusion, the world is in the midst of the COVID-19 pandemic. I've talked a lot in this book about the economic, social, and environmental fractures brought about by decades of neoliberalism. These fractures are being widened and deepened by COVID-19, especially when the response is marked once more by a lack of solidarity.

Differences exist across countries, of course. In some places, governments and citizens are responding by caring for the well-being of all—through such actions as making sure people who lose jobs still get paid, enforcing universal mask wearing, and a policy of massive testing, contact tracing, and quarantining the sick without burdening people with healthcare costs. In these countries, especially in Asia, COVID-19 has been contained and people protected. But these measures are not being applied everywhere. It also is especially clear to me that libertarianism is proving the mortal enemy of a solidarity-tinged response to the crisis. With few job protections, the US unemployment rate briefly spiked to levels last seen during the Great Depression. As middle-class people get to work from the comfort of their own homes, working-class people are forced to work on the front lines, exposing themselves to the virus every day. This lack of solidarity even reaches ludicrous levels, as a distinct minority even disdains the use of masks because it is seen as an impingement on their freedom. These actions are precisely how libertarianism inhibits virtue.

The record on state-led economic responses to the COVID-19 pandemic is more mixed. Here, we can see chips in the neoliberal armor, with politicians supporting measures that would have seemed unthinkable even a decade ago—most notably direct income support to workers and the unemployed, which in the United States took the form of direct checks. Likewise, the rapid development and deployment of vaccines in the United States demonstrates the power of both public-private partnerships and vigorous state capacity, concepts important to Catholic social teaching but left by the wayside during the neoliberal era. This necessary about-face is clear evidence that neoliberalism was simply not equipped to handle something like the pandemic.

This gives rise to a broader point: now more than ever, I would argue that we are at an inflection point in history. Four decades of neoliberalism, influenced by the discipline of neoclassical economics, have brought us to the brink of disaster. The global economy has proven capable of generating vast amounts of wealth but little in the way of virtue. Billions of people are excluded from the basics of human flourishing. And as the elites retreat into ever-smaller circles of solidarity, the economic forces of technological change and financialization, plus a pattern of globalization that favors corporations and financial institutions, lead to widening inequality and flattening opportunity. Some nations' lack of ability to respond effectively to the recent COVID-19 pandemic offers a sobering lesson on the loss of solidarity. And hovering over these health and financial disasters is the environmental crisis, which threatens to bring everything crashing down in a catastrophic fashion. Pope Francis is blunt: "Inequality and the lack of integral human development make peace impossible."[1]

History teaches us clear lessons in this regard. We know that economic frustration and anxiety can fuel demagogues and insular nationalists offering up scapegoats and easy answers. We are already seeing this in many countries. Political polarization in the United States is at levels not experienced in generations. I would even argue that we are at grave risk of a "1930s moment," in which faltering economic prospects and a shriveling common good lead to dire political dysfunctions. This backlash can manifest in different ways—sometimes directed inward against plutocrats and domestic elites, sometimes directed outward against immigrants and global financiers. Either way, this kind of backlash poses a major risk to domestic institutions and even to democracy; such anxiety and insecurity provides fertile ground for authoritarian leaders and demagogues. And the backlash has the potential to undermine not only the domestic common good but also the global common good, as nations turn inward and the institutions of postwar global governance weaken.

In this context, twentieth-century history presents clear warnings. The early decades of the previous century witnessed a collapse of the domestic and global common good, marked by a sharp turn toward authoritarianism—either the muscular nationalism of fascism or the radical leveling of communism. The tensions submerged by the first wave of globalization—underpinned by the international gold standard and its brutal demands on the domestic economy—eventually reached breaking point, and (to paraphrase William Butler Yeats) the center could not hold.[2] Then as now, rapid technological advance, a greed-fueled financial sector, and skyrocketing inequality in the context of libertarian ideology led to a major financial crisis and frayed social cohesion. It eventually led to war.

Of course, different countries reacted in different ways. The United States managed to avoid extremism and social collapse, thanks in large part to President Roosevelt's New Deal. Roosevelt understood that protecting human dignity and economic security was essential for preserving a market economy and even democracy. Hence he introduced government-provided work plus social insurance for old age, disability, and unemployment. The contrast between the United Kingdom and Germany is also instructive. As we all know, during the tumultuous period after the Great Depression, Germany produced Hitler while the United Kingdom retained a healthy democracy. There are many reasons for these sharply diverging paths, including stronger institutions in the United Kingdom and the ruinous reparations foisted on Germany by the World War I victors. But as noted by economic historian Barry Eichengreen, differing welfare provisions were also a contributing factor.[3] Britain had put in place a comprehensive unemployment insurance scheme that covered nearly all adult males by the 1920s. Not so Germany, where there was strong resistance to providing this kind of insurance on the grounds that it would promote laziness. Germany's pioneering welfare state from the late nineteenth century was really restricted to the old, the infirm, and the destitute. Germany finally managed to put in place a system only in 1927, just before the Great Depression. As a result, the system never really had a chance to get fully up and running before it was severely tested, and benefits were actually reduced in the process.

The lesson is that protecting people from the excesses of the free market through the power of government institutions is essential for economic and social stability—and even for democracy and peace. This lesson was much on the minds of the architects of the powerful "social democratic moment" that took root on both sides of the Atlantic after the Second World War. It was a moment motivated by a desire to establish peace and social cohesion through solidarity. And yet this lesson was lost over the past four decades as memories of war and Depression faded in the collective memory.

Given the warning signs on the horizon, a horizon that seems closer than ever, we surely need another "social democratic moment." Yet this moment must entail not a simple repetition of the past but rather a response tuned to current circumstances and contexts. In an insightful analysis, Thomas Piketty identifies three fault lines in the original social democratic model, fault lines that caused it to unravel: the failure to develop a more just approach to property ownership, especially as embodied by German-style worker sharing in business decision-making, the difficulty in extending progressive taxes on income and wealth to the era of enhanced globalization, and the inability to confront the challenge of inequality of education in an era of neoliberal "meritocracy."[4] I would argue that Catholic social teaching—with its ideas of joint vocation, the dignity of work, and an ethical globalization—is perfectly poised to deal with these fault lines.

"Political capitalism" as encapsulated by China is not a valid alternative. Like the communism of old, it promotes a stultifying form of solidarity that rejects subsidiarity and the dignity and agency of the human being. Just as the old social democratic moment rejected the old "twin rocks of shipwreck"—libertarianism and collectivization—so must the new response reject modern versions of these extremes.

Instead, this response should be based on the principles of Catholic social teaching, this time tinged by the prophetic witness of Pope Francis. I would argue that the only way out of the current conundrum is a new "virtue economics" that grounds the global economy in a new moral narrative, in a new social democratic consensus for the twenty-first century underpinned by what Pope Francis calls a new and universal solidarity. Certainly more urgent in light of the COVID-19 pandemic, this reform is also needed because of new and powerful mechanisms for manipulating information, which magnifies polarization and makes agreeing on a common good extremely difficult. Indeed, such social media-driven chaos means that not only has the notion of an objective good been cast into question but so has the very notion of objective truth. Given these circumstances, the response cannot merely be a technical response, which is likely to fail. It must be primarily a moral response, appealing to the moral and social nature of the human being. Our response cannot just be about protecting people from the vagaries of the market economy, no matter how important this is; it must also be about instilling virtue throughout all economic interactions.

In a sequence of remarkable talks, Pope Francis has tried to spell out what a post-COVID world must look like. He argues that the principles I have discussed in this book—principles such as the common good, the universal destination of goods, the preferential option for the poor, solidarity, subsidiarity, and care for our common home—are the ones that must guide us going forward.[5] He notes that "the pandemic has highlighted how vulnerable and interconnected everyone is" and that "if we do not take care of one another, starting with the least, with those who are most impacted, including creation, we cannot heal the world."[6] He locates the two obstacles to this solidarity as indifference and individualism: "Indifferent: I look the other way. Individualist: looking out only for one's own interest."[7] Looking ahead, he argues that while we must find a cure for COVID-19—a "small but terrible virus"—"we must also cure a larger virus, that of social injustice, inequality of opportunity, marginalization, and the lack of protection for the weakest."[8] He puts it bluntly: "Either we come out of it [the pandemic] better, or we come out of it worse. . . . We have an opportunity to build something different."[9]

In his post-COVID discourses, Pope Francis identifies the two main dysfunctions as inequality and environmental devastation—matching the messages of chapters 6 and 7 of this book. He argues that chief among the economic and social dysfunctions aggravated by the pandemic is inequality. "These symptoms of inequality reveal a social illness," he says. "It is a virus that comes from a sick economy."[10] He stresses that this illness in turn comes from unequal economic growth that disregards fundamental human values and decries the fact that "a few wealthy people possess more than all the rest of humanity."[11] Stressing that the same economic model is leading to environmental devastation, most notably climate change and biodiversity loss, he notes, "We are close to exceeding many limits of our wonderful planet, with serious and irreversible consequences."[12] In an echo of *Laudato Si'*, he argues that inequality and environmental devastation have the same root in a disordered economy based on "wanting to possess and wanting to dominate."[13]

For Pope Francis, the solution is solidarity, which, as I've stressed throughout this book, is more important than ever as the world grows more interconnected. Yet, argues Pope Francis, "we do not always transform this *interdependence* into *solidarity*. There is a long journey between interdependence and solidarity."[14] Instead, we get stuck in structures of sin. Yet solidarity, he argues, allows us to build "antibodies" against individualism, allowing us to heal injustice and oppression.[15] In line with traditional Catholic social teaching, he also stresses subsidiarity, which goes hand in hand with solidarity. In this context, Pope Francis emphasizes, subsidiarity for a just post-COVID world requires the voice and participation of all people, not just the wealthy and well connected. "To emerge better from a crisis, the *principle of subsidiarity* must be enacted," he insists, "respecting the autonomy and the capacity to take initiative that everyone has, especially the least."[16] For Pope Francis, subsidiarity includes intermediary bodies such as families, associations, unions, and small businesses.

Ultimately, the pope is interested in the common good. "The coronavirus is showing us that each person's true good is a common good, not only individual, and, vice versa, the common good is a true good for the person," he stresses.[17] Without an emphasis on the common good, we are left with egoism, which Pope Francis says is like building on sand. "To build a healthy, inclusive, just and peaceful society, he says, "we must do so on the rock of the common good."[18] For the pope this is a global common good; in an address to the United Nations in September 2020, he called for renewed multilateralism in the context of an ethical globalization to avoid the pitfalls of insularity and nationalism. Here is how he phrases this decisive challenge:

> We are faced, then, with a choice between two possible paths. One path leads to the consolidation of multilateralism as the expression of a renewed sense of global co-responsibility, a solidarity grounded in justice and the attainment of peace and unity within the human family, which is God's plan for our world. The other path emphasizes self-sufficiency, nationalism, protectionism, individualism and isolation; it excludes the poor, the vulnerable and those dwelling on the peripheries of life. That path would certainly be detrimental to the whole community, causing self-inflicted wounds on everyone. It must not prevail.[19]

This is the stark choice facing us: a new economy or the same reckless path that has created so many dangerous divisions, fault lines, and dysfunctions.

The goal of this book has been to flesh out what this new economy might look like, in both theoretical and practical terms. I began in chapter 1 by showing that the roots of modern Catholic social teaching lie in millennia past—in the injunctions to show justice to the poor in the Hebrew Scriptures; in the teachings of Jesus, especially as summed up in the Beatitudes; and in the attitude toward wealth demonstrated by the early Church. I also talked about the second lung of this Catholic ethical tradition: the ethics of the ancient philosopher Aristotle, who argued that true happiness can be equated with a life of virtue, identified with becoming our best selves, who we were born to be. And the great medieval philosopher Thomas Aquinas synthesized these two strands, arguing that happiness finds its ultimate end in God, justice is a central virtue of economic affairs, and the desire for wealth for its own sake is disordered. From these ancient roots, I then described the emergence of modern Catholic social teaching as a moral response to the great upheavals of the industrial revolution. This teaching can be seen as both conservative and progressive—conservative in the sense that it recognizes that virtue has been upended in the modern economy, and progressive in the sense that it seeks to yoke modern institutions to the traditional pursuit of solidarity and justice.

The next step was to contrast the assumptions of Catholic social teaching and neoclassical economics. In chapter 2, I isolated ten core principles of Catholic social teaching: the common good, integral human development, integral ecology, solidarity, subsidiarity, reciprocity and gratuitousness, the universal destination of goods, the preferential option for the poor, Catholic notions of rights and duties, and Catholic notions of justice. From this vantage point, a "moral economy" oriented around these principles would exclude no one, including future generations, and would seek the fullest development of all peoples in line with their capacities. It would recognize that the goods of the earth and human labor are designed to meet the needs of all and that economic success depends not on overall economic growth but on how the poor are faring. Moreover, it would recognize that all economic endeavors are human endeavors, marked by solidarity, reciprocity, and fraternity. All of these principles stand in stark contrast to neoclassical economics, which conjures up a vision of "rational economic man" seeking to maximize his preferences, typically equated with material goods, without any limit. There are no higher goals; there is no role for virtue or morality. And the vision of economic interaction is based not on cooperation but rather on competition through the marketplace. One of the central arguments of this book, drawn out in chapter 3, is that this vision of human nature is fundamentally flawed, as shown by recent evidence from behavioral economics, evolutionary biology, neuroscience, happiness studies, and psychology. The Catholic vision is far more in tune with human nature.

In the second half of the twentieth century, though, as described in chapter 4, neoclassical economics rose to increasing prominence and eventually gave rise to full-throated neoliberalism, an economy guided by its principles. This ideology has done immense harm, both to human beings and to whole economies. Because its vision of human nature is flawed, neoliberalism has spurred immense unhappiness, isolation, and mental health challenges. At the same time, it has generated massive fractures in society, leading to rising inequality, exclusion, and corporate power. This inequality in turn has undermined social cohesion and ignited some very dangerous flames. On top of these negative results, our quest for endless economic growth in the context of a virtue-free economy has fueled the environmental crisis, the greatest crisis of the century, which threatens the future of human civilization.

In the second half of the book, I moved from the theoretical to the practical, asking what an economy built on the principles of Catholic social teaching would look like. In chapter 5, I argued that it would break with libertarianism and would instead see a guiding role for the state in terms of fostering the common good. But I also argued that business and finance do not have complete freedom to pursue their own ends in a way that is disconnected from the common good. All economic activity must be oriented toward the common good, and it is a matter of prudence whether it is assigned to the public or private sector. Following this exploration, in chapter 6, I examined the problem of inequality and the related jobs crisis. I argued that inequality not only undermines economic

growth and the common good but also solidarity, compassion, and other virtues. Dealing with inequality must therefore be one of the central challenges of
economics, for a broader array of reasons than typically put forth. Chapter 7
looked into the environmental crisis, especially guided by the teachings of Pope
Francis. Again, it argued that solving this crisis must be a central challenge of all
economic activity. Finally, chapter 8 looked at the global dimension, the need
for expanded circles of solidarity in the context of an ethical globalization.

Let me conclude, then, by laying out ten key practical solutions of a "virtue
economy" influenced by Catholic social teaching.

First, move away from an excessive reliance on GDP and economic growth.
Replace it with newer measures of happiness and well-being, and reconsider—
in line with the thought of Pope Francis—whether we should be seeking endless
economic growth, especially in wealthier countries.

*Second, make sure that governments guarantee the material bases of human flour-
ishing*—food, housing, healthcare, education, and social protection (including
for workers in the informal sector). Move away from the idea that the role of
government is only to lay down the rules of the game, especially when those
rules are tilted toward capital and business.

Third, raise taxes on capital and wealthy individuals. This revenue would fund
needed investments in decarbonization and the material bases of human flourishing. Such taxation could also help instill virtue, especially since it establishes a
norm that there is a ceiling, as well as a floor, on the appropriate level of income
and wealth that a person should accrue.

Fourth, promote dignified employment as a central goal of policy. This solution
has implications for the funding of technological change, the function of central
banks, work-sharing schemes that keep workers on the books during bad times,
and the role of the state as employer-of-last-resort. As a leading example, a heroic
push for decarbonization will surely entail enormous employment opportunities.

*Fifth, make sure that businesses are responsible to a wider variety of stakeholders
than simply shareholders.* Including workers, customers, suppliers, the environment, and wider society, this reform would move away from the maximization of
shareholder value and could include support for worker cooperatives and hybrid
forms of enterprises that simultaneously make profits and pursue social ends.

Sixth, rebalance the relationship between capital and labor. Support strong
unions and collective bargaining. Promote democracy in the workplace through
worker representation on both boards of governments and in the internal management of enterprises.

*Seventh, restructure the financial sector to allow it to serve the productive econ-
omy rather than itself.* This change would include breaking up the large banks;
introducing a tax on financial transactions; reining in the worst excesses, such

as private equity and vulture funds; and supporting credit unions and small and regional banks.

Eight, support an ethical globalization. Such a change would rebalance power between capital and labor, creditors and debtors, and rich countries and poor countries. It would prioritize global commons such as climate change and pandemics and treat migrants and refugees with respect and dignity.

Ninth, recognize the centrality of the Sustainable Development Goals as the basic contours of a global common good. These goals recognize that economic progress must always go hand in hand with social inclusion and care for the planet. And financing these goals in poor countries requires stepped up global solidarity.

Tenth, solve the climate crisis and other environmental challenges. Again, this is a global challenge, under the auspices of the Paris Agreement on Climate Change and other international treaties. It requires, to the best of our ability, decarbonization of the energy system by midcentury at the latest. Without this achievement, the very basis of human flourishing will be fatally undermined.

This list of ten priorities is merely a basic flavor of the policies discussed in this book. What links them all is that they are not merely technocratic; they have as their goal the inculcation of virtue across all corners of the global economy. And while they are firmly rooted in the wisdom of Catholic social teaching, especially as infused by Pope Francis, I believe that these values can transcend confessional divides, appealing to those of all faiths and none. All that is required is an appreciation that the current model doesn't work and it doesn't work because it is based on the wrong values.

I don't want to appear naive. Changing the global economy along these lines is not going to usher in a utopia. But I do believe it can eradicate the worst excesses of neoliberalism, not only on the economy and society but on human psychology too. My basic contention is that neoliberalism inculcates and amplifies the wrong values. It is time to try something different. It is time to reform systems of education, especially in the domains of business and economics. Ultimately, what is at stake is not just the health of our economies and societies, or indeed personal happiness and flourishing, but peace itself. It is about successfully circumventing this "1930s moment."

I started this book with a quote from Pope Francis. So it is apt that I also end with his words. In his 2015 Popular Movements speech, Pope Francis calls for the poor to become "artisans of their own destiny" and notes that "the future of humanity does not lie solely in the hands of great leaders, the great powers and the elites. It is fundamentally in the hands of peoples and in their ability to organize."[20] Change is coming. But it is coming from the bottom, not the top. Let us hear and respond to the cry of the earth and the cry of the poor. And let us build something better.

Notes

1. *FT*, 235.
2. See Frieden, "Will Global Capitalism Fail Again?"
3. See Eichengreen, *Populist Temptation*, ch. 6.
4. Piketty, *Capital and Ideology*, ch. 11.
5. Pope Francis, General Audience, Vatican City, August 5, 2020.
6. Pope Francis, General Audience, August 12, 2020.
7. Pope Francis.
8. Pope Francis, General Audience, August 19, 2020.
9. Pope Francis.
10. Pope Francis, General Audience, Vatican City, August 26, 2020.
11. Pope Francis.
12. Pope Francis.
13. Pope Francis.
14. Pope Francis, General Audience, September 2, 2020.
15. Pope Francis.
16. Pope Francis, General Audience, Vatican City, September 23, 2020.
17. Pope Francis, General Audience, September 9, 2020.
18. Pope Francis.
19. Pope Francis, "Address of His Holiness Pope Francis to the Seventy-Fifth Meeting of the General Assembly of the United Nations."
20. Pope Francis, "Participation of the Second World Meeting of Popular Movements."

BIBLIOGRAPHY

Key Papal Documents

CA: *Centesimus Annus* (Pope John Paul II, 1991). http://www.vatican.va/content/john
-paul-ii/en/encyclicals/documents/hf_jp-ii_enc_01051991_centesimus-annus.html.

CIV: *Caritas in Veritate* (Pope Benedict XVI, 2009). http://www.vatican.va/content
/benedict-xvi/en/encyclicals/documents/hf_ben-xvi_enc_20090629_caritas-in
-veritate.html.

EG: *Evangelii Gaudium* (Pope Francis, 2013). http://www.vatican.va/content/francesco
/en/apost_exhortations/documents/papa-francesco_esortazione-ap_20131124
_evangelii-gaudium.html.

GS: *Gaudium et Spes* (Second Vatican Council, 1965). https://www.vatican.va/archive
/hist_councils/ii_vatican_council/documents/vat-ii_const_19651207_gaudium-et
-spes_en.html.

FT: *Fratelli Tutti* (Pope Francis, 2020). http://www.vatican.va/content/francesco/en
/encyclicals/documents/papa-francesco_20201003_enciclica-fratelli-tutti.html.

LE: *Laborem Exercens* (Pope John Paul II, 1981). http://www.vatican.va/content/john
-paul-ii/en/encyclicals/documents/hf_jp-ii_enc_14091981_laborem-exercens.html.

LS: *Laudato Si'* (Pope Francis, 2015). http://www.vatican.va/content/francesco/en
/encyclicals/documents/papa-francesco_20150524_enciclica-laudato-si.html.

MM: *Mater et Magistra* (Pope John XXIII, 1961). http://www.vatican.va/content/john
-xxiii/en/encyclicals/documents/hf_j-xxiii_enc_15051961_mater.html.

OA: *Octogesima Adveniens* (Pope Paul VI, 1971). http://www.vatican.va/content/paul-vi
/en/apost_letters/documents/hf_p-vi_apl_19710514_octogesima-adveniens.html.

PDMP: *Pacem, Dei Munus Pulcherrimum* (Pope Benedict XV, 1920). http://www.vatican
.va/content/benedict-xv/en/encyclicals/documents/hf_ben-xv_enc_23051920
_pacem-dei-munus-pulcherrimum.html.

PP: *Populorum Progressio* (Pope Paul VI, 1967). http://www.vatican.va/content/paul-vi
/en/encyclicals/documents/hf_p-vi_enc_26031967_populorum.html.

PT: *Pacem in Terris* (Pope John XXIII, 1963). http://www.vatican.va/content/john-xxiii
/en/encyclicals/documents/hf_j-xxiii_enc_11041963_pacem.html.

QA: *Quadragesimo Anno* (Pope Pius XI, 1931). http://www.vatican.va/content/pius-xi /en/encyclicals/documents/hf_p-xi_enc_19310515_quadragesimo-anno.html.

QAm: *Querida Amazonia* (Pope Francis, 2020). http://www.vatican.va/content/francesco /en/apost_exhortations/documents/papa-francesco_esortazione-ap_20200202 _querida-amazonia.html.

RN: *Rerum Novarum* (Pope Leo XIII, 1891). http://www.vatican.va/content/leo-xiii/en /encyclicals/documents/hf_l-xiii_enc_15051891_rerum-novarum.html.

SRS: *Sollicitudo Rei Socialis* (Pope John Paul II, 1987). http://www.vatican.va/content /john-paul-ii/en/encyclicals/documents/hf_jp-ii_enc_30121987_sollicitudo-rei -socialis.html.

References

Acemoglu, Daron, and Pascal Restrepo. "Robots and Jobs: Evidence from US Labor Markets." NBER Working Paper 23285, March 2017.

Acemoglu, Daron, and James A. Robinson. *Why Nations Fail: The Origins of Power, Prosperity and Poverty*. New York: Crown Publishers, 2012.

Aldred, Jonathan. *License to Be Bad: How Economics Corrupted Us*. London: Allen Lane, 2019.

Alston, Philip. "The Parlous State of Poverty Reduction." Report of the Special Rapporteur on Extreme Poverty and Human Rights. United Nations, June 15–July 3, 2020.

Alvaredo, Facundo, Lucas Chancel, Thomas Piketty, Emmanuel Saez, and Gabriel Zucman, eds. *World Inequality Report 2018*. Cambridge, MA: Belknap Press of Harvard University Press, 2018.

Anderson, Elizabeth. *Private Government: How Employers Rule Our Lives (and Why We Don't Talk about It)*. Princeton, NJ: Princeton University Press, 2017.

Annett, Anthony. "Connection, Disconnection, Reconnection: The Radical Vision of Laudato Si'." In *Laudato Si' and the Path to COP22*. Vatican City, September 28, 2016. http://www.pas.va/content/accademia/en/publications/scriptavaria/laudato_si _cop22.html.

Annett, Anthony. "Economía de la virtud y desafíos económicos actuales: El mapa caminero de *Caritas in veritate* y *Laudato si'*." In *Sociedad civil y bien común: Hacia una nueva articulación del mercado, el estado y la sociedad civil*. Vol. 2, edited by Juan Carlos Scannone, 221–74. Córdoba: Editorial de la Universidad Católica de Córdoba, 2018.

Annett, Anthony. "The Economic Vision of Pope Francis." In *The Theological and Ecological Vision of Laudato Si': Everything Is Connected*, edited by Vincent Miller, 160–74. London: Bloomsbury / T&T Clark, 2017.

Annett, Anthony. "Ethical Actions to End Poverty." In *Ethics in Action for Sustainable Development*, edited by Anthony Annett, Owen Flanagan, Jeffrey Sachs, Marcelo Sánchez Sorondo, Jesse Thorson, and William Vendley. New York: Columbia University Press, forthcoming.

Annett, Anthony. "Human Flourishing, the Common Good, and Catholic Social Teaching." In *World Happiness Report 2016: Special Rome Edition*. Vol. 2, edited by Jeffrey Sachs, Leonardo Becchetti, and Anthony Annett, 38–65. New York: UN Sustainable Development Solutions Network, 2016.

Annett, Anthony. "Laudato Si' and Inclusive Solidarity: The Ideology of the Market and the Reality of Inequality." In *Inclusive Solidarity and the Integration of Marginalized People*, edited by Stefano Zamagni and Marcelo Sánchez Sorondo, 36–58. Vatican City: Libreria Editrice Vaticana, 2017.

Annett, Anthony. "Our Common Responsibility for Our Common Home: The Activist Vision of Laudato Si'." In *Care for the World: Laudato Si' and Catholic Social Teaching in an Era of Climate Crisis*, edited by Frank A. Pasquale, 25–40. Cambridge: Cambridge University Press, 2019.

Annett, Anthony. *Resource Guide on Climate Change for Religious Communities*. New York: Religions for Peace, 2017.

Annett, Anthony, Owen Flanagan, Jeffrey Sachs, Marcelo Sánchez Sorondo, Jesse Thorson, William Vendley, eds. *Ethics in Action for Sustainable Development*. New York: Columbia University Press, forthcoming.

Annett, Anthony, Jeffrey Sachs, William Vendley, and Marcelo Sánchez Sorondo. "A Multireligious Consensus on the Ethics of Sustainable Development: Reflections of the Ethics in Action Initiative." T20 Policy Brief, May 2017.

Appelbaum, Binyamin. *The Economists' Hour: False Prophets, Free Markets, and the Fracture of Society*. New York: Hachette Book Group, 2019.

Aquinas, Thomas. *Summa Theologica*. 2nd, rev. ed., trans. Fathers of the English Dominican Province, 1920; New Advent, 2008.

Argandona, Antonio. "The 'Logic of Gift' in the Business Enterprise." In *Human Development in Business: Values and Humanistic Management in the Encyclical Caritas in Veritate*, edited by Domènec Melé and Claus Dierksmeier, 198–216. London: Palgrave Macmillan, 2012.

Aristotle. *Nicomachean Ethics*. Translated by J. A. K. Thomson. London: Penguin, 1953.

Atkinson, Anthony. *Inequality: What Can Be Done?* Cambridge, MA: Harvard University Press, 2015.

Baker, Dean. *Rigged: How Globalization and the Rules of the Modern Economy Were Structured to Make the Rich Richer*. Washington, DC: Center for Economic Policy Research, 2016.

Baumgarth, William P., and Richard J. Regan, eds. *Saint Thomas Aquinas: On Law, Morality, and Politics*. Cambridge: Avatar Books, 1988.

Becker, Gary. "The Economic Way of Looking at Life." Nobel Lecture, December 9, 1992.

Bentham, Jeremy. *An Introduction to the Principles of Morals and Legislation*, 1789. http://socserv2.socsci.mcmaster.ca/econ/ugcm/3ll3/bentham/morals.pdf.

Bereiter, Bernhard, Sarah Eggleston, Jochen Schmitt, Chirstoph Nehrbass-Ahles, Thomas F. Stocker, Hubertus Fischer, Sepp Kipfstuhl, and Jérôme Chappellaz. "Revision of the EPICA Dome C CO2 Record from 800 to 600 kyr Before Present." *Geophysical Research Letters* 42, no. 2 (2015): 542–49.

Berg, Andrew, Edward F. Buffie, and Luis-Filipe Zanna. "Robots, Growth, and Inequality." *Finance and Development* 53, no. 3 (2016): 10–13.

Blake, William, Frank Brewer Bemis, and Lessing J. Rosenwald Collection. *Milton, a Poem in 12 [i.e. 2] Books*. London 1804 [1815?]. https://www.loc.gov/item/48031331.

Bloodworth, James. *Hired: Six Months Undercover in Low-Wage Britain*. London: Atlantic Books, 2018.

Bloom, Paul. *Just Babies: The Origins of Good and Evil*. New York: Crown, 2013.

Bo, Charles. "Submission by Charles Cardinal Maung Bo." Presented at *Laudato Si' and the Path to COP22*, Vatican City, September 28, 2016. http://www.accademiascienze.va/content/accademia/en/publications/scriptavaria/laudato_si_cop22/bo.html.

Boulding, Kenneth. *The Meaning of the Twentieth Century: The Great Transition*. New York: Harper and Row, 1964.

Bowles, Samuel. *The New Economics of Inequality and Redistribution*. Cambridge: Cambridge University Press, 2012.

Bowles, Samuel. *The Moral Economy: Why Good Incentives Are No Substitute for Good Citizens*. New Haven, CT: Yale University Press, 2016.

Bowles, Samuel, and Herbert Gintis. *A Cooperative Species: Human Reciprocity and Its Evolution*. Princeton, NJ: Princeton University Press, 2011.

Brown, Peter. *Through the Eye of a Needle: Wealth, the Fall of Rome, and the Making of Christianity in the West, 350–550 AD*. Princeton, NJ: Princeton University Press, 2012.

Bruni, Luigino. *Civil Happiness: Economics and Human Flourishing in Historical Perspective*. New York: Routledge, 2006.

Bruni, Luigino. *The Wound and the Blessing*. New York: New City Press, 2012.

Bruni, Luigino, and Stefano Zamagni. *Civil Economy: Efficiency, Equity, Public Happiness*. Bern: Peter Lang, 2007.

Buchanan, James M. "The Constitution on Economic Policy." Nobel Lecture, December 8, 1986.

Burke, Marshall, Solomon M. Hsiang, and Edward Miguel. "Climate and Conflict." NBER Working Paper 20598, 2014.

Burke, Marshall, Solomon M. Hsiang, and Edward Miguel. "Global Non-linear Effect of Temperature on Economic Production." *Nature* 527 (2015): 235–39.

Burkhauser, Richard V., Jan-Emmanuel De Neve, and Nattavudh Powdthavee. "Top Incomes and Human Well-Being around the World." CEP Discussion Paper 1400, 2016.

Carbon Majors Database. *Carbon Majors Report, 2017*. Carbon Majors Database Report, July 2017.

Case, Anne, and Angus Deaton. *Deaths of Despair and the Future of Capitalism*. Princeton, NJ: Princeton University Press, 2020.

Cecchetti, Stephen, and Enisse Kharroubi. "Reassessing the Impact of Finance on Growth." BIS Working Papers 381, 2012.

Chappel, James. *Catholic Modern: The Challenge of Totalitarianism and the Remaking of the Church*. Cambridge, MA: Harvard University Press, 2018.

Chetty, Raj, Nathaniel Hendren, Patrick Kline, and Emmanuel Saez. "Where Is the Land of Opportunity? The Geography of Intergenerational Mobility in the United States." NBER Working Paper 19843, 2014.

Christakis, Nicholas A. *Blueprint: The Evolutionary Origins of a Good Society*. New York: Hachette, 2019.

Christiansen, Drew. "Pacem in Terris." In *Modern Catholic Social Teaching: Commentaries and Interpretations*, edited by Kenneth R. Himes, 226–52. Washington, DC: Georgetown University Press, 2018.

Chrysostom, John. "Second Sermon on Lazarus and the Rich Man." In *St. John Chrysostom on Wealth and Poverty*, translated by Catherine P. Roth, 39–55. Crestwood, NY: St. Vladimir's Seminary Press, 1984.

Clark, Meghan J. "Caritas in Veritate." In *Modern Catholic Social Teaching: Commentaries and Interpretations*, edited by Kenneth R. Himes, 482–514. Washington, DC: Georgetown University Press, 2018.

Clark, Meghan J. "Seeking Solidarity for Development: Insights from Catholic Social Teaching for Implementing the UN Agenda." *Journal of Catholic Social Thought* 13, no. 2 (2016): 311–28.

Clark, Meghan J. *The Vision of Catholic Social Thought: The Virtue of Solidarity and the Praxis of Human Rights*. Minneapolis: Fortress Press, 2014.

Climate Central. "The 10 Warmest Years on Record." Climate Central, January 15, 2020. https://www.climatecentral.org/gallery/graphics/top-10-warmest-years-on-record.

Cline, Eric H. *1177 BC: The Year Civilization Collapsed*. Princeton, NJ: Princeton University Press, 2015.

Cloutier, David. *The Vice of Luxury: Economic Excess in a Consumer Age*. Washington, DC: Georgetown University Press, 2015.

Coady, David, Ian Parry, Nghia-Piotr Le, and Baoping Shang. "Global Fossil Fuel Subsidies Remain Large: An Update Based on Country-Level Estimates." IMF Working Paper 19/89, 2019.

Cohn, Alain, Ernst Fehr, and Michel Andre Marechal. "Business Culture and Dishonesty in the Banking Industry." *Nature* 516 (2014): 86–89.

Collier, Paul. *The Future of Capitalism: Facing the New Anxieties*. London: Allen Lane, 2018.

Corak, Miles. "Income Inequality, Equality of Opportunity, and Intergenerational Mobility." *Journal of Economic Perspectives* 27, no. 3 (2013): 79–102.

Curran, Charles E., Kenneth R. Himes, and Thomas A. Shannon. "Sollicitudo Rei Socialis." In *Modern Catholic Social Teaching: Commentaries and Interpretations*, edited by Kenneth R. Himes, 429–49. Washington, DC: Georgetown University Press, 2018.

Dabla-Norris, Era, Kalpana Kochhar, Nujin Suphaphiphat, Frantisek Ricka, and Evridiki Tsounta. *Causes and Consequences of Income Inequality: a Global Perspective*. Washington, DC: IMF, 2015. https://doi.org/10.5089/9781513555188.006.

Daly, Daniel, J. "Structures of Virtue and Vice." *New Blackfriars* 92, no. 1039 (2011): 341–57.

Daly, Lew. "The Church of Labor." *Democracy: A Journal of Ideas* 22 (Fall 2011).

Daly, Lew. *God's Economy: Faith-Based Initiatives and the Caring State*. Chicago: University of Chicago Press, 2009.

Dao, Mai, and Prakash Loungani. "The Human Cost of Recessions: Assessing It, Reducing It." *IMF Staff Position Notes*, no. 17 (2010): 1. https://doi.org/10.5089 /9781462308163.004.

Darwin, Charles. *The Descent of Man and Selection in Relation to Sex*. Princeton, NJ: Princeton University Press, 1871. https://teoriaevolutiva.files.wordpress.com/2014 /02/darwin-c-the-descent-of-man-and-selection-in-relation-to-sex.pdf.

Dawkins, Richard. *The Selfish Gene*. Oxford: Oxford University Press, 1976.

Deck, Allan Figueroa. "Populorum Progressio." In *Modern Catholic Social Teaching: Commentaries and Interpretations*, edited by Kenneth R. Himes, 302–25. Washington, DC: Georgetown University Press, 2018.

Dembinski, Paul H. "Fecundity vs. Efficiency: Rediscovering Relations." In *Human Development in Business: Values and Humanistic Management in the Encyclical Caritas in Veritate*, edited by Domenèc Melé and Claus Dierksmeier, 98–116. London: Palgrave Macmillan, 2012.

De Neve, Jan-Emmanuel, and George Ward. "Happiness and Work." In *World Happiness Report 2017*, edited by John Helliwell, Richard Layard, and Jeffrey Sachs, 144–77. New York: UN Sustainable Development Solutions Network, 2017.

Descartes, René. *Discourse on Method and Meditations on First Philosophy*. Translated by Donald A. Cress. Indianapolis: Hackett Publishing Company, 1998.

Development Assistance Research Associates and the Climate Vulnerable Forum. *Climate Vulnerability Monitor: A Guide to the Cold Calculus of a Hot Planet*. 2012. https://daraint.org/wp-content/uploads/2012/09/CVM2ndEd-FrontMatter.pdf.

Dicastery for Promoting Integral Human Development. *Vocation of the Business Leader: A Reflection*. Vatican City: Dicastery for Promoting Integral Human Development, 2018.

Dierksmeier, Claus. *Reframing Economic Ethics: The Philosophical Foundations of Humanistic Management*. London: Palgrave Macmillan, 2016.

Dierksmeier, Claus, and Michel Pirson. "*Oikonomia* versus *Chrematistike*: Learning from Aristotle about the Future Orientation of Business Management." *Journal of Business Ethics* 88 (2009): 417–30.

DiLeo, Daniel. "Creation Care through Consumption and Life Choices." In *The Theological and Ecological Vision of Laudato Si': Everything Is Connected*, edited by Vincent Miller, 217–34. London: Bloomsbury / T&T Clark, 2017.

Donohue, John R. "The Bible and Catholic Social Teaching: Will This Engagement Lead to Marriage?" In *Modern Catholic Social Teaching: Commentaries and Interpretations*, edited by Kenneth R. Himes, 11–42. Washington, DC: Georgetown University Press, 2018.

Eberstadt, Nicholas. *Men without Work: America's Invisible Crisis*. Conshohocken, PA: Templeton, 2016.

Edlund, Lena, and Evelyn Korn. "A Theory of Prostitution." *Journal of Political Economy* 110, no. 1 (2002): 181–214.

Eichengreen, Barry. *The Populist Temptation: Economic Grievance and Political Reaction in the Modern Era*. New York: Oxford University Press, 2018.

Epstein, Gerald, and Juan Antonio Montecino. "Overcharged: The High Cost of High Finance." Roosevelt Institute. Study. July 12, 2016. https://www.peri.umass.edu /component/k2/item/729-overcharged-the-high-cost-of-high-finance.

Etzioni, Amitai. "The Moral Effects of Economic Teaching." *Sociological Forum* 30, no. 1 (2015): 228–33.

Evers-Hillstrom, Karl. "Lobbying Spending Reaches $3.4 Billion in 2018, Highest in 8 Years." *OpenSecrets.org*, January 2019.

Fagan, Brian. *The Long Summer: How Climate Changed Civilization*. New York: Basic Books, 2004.

Femia, Francecso, and Caitlin Werrell. "Syria: Climate Change, Drought, and Social Unrest." *Center for Climate and Security*, February 29, 2012. https://climateandsecurity .org/2012/02/syria-climate-change-drought-and-social-unrest/.

Finn, Daniel K. "Centesimus Annus." In *Modern Catholic Social Teaching: Commentaries and Interpretations*, edited by Kenneth R. Himes, 450–81. Washington, DC: Georgetown University Press, 2018.

Finn, Daniel K. *Christian Economic Ethics: History and Implications*. Minneapolis: Fortress Press, 2013.

Finn, Daniel K. "Nine Libertarian Heresies Tempting Neoconservative Catholics to Stray from Catholic Social Thought." *Journal of Markets and Morality* 14, no. 2 (2011): 487–503.

Finnis, John. "Aquinas' Moral, Political, and Legal Philosophy." In *The Stanford Encyclopedia of Philosophy*, edited by Edward N. Zalta, Summer 2020. http://plato.stanford .edu/entries/aquinas-moral-political/.

Firer Hinze, Christine. *Glass Ceilings and Dirt Floors: Women, Work, and the Global Economy*. Mahwah, NJ: Paulist Press, 2015.

Firer Hinze, Christine. "Quadragesimo Anno." In *Modern Catholic Social Teaching: Commentaries and Interpretations*, edited by Kenneth R. Himes, 158–82. Washington, DC: Georgetown University Press, 2018.

Frankl, Victor E. *Man's Search for Meaning*. Boston: Beacon Press, 2006.

Frey, Carl Benedikt. *The Technology Trap: Capital, Labor, and Power in the Age of Automation*. Princeton, NJ: Princeton University Press, 2019.

Frey, Carl Benedikt, and Michael A. Osborne. "The Future of Employment: How Susceptible Are Jobs to Computerisation?" Oxford Martin School Working Paper, 2013.

Frieden, Jeffry. "Will Global Capitalism Fail Again?" Bruegel Essay and Lecture Series, Brussels, 2006.

Furceri, Davide, and Prakash Loungani. "Capital Account Liberalization and Inequality." IMF Working Paper 15/243, 2015.

Galbraith, John Kenneth. *American Capitalism: The Concept of Countervailing Power*. Boston: Houghton Mifflin, 1962.

Gaspar, Vitor, David Amaglobeli, Mercedes Garcia-Escribano, Delphine Prady, and Mauricio Soto. "Fiscal Policy and Development: Human, Social, and Physical

Investments for the SDGs." *International Monetary Fund Discussion Notes, No. 19/03*, 2019. https://www.imf.org/en/Publications/Staff-Discussion-Notes/Issues/2019/01/18/Fiscal-Policy-and-Development-Human-Social-and-Physical-Investments-for-the-SDGs-46444.

Gilens, Martin, and Benjamin I. Page. "Testing Theories of American Politics: Elites, Interest Groups, and Average Citizens." *Perspectives on Politics* 12, no. 3 (2014): 564–81.

Gillespie, Michael Allen. *The Theological Origins of Modernity*. Chicago: University of Chicago Press, 2008.

Glasman, Maurice. "The Politics of Employment." Address to Centesimus Annus Pro Pontifice Foundation, 2013.

Gold, Lorna. *New Financial Horizons: The Emergence of an Economy of Communion*. New York: New City Press, 2010.

Goldin, Claudia, and Lawrence Katz. *The Race between Education and Technology*. Cambridge, MA: Harvard University Press, 2008.

Gordon, Robert J. *The Rise and Fall of American Growth: The U.S. Standard of Living since the Civil War*. Princeton, NJ: Princeton University Press, 2016.

Gould, Eric D., and Alexander Hijzen. "Growing Apart, Losing Trust? The Impact of Inequality on Social Capital." IMF Working Paper 16/176, 2016.

Graeber, David. *Debt: The First 5,000 Years*. Brooklyn, NY: Melville House, 2011.

Gregory, Brad S. *The Unintended Revolution: How a Religious Revolution Secularized Society*. Cambridge, MA: Belknap Press of Harvard University Press, 2012.

Groody, Daniel G. *Globalization, Spirituality, and Justice: Navigating the Path to Peace*. New York: Orbis Books, 2015.

Hall, Edith. *Aristotle's Way: How Ancient Wisdom Can Change Your Life*. London: Penguin Random House, 2018.

Hallegatte, Stephane, Mook Bangalore, Laura Bonzanigo, Marianne Fay, Tamaro Kane, Ulf Narloch, Julie Rozenberg, David Treguer, and Adrien Vogt-Schilb. *Shock Waves: Managing the Impacts of Climate Change on Poverty*. Washington, DC: World Bank, 2015.

Harper, Kyle. *The Fate of Rome: Climate, Disease, and the End of an Empire*. Princeton, NJ: Princeton University Press, 2017.

Harrington, Daniel, and James Keenan. *Jesus and Virtue Ethics: Between New Testament Studies and Moral Theology*. Lanham, MD: Sheed and Ward, 2002.

Hayek, Friedrich A. *The Constitution of Liberty*. Chicago: University of Chicago Press, 1960.

Helliwell, John. "Understanding and Improving the Social Context of Well-Being." NBER Working Paper 18486, 2012.

Helliwell, John, and Haifang Huang. "Comparing the Happiness Effects of Real and On-line Friends." Edited by Cédric Sueur. *PLoS ONE* 8, no. 9 (September 3, 2013): e72754. https://doi.org/10.1371/journal.pone.0072754.

Helliwell, John, Haifang Huang, and Shun Wang. "Social Foundations of World Happiness." In *World Happiness Report 2017*, edited by John Helliwell, Richard Layard, and Jeffrey Sachs, 8–47. New York: UN Sustainable Development Solutions Network, 2017.

Helliwell, John, Richard Layard, Jeffrey Sachs, and Jan-Emmanuel de Neve, eds. *World Happiness Report 2020*. New York: UN Sustainable Development Solutions Network, 2020.

Henley, Ben, and Nerilie Abram. "The Three-Minute Story of 800,000 Years of Climate Change with a Sting in the Tail." *Conversation*. Last modified June 12, 2017. https://theconversation.com/the-three-minute-story-of-800-000-years-of-climate-change-with-a-sting-in-the-tail-73368.

Himes, Kenneth R. *Modern Catholic Social Teaching: Commentaries and Interpretations*. Washington, DC: Georgetown University Press, 2018.

Hinson-Hasty, Elizabeth L. *The Problem of Wealth: A Christian Response to a Culture of Affluence*. New York: Orbis Books, 2017.

Hirschfeld, Mary L. *Aquinas and the Market: Toward a Humane Economy*. Cambridge, MA: Harvard University Press, 2018.

Hollenbach, David. *The Common Good and Christian Social Ethics*. New York: Cambridge University Press, 2002.

Hollenbach, David. "Gaudium et Spes." In *Modern Catholic Social Teaching: Commentaries and Interpretations*, edited by Kenneth R. Himes, 275–301. Washington, DC: Georgetown University Press, 2018.

Hopkins, Gerard Manley. *"God's Grandeur" and Other Poems*. New York: Dover Publications, 1995.

Hösle, Vittorio. "Ethics and Economics, or How Much Egoism Does Modern Capitalism Need? Machiavelli's, Mandeville's, and Malthus's New Insight and Its Challenge." *Archives for Philosophy of Law and Social Philosophy* 97, no. 3 (2011): 425–40.

Hudson, Michael. . . . *And Forgive Them Their Debts: Lending, Foreclosure and Redemption from Bronze Age Finance to the Jubilee Year*. Dresden: ILSET-Verlag, 2018.

Intergovernmental Panel on Climate Change. "AR5 Synthesis Report: Climate Change, 2014." Intergovernmental Panel on Climate Change, Geneva, 2014.

Intergovernmental Panel on Climate Change. "Global Warming of 1.5 Degrees C." Intergovernmental Panel on Climate Change, Geneva, 2018.

International Energy Agency. "Energy Technology Perspectives 2015." International Energy Agency, Paris, 2015.

International Labor Organization. "COVID-19 and the World of Work." In *ILO Monitor*. 7th ed., 1–35. Geneva: International Labor Organization, 2021.

International Labor Organization. "World Social Protection Report 2017–19: Universal Social Protection to Achieve the Sustainable Development Goals." International Labor Organization, Geneva, 2017.

International Monetary Fund. "How Big Is the Implicit Subsidy for Banks Considered Too Important to Fail?" In *Global Financial Stability Report*, April, 101–32. Washington, DC: International Monetary Fund, 2014.

International Monetary Fund. "How to Mitigate Climate Change." In *Fiscal Monitor*, October, 1–29. Washington, DC: International Monetary Fund, 2019.

International Monetary Fund. "The Rise of Corporate Market Power and Its Macroeconomic Effects." In *World Economic Outlook*, 55–76. Washington, DC: International Monetary Fund, April 2019.

Ivereigh, Austen. *The Great Reformer: Francis and the Making of a Radical Pope*. New York: Henry Holt and Company, 2014.

Ivereigh, Austen. *Wounded Shepherd: Pope Francis and His Struggle to Convert the Catholic Church*. New York: Henry Holt and Company, 2019.

Jaumotte, Florence, and Carolina Osorio Buitron. "Inequality and Labor Market Institutions." *IMF Staff Discussion Notes* 15, no. 14 (2015).

Johnson, Simon, and James Kwak. *Thirteen Bankers: The Wall Street Takeover and the Next Financial Meltdown*. New York: Pantheon Books, 2010.

Judt, Tony. *Ill Fares the Land*. New York: Penguin, 2010.

Judt, Tony. *Postwar: A History of Europe since 1945*. New York: Penguin, 2005.

Kahneman, Daniel, and Angus Deaton. "High Income Improves Evaluation of Life but Not Emotional Wellbeing." *Proceedings of the National Academy of Sciences* 107, no. 38 (September 21, 2010): 16489–493.

Kahneman, Daniel, Alan B. Krueger, David A. Schkade, Norbert Schwarz, and Arthur A. Stone. "A Survey Method for Characterizing Daily Life Experience: The Day Reconstruction Method." *Science* 306, no. 5702 (2004): 1776–80.

Katz, Lawrence, and Alan B. Krueger. "The Rise and Nature of Alternative Work Arrangements in the United States, 1995–2015." Working Paper 603, Princeton University, Industrial Relations Section, 2016.

Kelley, Colin P., Shahrzad Mohtadi, Mark A. Crane, Richard Seager, and Yochanan Kushnir. "Climate Change in the Fertile Crescent and Implications of the Recent Syrian Drought." *Proceedings of the National Academy of Sciences of the United States of America* 112, no. 11 (March 17, 2015): 3241–46.

Kennedy, Robert F. "Remarks at the University of Kansas." University of Kansas, March 18, 1968. https://www.jfklibrary.org/learn/about-jfk/the-kennedy-family/robert-f-kennedy/robert-f-kennedy-speeches/remarks-at-the-university-of-kansas-march-18-1968.

Keynes, John Maynard. *The Economic Consequences of the Peace*. London: Macmillan, 1919.

Keynes, John Maynard. "Economic Possibilities for Our Grandchildren." In *Essays in Persuasion*, 358–73. London: Macmillan, 1930.

Keynes, John Maynard. *The General Theory of Employment, Interest and Money*. London: Macmillan, 1936.

Kohli, Atul. *Imperialism and the Developing World*. Oxford: Oxford University Press, 2020.

Konyndyk DeYoung, Rebecca, Colleen McCluskey, and Christina Van Dyke. *Aquinas's Ethics: Metaphysical Foundations, Moral Theory, and Theological Context*. Notre Dame, IN: University of Notre Dame Press, 2009.

Kraut, Richard. "Aristotle's Ethics." In *The Stanford Encyclopedia of Philosophy*, edited by Edward N. Zalta, Summer 2018, Metaphysics Research Lab, Stanford University, 2018. http://plato.stanford.edu/entries/aristotle-ethics/.

Krekel, Christian, and George MacKerron. "How Environmental Quality Affects Our Happiness." In *World Happiness Report 2020*, edited by John Helliwell, Richard Layard, Jeffrey Sachs, and Jan-Emmanuel de Neve, 94–111. New York: UN Sustainable Development Solutions Network, 2020.

Kureethadam, Joshtrom Isaac. *The Ten Green Commandments of Laudato Si'*. Collegeville, MN: Liturgical Press, 2019.

Labaton Sucharow. "Wall Street, Main Street, Fleet Street: Corporate Integrity at a Crossroads." In *US and UK Financial Services Industry Survey*, 1–10. July 2012.

Lamoureux, Patricia A. "Laborem Exercens." In *Modern Catholic Social Teaching: Commentaries and Interpretations*, edited by Kenneth R. Himes, 403–28. Washington, DC: Georgetown University Press, 2018.

Lancet Commissions. "Health and Climate Change: Policy Responses to Protect Public Health." *Lancet* 386, no. 10006 (2015): 1861–1914.

Landes, Elisabeth M., and Richard A. Posner. "The Economics of the Baby Shortage." *Journal of Legal Studies* 7, no. 2 (1978): 323–48.

Langan, John P. "The Christmas Messages of Pius XII." In *Modern Catholic Social Teaching: Commentaries and Interpretations*, edited by Kenneth R. Himes, 183–98. Washington, DC: Georgetown University Press, 2018.

Layard, Richard. "Mental Illness Destroys Happiness and Is Costless to Treat." In *Global Happiness Policy Report, 2018*, edited by Jeffrey Sachs, 26–51. New York: Sustainable Development Solutions Network, 2018.

Levine, Amy-Jill. *Short Stories by Jesus: the Enigmatic Parables of a Controversial Rabbi*. New York: Harper One, 2014.

Levy, Frank, and Peter Temin. "Inequality and Institutions in 20th Century America." NBER Working Paper 13106, 2007.

Lohfink, Gerhard. *Jesus of Nazareth: What He Wanted, Who He Was*. Collegeville, MN: Liturgical Press, 2012.

Lothes Biviano, Erin, David Cloutier, Elaine Padilla, Christiana Z. Peppard, and Jame Schaefer. "Catholic Moral Traditions and Energy Ethics for the Twenty-First Century." *Journal of Moral Theology* 5, no. 2 (2016): 1–36.

Lynas, Mark. *Six Degrees: Our Future on a Hotter Planet*. Washington, DC: National Geographic, 2008.

MacCulloch, Diarmaid. *A History of Christianity: The First Three Thousand Years*. London: Allen Lane, 2009.

MacIntyre, Alasdair. *After Virtue*. London: Gerald Duckworth and Co., 1981.

Mandeville, Bernard. *The Fable of the Bees, or Private Vices, Publick Benefits: With An Essay on Charity and Charity-Schools, and A Search into the Nature of Society*. London: J. Tonson, 1729. First published 1714.

Mann, Michael. *The New Climate War: The Fight to Take Back Our Planet*. New York: Hachette Book Group, 2021.

Maritain, Jacques. *The Person and the Common Good*. New York: Charles Scribner's Sons, 1947.

Markovits, Daniel. *The Meritocracy Trap: How America's Foundational Myth Feeds Inequality, Dismantles the Middle Class, and Devours the Elite*. New York: Penguin Random House, 2019.

Maslow, Abraham H. "A Theory of Human Motivation." *Psychological Review* 50, no. 4 (1943): 370–96.

Mauss, Marcel. *The Gift: Forms and Functions of Exchange in Archaic Societies*. New York: Norton, 1967.

Mayer, Colin. *Prosperity: Better Business Makes the Greater Good*. Oxford: Oxford University Press, 2018.

Mayer, Jane. *Dark Money: The Hidden History of the Billionaires behind the Rise of the Radical Right*. New York: Doubleday, 2016.

Mayville, Luke. *John Adams and the Fear of American Oligarchy*. Princeton, NJ: Princeton University Press, 2016.

Mazzucato, Mariana. *The Value of Everything: Making and Taking in the Global Economy*. London: Allen Lane, 2018.

McKibben, Bill. *Falter: Has the Human Game Begun to Play Itself Out?* New York: Henry Holt and Company, 2019.

Medaille, John. *The Vocation of Business: Social Justice in the Marketplace*. New York: Continuum International Publishing Group, 2008.

Mian, Atif R., Ludwig Straub, and Amir Sufi. "The Saving Glut of the Rich and the Rise in Household Debt." NBER Working Paper 26941, 2020.

Mian, Atif, and Amir Sufi. *House of Debt: How They (and You) Caused the Great Recession and How We Can Prevent It from Happening Again*. Chicago: University of Chicago Press, 2014.

Mich, Marvin L. *Catholic Social Teaching and Movements*. Mystic, CT: Twenty-Third Publications, 1998.

Mich, Marvin L. "Mater et Magistra." In *Modern Catholic Social Teaching: Commentaries and Interpretations*, edited by Kenneth R. Himes, 199–225. Washington, DC: Georgetown University Press, 2018.

Milanovic, Branko. *Global Inequality: A New Approach for the Age of Globalization*. Cambridge, MA: Harvard University Press, 2016.

Milanovic, Branko. *Capitalism Alone: The Future of the System That Rules the World*. Cambridge, MA: Harvard University Press, 2019.

Milbank, John, and Adrian Pabst. *The Politics of Virtue: Post-liberalism and the Human Future*. London: Rowan and Littlefield International, 2016.

Moyn, Samuel. *Christian Human Rights*. Philadelphia: University of Pennsylvania Press, 2015.

New Maddison Project Database and World Bank. "World GDP over the Last Two Millennia." OurWorldInData.org. 2017. https://ourworldindata.org/grapher/world -gdp-over-the-last-two-millennia?time=1..latest.

Nowak, Martin A. *Super Cooperators: Altruism, Evolution, and Why We Need Each Other to Succeed*. New York: Free Press, 2011.

Nozick, Robert. *Anarchy, State, and Utopia*. Oxford: Blackwell, 1974.

Nussbaum, Martha. "Mill between Aristotle and Bentham." In *Economics and Happiness: Framing the Analysis*, edited by Luigino Bruni and Pier Luigi Porta, 170–83. New York: Oxford University Press, 2005.

Oreskes, Naomi, and Erik M. Conway. *Merchants of Doubt: How a Handful of Scientists Obscured the Truth on Issues from Tobacco Smoke to Global Warming*. New York: Bloomsbury Press, 2011.

Ostry, Jonathan D., Andrew Berg, and Charalambos G. Tsangarides. "Redistribution, Inequality, and Growth." *IMF Staff Discussion Notes* 14, no. 2 (2014): 1–30.

Oxfam. "World's Billionaires Have More Wealth than 4.6 Billion People." *Oxfam*, January 20, 2020. https://www.oxfam.org/en/press-releases/worlds-billionaires-have -more-wealth-46-billion-people.

Parker, Geoffrey. *Global Crisis: War, Climate Change, and Catastrophe in the Seventeenth Century*. New Haven, CT: Yale University Press, 2013.

Parrenin, F., V. Masson-Delmotte, P. Köhler, D. Raynaud, D. Paillard, J. Schwander, C. Barbante, A. Landais, A. Wegner, and J. Jouzel. "Synchronous Change of Atmospheric CO_2 and Antarctic Temperature during the Last Deglacial Warming." *Science* 339, no. 6123 (2013): 1060–63.

Piff, Paul, Daniel M. Stancatoa, Stéphane Côtéb, Rodolfo Mendoza-Dentona, and Dacher Keltner. "Higher Social Class Predicts Increased Unethical Behavior." *Proceedings of the National Academy of Sciences of the United States of America* 109, no. 11 (March 13, 2012): 4086–91.

Piketty, Thomas. *Capital and Ideology*. Cambridge, MA: Belknap Press, 2020.

Piketty, Thomas. *Capital in the Twenty-First Century*. Cambridge, MA: Belknap Press, 2014.

Polanyi, Karl. *The Great Transformation: The Political and Economic Origins of Our Time*. Boston, MA: Beacon Press, 2001.

Pomeranz, Kenneth. *The Great Divergence: China, Europe, and the Making of the Modern World Economy*. Princeton, NJ: Princeton University Press, 2000.

Pope Francis. "Address of His Holiness Pope Francis to Delegates from the Italian Confederation of Workers' Unions (CISL)." Vatican City, June 28, 2017. http://www .vatican.va/content/francesco/en/speeches/2017/june/documents/papa-francesco _20170628_delegati-cisl.html.

Pope Francis. "Address of His Holiness Pope Francis to Participants at the Meeting for Executives of the Main Companies in the Oil and Natural Gas Sectors, and Other Energy Related Businesses." Vatican City, June 9, 2018. http://www.vatican.va /content/francesco/en/speeches/2018/june/documents/papa-francesco_20180609 _imprenditori-energia.html.

Pope Francis. "Address of His Holiness Pope Francis to Participants in the Meeting 'Economy of Communion' Sponsored by the Focolare Movement." Vatican City,

February 4, 2017. http://www.vatican.va/content/francesco/en/speeches/2017
/february/documents/papa-francesco_20170204_focolari.html.

Pope Francis. "Address of His Holiness Pope Francis to the Seventy-Fifth Meeting of the
General Assembly of the United Nations." September 25, 2020. https://w2.vatican
.va/content/francesco/en/messages/pont-messages/2020/documents/papa-francesco
_20200925_videomessaggio-onu.html.

Pope Francis. "Audience to Representatives of the Communications Media." March 16,
2013. http://www.vatican.va/content/francesco/en/speeches/2013/march/documents
/papa-francesco_20130316_rappresentanti-media.html.

Pope Francis. General Audience, Vatican City, August 5, 2020. http://w2.vatican.va
/content/francesco/en/audiences/2020/documents/papa-francesco_20200805
_udienza-generale.html.

Pope Francis. General Audience, August 12, 2020. http://w2.vatican.va/content/francesco
/en/audiences/2020/documents/papa-francesco_20200812_udienza-generale.html.

Pope Francis. General Audience, August 19, 2020. http://w2.vatican.va/content/francesco
/en/audiences/2020/documents/papa-francesco_20200819_udienza-generale.html.

Pope Francis. General Audience, Vatican City, August 26, 2020. http://w2.vatican
.va/content/francesco/en/audiences/2020/documents/papa-francesco_20200826
_udienza-generale.html.

Pope Francis. General Audience, September 2, 2020. http://w2.vatican.va/content
/francesco/en/audiences/2020/documents/papa-francesco_20200902_udienza
-generale.html.

Pope Francis. General Audience, September 9, 2020. http://w2.vatican.va/content
/francesco/en/audiences/2020/documents/papa-francesco_20200909_udienza
-generale.html.

Pope Francis. General Audience, Vatican City, September 23, 2020. http://www.vatican
.va/content/francesco/en/audiences/2020/documents/papa-francesco_20200923
_udienza-generale.html.

Pope Francis. "Letter of His Holiness Pope Francis to the Popular Movements." Vatican City, April 12, 2020. http://www.vatican.va/content/francesco/en/letters/2020
/documents/papa-francesco_20200412_lettera-movimentipopolari.html.

Pope Francis. "Meetings with Members of the General Assembly of the United Nations
Organization: Address of the Holy Father." New York, September 25, 2015. http://
www.vatican.va/content/francesco/en/speeches/2015/september/documents/papa
-francesco_20150925_onu-visita.html.

Pope Francis. "Message from the Holy Father to the Participants in the Plenary Session
of the Pontifical Academy of Social Sciences." Vatican City, April 28, 2017. https://
press.vatican.va/content/salastampa/en/bollettino/pubblico/2017/04/28/170428h
.html.

Pope Francis. "Message of His Holiness Pope Francis for the Celebration of the 51st
World Day of Peace." Vatican City, January 1, 2018. http://w2.vatican.va/content
/francesco/en/messages/peace/documents/papa-francesco_20171113_messaggio
-51giornatamondiale-pace2018.html.

Pope Francis. "Participation of the Second World Meeting of Popular Movements: Address of the Holy Father." Santa Cruz, Bolivia, July 9, 2015. http://www.vatican.va/content/francesco/en/speeches/2015/july/documents/papa-francesco_20150709_bolivia-movimenti-popolari.html.

Pope, Stephen J. "Overview of the Ethics of Thomas Aquinas." In *The Ethics of Thomas Aquinas*, edited by Stephen J. Pope, 30–53. Washington, DC: Georgetown University Press, 2002.

Putnam Robert D. *Bowling Alone: The Collapse and Revival of American Community*. New York: Simon and Schuster, 2000.

Rainforest Action Network. "Banking on Climate Change: Fossil Fuel Finance Report 2020." 2020. https://www.ran.org/bankingonclimatechange2020/.

Ramanathan, Veerabhadran. "The Two Worlds Approach for Mitigating Air Pollution and Climate Change." In *Sustainable Humanity, Sustainable Nature: Our Responsibility*, edited by Partha Dasgupta, Veerabhadran Ramanathan, and Marcelo Sánchez Sorondo, 285–300. Vatican City: Pontifical Academy of Sciences, Extra Series 41, 2014.

Rasmussen, Dennis. "Adam Smith on What Is Wrong with Economic Inequality." *American Political Science Review* 110, no. 2 (2016): 342–52.

Reeves, Richard V. *Dream Hoarders: How the American Upper Middle Class Is Leaving Everyone Else in the Dust, Why That Is a Problem, and What to Do about It*. Washington, DC: Brookings Institution Press, 2017.

Reich, Robert. *Saving Capitalism: For the Many, Not the Few*. New York: Alfred A. Knopf, 2015.

Ricard, Matthieu. *Altruism: The Power of Compassion to Change Yourself and the World*. New York: Little, Brown and Company, 2015.

Rockström, Johan et al. "A Safe Operating Space for Humanity." *Nature* 461 (1999): 472–75.

Rodrik, Dani. "Populism and the Economics of Globalization." NBER Working Paper 23559, 2017.

Rodrik, Dani. *Straight Talk on Trade: Ideas for a Sane World Economy*. Princeton, NJ: Princeton University Press, 2018.

Rodrik, Dani. "What Do Trade Agreements Really Do?" NBER Working Paper 24344, 2018.

Roos, Jerome. *Why Not Default? The Political Economy of Sovereign Debt*. Princeton, NJ: Princeton University Press, 2019.

Ryan, Richard, Veronika Huta, and Edward L. Deci. "Living Well: A Self-Determination Theory Perspective on Eudaimonia." *Journal of Happiness Studies* 9 (2008): 139–70.

Sachs, Jeffrey D. "Addiction and Unhappiness in America." In *World Happiness Report 2019*, edited by John Helliwell, Richard Layard, and Jeffrey Sachs, 122–31. New York: UN Sustainable Development Solutions Network, 2019.

Sachs, Jeffrey D. *The Age of Sustainable Development*. New York: Columbia University Press, 2015.

Sachs, Jeffrey D. *The Ages of Globalization: Geography, Technology, and Institutions*. New York: Columbia University Press, 2020.

Sachs, Jeffrey D. "America's Health Crisis and the Easterlin Paradox." In *World Happiness Report 2018*, edited by John Helliwell, Richard Layard, and Jeffrey Sachs, 146–59. New York: UN Sustainable Development Solutions Network, 2018.

Sachs, Jeffrey D. "Climate Change and New Evidence from Science, Engineering, and Policy." Paper presented at Pontifical Academy of Sciences meeting, May 27, 2019. http://www.accademiascienze.va/content/accademia/en/events/2019/climatechange.html.

Sachs, Jeffrey D. "Investing in Social Capital." In *World Happiness Report 2015*, edited by John Helliwell, Richard Layard, and Jeffrey Sachs, 152–66. New York: Sustainable Development Solutions Network, 2015.

Sachs, Jeffrey D. "Restoring American Happiness." In *World Happiness Report 2017*, edited by John Helliwell, Richard Layard, and Jeffrey Sachs, 178–84. New York: UN Sustainable Development Solutions Network, 2017.

Sachs, Jeffrey D. "Social Conflict and Populist Policies in Latin America." NBER Working Paper 2897, 1989.

Sachs, Jeffrey D. *To Move the World: JFK's Quest for Peace.* New York: Random House, 2013.

Sachs, Lisa, Lise Johnson, and Ella Merrill. "Environmental Injustice: How Treaties Undermine Human Rights Related to the Environment." *La Revue des Juristes de Science Po*, no. 18 (2020): 90–100.

Saez, Emmanuel. "Striking It Richer: The Evolution of Top Incomes in the United States (Updated with 2014 Preliminary Estimates)." *Technical Notes* 201506, World Inequality Lab, 2015.

Saez, Emmanuel, and Gabriel Zucman. *The Triumph of Injustice: How the Rich Dodge Taxes and How to Make Them Pay.* New York: W. W. Norton and Company, 2019.

Sahay, Ratna et al. "Rethinking Financial Deepening: Stability and Growth in Emerging Markets." *IMF Staff Discussion Notes* 15, no. 8 (2015): 1. https://doi.org/10.5089/9781498312615.006.

Sánchez Sorondo, Marcelo. "The Church as Intrinsically a Social Movement to Make the Last First." Paper presented at meeting, Ethics in Action, Vatican City, November 2016.

Sandel, Michael. *Justice: What's the Right Thing to Do?* New York: Farrar, Straus, and Giroux, 2009.

Sandel, Michael. *The Tyranny of Merit: What's Become of the Common Good?* New York: Farrar, Straus, and Giroux, 2020.

Sandel, Michael. *What Money Can't Buy: The Moral Limits of Markets.* New York: Farrar, Straus, and Giroux, 2012.

Sapolsky, Robert M. *Behave: The Biology of Humans at Our Best and Worst.* New York: Penguin, 2017.

Scheidel, Walter. *The Great Leveler: Violence and the History of Inequality from the Stone Age to the Twenty-First Century.* Princeton, NJ: Princeton University Press, 2017.

Schneider, Nathan. *Everything for Everyone: The Radical Tradition That Is Shaping the Next Economy.* New York: Nation Books, 2018.

Seligman, Martin. *Flourish: A Visionary New Understanding of Happiness and Well-Being*. New York: Atria, 2012.

Sen, Amartya. *Collective Choice and Social Welfare*. San Francisco: Holden-Day, 1970.

Sen, Amartya. "Rational Fools: A Critique of the Behavioral Foundations of Economic Theory." *Philosophy and Public Affairs* 9, no. 4 (1977): 317–24.

Shadle, Matthew. *Interrupting Capitalism: Catholic Social Thought and the Economy*. Oxford: Oxford University Press, 2018.

Shah, Aniket. "The Foundations of Development Banking: A Critical Review." In *The Routledge Handbook of Financial Geography*, edited by Janelle Knox-Hayes and Dariusz Wójcik, 352–77. Abingdon, UK: Routledge, 2021.

Shannon, Thomas A. "Rerum Novarum." In *Modern Catholic Social Teaching: Commentaries and Interpretations*, edited by Kenneth R. Himes, 133–57. Washington, DC: Georgetown University Press, 2018.

Shapiro, Ian. *The Moral Foundations of Politics*. New Haven, CT: Yale University Press, 2003.

Shaxson, Nicholas. *The Finance Curse: How Global Finance Is Making Us All Poorer*. London: Bodley Head, 2018.

Shaxson, Nicholas. "Tackling Tax Havens." *Finance and Development* 56, no. 3 (2019): 6–10.

Simon, Herbert. "Public Administration in Today's World of Organizations and Markets." Pittsburgh, PA: Carnegie Mellon University, 2000.

Sinclair, Upton. *I, Candidate for Governor: And How I Got Licked*. Los Angeles: End Poverty, 1935.

Smith, Adam. *An Inquiry into the Nature and Causes of the Wealth of Nations*. 1776. Retrieved from https://www.ibiblio.org/ml/libri/s/SmithA_WealthNations_p.pdf.

Smith, Adam. *The Theory of Moral Sentiments*, 1759. https://www.ibiblio.org/ml/libri/s/SmithA_MoralSentiments_p.pdf.

Snyder, Carolyn W. "Evolution of Global Temperature over the Past Two Million Years." *Nature* 538 (2016): 226–28.

Spence, Michael, and Sandile Hlatshwayo. "The Evolving Structure of the American Economy and the Employment Challenge." Working Paper, Council on Foreign Relations, 2011.

Stern, Nicholas H. *The Economics of Climate Change: The Stern Review*. Cambridge: Cambridge University Press, 2007.

Stiglitz, Joseph E. *The Price of Inequality: How Today's Divided Society Endangers Our Future*. New York: W. W. Norton and Company, 2012.

Stiglitz, Joseph, Jean-Paul Fitoussi, and Martine Durand. *Measuring What Counts: The Global Movement for Well-Being*. New York: New Press, 2019.

Stoller, Matt. *Goliath: The 100-Year War between Monopoly Power and Democracy*. New York: Simon and Schuster, 2019.

Stout, Lynn. *Cultivating Conscience: How Good Laws Make Good People*. Princeton, NJ: Princeton University Press, 2011.

Sustainable Development Solutions Network. "America's Zero Carbon Action Plan." Sustainable Development Solutions Network, New York, 2020.

Sustainable Development Solutions Network. "SDG Costing and Financing for Low-Income Developing Countries." Report. Sustainable Development Solutions Network, New York, 2019.

Sustainable Development Solutions Network and Institute for Sustainable Development and International Relations. "Pathways to Deep Decarbonization: 2015 Report." Sustainable Development Solutions Network, New York, 2015.

Tirole, Jean. *Economics for the Common Good.* Princeton, NJ: Princeton University Press, 2017.

Tokarska, Katarzyna B., Nathan P. Gillett, Andrew J. Weaver, Vivek K. Arora, and Michael Eby. "The Climate Response to Five Trillion Tonnes of Carbon." *Nature Climate Change* 6 (2016): 51–55.

Tooze, J. Adam. *Crashed: How a Decade of Financial Crises Changed the World.* New York: Viking, 2018.

Trivers, Robert L. "The Evolution of Reciprocal Altruism." *Quarterly Review of Biology* 46, no. 1 (1971): 35–57.

Twenge, Jean M. "The Sad State of Happiness in the United States and the Role of Digital Media." In *World Happiness Report 2019,* edited by John Helliwell, Richard Layard, and Jeffrey Sachs, 86–95. New York: UN Sustainable Development Solutions Network, 2019.

United Nations. *The Millennium Development Goals Report 2015.* New York: United Nations, 2015.

United Nations. "Transforming Our World: The 2030 Agenda for Sustainable Development." Resolution Adopted by the General Assembly, September 25, 2015.

United Nations. *World Social Report 2020: Inequality in a Rapidly Changing World.* New York: United Nations, 2020.

United Nations Conference on Trade and Development. "From the Great Lockdown to the Great Meltdown: Developing Country Debt in the Time of Covid-19." *Trade and Development Report Update,* 2020. https://unctad.org/system/files/official-document/gdsinf2020d3_en.pdf.

United Nations Conference on Trade and Development. "Roadmap toward Sustainable Sovereign Debt Workouts." 2015. https://unctad.org/system/files/official-document/gdsddf2015misc1_en.pdf.

United Nations World Food Program. "COVID-19 Will Double Number of People Facing Food Crises unless Swift Action Is Taken." UNWFP, April 21, 2020. https://www.wfp.org/news/covid-19-will-double-number-people-facing-food-crises-unless-swift-action-taken.

US Bishops National Catholic War Council. "Program for Social Reconstruction." National Catholic Welfare Council, 1919. https://www.stthomas.edu/media/catholicstudies/center/ryan/Ryan_1919_Program_Social_Reconstruction.pdf.

Vatican. *Final Document of the Synod on the Amazon,* 2019. https://www.vaticannews.va/en/vatican-city/news/2020-02/final-document-synod-amazon.html.

Veblen, Thorstein. *The Theory of the Leisure Class*. New York: Penguin Books, 1994.

Vedel, Anna, and Dorthe K. Thomsen. "The Dark Triad across Academic Majors." *Personality and Individual Differences* 116 (2017): 86–91.

Verhaeghe, Paul. *What about Me? The Struggle for Identity in a Market-Based Society*. London: Scribe Publications, 2014.

Wagner, Gernot, and Martin L. Weitzman. *Climate Shock: The Economic Consequences of a Hotter Planet*. Princeton, NJ: Princeton University Press, 2015.

Waldfogel, Joel. "The Deadweight Loss of Christmas." *American Economic Review* 83, no. 5 (2001): 1328–36.

Wallace-Wells, David. *The Uninhabitable Earth*. London: Allen Lane, 2019.

Ward, Kate. "Wealth, Poverty and Inequality: A Christian Virtue Response." PhD diss., Boston College, 2016.

Wight, Jonathan B. *Ethics in Economics: An Introduction to Moral Frameworks*. Stanford, CA: Stanford University Press, 2015.

Wilkinson, Richard, and Kate Pickett. *The Inner Level: How More Equal Societies Reduce Stress, Restore Sanity and Improve Everybody's Wellbeing*. London: Penguin Random House, 2018.

Wilkinson, Richard, and Kate Pickett. *The Spirit Level: Why More Equal Societies Almost Always Do Better*. London: Allen Lane, 2009.

Wilson, Edward O. *The Meaning of Human Existence*. New York: Norton, 2014.

Wootton, David. *Power, Pleasure, and Profit: Insatiable Appetites from Machiavelli to Madison*. Cambridge, MA: Harvard University Press, 2018.

World Bank. "Reversals of Fortune." *Poverty and Shared Prosperity 2020*. Washington, DC: World Bank Group, 2020. https://openknowledge.worldbank.org/bitstream/handle /10986/34496/9781464816024.pdf.

Wright, Tom, and Bradley Hope. *Billion Dollar Whale: The Man Who Fooled Wall Street, Hollywood, and the World*. New York: Hachette, 2018.

Zamagni, Stefano. "Catholic Social Thought, Civil Economy, and the Spirit of Capitalism." In *The True Wealth of Nations: Catholic Social Thought and Economic Life*, edited by Daniel Finn, 63–93. Oxford: Oxford University Press, 2010.

Zamagni, Stefano. "On the Birth of Economic Science during the Italian-Scottish Enlightenment: Two Paradigms Compared." Mimeo, University of Bologna, January 2021.

Zenner Peppard, Christiana. "Laudato Si'." In *Modern Catholic Social Teaching: Commentaries and Interpretations*, edited by Kenneth R. Himes, 515–50. Washington, DC: Georgetown University Press, 2018.

Zhang, Tao. "Opening Remarks by Deputy Managing Director Tao Zhang at the 2019 Seminar on Climate Resilience for Small Islands States." December 4, 2019. https:// www.imf.org/en/News/Articles/2019/12/04/sp12022019-2019-seminar-on-climate -resilience-for-small-islands-states.

INDEX

Note: Figures and tables are indicated by page numbers in *italics*.

ABOUT THE AUTHOR

Anthony M. Annett is a Gabelli Fellow at Fordham University. He has a BA and an MLitt from Trinity College Dublin and a PhD in economics from Columbia University. He spent two decades at the International Monetary Fund, including as speechwriter to two managing directors. He is also a member of the College of Fellows of the Dominican School of Philosophy and Theology in Berkeley.